The Keynesian Episode
A Reassessment

The Keynesian Episode
A Reassessment

W. H. Hutt

Liberty Fund
Indianapolis

This book is published by Liberty Fund, Inc., a foundation established to encourage study of the ideal of a society of free and responsible individuals.

The cuneiform inscription that serves as our logo and as the design motif for our endpapers is the earliest-known written appearance of the word "freedom" (*amagi*), or "liberty." It is taken from a clay document written about 2300 B.C. in the Sumerian city-state of Lagash.

Library of Congress Cataloging in Publication Data

Hutt, William Harold, 1899–
    The Keynesian episode.

    Includes index.
    1. Keynesian economics.   I. Title.
HB99.7.H88   330.15′6   79–4150
ISBN 0–913966–60–6 (hardcover edition)
ISBN 0–913966–61–4 (paperback edition)

11   10   09   08   07   06   05   04   03   80   C   5   4   3   2   1
12   11   10   09   08   07   06   05   04   03   P   7   6   5   4   3

Contents

Preface

The present work began with an attempt to prepare a second edition of my 1963 book, *Keynesianism—Retrospect and Prospect.* I set out to retain, as far as could be consistent with my revisions, omissions, and additions, the original arrangement of that book and the same order of chapters. But I was soon led to write three additional chapters, to omit four, and drastically to curtail two others. This and other changes in the text I thought necessary eventually made it clear that I was writing a new book.

Even so, I have allowed some parts of the text of my original book to stand unrevised; but I have generally tried to improve exposition. I have retained the chapter titles in many cases. I have omitted a chapter I called "The Say Law"[1] because I have recently published *A Rehabilitation of Say's Law,* which deals so much better (I hope) with the same vital issue. I have omitted the chapter entitled "The Acceleration Fallacy" and substituted a much shorter version, partly because the phenomenon plays so unimportant a role in Keynes' own theoretical system. And finally, I have omitted the chapters "Depression and Boom," "Capital Saturation," and "Anticipated Inflation." This is because these phenomena are incidentally but adequately (in my present judgment) dealt with in passages which I have revised or added at different places in the text. In some cases, however, I have referred the reader to passages in the 1963 book, which I shall henceforth call *Keynesianism.*

I decided to omit the chapter "Anticipated Inflation" with some

---

[1] I cannot explain why I used that term for "Say's law." I think my old teacher Edwin Cannan must have used those words in his teaching. He never mentioned the law in writing, although he often referred to J. B. Say.

sadness because I thought that it was one of the least unsatisfactory parts of my contribution. When I wrote it, first in the late 1950s, the points I was making seemed still highly controversial. Today they seem to me to be almost universally accepted. I have, however, thought it wise throughout to continue to distinguish sharply between unanticipated inflation, which can have coordinative effects in a discoordinated economy, and anticipated inflation, which cannot.

I have thought it appropriate to include a prologue, in which I deal among other things with the psychology of opinion and the genesis of intellectual fashions. In this prologue, I explain how I was persuaded (by myself, not others) to write both *Keynesianism* and the present book. In this book I have also incorporated an adaptation of an article which was first published in 1971, in a symposium entitled *Toward Liberty* published by the Institute of Humane Studies, in honor of the 90th birthday of Ludwig von Mises. Its title was "Reflections on the Keynesian Episode." I have used these words, "The Keynesian Episode," with the permission of the institute, in the title of the present work.

The article commented among other things on the remarkable personality of Keynes, whose work, and the development of whose work, revolutionized subsequent economic theory, an effect which he himself confidently predicted.[2] I call it "On Keynes." It makes up the greater part of Chapter 1. In Chapter 2, which is also new but incorporates some passages from the same article, I explain my position on the intellectual harm to the useful development of economics by the extraordinary attempt by the great majority of professional economists to accept Keynes' *The General Theory of Employment, Interest, and Money* as though it were the new *Wealth of Nations* and remodel their teachings on it. Chapter 3 also is a wholly new contribution. It treats certain vices as well as the forgotten virtues of much pre-Keynesian economics.

I now believe that there are big advantages in supplementing what were Chapters 1 and 2 in my *Keynesianism* by explaining rather more fully, in advance, some of my objections to such Keynesian notions as survive in so many of today's textbooks. The reader will find many references to articles and books of mine which record developments in my thinking since 1928, when I entered academic life. The subject of coordination of the economic system via the pricing system, which

---

[2] In a letter to George Bernard Shaw shortly before publication of *The General Theory.*

is the true issue with which *The General Theory* was concerned, dominated nearly all my studies subsequent to 1930.

Keynes himself described those he criticized as "classical economists." The usage is far from ideal. Between Adam Smith and his disciples on the one hand, and the bulk of the economists in the early 1930s on the other hand, there had been formidable developments in understanding; moreover, there were really big differences on some things among the "Cambridge School" (Alfred Marshall), the "Austrian School" (Mises and Hayek), and the "London School" (Cannan and Robbins) in those days. And different members of these groups by no means agreed with one another on all issues! Nevertheless, there were some important notions which, I feel, nearly all pre-Keynesians would have accepted, say, before 1936. Accordingly, I shall from now on refer simply to "pre-Keynesian" economics when I am discussing this consensus among teachers of economics prior to the publication of *The General Theory*.

From the beginning I have found it necessary to refer to the "release" or the "withholding" of *productive capacity,* terminology which I had used in my *Theory of Idle Resources* (1939).[3] I should explain, however, at this stage, that by "release" of capacity I shall mean the reduction of a price of any input or output which is initially in excess of its market-clearing value; and by "withholding" of capacity, I shall mean the raising of a price to above, or further above, its market-clearing level, or its maintenance at such a level.[4]

By "services" I mean throughout *productive* services of men or assets. They are "productive" if they have value, and that means if they can command something else of value in exchange (in a money economy, through the medium of the purchase-sale process); or if the men or assets are offering in prospect, passively or in cooperation with complementary assets or other persons, a contribution to an income stream.

A notion which I have introduced in this book and have found useful in clarifying the issues which arise in the study of "consumption-saving" decisions is that of a classification of assets according to their life expectancies (which end in consumption). The process of production, which is "the creation of value," occurs through the

---

[3] The second edition of this book appeared in 1977, published by Liberty Fund, Inc. (Indianapolis).

[4] Further clarification of the notion of the withholding or the releasing of capacity is given on pp. 148n, 178–80, 218–23; in my *Theory of Idle Resources,* 2d ed., chap. 10; and my *A Rehabilitation of Say's Law,* chap. 5.

embodiment of the services of men and of assets into an aggregate assets stock, or the embodiment of assets of relatively short life expectancies into assets of longer life expectancies. The stock of assets is in process of current accumulation and consumption, the latter through the extermination of value and replacement (partially, fully or more than fully, by the same embodiment process). Services directly consumed are products of zero life expectancy, a concept to be explained.

I use the term "consumption" in Say's sense, namely, "the extermination of value," whether that of services or of assets. "Production" to replace or more than replace the value of consumption can be regarded as a stimulus. Consumption, although the ultimate end or purpose of all production, ought, I shall argue, always to be regarded as a depressant.

Several small changes (unimportant but not inappropriate) have been made from the terminology of *Keynesianism,* such as "labor unions" for "trade unions" and the omission of the word "recent" for books published more than twenty years earlier. Also, I have eliminated a number of "asides"—interpolations which, although relevant, I now judge to cause an undue interruption in a chain of argument. And I have resorted to a greater extent to the expositional device of brief repetitions of points made earlier. This is to eliminate serious misunderstandings such as I illustrate in the prologue and which occurred in interpretations of *Keynesianism* by economists of stature.

In my references to well-known economists, I have omitted their initials except where this might otherwise lead to confusion. Finally, I have omitted titles. British economists have been widely honored in this way—thus, Lord Robbins, Sir Roy Harrod and so forth. But most of my references to them are to their contributions made long before they acquired titles.

In the preface of my *Keynesianism,* I expressed my indebtedness to many well-known economists. Since the publication of that book, I have gained greatly from the criticisms and appreciations of so many economists (through personal contacts and published contributions) that it would require more space than would be appropriate even to list their names.

I cannot refrain from mentioning my appreciation and gratitude to my secretary, Mrs. Joan LeBel, for her role in dealing with the many rearrangements and revisions of the text I now present.

Prologue

The reasons for the extraordinary seductiveness of the notions which Keynes' disciples gradually systematized into "Keynesianism" and later rehabilitated into "neo-Keynesianism," concern the psychology of opinion—the genesis of intellectual fashions, creeds, and ideologies. The broad topic is one which began to interest me as a young man, very soon after I had entered academic life in 1928. In 1936 I recorded the results of my early endeavors to clarify my thoughts on the subject in my *Economists and the Public*.[1] While that book was in the press, *The General Theory of Employment, Interest, and Money*, was published.[2] I read quickly through such parts of Keynes' book as I could then follow, and I managed to insert an additional, last-minute passage in my own book, which recorded my rapidly acquired impressions. Already in 1936, although I had been bewildered by it, I had seen clearly and predicted that *The General Theory* would have a quite unparalleled influence *by reason of what I judged to be its demerits as a contribution to thought*. Its policy implications appeared to have been chosen for their political attractiveness. Its misrepresentations of the "classical" economists seemed certain to have a powerful appeal (because the teachings of the "dismal science" had at all times been accepted reluctantly by many who were unable to refute them). Moreover, the obscurities of the *General Theory* (which I have *since* come to recognize as due, in every case, to defective thinking), expressed as they were in the *language* of

---

[1] W. H. Hutt, *Economists and the Public: A Study in Competition and Opinion* (London: Jonathan Cape, 1936), pp. 245–47.

[2] John Maynard Keynes, *The General Theory of Employment, Interest, and Money* (New York: Harcourt, Brace, and Company, 1936).

science, appeared likely to enhance its reputation (for all too many people in all spheres—the academic sphere not excluded—are apt to accept obscurity for profundity).

During the decade preceding the publication of my *Keynesianism,* Keynesian doctrine seemed to command more confident and uncritical respect than ever in *governmental* circles, despite a clear retreat in *academic* circles. Depression or recession could be met, it was believed, either by encouraging consumption or by taking steps to ensure a more rapid rate of spending. It was the stereotypes which had been formed in this background that I endeavored, in 1963, to challenge. Such ideas were bringing about, I believed, grievous harm in the Western world; and I felt, rather naively perhaps, that my contribution could do something at least to stem the tide.

My main thesis was that the intellectual developments for which Keynes' *General Theory* appeared to be responsible had caused a setback to scientific thinking about human economic relations at a crucial epoch. In enunciating this charge, I referred (in the final chapter) to a growing but already clear tendency to abandon crucial theoretical tenets in Keynes' system. Nevertheless, I emphasized that concepts, analytical apparatus, and policy implications which had been erected on apparently then discarded tenets, were surviving in the form of a neo-Keynesian orthodoxy. Meanwhile, the retreat has continued, although, apart from Axel Leijonhufvud's impressive and scholarly critique of ten years ago,[3] I am aware of no further direct attack on the Keynesian system. But many economists do show that they have abandoned it. T. W. Hutchison's *Keynes Versus the Keynesians*[4] does not directly criticize *The General Theory*. It deals, very convincingly I think, with the wide discrepancies between Keynes' own post–*General Theory* arguments and the teachings of his most eminent British disciples. Although I do not wholly agree with Hutchison's opinions on Keynes' ideas, I am deeply grateful for his important contribution. Otherwise, the most important contributions on the topic since Leijonhufvud's fine book have been by Don Patinkin,[5] John R. Hicks,[6] Donald E. Moggridge, and Hyman P.

[3] Axel Leijonhufvud, *On Keynesian Economics and the Economics of Keynes* (New York: Oxford University Press, 1968).

[4] T. W. Hutchison, *Keynes Versus the Keynesians* (London: Institute of Economic Affairs, 1977).

[5] Don Patinkin, *Keynes' Monetary Thought: A Study of Its Development* (Durham, N.C.: Duke University Press, 1976).

[6] John R. Hicks, *The Crisis in Keynesian Economics* (New York: Basic Books, 1974).

Minsky. In spite of their many merits, they have not caused me to abandon any of the positions I took in 1963 (although I was quite prepared to). Indeed, my own subsequent thinking has been influenced less by new theoretical contributions and the new material now available concerning Keynes' speculations during the pre–*General Theory* period and subsequent to it, than by the abject failure everywhere of Keynesian policy. But nearly all my own publications over the last fifteen years have recorded developments in my understanding of the issues. I shall, on occasion, refer to these contributions. They all treat among other things the causes which created originally, and have since been perpetuating, the hold that Keynesianism and neo-Keynesianism have acquired in the universities.[7]

I can now claim, I think, that my insights were superior to those of economists who initially rejected my thesis. It is relevant to quote the former prime minister of Britain, James Callaghan, who openly confessed in 1977:

> We used to think that you could spend your way out of recession. . . . I tell you, in all candor, that that option no longer exists, and that insofar as it ever did exist, it only worked by injecting bigger doses of inflation into the economy followed by higher levels of unemployment as the next step. That is the history of the past twenty years.

And that, roughly, *is* the case I put forward in 1963. Yet, British inflation has now continued apace. I argued then, and do so today with even greater confidence, that the whole problem concerns pricing, not demand. At the policy level, instead of trying to "stimulate" the economy through spending, government responsibility should be confined, ideally, to attempts at improving the working of the pricing system. And governments should be trying also to remove obstacles imposed by private coercion—boycotts, strike threats, physical intimidation, and the like—on the guidance of men and assets to where their prospective yields are greatest, while themselves refraining from imposing such obstacles for private or sectional advantage.

In the preface to my *Keynesianism,* I explained that my aim was that of devising a method of exposition which was "so simple that errors of premises or logic (could) be pinpointed." Well, no critic has yet ventured to pinpoint any error, either in my premises or my reasoning. A review in the *Economic Journal* of June 1964 referred

---

[7] The political causes are discussed in my *Politically Impossible . . . ?* (London: Institute of Economic Affairs, 1971).

to my "invincible *ignorance*" *of,* not my alleged *misunderstanding* of, Keynes' views on any specific topic. I am convinced that the reviewer in this case had not read but merely scanned my book. He may well have been shocked and angered by some of my conclusions, and especially at my rejection of "the notion that insufficient spending (as distinct from defective pricing) creates unemployment."

I was eager for reasoned objections to my rigorously stated case. In 1963 I anticipated harsh criticism, even devastating, ruthless refutation. Reasoned objections never came. Nor did a subsequent article of mine,[8] which further documented a retreat by major proponents of the Keynesian gospel, evoke any reply.[9] I was not, however, expecting mere vituperation and slander in the official journal of the Royal Economic Society. I took the probably unprecedented step of requesting an editorial apology for *the tone* of the review published. My request was refused.

While the review referred to my "invincible ignorance," it included no comprehensible challenges. However wrong my argument may have been on some crucial issues, it was the outcome of more than a quarter century of patient thought and study. It deserved courteous treatment. In the *Economic Journal,* it received wholly unexplicit disparagement. But if *I* was "invincibly ignorant" about what Keynes had said, so were others. Indeed, in the hope of avoiding such charges, I quoted from Keynes' disciples, although seldom from his "circus,"[10] on several occasions to illustrate what I could not accept. For instance, I quoted Kenneth Boulding as saying (1) that Keynes' great contribution showed that "under certain circumstances there may be a deficiency of purchasing power or of consuming power, in the sense that the public is not willing to buy at existing prices the total volume of goods that are offered for sale"; and (2) that the Keynesian Revolution . . . consists in the explicit recognition of . . .

---

[8] "Keynesian Revisions," *South African Journal of Economics,* June 1965, pp. 101–13.

[9] I do not, of course, accept mere disparagement and misrepresentation (of which there has been plenty) as reply or criticism. Subsequent to the publication of my 1963 book, J. H. Botha published a courteous criticism of an earlier contribution of mine, "The Significance of Price Flexibility," which appeared in Henry Hazlitt, ed., *The Critics of Keynesian Economics* (Princeton, N.J.: D. Van Nostrand Company, 1960), pp. 386–403. This created the first opportunity I had of hearing and answering explicit Keynesian objections to my argument. See J. H. Botha, "The Critics of Keynesian Economics," *South African Journal of Economics,* June 1963, pp. 81–101, and W. H. Hutt, "The Critics of Classical Economics," *South African Journal of Economics,* June 1964, pp. 81–94.

[10] Keynes' "circus" was the nickname which became attached to a group of young advisers, mainly in Cambridge.

the simple truth that "every *transfer* of money is at the same time income to the person who receives it and expenditure to the person who gives it. . . ." No Keynesian, as far as I know, has objected to these assertions in Boulding's deservedly influential book; and these words do state succinctly two main theses of *The General Theory* which, I argue now, as I did in 1963, were wholly untenable.

For the same reasons, at an important stage of my 1963 argument I used the text of Michael Polyani's successful popularization *to illustrate* a fundamental defect in popular Keynesian thinking. Polyani was famous as a physicist, physical chemist, and social philosopher; and he was erudite in many fields. But I do not regard him as I would a professional economist. It is a tribute to his genius that he perceived the enormous importance of *The General Theory*. I used his exposition solely because, in my opinion, he explained more clearly than other popularizers (for example, Dudley Dillard, Alvin H. Hansen, Kenneth Boulding, and Abba P. Lerner) the crucial nature of Keynes' originalities; and, approving them, he presented them with remarkable elegance. I regard Polyani's book as the most brilliant, simple, self-consistent, and persuasive exposition of unperceived, subtle error that I have ever read.

The belittlement of my contentions in the *Economic Journal* should, I suggest, be judged in relation to "the refusal of debate"—a striking phenomenon of the present age. My book was reviewed in hardly any of the English-language economic journals. I have been informed that several well-known economists refused to review it. Why?

In September 1975, I received a splendid letter from D. A. Wilhelmson, who was then a complete stranger, commenting on the "refusal of debate" on the subject I am treating. I quote (with permission) from it.

> I would be very much interested in your thoughts on another aspect of the dispute, which I have never seen discussed.
>
> Your point is certainly well taken that economists are too easily intimidated by the prevailing mythology, and should at least state the facts of life plainly, along with the discouragingly constrained alternatives they feel led to propose. But I can't escape the conclusion that the primary obstacle to the acceptance and implementation of classical liberal principles is a related, but more fundamental, defect in the liberals' whole approach to controversy. It seems to me that they have not even tried to devise a strategy which offers any realistic hope of changing the opinions of their adversaries.
>
> A considerable volume of sound economic analysis and criticism

is published, but its impact is pretty much limited to those who already share the views expressed. Few people read anything contrary to their own convictions, and when they do, can easily dismiss all disquieting facts and arguments with unchallenged rationalizations. It is simply asking too much of human nature and intellectual integrity to expect a person voluntarily to accept the logical implications of adverse evidence and argument. And with a half-dozen or so contradictory schools of thought in economics, and countless variations and shadings of these philosophies, even the most intelligent, well-educated and conscientious citizen or public servant will find it a staggering task to set aside his own biases and research the subject with an open mind, searching out rebuttals to each thesis, and evaluating the competing theories, evidence and arguments thoroughly enough to recognize the truth with any confidence. A radically different approach is needed; some kind of mechanism in our society for threshing out these disputes in a systematic fashion which will make it difficult for economists, politicians and the electorate to preserve their misconceptions.

An intensive and extended debate type of format seems to be the only possible way of forcing partisans to examine their own convictions, and to face up to their delusions. The trouble with present-day debate is that it is never pursued far enough to change opinions appreciably. The confrontation is so superficial that participants and spectators alike are left perfectly free to indulge their original prejudices.

It seems to me that the very survival of freedom, to say nothing of its extension, will depend on the initiation and dissemination of exhaustive and definitive debate on economic issues. Debate in format which is specifically designed to force a direct confrontation between the opposing viewpoints, to thresh out every argument that is raised, and to pursue each one doggedly to the point where a concession by one side became inescapable. This approach probably would not lend itself well to oral contests or one-shot publications, but would require longer-term projects, involving a continuing exchange of carefully prepared arguments between teams of qualified authorities, headed or sanctioned, as far as possible, by prominent and acknowledged spokesmen.

Accordingly, I am taking the unusual step of asking whether my readers might assist in the precipitation of debate. My book teems with assertions which, if the consensus of Keynesian teaching of economics has any justification, ought to be refuted in the most explicit manner. In this book I have tried even harder to facilitate challenge. This is because I must frankly admit to a failure in communication in my 1963 *Keynesianism*. My argument failed to get across, on some points, even to my friends.

For instance, the late David McCord Wright's review[11] was in part favorable, but in part unfairly caustic, I thought. He praised my "valuable chapters on the nature of money and the functioning of the pricing system," and he wrote that, in taking as my basic target Harrod's summarization of the kernel of Keynes' argument, I had "no difficulty in demolishing this thesis" (Harrod had stated the thesis as follows, that "if a certain level of interest is established, which is inconsistent with full activity, *no flexibility or immobility in other parts of the system will get the system to move to full activity"*). Yet Wright claimed that his own *The Keynesian System* does the job much better and shows why. On some issues, I readily agree. But his book appeared while mine was in the press; and I had little opportunity of revising my text. I could do no more than mention in the preface that my task would have been facilitated had his book appeared earlier.

Where I failed most seriously, however, was in leaving my critic with the impression that I am "a hard-shell, sound money, and price-flexibility man *who would never increase M or certainly not MV"* (my italics). Wright did perceive that some of my "qualifications" conflicted with any such judgment. But a large part of what I was trying to communicate was *exactly the opposite*—to show that, whereas in Keynes' equations M was a constant, I regarded it as a policy variable. I hope that the changes that I have made to parallel passages in the present text demonstrate this beyond all possible doubt.[12]

Wright's gravest criticism, however, was that I "frequently" misstated Keynes. Shortly after his review appeared, I happened to ride with him by train from Stresa to Rome, and I asked him to send me a list of any misquotations he had noticed. He seemed then not to remember having written the phrase challenged, but said that what he actually meant was that I had, at times, misrepresented Keynes' position. *I have carefully rechecked all my quotations, which still seem to be literally correct and not out of context.* But if any reader does find a mistake, I sincerely hope that he will inform me.

---

[11] *American Economic Review,* June 1964, pp. 431–32. See appendix to chap. 18.

[12] I did and still do place stress on the great advantage to any free community of a measuring rod of money which has some defined value whereas, almost to the last, Keynes regarded any such money unit as a restraint on a nation's monetary autonomy.

My critic was in fact smouldering under the same feeling of in-justice at the hands of the Keynesians that I myself had experienced. My main criticism of *his* fine work is that when David (that is, David McCord Wright) faces Goliath he ought, above all, not to be timid. I hinted that he and other named critics tended to be unduly lenient when it came to refuting so powerful an adversary. Keynes had great power. He knew it; and he himself had been ruthless. (See pp. 27, 34.)

A very recent criticism of some of my ideas in general has ap-peared in *The Economic Record,* June 1977, by C. S. Soper, who argues that Keynes really accepted Say's law. A much more dog-matic Keynesian than Soper, Paul M. Sweezy, once declared that all the arguments of *The General Theory* "fall to the ground if the va-lidity of Say's law is assumed." Is that not evidence of grave con-fusion somewhere? *The Economic Record* has refused to publish my reply, on the grounds that it cannot accept replies to reviews. The economic journals of the world abound with replies to reviews and, in the light of the importance of the topic, I cannot help feeling that we have here a clear instance of the *"refusal of debate"* to which D. A. Wilhelmson refers. I do not of course blame Soper.

I intended the term "Keynesianism" in the title of that book to refer to the doctrines which emerged, somewhat changed, out of the teachings of *The General Theory.* I recognized that there had been, before 1963, an undeniable retreat on the part of Keynesians as a whole; and I emphasized evidences of a retreat by Keynes himself during the decade between the publication of his *magnum opus* and his death. I had felt that where it had been open to his closest dis-ciples (especially members of "the circus"), to expose errors in their master's work and no such exposure had been ventured, I was justified in assuming that their broad acceptance of *The General Theory* teachings could be safely assumed. Some important articles by Keynes appeared in the London *Times* in December 1937. These articles suggest, superficially at least, a quite remarkable change of viewpoint. I quoted from one in *Keynesianism,* but became aware of their true importance only when T. W. Hutchison's *Keynes Versus the Keynesians* was published. Moreover, in the light of the recent publication of Keynes' papers, the subsequent comments they have inspired, and especially Hutchison's and Moggridge's scholarly contributions, I have thought it necessary here to try to interpret some of the different forms which post-Keynesian Keynesianism has now taken. In 1968, however, the very title of Leijonhufvud's *Keynesian Economics and the Economics of Keynes* had brought home to me the fact that the words in my title, *Retrospect and Prospect,* did not sufficiently differentiate between Keynes and his successors.

Hutchison now argues cogently, however (in the words of the editor's preface of his book), that "Keynes would not have supported" the policy views Keynesians have subsequently proclaimed on his authority. "Keynes' name and repute have been used to support policies not justified by his writings."[13] I do not at the moment accept that this is true of his *General Theory;* though it is true, as Hutchison himself puts it, that there are "wide divergencies between the policy objectives which Keynes formulated *in the last decades of his life* and those propagated in his name in the decades after his death"[14] (my italics).

In the opening paragraph of Hicks' elegant work, *The Crisis in Keynesian Economics,*[15] Hicks expresses his belief, justified in my opinion, that it was after Keynes' death that he had "his greatest impact upon the world." But it was not his later writings which had an impact on policy. It was his *General Theory.* And it was to be expected. The impact has been disastrous. It was the conceptual confusions of that book which, I shall argue, befuddled not only economists but lay opinion makers and decision makers. The truth is that Keynes' retreat, which began immediately after publication of *The General Theory*, and continued until his death, had lacked adequate explicitness to undo the harm. His disciples were hardly likely, for example, to explain to the world with sufficient candor that his several respectful references to "the classical medicine" in 1946 actually implied an almost incredible retraction.[16] Viner tells us that the suppression of his last, posthumous article, which appeared to emphasize his change of attitude, was seriously considered.[17] It was the fanatical fervor with which his most eminent British disciples had become attached to Keynes' 1936 thinking that, in my own judgment, has been largely to blame for bringing Britain to her present plight.

My own interpretation of Keynes' recommendations on policy matters subsequent to *The General Theory* differs, however, from that of Hutchison. Certainly I accept the latter's view that Keynes' later pronouncements clashed with "the conventional unwisdom of

---

13 Hutchison, *Keynes Versus the Keynesians,* p. x.

14 Ibid., p. 4.

15 Hicks, op. cit.

16 "The classical medicine" was how he had surprisingly described the teachings he had originally, and only a decade earlier, disparaged.

17 Hutchison, op. cit., p. 23 n.

the 1950s and 1960s" (Hutchison's words).[18] In my judgment, however, from 1936 to 1945, Keynes increasingly ignored the theories he
had developed in his famed work. While occasionally quoting
passages from his own gospel (in order to soften, I think, the blow
to his disciples), he relied on common sense and a fine grasp of the
facts. For, as I suggest in Chapter 1, Keynes was the complete prag-
matist. His recommendations were, as I shall shortly suggest, characterized by impatience for influence[19] and by the cynical sophism, "In
the long run we are all dead." He may well have been prepared to
risk the possibility of a rapid governmental drift toward the left,
which the centralization of monetary control recommended in *The
General Theory* would obviously have facilitated. But he seems to
have developed an inkling of the relative but consequential economic
chaos and decay which were, following his death, actually to be
experienced in Britain. If so, that would explain his apparent defec-
tion during his final years.

Nevertheless, if we can rightly accept as a guide Keynes' policy
dicta from 1937 onward, Hutchison can rightly claim, I feel, that
Keynes would probably, on many issues, have rejected the post–
World War II advice of many of those who claimed to be his
disciples.

On the other hand, if *The General Theory* is regarded as the
Keynesians' Bible, his respectful references, in 1946, to "classical
medicine" and to the wisdom of Adam Smith, and his praise of "the
invisible hand," ought to have caused his faithful apostles to shout
"heresy"! Import controls and exchange controls are, he then said,
"expedients" which would be less necessary if the "classical medicine"
were allowed to work. Had he lived, he might *perhaps* have gone
even farther. "I was the only non-Keynesian there," he is said to have
remarked after meeting with Washington economists in 1944. But,
remarks Robert Skidelsky, although if Keynes had lived, "he would
have remained more flexible than his disciples. . . . There was no
more chance of him becoming 'pre-Keynesian' than there was of
Copernicus once more becoming a flat-earther."[20] I am *inclined* to
agree, but I sometimes wonder.

What *is* beyond question is that, although Keynes favored enlarg-

---

18 Ibid., p. 19.
19 Donald E. Moggridge refers to Keynes' "almost desperate desire to influence
policy." *John Maynard Keynes* (New York: Penguin Books, 1976), p. 31.
20 Robert Skidelsky, *Spectator,* August 7, 1976, p. 8.

ing the sphere of government, he would certainly never have approved of using inflation *deliberately* to wreck the institutions of a society in which a measure of economic freedom survived; and some of the neo-Keynesians made no bones about such an aim. I agree further when Hutchison charges: "Although pseudo-Keynesian economists did not, of course, *want* inflation, some of them—*quite unlike Keynes himself*—wanted very much indeed its usual fruits and consequences in the form of wage- and price-controls, regulation of profits, widespread subsidization, import controls, etc., for which inflation provides a pretext." The *older* Keynes certainly seemed to be warning against such expedients.

In January 1937, however, Keynes was actually advocating a policy which *superficially* resembled the Austrian advocacy of preventing slumps by curbing inflationary booms. This was in remarkable contrast to the then current general interpretations of his philosophy (or at least popular interpretations of it). *With unemployment of 12½ percent,* Keynes was arguing that any "general stimulus" would be wrong, and that new public works projects should be abandoned. Yet the British economy *was* apparently booming. On this occasion he was seemingly regarding booms more as "overactivity" or (although he did not use this term) "overprosperity."[21] In spite of exceptionally high unemployment, attempts to increase "aggregate demand" should, he thought, be abated.

But it was not overactivity, in the sense that the product of a large real income would eventually create an inevitable glut and subsequent slowdown. It was a situation which, for the maintenance of a politically expedient value for the money unit; or for the honoring of a convertibility obligation; or for the preservation of a money unit value at parity with one or more foreign currencies, required monetary contraction. *Ceteris paribus,* greater "activity"—greater use of men and assets—always validates credit expansion (in the light of a nondeflationary, noninflationary ideal). Keynes had, it seems, grown so used to unanticipated inflation being accompanied by the release of capacity, and the greater activity so secured that, at times, he (and many of his disciples) treated "inflation" as the same thing as "overactivity." Expressing the situation in terms of the Fisher identity of exchange, inflation occurs when MV increases in relation to T. But "overactivity," if it has any meaning at all, causes T to rise

---

[21] I examine this notion and that of "overfull employment" on pp. 423–25.

in terms of *MV!* It alleges a *deflationary* situation. Such is the muddle that the Keynesian revolution has created.

Already, some readers may be inclined to ask: What is the purpose of all this effort and argument when it is obviously politically impossible to bring inflation to an end? On pp. 166–77 I have outlined a scheme which, although I admit seems on the face of it to be politically unthinkable, could otherwise eliminate inflation *and* involuntary unemployment in the United States. It is based on a plan for the coordination of the economic system which would maximize the wages and income flow and minimize inequalities of income.

Now it is important always to bear in mind, as Hayek once tried to remind us (referring to the fact that inflation harms creditors and benefits debtors), that "the most important and numerous class of creditors are the wage and salary earners and the small savers."[22] That is, the system created by Keynesianism has been flagrantly damaging the overwhelming mass of ordinary citizens. At the same time, says Hayek, "there is no problem of stopping inflation. If the monetary authorities really want to . . . they can do so practically overnight." However, "more and more people . . . have resigned themselves to the inevitability of indefinitely continued inflation."[23]

Nevertheless, Hayek shows that "we *must* stop inflation if we are to preserve a viable society of free men. Once this urgent necessity is fully understood, I hope people will also gather the courage to grasp the hot irons which must be tackled if the political obstacles are to be removed." And here Hayek's insights coincide with mine. "The hot irons" are "the power of the unions over wages."[24] "So long as this fundamental issue is not resolved," Hayek continues, "there is little to be hoped from any improvement of the machinery of monetary control."[25] Such virtues as my own plan may have are derived from what I think is an identical recognition and interpretation of the working of modern society.

The real problem may well be to convey the truths (as I see and present them in this book) to the masses of relatively poor voters who have been indoctrinated into believing that the remuneration of the relatively affluent (about one-fifth of American wage earners) has been to the disadvantage of the rest. The present book certainly cannot do this directly. But its readers could.

---

[22] F. A. Hayek, *The Austrian Theory of the Trade Cycle and Other Essays* (New York: Center for Libertarian Studies, 1978), p. 36.

[23] Ibid., p. 35.

[24] Ibid., p. 43.

[25] Ibid.

The Keynesian Episode
A Reassessment

1

On Keynes

I shall never forget the extraordinary impression that the brilliant preface of *The General Theory* made on me. Keynes' previous writings had struck me as forceful and challenging yet superficial and, at crucial points, very difficult to follow. I had spent more time struggling with his *Treatise on Money* than I had devoted to any previous work. But I felt that, in spite of a masterly discussion of index numbers,[1] and many eloquent passages, it was a badly planned, rambling, and (I came to fear) an ephemeral work. Some of Keynes' previous works, such as *The End of Laissez-Faire*, had impressed me as shallow to the point of irresponsibility. Yet the persuasiveness of that preface to *The General Theory* remained with me. It seemed to announce a critical, revolutionary contribution of great intellectual courage. I started reading, I remember, prepared for an exhilarating challenge. As I read, my attitude changed quickly to bewilderment and dismay. At the outset I predicted that the work, in spite of its obscurantism, would have a tremendous and unprecedented impact.[2]

Austin Robinson explains how the Keynesian revolution "consisted

---

[1] This discussion was based on work done very much earlier.

[2] Hutt, *Economists and the Public*, pp. 245–47. Gottfried Haberler has passed a similar judgment. He suggests that "the *General Theory* would have been much less influential . . . had it built on existing foundations and had it done justice to earlier writers; had its author refrained from setting up a caricature of 'the classical economics' as a straw man to be knocked down; in other words, had Keynes written a scholarly, well-balanced treatise instead of providing an *ad hoc,* makeshift theory serving as underpinning for a combination of a policy tract, a passionate call for economic reforms, and an impassioned indictment of orthodoxy." Gottfried Haberler, "Sixteen Years Later," in Robert Lekachman, ed., *Keynes' General Theory: Reports of Three Decades* (New York: St. Martin's Press, 1964), p. 294.

in inducing a reluctant body of dedicated but perhaps rather cautious, critical, and conservative thinkers to abandon a large part of what they had given their lives to learning and teaching, and to accept, as one complete (or virtually complete) package, a set of new and highly debatable propositions and of new ways of handling familiar problems."[3]

I am very much aware that, in 1963, I also was attempting to induce equally dedicated scholars to discard the intellectual capital into which they had invested years of study and lecture preparation. In my case such a task seemed herculean—almost quixotic. Whereas Keynes was well aware of how popular the policy implications of *his* teachings would be, I was equally aware of how unpopular *mine* would probably become. Robinson admits the difficulty of explaining the how and why of the Keynesian revolution.

Harrod and Robinson have convincingly portrayed Keynes as a grand person—gentle, generous, a *bon viveur,* witty, magnetic, venturesome, scholarly and—among his friends—loyal, kindly, and modest. He was also ambitious, impatient for influence, acquisitive (from a longing for elegant living and those noble things to which wealth gives access), ruthless, and casuistic. These are dangerous qualities in an economist, especially in one who, by reason of background, personal charm, and knowledge of the world, moved in influential circles.[4] Already, Keynes had become an international celebrity.[5] I have come to think of him as a strange combination of philosopher, economist, and adventurer. His writings as a whole, I believe, reveal a concern with "intellectual tactics." In his campaign among economists and in his public life he watched and calculated reactions, devising his career strategy accordingly.

As a thinker, he was original, scintillating, and facile rather than profound or dedicated. His temperament and his zeal to change the course of events militated against profundity. He skated brilliantly on the surface, failing to plumb the depths. Of exceptional intellect,

---

[3] E. A. G. Robinson, "Could There Have Been a 'General Theory' Without Keynes?" in Lekachman, op. cit., p. 93.

[4] Moggridge, *John Maynard Keynes* (New York: Penguin Books, 1976), p. 52, reports that Keynes "moved in the highest circles. . . . his letters to his parents are full of reports of dinners with Lloyd George, weekends with Lord Cunliffe (the governor of the Bank of England), the Asquiths, and the McKennas, to name only a few."

[5] Ibid., p. 72. Press clippings preserved by his mother show that, when he married Lydia Lopokova of the Russian Ballet, the event "was as widely reported as many recent events in the film world, with large notices and pictures."

yet essentially a man of action, he could master rapidly those arguments and teachings which did not clash with his settled convictions. Economists whose views radically differed from his he dismissed contemptuously, reading their contributions hastily—if at all—and with little effort at sympathetic understanding. In his eagerness to bend policy in the direction he favored, he seems to have hidden from himself his failure really to understand what he called "classical" teaching.[6] To refute that teaching he resorted to dialectical tricks, recklessly imputing to the "classical" writers opinions which they could never be shown, by actual quotation, to have held.[7] His references to the teachings of the "classical" or "orthodox" economists in his tract, *The End of Laissez-Faire,* and in *The General Theory,* are almost invariably flagrant misrepresentations. The tendency to attribute to a school of thought one is attacking opinions which any member of that school would indignantly deny is hardly a quality of the detached scholar. Yet Keynes appeared to have delighted in a challenging perverseness.

Supremely confident, conscious of his reputation and rhetorical skill, he appears to have been self-critical only when his previous speculations had tended to lead him away from instead of toward conclusions to which he was intuitively attached. When he discarded concepts and apparatus which he had earlier introduced, it was because he had found more convincing ways, although sometimes quite different and *inconsistent* ways, of stating a case which, in its essence, he had not modified. Austin Robinson regarded him as "remarkably consistent in his strategic objectives, but extraordinarily fertile in tactical proposals for achieving them."[8] I should say rather that while his convictions about *policy* seem indeed to have been unshakable, he constantly changed the arguments, assumptions, terminology, and formulas which could be used to justify those convictions. In other words, his fundamental ideas were subject to change only

[6] Roy F. Harrod, *The Life of John Maynard Keynes,* 2d ed. (New York: Harcourt, Brace, and Company, 1952), p. 453, confesses that it seemed to him that Keynes was "in some confusion about what the classical position really was; that he had not fully thought it through."

[7] Perhaps the most indefensible misrepresentation was his quotation of John Stuart Mill in his attempt to refute Say's law (as Benjamin M. Anderson, Emil Korner, Don Patinkin, and others have pointed out): he ended the quotation just where its continuance would have led to a wholly different view of Mill's contention. (See W. H. Hutt, *A Rehabilitation of Say's Law* [Athens: Ohio University Press, 1975], chap. 3, p. 3.)

[8] "John Maynard Keynes, 1883–1946," *Economic Journal,* March 1947, p. 45.

in respect of the particular concepts, formulas, or jargon in which he dressed them.[9]

Harrod, Keynes' loyal biographer, says that one gets the feeling, from earlier works, that "he was tentatively and no doubt hurriedly searching for arguments to support a conviction, which was itself more solidly based than the supports which he outlined. It was in fact what we have come to call a 'hunch.'"[10] I share this feeling that Keynes was "searching for arguments to support a conviction." But I have it about the whole body of what was original in his economic writings. His "hunch" throughout was that control of expenditure through monetary and fiscal policy could solve the problems of maladjustment expressed in unemployment. And he seems originally to have believed that this could be done *without* the disastrous sociological consequences of a gradual depreciation of the currency. His intellectual speculations consisted, I think, of a groping around —with great ingenuity—for ways of thinking which appeared to support his "hunch," selecting and eagerly clutching those which appeared to do so, and inhibiting those which did not. The process was unconscious. I do not impugn his honesty as a scholar.

Harrod tells us also that Keynes "had completed the outline of the public policy which has since been specifically associated with his name" as early as 1924, and that he advanced his proposals then, "before being in a position to give a full theoretical justification of them." This was, continues Harrod, no doubt "because he deemed it urgently needful for Britain to act with speed. It must not be inferred [that his recommendations] were thrown out at random. . . . Did he in some primitive sense already know the theoretical conclusions that he was later to articulate? . . . Is it possible for the mind to jump from the data which are the premises of an argument to the practical conclusions, without being conscious oneself of the theoretical conclusions, which are nonetheless the logical link between the premises and the practical conclusions?"[11] Could it not be that Keynes' "primitive sense" militated against rather than promoted truly constructive thinking?

For instance, the desirability of stimulating and controlling internal investment, with public works and limitations on foreign investment, etc., formed an important part of his contribution to the

---

[9] This assertion is less true of Keynes subsequent to *The General Theory*.
[10] Harrod, op. cit., p. 467.
[11] Ibid., pp. 350–51.

influential 1928 "Liberal Yellow Book." Even in mid-1928 (which *some* would regard as a boom year in Britain), he was continually advocating capital expenditure on public account (to rectify the chronic unemployment which, under the paradoxical situation created, had persisted in spite of phenomena which suggested prosperity). As early as 1924, he had advocated a public works policy, and in 1928, when David Lloyd George and his advisers thought that public works would be a good issue for the coming election, he wholeheartedly supported them.

Again, his *Treatise on Money* (1930) was an attempt to find methods of eliminating cyclical fluctuations *under conditions of price stability*. It was intended to refute the "classical" (more specifically, "Austrian") view that, to prevent a depression *under currency convertibility,* it is essential to prevent the boom. In *The General Theory,* however, he quietly abandoned any suggestion that his proposals were consistent with long-run price stability, which could be broadly assumed in the *Treatise*. In doing so, he shifted attention from all the issues which arise when monetary or fiscal steps taken in the interests of stability of employment have to be limited by the ideal of stability of prices or the necessity to honor convertibility obligations.

Keynes has often been hailed as a genius. I enthusiastically agree that he *was*. He was an extraordinarily intelligent and able person in many ways. But his genius was compounded, I judge, of forensic and diplomatic powers, rhetoric, wit, close-range logic, flair for publicity, vitality, and personal charm. He virtually hypnotized most economists who came into close contact with him. In conversation the critical abilities of those who had dealings with him seem often to have evaporated.[12] He could move people in conversation where he could never have moved them in print. He won the devotion, indeed idolatry, of his disciples. When I think of the extraordinary effect he had upon some who were once (before *The General Theory*) my intellectual friends, I am inclined to feel that I also may have succumbed had I known him personally.

Keynes was also a master of prose. When he was thinking clearly no writer could express himself more aptly, more lucidly, or more gracefully. He was capable of expressing great nobility of ideas, often with almost poetic eloquence. But in his theoretical analyses, in the prose passages which link together his passages of mechanical or

---

[12] Robinson refers to the remark of a momentary opponent: "Keynes can persuade me of anything, however wrong-headed I believe it to be." Op. cit., p. 67.

mathematical exposition, there is much obscurity; and in Keynes' case, verbal obscurity usually signaled intellectual confusion. The passages in the *Treatise on Money* and *The General Theory* which caused so many headaches to his readers are just those passages in which, I have maintained, his thinking went seriously astray—cryptic sentences or paragraphs which cannot be explained, only explained away. In the intervening passages, in which his *hypotheses* are largely conclusions invalidly reached, his exposition is as easy to follow as anything which has ever been written in economics.

To Moggridge, for example, *The General Theory* "for all its flashes of brilliance and elegance, is perhaps the most obscurely written of Keynes' contributions to economics."[13] And even those admirers who regard *The General Theory* as a work of genius sometimes agree (Samuelson's words) that it "is a badly written book, poorly organized . . . arrogant, bad-tempered, polemical. . . . It abounds in mares' nests and confusions;" that Keynes "seems to have left no mark on pure theory," and that such originalities as are to be found in his writings "are novel at best only in terminology and emphasis."[14]

"Arrogant," "bad-tempered," "polemical"—these words do not overstate the tone of Keynes' attack on economists whose authority he wished to destroy. To "blast the classical foundations"[15] he set up "the sort of caricatures which are typically set up as straw men for purposes of attack in controversial writing," his writing at times being "more like the language of the soap-box reformer than that of an economist writing a theoretical tome for economists."[16] And his methods of ridicule and misrepresentation have at times been borrowed by his followers. Moreover, *the neo-Keynesians are certainly following his example in constantly shifting the grounds on which they support given policy implications.*[17]

During the decade following *The General Theory,* most of the

[13] Moggridge, op. cit., p. 91.

[14] Paul A. Samuelson, "Lord Keynes and the General Theory," *Econometrica,* July 1946, p. 190.

[15] Thomas Wilson, *Fluctuations in Income and Employment, with Special Reference to Recent American Experience and Postwar Prospects,* 3d ed. (New York: Pitman Publishing Company, 1948), p. 19.

[16] F. H. Knight, "Unemployment: And Mr. Keynes's Revolution in Economic Theory," *Canadian Journal of Economics and Political Science,* February 1937, pp. 101, 119.

[17] For clear instances, see my article, "Critics of the 'Classical Tradition,'" *South African Journal of Economics,* June 1964, pp. 81–94.

conventional economists who discussed this work seemed to suspend their normal critical approach—almost as though they were afraid of its author. It had been known for some years that his *magnum opus* was on its way, and I am certain that no work on economics was ever so rapidly or eagerly purchased on its publication. Having obtained the book, economists generally endeavored patiently to find every possible new insight, every new concept, or every new and workable apparatus in his contribution. This was in spite of its distressing obscurities, its slovenly plan, its apparent resuscitation of long discarded fallacies, and the indignation it aroused by its misrepresentations. If Keynes' readers could find any point of detail on which favorable comment was possible, they usually went out of their way to praise it. Even his strongest critics tended on occasion to give him unmerited credit for novelty.

Harrod refers to a "rabble of detractors" of Keynes and contends that they have falsely accused him of inconsistency.[18] I wish Harrod had named the rabble. Those economists who had the intellectual courage to challenge Keynes have never, apart from myself, I believe, been accused of having *misrepresented* Keynes' arguments when they tried to show that they are untenable. And I do not think that any economist of the old school would ever have *disparaged* another for changes of *intellectual conviction*. The only kinds of inconsistency with which I can recall Keynes having been explicitly charged, are those which concern definitions,[19] and changes in argument to support unchanged conclusions which disciples such as Robinson and Harrod themselves have admitted.

And other Keynesians have referred, also in emotive language, and *without mentioning names,* to those who have dared to criticize their leader. For example, Seymour E. Harris suggested more than twenty-five years ago that the reaction against Keynesianism then discernible consisted of "unfriendly interpretations and destructive criticisms." He wrote of "Keynes baiters."[20] I am about to examine this charge. But surely, if the term "baiter" can be appropriately used of any economist, it must be applied to Keynes himself. Austin Robinson describes him as "the great iconoclast."[21] And Harrod also refers

---

[18] Harrod, op. cit., p. 467.

[19] The most strongly worded attack I can remember on this issue came from A. C. Pigou. See his article in *Economica*, May 1936, pp. 115–32.

[20] Seymour E. Harris, ed., *The New Economics: Keynes' Influence on Theory and Public Policy* (New York: Alfred A. Knopf, 1947), pp. 3, 7.

[21] Robinson, "John Maynard Keynes," in Lekachman, ed., op. cit., p. 87.

to "a streak of iconoclasm. To tease, to flout, finally perhaps to over-throw, venerable authorities—that was a sport which had great appeal for him."[22] Harrod excuses Keynes' "barbed utterances,"[23] his "mischievous pleasure . . . in criticizing revered names," on the grounds that "this was done of set purpose. It was his deliberate reaction to the frustrations he had felt, and was still feeling, as the result of the persistent tendency to ignore what was novel in his contribution. He felt that he would get nowhere if he did not raise the dust."[24]

But *were* Keynes' "novelties" ignored? Even before *The General Theory* no economist at any time had ever had his contributions examined with greater care and sympathy, and a more obvious desire to find acceptable developments in them. To take my own case. As I have said before, I devoted more time to Keynes' *Treatise on Money* than to any other book I ever studied prior to *The General Theory*. I felt compelled to do so because of the extraordinary respect and attention accorded this work by economists whose opinions I respected. What other economist has ever had his writings subjected—during the decade in which he had written—to such detailed and painstaking analysis as is found in Arthur W. Marget's monumental work, *The Theory of Prices?* After a survey of the general tone of the critical literature, I am very doubtful whether Seymour Harris' charge of "unfriendly" interpretations and "destructive" criticisms can be substantiated. At any rate, the only criticisms which made any impression on my own thinking stand in the sharpest contrast to Keynes' own references to the "classical" school, in that they have been sober, lenient, tactful, and respectful analyses.[25] Keynes' critics never hit back with his own weapons. On the contrary, they apparently strove to give every possible grain of credit to his viewpoint and that of his followers. If the exposure of error is to be regarded as "unfriendly" or "destructive," academic discussion can hardly proceed.

On the other hand, Keynes' disciples showered him with almost idolatrous praise. They excused the slipshod exposition of the book

---

[22] Harrod, op. cit., p. 88.

[23] Ibid., p. 367.

[24] Ibid., p. 451.

[25] For example, those of Fritz Machlup, Gottfried Haberler, Jacob Viner, David McCord Wright, Franco Modigliani, Axel Leijonhufvud and Henry Hazlitt. I do not think that A. C. Pigou's angry article in 1936 or Knight's hard-hitting review in 1937 can be regarded as exceptions. Every harsh word of the latter was justifiable.

which is supposed to have revolutionized economic science on such dubious grounds as: "His instinct was . . . to get his present thinking into the hands of readers before the policies that he was seeking to influence were crystallized. He was a pamphleteer rather than a procrastinating and perfectionist pedant."[26] And they explained away his extravagances with a tolerance which would never have been extended to a writer with a lesser reputation. We were told that his misrepresentation and ridiculing of what he called "classical" think-ing—described by Lorie Tarshis as emphasizing "his break from the earlier doctrines—must be regarded as a tactic of persuasion rather than as an objective statement of the relation between his own work and conventional doctrine."[27] The offensive parts of his work are described as its "satiric aspect," an aspect which enhances the "en-tertainment value" of *The General Theory*[28]—his "showmanship,"[29] mere "sport" on his part,[30] his deliberate attempt to "raise the dust."[31] We are asked not to reject his "theory" because we are forced to reject his "personal opinions."

There was no need for Harrod to apologize for Keynes' "criticism" of revered names, or even for the "mischievous pleasure" it afforded him, had it merely been *criticism*. But Keynes' "deliberate reaction," his ridiculing of disinterested scholars in order to "raise the dust" was his method of dealing with those whose writings he felt intuitively (rather than by force of reason backed by careful study) were untenable. Harrod tells us how Keynes could make the most reckless, preposterous, and unjust assertions.[32] Yet he is almost naive in his excuses. He describes Keynes' impetuosity and his tendency to speak

---

[26] Robinson, "Could There Have Been a 'General Theory' Without Keynes?" in Lekachman, ed., op. cit., p. 94.

[27] Lorie Tarshis, "A Consideration of the Economic and Monetary Theories of J. M. Keynes," *American Economic Review, Papers and Proceedings,* May 1948, p. 261.

[28] John R. Hicks "Mr. Keynes and 'Classics': A Suggested Interpretation," *Econometrica,* April 1937, p. 147.

[29] John H. Williams, "An Appraisal of Keynesian Economics," *American Economic Review,* May 1948, p. 289.

[30] Harrod, op. cit., p. 88.

[31] Ibid., p. 451.

[32] For example, to the effect that Cambridge "was the only place where they knew anything about economics. The London School of Economics . . . was pushed aside . . . [T]hey knew nothing at all of economics on the Continent" (Harrod's words, ibid., p. 319). Harrod confesses that Keynes' whole exposi-tion "was so drenched in friendly feeling" toward himself "that it was impossi-ble to be critical" (ibid.).

beyond his book as "minor failings."[33] They are *major* failings in a person on whose responsibility and insight the intelligentsia are prepared to place the greatest reliance. Harrod says that Keynes, in the latter part of *The General Theory,* "may have allowed himself to be carried too far by the exhilaration due to emancipation from old fetters."[34] That Keynes was exhilarated is understandable. He had found arguments *to support policies* which he knew were bound to be extraordinarily popular and influential, and "the circus," his small trusted group of brilliant young advisers, had been unable to see serious flaws or unable to convince him of the flaws. No wonder he was exhilarated! But Keynes' attempt to "shake up" the economists somehow led a whole generation of students of economics to despise rather than examine the great tradition which constituted "classical" economic science (as Keynes used the word "classical," that is, pre-Keynesian).[35]

In his editorial introduction to an evaluation published about twelve years ago (by nine leading economists) of Keynes' *General Theory,* Robert Lekachman remarks quite casually, "everybody is a Keynesian now."[36] Well, the Keynesians have been claiming this, from time to time, ever since it began to be obvious that the very roots of Keynes' teachings were being cogently challenged, and in spite of the clearly observable retreat to which I referred at the outset.[37] Lekachman should have added the words, "although they are no longer prepared or able to defend Keynes' revolutionary propositions from devastating criticisms." For as I have already stressed, since 1946 Keynes' followers appear to have been spasmodically relinquishing reliance on the theoretical structure of *The General Theory* while mostly clinging to its terminology, its form, and its policy implications.

To some extent the theoretical retreat has been forced by the expression of spontaneous skepticism from within the Keynesian

---

[33] Ibid., p. 373.

[34] Ibid., p. 460.

[35] The typical student of today seems to have been indoctrinated with the belief that pre-Keynesian economists somehow relied upon divinely inspired guidance—"mythical automatic stabilizers" as one Keynesian put it—to produce order out of laissez-faire chaos.

[36] "Introduction," in Lekachman, ed., op. cit., p. 10.

[37] The retreat is continued in the book which Lekachman edited. The reader will find several passages in his introduction which illustrate this, particularly on pp. 2, 4, and 9. The retreat has accelerated during the last twelve years. I deal with it further in Chapter 18.

camp. In part it has been induced by the need to answer obviously non-Keynesian objections. But in my judgment the main pressure has come through the march of events as they have seemed to contradict the Keynesian thesis. Non-Keynesians in the 1920s and early 1930s who argued that recourse to the "cheap money" that Keynes had been advocating was a reform in the wrong direction—and that it would lead to the gradual depreciation of the measuring rod of value, the emergence later of a proliferation of centrally imposed controls, and the magnification of governmental power—have been proved right.[38]

For instance, in October 1933 President Roosevelt inaugurated a monetary policy which can be said to have embodied the policy recommendations of Keynes' *Treatise,* which had appeared three years previously. The aim, declared Roosevelt, was to "maintain a dollar which will not change its purchasing power during the succeeding generation."[39] And other events continue to mock Keynesian teachings. During 1958 it was noticed with surprise that cheap money and rapidly rising prices in the United States were accompanied by worsening unemployment. Thereafter, almost uninhibited reliance on every conceivable form of Keynesian apparatus brought no success in eliminating the chronic unemployment of more than 5½ percent of the labor force until a rapid inflation was inaugurated in 1965. Unemployment in the United States had then been maintained at above this figure for nearly seven years. Yet, commented Paul W. Mc-Cracken in 1964, "one can find no period in the so-called 'boom-bust' days, before we exercised our business-cycle taming talents, when unemployment was this high for such a long span."[40] Under

---

[38] Keynes seems himself to have been warning, in the largely contradictory last chapter of *The General Theory,* of the dangers of his own policy recommendations. The same fears appear to be reflected in several of his post–*General Theory* assertions, and especially in his last *Economic Journal* article, in his references to the "wholesome long-run doctrine" and "classical medicine" (the latter no fewer than four times). (Keynes, "The Balance of Payments of the United States," *Economic Journal,* June 1946, pp. 172–87. See below, pp. 42, 64.)

[39] In 1958, reminding the American people of the warnings issued by "experienced monetary economists" at the time, Walter E. Spahr asked: "Do the Keynesians shout from the housetops that F.D.R. has been proved wrong and that we should therefore change our course? Not at all. . . ." (Quoted from Spahr, *Monetary Notes,* Economists' National Committee on Monetary Policy, December 1964.)

[40] McCracken, "Unemployment in an Expanding Economy—The Long View," *Michigan Business Review,* July 1964. Regarding unemployment, the "bad old days" were by no means as black as they have been painted. For instance, in the United States, in two-thirds of the identifiable recessions from the 1890s to the 1930s, real income was higher in the recession year than it had been in the

Keynesian experience, "the tolerable level" of unemployment has indeed shown, in Lekachman's words, "a secular tendency to rise."[41]

The failure seems to have been abject; and without a more rapid drift toward totalitarian government, it is unlikely, I suggest, that Keynesian policy will again achieve the same appearance of success in the Western world; for it will be necessary for government to suppress reactions to the expectation of inflation over an ever-expanding area of the economy. The suppression of such reactions ought by this time to have been clearly recognized as the *raison d'être* of every Keynesian "persuasion" or "control." Let the reader ask himself whether every "success" achieved by cheap money in the past has not been due to the mass of people not expecting it, or not expecting its planned duration or speed; or through more people having been prevented, by authority, from behaving rationally in the light of their predictions.

It may well be that if Keynes had never lived, contemporary history —of thought and action—would hardly have differed. If *he* had not provided a supposed justification for the various media through which inflation can be engineered, with the whole range of "central controls" needed to make the chronic, creeping, crawling rise of prices politically acceptable, some other prophet could conceivably have provided supposedly scientific authority, with different jargon and formulas. To retain office, governments had to compete with policies which were both plausible and not unacceptable to the more powerful pressure groups, such as labor and organized agriculture. Keynesianism has proved to be a stratagem which enabled governments to do this without early disaster. "A great change in outlook was required," wrote Thomas Wilson. It was Keynes' "rhetoric and new mystique which carried the day."[42]

---

previous peak. (Ibid., p. 8.) Moreover, in two of the recessions in which this was not the position (1894 and 1921) drastic coordinative price adjustments were laying the foundations for prolonged prosperity (in the 1921 recession, following an unprecedented but remarkably effective deflation to reestablish the integrity of the dollar); and of the other two cases, in 1908 and 1914, the first was the consequence of a financial panic and the second was due to disturbances of world trade caused by the outbreak of World War I.

[41] Lekachman, op. cit., p. 2. I do not here deal with the tendency to discuss "unemployment," as variously defined in different countries and at different times, as though it were usefully measurable for the purposes to which such "measurement" is put.

[42] T. Wilson, "Professor Robertson on Effective Demand and the Trade Cycle," *Economic Journal*, September 1953, p. 570.

There is no doubt at all that Keynes' contribution has served *governments* well. But for *the governed* the consequences would have been disastrous, had it not been for continued economization as a result of technological progress and the persistent search for and discovery of new riches in the earth and under the sea. And Keynesian stereotypes remain the great obstacle to more effective coordination everywhere.

2

The Keynesian Obstacle

In this chapter I shall be developing my suggestion that the intellectual repercussions generated by *The General Theory* greatly hindered a much-needed sharpening of the tools of economic analysis in the 1930s. Thinking of this assertion, and especially of the Keynesian jargon, I suggested in the preface of my *Keynesianism* that "there are some kinds of language the habitual use of which hinders the perception of certain things as well as the saying of them." But to hinder is not to prevent, and many writers persevering with what seem to me to be conceptually woolly Keynesian terms and models have independently recognized, I believe, some of the fallacies that I have tried to expose.[1] Hence the sharpening process has never ceased; while the Keynesian camp itself has supplied some new and useful insights.

I continue here to develop my own contribution to the "sharpening" process. In doing so, I shall, I think, show why pre-Keynesian notions were, in general, superior to any Keynesian or neo-Keynesian innovations.

Although Keynesian influences still dominate the teaching of economics, a vigorous controversy seems to have been occurring among neo-Keynesians during the last decade regarding their posture on their master, and on pre-Keynesian teachings. Two recent contributions illustrate my point.[2]

---

[1] I think here first of the impressive contributions of Milton Friedman, Harry G. Johnson, Axel Leijonhufvud, Gottfried Haberler, Fritz Machlup, Don Patinkin, Leland B. Yeager, Robert W. Clower, and David McCord Wright.

[2] Minsky, *John Maynard Keynes;* Hutchison, *Keynes Versus the Keynesians.*

Hyman P. Minsky, like T. W. Hutchison, holds that the Keynesianism of today (1978), violates "both the spirit and the substance *of Keynes' work.*" Hutchison in his recently published work agrees. *But Minsky holds this opinion for reasons almost antithetical to those of Hutchison!* Thus, Minsky regards as deplorable today's growing acceptance of the validity of the quantity theory of money, while Hutchison recognizes the true Keynes as having perceived that the "classical medicine" *would* be effective if only "effective demand" could be ensured (this insight being discernible especially from Keynes' post–*General Theory* contributions).

However, through returning to quantity theory ways of thinking, says Minsky, "academic economics has recaptured much of the sterility and irrelevance with respect to the operation of the real-world economy which characterized the discipline prior to the appearance of *The General Theory.*"[3] To him Keynes' great insights were derived from a recognition of the "essential characteristics of a capitalist economy," in which "nothing useful could be done to counteract depressions."[4]

This very common charge, that pre-Keynesian *economists* thought that "nothing could be done to counteract depression," cannot be substantiated, except in the sense that some pre-Keynesians may have inhibited thought about more obvious remedies because they feared that politics stood in the way. In my *Economists and the Public* I wrote that economists in what Keynes called "the classical tradition" felt in those days that "nothing they could do or say could have the slightest effect in checking the accumulation of wrong ideas and false policies which they bring forth. . . ." The economist's "only way to permanent influence is," I said, "to take a line which will be consistently acceptable to some powerful group. . . ."[5] This challenge expressed my opinion in the mid-1930s. (I return to the significance of politics on pp. 77 et seq.)

On this broad issue, however, it may at first appear that Minsky's views coincide with Hutchison's. There was, says the latter, "no effective alternative to Keynes' proposals in the interwar years." While "Keynes' policy doctrines were not without weaknesses and dangers, . . . in a profoundly and acutely critical world economic situation they were the best, and almost the only coherent proposals

---

[3] Minsky, op. cit., p. 4.

[4] Ibid., pp. 6–7.

[5] Hutt, *Economists and the Public*.

in Britain at the time."[6] Certainly they may have been the only *politically easy or possible* proposals. But that is a rather different suggestion. Yet even Keynes' severest critics recognized that in "acutely critical" situations, as when a policy of mere drift has been followed over a long period of indisposition, and the patient is now delirious and in pain, it may well be wise to treat him immediately with an addictive drug. In 1931, for example, a group of typical non-Keynesians in the United States recommended "inflation" for the languishing economy, *and they called it just that.*[7] Prior to *The General Theory,* however, Keynes himself never described any of his proposals as "inflationary." And he made it clear that, although *the treatment* he prescribed was primarily concerned with control of spending, he diagnosed *the illness to be cured* in nonmonetary aspects of the marketing system. Nevertheless, the inflation element in economic policy since the mid-1930s *has* certainly worked everywhere very much like an addictive drug.

While some economists of major importance still believe that Keynes' answers to the questions arising in Britain during the troubled 1930s (although admittedly seriously defective in some respects) were necessary for Britain's very survival, neo-Keynesians today, in trying to suggest "operational" policies, are suddenly realizing that they are prescribing pre-Keynesian advice. Thus, Moggridge refers to the recent dissatisfaction of neo-Keynesians over "increased formalization of economic theory along what those concerned regard as pre-Keynesian lines."[8] Well, the neo-Keynesians do seem rather reluctant to realize that much of their revisionist thinking had been anticipated well before *The General Theory.*

Hutchison holds,[9] however, that "with the benefit of hindsight, inadequacies and dangers can certainly be discerned in Keynes' doctrines' (in *The General Theory*). I maintain, on the contrary, that it was possible, through pre-Keynesian insights, to perceive fundamental "inadequacies" immediately following publication of that book.

---

[6] Hutchison, op. cit., pp. 7–8. The late Harry Johnson held a very similar opinion.

[7] J. Ronnie Davis, "Chicago Economists, Deficit Budgets, and the Early 1930s," *American Economic Review,* June 1968, pp. 476–82. The group included Frank H. Knight, Henry C. Simons, Jacob Viner, Aaron Director, and Lloyd W. Mints.

[8] Moggridge, *John Maynard Keynes,* pp. 164–65.

[9] Hutchison, op. cit., p. 8.

Keynes had claimed, in 1936, complete generality for his propositions, as did most of his disciples for many years. We can now see that this was a quite preposterous claim. Only when the march of events seemed to reduce the essence of orthodox Keynesianism to an absurdity did we become aware of cautious changes of attitude on his part. Even Keynes himself already appeared to be retreating, especially in the last chapter of *The General Theory,* in his *Economic Journal* debates with Frank D. Graham and F. A. Hayek,[10] and in his last, posthumous article.[11] But we now have much more evidence of a quite striking change in Keynes' attitude toward policy subsequent to *The General Theory* and during the final decade of his life; and we are specially indebted to Hutchison, Moggridge and Patinkin for additional information and shrewd comment relevant to the changes.

Possibly because today's surviving Keynesians and neo-Keynesians now feel more and more bound to recommend "classical medicine" for ailing economies, they tend to stress all the differences they can between their own and the pre-Keynesian ideas they are discovering, instead of emphasizing points of agreement. And on occasion they allege *quite imaginary differences.* For example, Minsky states that *The General Theory* showed that "the price level does not depend solely or even mainly on the quantity of money. . . ."[12] This passage is proclaimed as though it were enunciating an important innovation!

Pre-Keynesians generally believed that, *if* the demand for money is assumed not to change, "the price level" certainly *depends* on the "quantity of money." That is if T and V are given, a rise in M *does imply* a rise in P. That is one simple form of the old "quantity theory," an essential part of pre-Keynesian economics which Minsky is criticizing. But perception of the usefulness of the identity, $MV \equiv PT$, does not rule out a recognition that there are many factors which influence prospective yields from investment in money, and hence demands for money, and hence changes in T or V.

So severely have Keynes' doctrines been treated, however, that some economists, although seemingly reluctant to renounce the

---

[10] Hayek, "A Commodity Reserve Currency," *Economic Journal,* June-September 1943, pp. 176–84; Keynes, "The Objective of International Price Stability," ibid., pp. 185–86; Graham, "Keynes *vs.* Hayek on a Commodity Reserve Currency," December 1944, pp. 422–29; Keynes, "Note," ibid., pp. 429–30.

[11] "The Balance of Payments of the United States," *Economic Journal,* pp. 172–87.

[12] Minsky, op. cit., p. 2.

Keynesian approach, have nevertheless been suggesting during the last two decades that all these controversies belong to the past. We are now "well into the post-Keynesian era,"[13] they are apt to say. Yet others (speaking rather from the non-Keynesian camp) sometimes declare that "we are all Keynesians now." The truth is, I think, that most economists now feel themselves forced to talk and teach in what has become the modern economic language in order to retain respect and get a hearing, *in spite of the unsatisfactory concepts and misleading terminology to which they are thereby committed.* Through a powerful urge to follow well-worn trails in academic discussion, economists have found themselves in a Keynesian quagmire. They mostly realize now that they have for too long followed a leader who was himself lost; but many appear to be resigned to their fate—unwilling to try to extricate themselves from their entanglement.

Some perhaps try to rationalize their predicament, saying that however fallacious Keynesian theory may be, the policies it implies are, *for political reasons,* "wiser" than "classical" policies. Even so, if that is an economist's conviction, it is still his duty to explain *why* "classical" remedies must be held to be defective from the angle of political acceptability.[14]

We can consider the position of the late Harry G. Johnson, who, like so many former Keynesians, appeared to admit that the vital originality of *The General Theory*—the unemployment equilibrium thesis—is untenable. He did not argue that Keynes' *economics* is defensible but that his "polemical instinct was surely right . . ."; for, "neo-classical ways of thinking were then" (i.e., in 1936) "a major obstacle to sensible antidepression policy."[15] In other words, in spite of the fundamental fallacy on which, he agreed, Keynes' thought was based, it did serve a beneficial purpose; for the *authority* of "classical" antidepression thought, which Johnson held had not been "sensible," was dealt a necessary blow.

But exactly how can it be held that the policy implications of pre-Keynesian economics were not "sensible"? After all, *they were never put to the test.* The passage from Johnson may perhaps mean that,

---

[13] For example, Harry G. Johnson, "The General Theory After Twenty-five Years," *American Economic Review, Papers and Proceedings,* May 1961, p. 26.
[14] This is a main theme of my *Politically Impossible. . . ?*
[15] Johnson, op. cit., p. 3.

although "neo-classical" remedies *could* undoubtedly have restored prosperity in the thirties, it was hopeless to expect an electorate (and hence politicians) either to understand or to adopt those remedies. Certainly economists who regard pre-Keynesian teachings as not being "sensible," may be thinking simply of the admitted difficulty or the supposed impossibility of winning political consent for the reforms to which those teachings were pointing. That being so, they may believe Keynes' polemics to have helped persuade the community to be "sensible," in the sense (1) of acquiescing in inflation whenever unemployment or recession is threatening, *and the intention to inflate the currency can be hidden,* as a crude means of confiscating the real gains from money wage rates forced above market-clearing values, or (2) of acquiescing in authoritarian "incomes policies," "controls," "ceilings," "persuasions," and "guidelines" intended to curb the traditional tendency of labor unions to reduce the flow of uninflated wages. If that is the case, the neo-Keynesians should make it clear beyond doubt.[16]

It is possible, however, that pre-Keynesian remedies are held not to have been "sensible" because of some radical weakness (which Keynes himself did not discern) in the abstract reasoning which inspired them. That is a quite different point. Pre-Keynesian anti-depression teachings are to the effect that unemployment (as a short-term phenomenon) and depression are due to a contraction of the flow of wages and other income through some discoordination of the pricing system. Discoordination is blamed on too many wage rates (and hence final prices) being fixed above market-clearing levels, that is, too high in relation to income or inconsistently with price expectations. Labor unions and, in some countries, a form of subsidized unemployment "insurance" are usually diagnosed as the major factors which encourage the pricing of the flow of productive services inconsistently with full or optimal use of men and other resources. More generally, pre-Keynesian thought implied that the avoidance of depression is to be most wisely achieved through (1) the avoidance of inflation which, under any system in which the money unit has some defined value (or some politically expedient value), will have to be corrected by deflationary rectifying action and (given rigidities in the wage and price system) a decline in activity generally; and (2) the deliberate planning of institutions conducive to market-selected price and wage-rate adjustments in response to economic change, in order to maintain or enhance the flow of unin-

---

[16] See my *Politically Impossible. . . ?* part 5.

flated wages and income. But once the persistent ignoring of "classical" precepts has precipitated chaos, and *insurmountable* political obstacles obviously block the way to noninflationary recovery, only a pedant would oppose inflation.[17] (See pp. 30–32.)

Now there may be one or more serious flaws in the pre-Keynesian theory which I have so briefly stated. If so, I know of no serious exposition which sets out to indicate the flaws, *apart from the Keynesian unemployment equilibrium thesis, which appears now to have been discarded.* Yet the neo-Keynesians seem prepared neither to provide new (non-Keynesian) criticisms of the pre-Keynesian, "classical" case nor overtly to return to it.

The chief tragedy of what, I believe, will ultimately come to be regarded as the Keynesian *episode* in the history of academic economics is that to which I referred earlier in this chapter. It hampered the development or refinement of theory during an epoch in which institutional changes required a sharpening of the tools of analysis.

What seems to have been happening since 1936 is that "fundamental economics" (which had been concerned with the devising of tools for studying the causes of observable economic phenomena) has been branching—not improperly—into "operational economics." In other words, the trend was toward formulations of economic analysis suitable for application *in already adopted governmental economic policy,* making abstraction of the rationality of that policy. But "operational economics" quickly degenerated—*via* Keynesian influences—into "economic apologetics." By that, I mean the devising of concepts and theoretical constructions which can be used to justify policies which have the virtue (or the reverse) of being politically acceptable.

I should be the last to decry the development of the government's sphere in the acquisition and interpretation of the data relevant to the guidance of its own coordinative activities and those of private entrepreneurs.[18] This is the valid role of "operational economics."

---

[17] In my judgment, however, the political obstacles were *not* insurmountable in Britain in 1931. If Lord Passfield (Sidney Webb) had had the courage that year to state in the House of Lords what he and Beatrice Webb privately believed about the British trade unions, he might have brought down the government of which he was a member, but his action could well have saved the pound sterling. (See my article, "Critics of the 'Classical Tradition,' " *South African Journal of Economics,* June 1964, p. 84.)

[18] In my *Plan for Reconstruction: A Project for Victory in War and Peace* (New York: Oxford University Press, 1943), I envisaged the establishment of an expanded statistical service to collect, analyze, and disseminate data required for purposeful planning and coordination (whether by collective or

Much of the effort expended in the collection of the information employed in national accounting is of value not only to the administrators of the credit system (especially if they are contractually bound to maintain a money unit of some defined value) but to decision makers in whose calculations the future money valuation of income is important.

Fulfillment of this task requires a supply of economist-technicians, and not unnaturally the faculties of economics in the major universities of the Western world have been under pressure to become schools for the training of such "economists" or "economist-statisticians." But are the students who receive this training being taught to perceive clearly the coordinative role of the pricing system? Or are they being indoctrinated with the view that it is their task to help use the data collected to correct, through the "control of expenditure," an inherent tendency to equilibrium with unemployment in a free market system, or to offset discoordinations caused through the pricing of labor (or other sources of output) having been exempted from the sanctions of social (that is, market) discipline?

The defensible scope of central direction and leadership ("indicative planning") in a free market economy cannot be perceived, nor can the techniques employed be made fruitful, as long as Keynesian notions befog the issues. In almost all the universities everywhere today, the Keynesian approach seems still to dominate, with competing ideas virtually excluded.

I attempted to arouse interest in this situation in 1964, after I had thought about the reception accorded my *Keynesianism.* I wrote:

> It was about 25 to 30 years ago that most of the younger skeptics who expressed misgivings about the "new economics" began to be eliminated from academic life. There was no inquisition, no discernible or intentional suspension of academic freedom; but young non-conformists could seldom expect promotion. They appeared rather like young physicists who were arrogant enough to challenge the basic validity of revolutionary developments which they did not properly understand. To suggest that Keynes was wrong was like questioning the soundness of Einstein or Bohr. The older economists could perhaps declare their doubts without serious loss of prestige,

---

"private" entrepreneurial initiative). This suggestion was discussed further in my article "Plan for Economic Research in the Union" (*South African Journal of Economics,* June 1944, pp. 81–100, reprinted as a pamphlet by the Association of Scientific Workers of South Africa, 1944).

but any dissatisfaction on the part of the younger men seemed to be evidence of intellectual limitations.[19]

The position then was that a relatively small but clearly growing group of economists, scattered through the universities, seemed to be returning to the time-honored traditions of "classical" economics. But as I have said, even they tended mostly to use Keynesian terminology to the detriment (I believe) of their own and their students' thinking. Moreover, most teachers of economics seemed never really to have learned, or to have forgotten, what the pre-1930 economists were explaining.[20] For the younger men to question the currently fashionable approach demanded not only a rare insight but intellectual courage, and I have an uneasy feeling that, for those of junior status, it demanded also a willingness to sacrifice professional prospects in the interests of scientific integrity. I do not of course imply that there have been *no* outlets for the expression of dissenting thought. But there was no longer, I believe, anything resembling an open market of ideas in academic circles generally.

Economists of the great universities ought, I suggest, to ask themselves whether, in their own institution, academic freedom is really being effectively preserved. Are they certain, for instance, that junior staff who might feel some sympathy with ideas such as I here express or even with Axel Leijonhufvud's analysis (which is less iconoclastic than mine) could openly confess to that sympathy without damaging their academic careers? In some cases they might well answer affirmatively. There *are* a few universities in which such confidence would be fully justified. But discussions with economists who share my fears convince me that, in Britain and the United States at any rate, the setup is seldom conducive to any candid reassertion of pre-Keynesian ideas. Even senior economists have at times confessed to me that they are subject to powerful pressures to conform to fashion. Some feel under an obligation to train their most promising students along lines which are likely to make them acceptable as teachers in other universities, or as public servants in administrations dominated by surviving Keynesian convictions.

---

[19] Hutt, "Critics of the 'Classical Tradition.'" There may well have been occasional discriminations of a similar kind (equally difficult to substantiate) against the Keynesian type of thinking during the days when classical thinking was dominant.

[20] For instance, one of the most able of today's economists, Donald E. Moggridge, began the study of economics by studying *The General Theory*.

Others feel that any existing consensus of opinion carries its own authority. A young British economist with whom I was discussing some of my ideas about fifteen years ago made no attempt to answer any of the points I was making. He simply asked, "How many economists would agree with you today?" Others still are intimidated by the power-holding establishment. In 1964, I asked a distinguished middle-aged American economist, who seemed to appreciate my misgivings on many issues, whether he would not express his views in writing. He answered, "I dare not. I should probably be blacklisted." And about the same time I asked a brilliant youngish economist in Britain who, I had good reason to believe, would have been inclined to accept the heresies I have been propounding, why he did not himself openly challenge the Keynesians. He replied, "I am scared. They are much too powerful."

The modern emphasis on macroeconomics, the validity of which depends—as few writers in the field seem to realize—upon its reconciliation with microeconomics, aggravates the situation. For macroeconomics, which is particularly amenable to mathematical enunciation, is now being taught at an early stage in the typical curriculum; and the young student tends, I fear, to spend more time grappling with mathematics than with economics, the *difficulties* of which are not mathematical. His attention is diverted from rigorous thought about the phenomena of scarcity and price, and the stabilizing and coordinative role of the price system, to the study of complex truisms. When he graduates, he may have learned very little of basic economic science. If he tries to reconcile in his mind the apparent conceptual confusions which *most* macroeconomists elaborate, he is, as I have already suggested, likely to prejudice his academic record. Students with a lively and critical intelligence have admitted to me that they have felt it expedient (in the struggle for good symbols) to echo current texts and teachings mechanically, inhibiting all concern with their validity. It is of course *possible* to express pre-Keynesian thought in macro terms.[21] But that does not affect the present argument.

Despite my conviction that an economic creed has become entrenched within most of the universities—a Keynesian priesthood determined to retain its hold—I have no doubt that most economists in all the universities are sincerely convinced that the greatest possible opportunity for the free expression of divergent ideas *by those whom*

---

[21] See, for example, R. Garrison's recently published *Austrian Macroeconomics* (Menlo Park, Calif.: Institute for Humane Studies, 1978).

they regard as competent critics has been preserved. But critiques of Keynesian concepts which have appeared during the last two decades do render obsolete an enormous collection of apparatus, constructed through the expenditure of formidable scholarly effort since 1936. This alone must have created strong motives for resistance to competing teachings which threaten to precipitate widespread obsolescence in academic capital.[22]

The *genuineness* of the ever-present resistance to heresy does not, then, weaken the force of my charge. And are not the dangers to academic freedom to which I have referred magnified when university economists are hoping for influence as advisers of governments? Even if we assume that there is no question of bias due to pecuniary interest, a more elusive problem remains. Governments tend notoriously to disregard economists whose advice they believe it would be politically inexpedient to follow; and in the endeavor to exercise at least *some* guidance on the course of events, economists may all too easily be led to a compromise which ultimately weakens the force of disinterested and expert teachings.[23]

A barrier to the communication of ideas needs to be broken. This might happen through initiatives from among the economists themselves; through deliberate action on the part of the governing bodies of universities anxious to avoid the slur of indoctrination; or through growing pressure from independent-minded graduate or undergraduate skeptics who recognize and resent an indoctrination which remains to this day without effective challenge[24] and, I believe, a disastrous obstacle to a coordinated economic system.

---

[22] In 1947, Seymour Harris (*The New Economics,* p. 3) contended that academic opposition to Keynes originated from "the vested interests of scholars in the older theory." There is no doubt at all that the sheer burden of the readjustment of thought and the recasting of teachings hindered the more rapid adoption of an economics which now employs Keynesian concepts and models. But when economists cling, as they do today, to the Keynesian apparatus (with its policy implications) when the manifest untenability of its central tenet (unemployment equilibrium) has been demonstrated, Harris' charge is reversed.

[23] In my *Politically Impossible. . . ?* I suggest that the remedy is for economists' assumptions about the vote-acquisition process always to be explicitly announced and evaluated.

[24] In order to prevent possible misunderstanding, I must explicitly disclaim any suggestion that teaching the economic doctrines which I tried to show are untenable should be suppressed! When I maintained for instance, in *Keynesianism,* that the *multiplier* and the *accelerator* theorems should be expunged from the textbooks, I was not recommending any expurgation or censorship. My suggestion was merely that authors would soon be forced to abandon such notions if criticisms of them were *fairly* presented, side by side.

3

The Weaknesses of
Pre-Keynesian Economics

In this chapter the reader is asked to consider some alleged defects, as well as some great virtues in what Keynes called "classical" economics, which I called in my *Keynesianism* "orthodox," but which I now prefer generally to call "pre-Keynesian."[1] I feel now that I did not adequately defend the general body of pre-Keynesian economic thought which Keynes ridiculed. The present chapter is devoted to this topic. But it draws attention to certain important flaws in the system which Keynes did *not* mention explicitly, although they were, I think, causing him some uneasiness!

To adjudge the pre-Keynesian economists' teachings as a whole, during the period from World War I to *The General Theory* (1936), we must remember that, before that war, economists had not regarded unemployment as very important or very interesting. Sooner or later the workers found jobs if they really wanted to work, although politicians had already perceived joblessness to be a valuable phenomenon for exploitation in elections. For one thing, no theoretical work devoted explicitly to the phenomenon had been published. Beveridge's world-famous book on unemployment[2] was a beautifully written descriptive, empirical study with no analytical content. Because of the absence of any general analysis of the *concept* of unemployment, I was moved to contribute, in 1939, when conditions were very differ-

---

[1] My knowledge of the pre-Keynesian textbooks is derived from a rather random selection of authors. But I have read sufficiently carefully in such pre-Keynesian works as Keynes himself mentioned to form what I think are trustworthy judgments.

[2] W. H. Beveridge, *Unemployment; a Problem of Industry* (London: Longmans, Green, and Company, 1908).

ent, my own *Theory of Idle Resources,* which I claimed was "pure orthodoxy."[3]

Before World War I the workers' alternatives to employment had been less favorable than they were subsequently. After the war, however, *relatively* liberal unemployment compensation was widely available, and the subsidization of the occupation of being unemployed had (hardly surprisingly) greatly increased the numbers in that occupation. Moreover, the unemployed were voters—a truth which still further increased their numbers. For a decade, I myself observed the phenomenon in Britain, from 1918 to 1928; and Keynes' exposition, from his earliest works, was certainly shaped by the experiences of that period. His sympathy for the unemployed was, I believe, genuine. But the non-Keynesians of those days held that unemployment both of men and of assets was a question of defective pricing of labor and in no sense a question of inadequacies in the expression of demands.[4] I shall try to express the "pre–*General Theory*" ideas of non-Keynesian economists, as I understand them, about the "full use" of society's resources. In doing so, I shall use concepts which have been refined since those days and are influenced by the Keynesian controversies.

If through sheer inertia encountering a decline of demand at one extreme, or the deliberate use of strike power at the other extreme, wage rates in excess of values consistent with market clearance of previous outputs have been determined, that is, if wage rates exceed the workers' marginal prospective productivity, then some workers will be laid off. Of course, few managements think in such rigorous economic terms. They think simply in terms of the prospective loss to be avoided through sacrificing the product and saving the cost of each employee discharged. Almost universally, however, they do compare *prospective* sales with existing costs. And when current sales of a particular product fall, or when prices charged by their competitors fall, they react immediately. Some workers may at once be laid off or offered new contracts.

Managements realize that "recession" or "depression" occurs when asking too much becomes general. They also realize that unemployment is infectious. They vaguely perceive that the curtailment

---

[3] *The Theory of Idle Resources: A Study in Definition* (London: Jonathan Cape, 1939; 2d ed., Indianapolis: Liberty*Press*, 1977).

[4] A. C. Pigou was, I think, an exception.

of activity in their own enterprise attenuates their contribution to demands for the products of *other* workers in noncompeting fields.

This brings me to what I think is an important error of Keynes and his disciples. They are apparently blind to this last truth, which is a vital one. They do not recognize what I judge to be the most important "economic law" of all, namely, "the law of markets" or "Say's law." Quite a number of *non*-Keynesian economists, both before and since Keynes' death, recognized "the law of markets" without thinking of it as a law or explicitly perceiving its implications. This explains, I suggest, partly why few pre-Keynesian economists drew attention to the power of free market incentives to correct any nonuse of *valuable* (and hence *demanded*) resources of men or assets.

Unless frustrated by government edicts, or fear of subsequent strikes or strike threats, the expression of loss-avoidance motives following a reduced demand for a particular product tends, through the initiatives of both managements (on behalf of stockholders) and labor, to reduce margins and wage rates. Input and output prices will be forced to levels which can secure the continuance of workers in their existing jobs until demand recovers, and while they are, in the meantime, engaged in searching for other employment outlets during their leisure hours.

Admittedly, in the course of entrepreneurial decision making, what we now call *"market signals" need time to be observed and acted upon.* The demand for a certain product might well be observed to be falling, and inventories of it to be accumulating, for some time before a firm's management could feel reasonably certain that the long-run demand for that product had indeed fallen. Demands for particular products often fluctuate unpredictably over time. But we must beware of giving too much weight to this point, for no item in a firm's budgetary accounts is more carefully watched than the projected sales per week or month of each item in its inventories of finished goods. And when sales have fallen off, the firm will, in the meantime, normally take the risk of investing in greater inventories. However, the firm may often have no way of telling whether the decline in demand is the result of a competitor's price cutting, or of a transfer of demand to some quite different product (resulting from a change in preference), or whether the decline in demand is caused by the beginnings of a general recession.

If the decline in demand *is* judged to be the result of a general recession, the most typical reaction of managements in nonunionized firms will be to retain their personnel for as long as possible, at existing wage rates—especially if early recovery is expected. Managements will be concerned, above all, with the maintenance of employee goodwill, as well as with the avoidance of the costs of re-recruitment. *And finally, managements will be subject to the most powerful of all economic incentives, namely, as far as possible to maintain their assets in productive operation, whatever happens to demand for the product.*[5] At reduced wage rates, firms may retain their present employees, and so provide a continuing income for workers who are searching for alternative opportunities, as well as secure the continued full employment of their assets. There is indeed the same incentive for the owners of assets as for the suppliers of efforts and skills (1) to be alert to any fluctuation in demand for a particular product, and (2) as soon as its manifestations are clear, to react rationally to the change. For the workers, such action would be for them to accept a pricing of their services at the levels needed to retain employment, in face of demand for their services having obviously fallen. But such cost cutting (and price cutting) does more than provide continuous employment for a firm's employees. It enables a continuous contribution to the earnings of the firm concerned; and this continuity of incomes keeps going a contribution to demands for the product of others over an enormous field.

Of course, the harmonizing reactions which I have just described are all upset when the working of these very humane social forces, bringing input prices into line with output prices, are superseded by such things as subsidized unemployment compensation and the maintenance of wage rates under private coercion or governmental edict. When governments intervene, they usually substitute protection for some, with cynical unconcern about the injustices inflicted upon any who may be laid off. "Welfare activities" often have deplorable effects; but worst of all, I feel, they subsidize the "occupation of being unemployed" and cause the numbers of those officially described as "unemployed" to rise.

But when recession first begins to threaten, unless the cutting of input prices is prompt and adequate (which usually means courageous enough), the self-aggravating process under which prices in key activities come to diverge still further above market-clearing levels can get almost completely out of hand. In the total situation, indeed, it may appear as though nearly all prospective yields are falling.

---

[5] This incentive is examined further on pp. 72–73.

Entrepreneurs everywhere are justifiably pessimistic. Unless governments are prepared to act ruthlessly against those guilty of repressing the income flow, the condition of withheld capacity in a community will go from bad to worse. But in these circumstances, in *pseudo*-democracies,[6] the path to political power may be facilitated by the very process which is aggravating unemployment and depression. That is the political dilemma.

Now even when matters are at their worst, even when entrepreneurs generally fear that if they provide jobs for the unemployed, they might not cover their additional costs, i.e., even when they feel that expenditures merely for replacements or simply covering depreciation might not be recoverable, they might still be prepared to shoulder the risks if only labor were generally prepared to accept wage rates which equated with labor's temporarily low marginal *prospective* product.[7] *Simply through reliance on the universal incentives to avoid waste—the nonuse of the potential services of people's assets, or their efforts and skills—wasteful unemployment is eradicable without inflation.*

Such is the broad pre-Keynesian view of the phenomenon of widespread unemployment and depression. It is admittedly oversimplified. It does not deal, for instance, with monetary or fiscal policy. But pre-Keynesians would have denied that a good monetary system, like a good transport system, was *specially* relevant to the problem of full utilization of resources—men and assets. Nor were they blind to the reality that, if governments could get control of the monetary system, they could use it for private objectives such as the achievement of employment of labor (at a cost which exceeded the benefits) and the winning of elections.

But there is another aspect of pre-Keynesian economics which is of even greater importance. There remained at all times the great risk that pre-Keynesian economists were so loath to perceive, or admit, or discuss—the risk to investors of large chunks of capital being confiscated by future strike threats or strikes. There is no doubt

---

[6] By "*pseudo*democracy" is meant a society in which majorities or politically powerful groups may enrich themselves at the expense of minorities or the politically weak, by using the machinery of representative government and taxation to seize "private property."

[7] So many economists fail to give due weight to that word "prospective" that it is necessary to stress that, through *justifiable* entrepreneurial pessimism, the prospective product of labor may be extremely low *initially*. But the greater the willingness to face the facts and grasp the nettle, the earlier will be the recovery and the smaller the required downward price adjustments needed.

whatsoever that the constant menace of exploitation of the suppliers of assets by such methods has continuously been a major deterrent to the initiation of recovery, which it was recognized that pure market forces could otherwise have permitted.

Finally, pre-Keynesian economists certainly understood that, in acquiring inputs, entrepreneurs compared the input prices they were forced to pay with prospective yields from sales. And in times of general pessimism—widespread idleness of productive power, due chiefly to resistances to downward price adjustments—entrepreneurs could offer very much less than they would be able to (and compelled to) pay for labor later on, when the economic system had recovered. (See pp. 54, 162–63.)

While I have emphasized above widespread agreement on fundamentals among the pre-Keynesians, I must not leave the impression that, during the 1920s and 1930s, they were virtually unanimous. On quite a number of topics they differed very much among one another—at times on rather important issues. In many cases, they were undoubtedly wrong. Certain theorists of high reputation, for example Irving Fisher,[8] showed remarkably poor judgment in forecasting the consequences of economic blunders. But on money and monetary policy, their contributions were, on the whole, particularly penetrating; they were not guilty, I shall argue, of the specific sins which have been attributed to them by Keynesians.

It has been claimed, however, that in one respect at least Keynes brought about a notable advance, namely, in the principles of money. Before the great new insight brought to us by his *Tract on Monetary Reform* in 1923, his *Treatise on Money* in 1930, and his *General Theory,* it is suggested, monetary theory had been in an unsatisfactory state.

Of course, every branch of a science is always capable of progress. Yet in my judgment, ever since the remarkable contributions of Locke and Hume, monetary theory has been one of the least unsatisfactory branches of economics. "On what subject do modern specialists find the classical economics most impressive and instructive?" asks George J. Stigler. He answers, "Without question it is money and banking. A whole series of modern scholars—Angell, Gregory, Viner, Wood, and Mints, to name only five extensive explorers of the last

---

[8] Fisher's erroneous optimism about the future of stock prices in the United States stock market at the time of the 1929 crash has often been quoted to ridicule the traditional economists of the pre-Keynesian era.

twenty-five years—have concurred in the high quality of this discussion."[9] And the major contributions subsequent to Hume in this field (I think first of Adam Smith, J. B. Say, Henry Thornton, James Mill, David Ricardo, Robert Torrens and John Stuart Mill) evolved out of the insight recorded in those earlier expositions. Although subjected to far-reaching developments by such economists as Knut Wicksell, Léon Walras, Alfred Marshall, F. von Wieser, Ludwig von Mises, Edwin Cannan, Dennis Robertson, A. C. Pigou, and Irving Fisher, the core of classical teaching about money had not been seriously challenged before Keynes' "debunking."

But after about 1925, there does seem to have been a great deal of intellectual groping. It began about the time when Keynes started contributing. The uneasiness which it reflected was due less to dissatisfaction with what had been already established than to a feeling that, while the general substance of previous teaching was beyond challenge, it did not permit a complete explanation of all the phenomena of the time. The situation did not seem to be one which called for a *revolution* but one which suggested that careful development was needed. A number of speculations of promise were made in this spirit. They mostly ran into difficulties, and there was undoubtedly scope for and need for a major work of refinement and synthesis.

About the time *The General Theory* appeared and gradually led the majority of economists into a maze in which many are still lost, the time had become ripe, as I suggested in Chapter 2, for independent, constructive thought to clear up conceptual muddles. Refinements *were* being perceived to be urgently necessary. One important example concerned the nature of the issue and withdrawal of credit by holders of bank deposits and fiduciary money, one of the topics I treat in Chapter 8, "The Nature of Money." It was, I think, Keynes' *magnum opus* which diverted economists' attention from the theoretical refinements needed. I must explicitly exempt the "Austrian school" of economists and those who now call themselves "monetarists" from my charge here. But, with great humility, I suggest that even the monetarists' original, independent, and important contributions have been *affected by* (perhaps the most appropriate phrase would be *infected by*) their (the monetarists') use at times of Keynesian terminology to put a non-Keynesian case.

---

[9] George J. Stigler, *Five Lectures on Economic Problems* (New York: Macmillan Company, 1950), p. 35.

I have, however, already frankly admitted that, on one set of issues, there was a very serious weakness in typical pre-Keynesian economics—a weakness that Keynes himself felt but failed, I contend, to identify, namely, the implications of the private use of coercive power by unions. I regard this as the basic weakness of pre-Keynesian thinking. Economists generally had not, I believe, perceived clearly enough, or at any rate they had not explained, the self-aggravating nature of the withholding of supplies caused by every restraint imposed on competitive pressures. They did not realize the extent to which each individual pricing of an input or output above the market-clearing level is depleting the source of demands for noncompeting inputs or outputs. There *were* economists who perceived this truth. But they were not conspicuous. They did not have the influence they ought to have had, possibly because the implied remedy seemed to be painful (so easily describable as "cruel"). Nevertheless, the great majority of pre-Keynesian economists appear to have perceived the working of Say's law, without consciously evoking it, taking it for granted, so to speak. Had it been put to them, they would most likely have said, "Yes, but that is so." But Keynes, as we know, contemplating the depressed British economy of the mid-1930s, tried to lead his colleagues in a diametrically opposite direction.

The field in which the self-aggravating or self-perpetuating nature of pricing inconsistently with the full or optimal utilization of the community's resources was exemplified, then, above all in the consequences of the actions of organized labor. The topic was one on which few economists had pressed their thinking through to where it seemed to be leading them. Generally, they failed to perceive the harm wrought to aggregate income by the strike-threat system. They gravely underestimated the strength of organized labor, the inegalitarian consequences of its activities, and its responsibility for the losses due to wasteful idleness of assets and men in noncompeting fields.

In my *Keynesianism,* I myself largely withheld my criticism of the pre-Keynesians on this issue, as I did on several other questions that seemed not to be too closely concerned with Keynes' teachings. Today I think it urgently necessary to discuss the issue, which we now tend to call "wage-push," with the utmost candor. In 1933, Edwin Cannan made the point that "general unemployment appears when asking too much is a general phenomenon," and he referred in particular to the "extravagant pretensions" of the unemployed workers. Each group of producers, in pricing itself out of the market, priced out others also.[10] Lavington had made the same point earlier,[11] and I should guess that most economists who had read J. B. Say or James Mill accepted the argument. Yet to the politicians Keynes appeared to be offering a politically much less difficult remedy; and after 1936, economists nearly all forgot about Say, and in their rush not to be out of fashion— and to jump on the accelerating Keynesian bandwagon—*they nearly all tacitly dismissed consideration of a remedy which would have involved an unthinkable operation, such as a heart transplant.*

It was this very topic which, I sometimes think, attracted me into academic life in 1928. It certainly had me worried. *Nineteen twenty-five ought to have been regarded by British economists as the "year of triumph"; it was then that Great Britain had finally honored her word and resumed payments in gold at the contractual parity. But there followed six years of sabotage by organized labor of the great achievement,* the first three years of which I observed at fairly close quarters.

Being wise after the event and keeping silent about the significance of Britain's concrete experiences during those six years, economists, even some for whom I have the highest respect, have found it fashionable to blame Britain for having restored the gold standard at "an unrealistic parity." No one doubts that fraudulent bankruptcies can be for the advantage of the defaulters; but no economist has yet shown why it became *ethical,* in certain circumstances of the time, for a powerful nation to break its word. I suggest that *the crucial issue was a very simple one, namely, morality.* In its borrowing during the war years, the British Treasury had denied that the gold standard had been abandoned; and one still thought then of nations, as well as individuals, keeping promises. Britain borrowed cheaply while the war was raging because she had been trusted.[12]

There were great misgivings in Britain about her breach of faith in September 1931. For instance, it was widely feared that the transfer of monetary discretion to governments (apart from a purely in-terpretative discretion)[13] would be, as indeed it has turned out to be,

---

[10] Cannan, *Economic Scares* (London: P. S. King and Sons, 1933), pp. 31–38.

[11] F. Lavington, *The Trade Cycle* (London: P. S. King and Sons, 1922), p. 23.

[12] During the war, under the shadow of the Defense of the Realm Act, Edwin Cannan (an old-fashioned patriot) had been "reprimanded" for spreading alarm and despondency, by merely warning of the extent to which the gold value of sterling had declined.

[13] Under any system in which the money unit has a defined or contractual

the first step toward monetary policy becoming a tool of government. Quite naturally, the money system soon came to be utilized in the private interests of the small group of men who form governments, or the private interests of supporters who finance the politicians' campaigns.

We must remember, as I insisted in my *Keynesianism,* that before the publication of the *Treatise* (1930), even Keynes dared not recommend unequivocally the abandonment of the parity which had been restored in 1925. This was in spite of his having recommended in the *Treatise* policies which were ultimately incompatible with its survival. Had it not been for the politicians' then current attitudes toward the honoring of obligations solemnly incurred, pre-Keynesians like Cannan would, I think, have preferred the adoption, during a transitional period, of what Cannan used to call the "general prices standard." Like Keynes, he regarded the gold standard as a primitive form of money. But, he said, contemplating Western governments, "We do have a barbarous system of government and the gold standard is, *inter alia,* a most effective safeguard against inflation"[14] (although he never contemplated in those days, immediately following World War I, the irresponsible competitive depreciation of currencies set going in the world after September 19, 1931).

The facts are that, simply because the world trusted British monetary policy in the early 1920s, speculative forces rendered the establishment of the prewar parity for sterling extraordinarily easy. The trust in Britain had given her a breathing space which she needed to foster the flow of uninflated wages and incomes, together with the achievement of greater equality of income (which would have been its incidental concomitant). The eradication of wage-push could have initiated *a noninflationary boom,* and have provided the collateral necessary to back the eventually established parity in 1925. With good political leadership, a greater real income could have created the purchasing power needed to give content to a larger money-spending power.

---

value, central banks or "commercial banks of issue" must exercise *an interpretative judgment* in the process of disciplining receivers of credit (on behalf of the issue or withdrawal of credit by depositors or holders of fiduciary money, who are the ultimate issuers). But banks and financial institutions are themselves disciplined through rewards for wise or lucky judgments and penalized for unwise or unlucky judgments. (See Chapter 8.)

[14] "Annual Meeting of the Royal Economic Society: Discussion on Monetary Reform," *Economic Journal,* June 1924, pp. 160–61.

This last objective was easily definable. But it would have meant the provision of security for investors (especially for investors in unversatile but wage-multiplying assets) against exploitation by private coercive power. For unexpected strikes or strike threats can always confiscate a large part of the value of specific assets supplied. Hence investments in such assets simply do not occur. A really great statesman, with wise and courageous advisers, could have firmly announced *an irrevocable determination to restrain the use of private force which reduces the wages flow by raising key wage rates.* Market-selected adjustments to wage-rate levels consistent with market clearing would, *first, have restored outputs* in industries with overpriced inputs and outputs; and, *second, have raised demands for inputs and outputs in noncompeting activities.* And above all, such a policy would have brought about the gradual transfer of workers in suboptimal activities to occupations which had been previously monopolized by privileged workers (monopolized through private enforcement of "the rate for the job").

Unfortunately, the unions were permitted to carry on with their wages-reducing, poverty-creating pressures on the economy through the labor market. Technological and managerial ingenuities economized assets and labor, playing their role by raising the real value of employment outlets generally (by magnifying real income). But *not a single governmental step toward multiplying the wages flow was taken between 1925 and 1931,* and the spirit of enterprise was dampened in every way. On the contrary, the process of general impoverishment and perpetuation of avoidable inequality through strike-threat pressures was continued and intensified, while most economists seemed to inhibit any realistic discussion of this phenomenon.

The accelerated speed of the final return to the traditional parity in Britain was due, then, first to the trust which was, in 1925, still placed in the moral integrity of British statesmen, and second to the benign pressures from speculators. Speculation always assists in the monetary field when the aim of monetary authority is correctly perceived. The British were surprised at the strength of sterling. I do not think that Moggridge, who has done a great deal of research in this field, is quite fair in blaming the "impatience" of the British monetary authorities for precipitously advising the final step. For even when the objective of honoring the promise to restore the gold backing of British currency was explicitly and pointedly reaffirmed, most economists had still believed that the process would have to be very slow, taking at least a decade for its ultimate fulfillment. Naturally, therefore, when in 1925 speculation had brought the gap to what appeared to be a ridiculously small margin, the pressures to go all the way must have been extremely powerful. But in deciding to grasp the nettle and take the final plunge, both the Treasury and the Bank of England knew that quite drastic price and wage-rate adjustments might be forced upon the economy during a transitional period, if the hoped-for advantages achieved were to be enjoyed. But the required adjustments were not allowed to occur.

Even if Keynes had regarded the adjustments needed as practicable, he would almost certainly have regarded them as self-defeating, at least at the time when he wrote *The General Theory*. But let us assume that we do not have to concern ourselves with the now almost wholly discredited "unemployment equilibrium" notion. Then there is no *theoretical* argument left to show that the aim of pricing the services of all assets and workers at their market-clearing levels is inherently contradictory. Nor are there any grounds for regarding such a process as necessarily deflationary: In the absence of a commitment to convertibility, the value of the money unit is purely a question of monetary policy. I shall deal later with the practicability issue.

The crucial period during which the backing of the pound sterling, as reestablished in 1925, could have been provided (through an increase of real income and the real wages flow) was actually a period which was, characteristically, greeted by two of the most disastrous strikes in British history, a coal strike and a general strike. It was a period in which, some months before the tragedy of devaluation (September 1931) brought the era to an end, even Lord Passfield (Sidney Webb) could privately, not publicly, describe the General Council of Trade Unions as "pigs, pigs, pigs!"[15]

Six years after Britain's return to gold, conditions in Britain had demonstrated how the multiplication of market restraints, largely through trade union aggression, especially in *"the sheltered* indus-

---

[15] *Beatrice Webb's Diaries,* 1924–1932, edited by Margaret I. Cole (London: Longmans, Green, and Company, pp. 253–54. Curiously, in his tract *Liberalism and Labour* (1929), Keynes had described "trade unionists" as "once the oppressed, now the tyrants, whose selfish and sectionalist interests need to be bravely opposed." But he never carried his own fight beyond that. The notion that unions were "once the oppressed" is pure myth; it was originally derived, I think, from the slanted writing of economic history and a tradition of slanted teaching on the topic. (See Chapter 3 of my *The Strike-Threat System: The Economic Consequences of Collective Bargaining* [New Rochelle, N.Y.: Arlington House, 1973].)

tries," had braked or reversed the growth of earning power and caused unrest in *"the unsheltered* industries." In so doing it had brought in its train apparently chronic unemployment of men and assets. *Then the obvious willingness of the government to accept the Keynesian kind of thinking,* even before *The General Theory* made an inflationary solution respectable, *caused otherwise avoidable deflation to be essential,* prior to the great devaluation, in order to protect the pound sterling.[16] Yet, however bad the situation was in 1931, the proclaimed acceptance of an untrammeled market system could have worked wonders. Even in those circumstances, it could have preserved conditions under which wise government would have been able to prevent the world disaster of the British abandonment of gold.

This was the lesson that pre-Keynesian economic theory appeared at that time to be teaching. The tremendous power of the loss-avoidance incentives in causing the residual claimants on the value of the product of industry,[17] that is, the entrepreneurs, to price for full utilization of men and assets was frustrated by even more powerful pressures from organized labor. Keynes might have perceived this, but could think of no effective manner in which to speak out against the practices (governmental and private) which he was beginning to realize were causing the depression. I cannot justify this suggestion by any passage in *The General Theory,* but I shall be able to do so from Keynes' statements during the decade which followed that book, and by assertions by members of his "circus" after his death.

In my judgment there is not the slightest doubt that, in the absence of "the sabotage of British industry" which Beatrice Webb (in those words) so deplored in 1931, Britain could have sailed to prosperity under free market discipline and the pre-1914 gold parity. Had Lord Passfield stated in the House of Lords what he had growled privately to Mrs. Webb, he would have brought down his government. But in all probability the pound sterling could then have been saved, the wave of competitive devaluations which the British de-

---

[16] Edwin Cannan remarked to me the last time I saw him (in January 1932), "You know, I sometimes think that we could have come through had it not been for the extraordinary influence of that man Keynes."

[17] In a truly democratic society, the residual claimants on the value of outputs have the right to make wage offers on behalf of the consumers to whom they are subject. The failure of society to recognize this truth has been a major cause of poverty precipitation and poverty perpetuation.

valuation precipitated in other countries would have been avoided, the rise of Hitler might then never have occurred, there would then have been no World War II, and the reader may now continue the fantasy, if he wishes.

It *is* reasonable to conclude that, if the constraints on coordination, imposed mainly by private coercion, could have been avoided in the 1920s and 1930s, market incentives would have led to the pricing of inputs in the sheltered industries nearer to their market-clearing values. That would have led in turn, in each case, (1) to a rise in demand for inputs and outputs in unsheltered and noncompeting activities; (2) to a transfer of labor from suboptimal pursuits to more productive (better remunerated) occupations; and (3) a transfer from unemployment in many occupations to remunerated activities. Had these changes been permitted to occur, the pound sterling could have been saved.

It was not defective monetary policy which brought Britain to the disaster of September 1931, but defective economic policy generally; and that policy was justified by the myth that only the tolerance of strike-threat power, or the government's determination of particular costs and prices, could protect the worker from "exploitation." And in practice the honoring of this myth came to mean the inherent right of every "organized" labor group to squeeze as much as its leaders regarded as expedient out of the common pool of income. This "inherent right" was tacitly (seldom explicitly) accepted as something which all could and should accept. Why? No one *really* tackled the question of *how far* the price of labor in an occupation could properly be raised under duress.[18]

The only attempts to specify the limits to private coercive power I have seen, have suggested that the *unionized workers should not "go too far."* Where can we find the criteria of "too far"? Otherwise solemn *caveats* and dehortations have lacked explicit content and have all been treated with contempt.

Until after the publication of *The General Theory,* Keynes was always scornful in his references to Adam Smith's "invisible hand." I sometimes think, however, that his dissatisfaction with his predecessors and contemporaries was due to their failure to show sufficiently clearly that, *as long as the private use of coercive power is*

---

[18] Eugen Böhm-Bawerk's important *Control or Economic Law,* and Mises' relevant contributions had not then been translated into English, and H. C. Simons' seminal *Economic Policy for a Free Society* did not appear until 1948.

tolerated (physical violence and intimidation, boycotts, strikes, predatory pricing, etc.), *the "invisible hand" is prevented from operating spontaneously or efficiently.* The pre-Keynesians could hardly suggest designs for institutions calculated to release *pressures to* "optimal" utilization of resources, and thus enable the market mechanism to perform its allocative function properly, unless they first recognized and explained that private physical force, or use of strike-threat power, was preventing efficient and peaceful cooperation among men and was therefore imposing *a measure of anarchy* upon the coordinative mechanism of the market system.

Keynes once suggested that what was wrong with pre-Keynesian economics was that it "was worked out on the hypothesis of laissez-faire and free competition to a society which is rapidly abandoning these hypotheses."[19] But why did he not see that *the fact of that abandonment was just what was wrong?* What Keynes *should* have said, writing as an economist, was something like this:

> Our difficulties today are due to a degeneration of democratic political activity which has led decision-makers to abandon vital principles. We economists have been developing and refining these principles since Adam Smith. But the politicians have now been discarding our teachings for so long, in so many fields, that actual policies have been pragmatic only. We have been trying to solve short-term issues in the politically simplest ways, while the longer-term issues have become increasingly intractable.
>
> There are now only two courses open to us, if we are convinced that at root the discarded ideas can still assist us in fighting unemployment. *One,* we can rapidly restore prosperity by deliberately repealing recently-imposed income-reducing legislation. In the name of "social justice," we have encouraged the pricing of our key services and products, including labor, at above market-clearing values. The simple repeal of such legislation will not only restore prosperity but produce greater economic justice (if the achievement of greater equality of opportunity and condition is taken to be conducive to improved justice). *Two,* if reforms of this kind are held to be politically impossible, then we have no option but to adopt *a policy of rectifying the relationships of different prices to one another by subterfuge*—depreciating the value of our money unit. In adopting that course of action, we shall have to hide our intentions (for the perception of our aim by the man in the street would be strongly inclined

---

[19] Quoted in Moggridge, *John Maynard Keynes,* p. 71.

to defeat our purpose). And we must warn the electorate that we are prescribing a habit-forming drug. We deem it necessary to do so just in order to buy time. We act to head off disaster in a society that is already addicted to the very remedy we recommend.

The debasement of our money, which we frankly advocate as a short-term expedient, will give us time to legislate against all future attempts to impose prices which exceed market-clearing values. The reforms envisaged will greatly increase the flow of wages, and hence the source of demands; and they will also increase (in approximately the same proportion) profit-yields and interest. We recognize now that, since the early days of industrialism, strikes and strike threats have been poverty-creating—rendering the poor still poorer and the affluent still more affluent.[20] Our aim is to reverse this trend and gradually thereby achieve greater equality of opportunity and condition.

To attempt to put things right along such lines, a great leader could, in other words, have proclaimed the validity of Say's law, instead of dismissing it with mere disparagement. The people could have been taught the vital truth (if Say's law is indeed valid) that the withholding of capacity in any one part of the economy (for example, raising input prices by duress) sets going an apparent automatic tendency to self-aggravating unemployment of men and assets. Keynes' remarkable literary skill could have been used to communicate this thesis. But this explanation of depression, which I maintain is the true explanation, received no consideration from Keynes *at all*.[21]

This was the situation which existed in Britain in the mid-1930s. It was pointing to the need for a general expansion of utilized productive power. But the general public and the politicians were not being informed, or informed clearly enough, that each individual addition to output (priced at a market-clearing level) was creating an addition to demand for such noncompeting things as the increases in real income were destined to purchase.

Of course, it seems absurd to imagine Keynes as "the great leader" —as a champion of Say's law,[22] especially because most of his

---

[20] See my *The Strike-Threat System,* chap. 3, and *The Theory of Collective Bargaining* (2d ed.; London: Institute of Economic Affairs, 1975).

[21] Keynes did of course argue eventually that, provided we maintained "effective demand," "classical economics" would "come into its own." (See above, p. 34 n. 35, and below, p. 417.)

[22] As we have seen, Keynes mentioned that law—to reject it—but can hardly be said to have explained or examined its logic.

contemporaries appeared neither to understand nor to be able to communicate the law. But I rather think the pre-Keynesians understood it intuitively or regarded it as obvious, and assumed that others did. Preventable underutilization in one activity (or in many activities) caused reduced demands for outputs (and thus for inputs) *in noncompeting occupations.* Then, because the same kinds of discernible conduct are present in *other* occupations, cumulative underutilization tends to result.[23]

But Keynes' dissatisfaction with what seemed to be academic passivity in the actual situation of the mid-1930s, combined with his own even stronger inhibition against blaming organized labor too explicitly, caused him to attribute the depression and unemployment of his age to what I shall show are *imaginary defects* in the free marketing system. *The great undiscerned truth is that the free, or competitive system is the only coordinative mechanism which is compatible with the achievement of heterogeneous ends from heterogeneous means under freedom.*[24] Yet Keynes either did not perceive or never candidly referred to the "measure of anarchy" which I mentioned a few pages above, or to its origin.

Admittedly, *had* Keynes pinpointed the private use of coercive power as the crucial discoordinating factor, he could well have destroyed all his hopes of retaining, let alone adding to, the extraordinary respect which his pronouncements were then commanding in political circles. He could have expected to be called a crank and ridiculed in all sorts of ways. He would certainly have shocked public opinion and most of his friends. But his action would have served as a catalytic among academic economists. It would, I believe, have spurred their interest in the development of pre-Keynesian trends in economic thought, instead of discouraging or overshadowing those trends. I cannot refrain from again referring here to the parallel I mentioned above—the silence of Sidney and Beatrice Webb (the Passfields) in early 1931, when we know from Beatrice's diary of their perception that the labor unions were, in her words, "sabotaging British industry." (See *Beatrice Webb's Diaries,* ed. M. Cole [Longmans, 1956], vol. 2, pp. 283–84.)

---

[23] If the validity and importance of my own contributions to this topic should ever be recognized, it will, I think, be accepted that they consist in the stress I place on this aspect—namely, the implications of Say's law of markets.

[24] The word "freedom" here refers to "consumers' sovereignty" in determining ends and "responsible" entrepreneurial choice in determining the use of means. I explain the word "responsible" below (p. 76).

One of the most puzzling aspects of Keynes' criticism of pre-Keynesian thinking lies in his attitude toward what was then called "the profit system," but which I prefer to call "the loss-avoidance, profit-seeking incentives." In full perspective, these incentives can be seen to describe the mainspring of all rational action—that is, all action to achieve each objective (or product) up to the point at which other products (other objectives) become preferred. Such incentives constitute therefore the motive force which operates in any economic system in which personal freedom and equality of opportunity are regarded as virtues. I can claim, however, that pre-Keynesian economists did rely on "the profit motive," or "entrepreneurship," to explain the economic harmonies achieved through resolving the use of scarce, heterogeneous means for the achievement of the heterogeneous ends of mankind via the marketplace.

At the same time, identical incentives certainly play some part in Keynes' own scheme. Admittedly, their role in *The General Theory* is sometimes a rather vaguely discernible one. Often its operation is tacitly assumed (as it is with many pre-Keynesians). But during the last decade of Keynes' life, it seems that, at times, he recognized the need for these fundamental incentives exactly as his predecessors had done. Unfortunately he was never led to explain explicitly that, unless "the profit motive" (as it was usually described by pre-Keynesians) was overruled directly by government edict, or by tolerated private coercion, it continuously exerted pressures for fuller and more productive utilization of resources.

In the *Treatise* and even more clearly in *The General Theory,* then, Keynes was throughout quietly assuming profit-maximization as a vital force, if not as *the* basic force. And the whole purpose of his antidepression policy was to raise prospective yields (profits) to the entrepreneurial intermediaries through increased spending, that is, through what amounts to raising prospective output prices in relation to present and prospective input prices. Thus, Keynes' attitude toward profits constitutes the great unresolved contradiction which baffles all who try to interpret his writings. And a passage in his last chapter of *The General Theory* (which seems to me to be the most inconsistent of all the inconsistencies in that chapter with his argument in earlier chapters) is in fact a remarkable tribute by Keynes himself to the operation of the free market in its "allocative function," that is, in distributing the resources of men and assets in accordance with the myriad competing and complementary desires of the people in their consumer role. It reads as follows:

. . . I see no reason to suppose that the existing system seriously misemploys the factors of production which are in use. There are, of course, errors of foresight; but these would not be avoided by centralizing decisions. . . . It is in determining the volume, not the direction, of actual employment that the existing system has broken down. . . . The advantage to efficiency of the decentralization of decisions and of individual responsibility is even greater, perhaps, than the nineteenth century supposed; and the reaction against the appeal to self-interest may have gone too far. But, above all, individualism, if it can be purged of its defects and its abuses, is the best safeguard of personal liberty in the sense that, compared with any other system, it greatly widens the field for the exercise of personal choice. It is also the best safeguard of the variety of life, which emerges precisely from this extended field of personal choice, and the loss of which is the greatest of all the losses of the homogeneous or totalitarian state.[25]

Keynes' important qualifications in this passage—that is, his distinction between "the volume" and "the direction" of employment, and his references to the system "purged of its defects and its abuses" —obviously refer to what he believed he had shown, not in that context, but in *The General Theory* as a whole. But we look in vain among his rigorous passages in his argument to find any clarification of what "abuses" special to capitalism, other than idle capacity, he had in mind.

Thus neither Keynes' own exposition nor that of his disciples, as far as I can recall, drew explicit attention to the manner in which *the increase in money-spending power* which they were recommending for a depressed economy might lead to *the increase in purchasing power* which they simply *assumed* would follow, and thus cause a rise in prospective profits. They did not explain that, in a crude way, unanticipated inflation itself releases market-selected pressures upon prices of inputs and outputs in the direction of market-clearing values; although some of Keynes' post–*General Theory* remarks may have had that implication.[26]

I repeat therefore my suggestion that the distortion I diagnose in Keynes' thinking (and that of his followers) might have been due to his pessimistic but silent judgment about the political difficulties of

---

[25] *The General Theory*, pp. 379–80.

[26] That is, that the maintenance of "effective demand," meaning sufficient depreciation of the money unit, will validate "classical economics," so that the "classical medicine" will work.

weakening restraints which prevent market-selected wage-rate reductions—adjustments which, I argue, *could* have raised the wages-flow and income generally without inflation.

At nearly all times, I believe, pre-Keynesian economists, as well as Keynesians, recognized that depressions are stupidly wasteful and avoidable. But whether they realized that it was politics which frustrated attempts to eradicate slumps may be doubtful. They were, however, absolutely correct in their conclusions that, when the money unit had some official, defined value, the avoidance of booms was the wise way of preventing slumps; while they were equally correct in the view that booms were the consequence of previous cheap money; while cheap money was, in turn, ultimately responsible for the inevitable *corrective deflation*. But again, it is doubtful whether they saw that if a period of cheap money had been inadvertent, unrecognized as such, corrective deflation could be avoided *via deliberate reforms* to facilitate market-selected downward cost and price adjustments where prices exceeded market-clearing levels.

But had Keynes (or someone else with equal power) not offered a politically easy solution, I suggest that the pre-Keynesian economists *would* have come to perceive that the restoration of outputs, and hence a recovery in the source of demands from income, would permit *a noninflationary expansion* of the nominal money supply. If there is much withheld capacity initially, the real value of the aggregate money stock will rise when that capacity is released by the charging of market-clearing values for its services. As I have said, the real weakness of pre-Keynesian economics lay in its failure to perceive or place sufficient emphasis on this point—a weakness which Keynes *seems* not to have recognized.

Here we again run into the belief of some economists that any policy which aims at the removal of man-made barriers, which frustrate powerful motives to the pricing of outputs at market-clearing levels, is politically impossible. It may indeed be. But those who do so argue ought to recognize the objective, even if they believe that it is unachievable; and they should explicitly explain exactly why they hold that such a policy (the planned removal of barriers to freedom in pricing) must necessarily fail. Remember that it aims at the restoration of real income through releasing free market pressures to cause all inputs and outputs to be priced nearer to or at market-clearing levels. Have we not every right to expect opponents of such a solution to identify, in the clearest manner, such individuals or groups whose actions, they allege vaguely, will stand in the way?

Thus, if we believe that, because the high cost of steel in the United States limits demands for labor in other industries, in large or small degree, then we must be prepared to show that the raising of steel labor costs under duress may be causing hundreds of thousands, or even millions of Americans to have to be content with lower earnings in order to be able to retain employment. Could we not then legitimately identify any organized group which is so acting as to divert assets or labor to suboptimal employments or to maintain them in unemployment?

I am here criticizing certain essential, admitted weaknesses of some expositions of pre-Keynesian economists. It is true, I sometimes think, that because economists in general saw no way of making "operational" what they were on the brink of perceiving, they inhibited concern with it and sought in vain for other causes of unemployment and avoidable inequalities. If that suggestion is just, they were in the same position as I believe Keynes to have been.

But Keynesians' or neo-Keynesians' misgivings about market control through democratic consumers' sovereignty have not been obviously concerned with such issues as I have just discussed. Politics apparently barring such solutions, they have groped for other diagnoses. And Keynes himself diagnosed what was wrong in what I have just called "imaginary defects" in the market mechanism.

These defects were: (a) what Keynes thought of as *deleterious preferences* (the valuation of consumption in the more distant future too highly in relation to consumption in the immediate future), and (b) a *deleterious ratio,* the rate of interest which, due to those preferences, he felt was causing valuable assets and men to lose their value. Admittedly, Keynes himself did not recognize that this was the true nature of his diagnosis; and Keynesian critics may hold that my *reductio ad absurdum* is flagrant misrepresentation. Nevertheless, I hope to justify my assertion in subsequent chapters.

I hold that there is nothing at all, *under market freedom,* to prevent the system from harmonizing current price offers for inputs with prospective prices for outputs, even in confrontations with large changes in consumption preference or, the same thing, in saving preference. But suppose *market freedom* is denied. Suppose some workers are forbidden by their unions, or forbidden by governments on behalf of politically powerful unions, from accepting offers made, then the market's coordinating function is severely constrained. The "element of anarchy" to which I referred above is imposed upon the coordinative mechanism of the pricing system, braking any current rate of increase of aggregate income, or even causing aggregate income to contract. Moreover, a cumulative decline in the flow of profitably supplied goods and services priced for market clearance can be set in motion.[27]

Actually, I think I can claim that pre-Keynesian notions about boom and depression were "fundamentally correct." Broadly, taking the gold standard as given, the pre-Keynesians held that depression was avoidable only (1) through the avoidance by the monetary authority of inadvertent monetary inflation (because it must then eventually require rectifying deflationary action, which must magnify the pains of recovery); or (2) if wasteful idle productive capacity had inadvertently emerged, (a) to recognize and encourage the strong incentives of both parties—workers and entrepreneurs[28]—to restore employment by reducing those wage rates and prices which were judged to be fixed above market-clearing values; and (b) to take general remedial action to remove price barriers to recovery, in the understanding that the value of one man's employment and products provided a demand for another's employment and products.

It was because this policy was not or could not be vigorously followed that unemployment was a pre-Keynesian phenomenon, although never as serious as the unemployment experienced when Keynesian policies have been consistently followed for long periods. The "remedial action" I envisage can be classified as emergency and basic.

In emergency situations, political considerations may well outweigh economic considerations in the pre-Keynesian economist's prescription. Thus, the secret use of inflation might be attempted as a short-run expedient to boost profits in the interests of restoring the wages flow. Again, as an emergency measure, even recourse to incomes policies might be defensible—raising the wages flow by forcing down wage rates which had been raised under duress during a stipulated previous period. But, by reason of the great defect in pre-Keynesion economics which I referred to above (on pp. 57–58),

---

[27] Such a reaction is, however, equally likely to be the response to *any* large change in consumer preference. It is not *specially* probable because saving preference is involved.

[28] In contracting to accept any wage offer an entrepreneur may make, workers also are performing an entrepreneurial function.

there was another emergency step which was indicated by the situation but never put forward. In order to restore the employment of labor, a courageous government could have relied upon the crude device of calling upon all *employed* workers to accept longer hours of employment without additional pay (because their enlarged and cheapened outputs would increase the source of demands for unemployed workers in other occupations and raise the value of employment outlets in noncompeting activities generally). These are, however, merely emergency remedies, not normally to be contemplated.

Regarding *basic reforms,* the action required implies the replanning of social institutions with a view toward minimizing general instability and uncertainty. The method is that of promoting fluidity in price and cost adjustments. We are all in favor of that. But what Keynes did *not* appear to perceive was that the social framework needed for maximum stability requires a *decentralization* of the decision-making function and not its *centralization.* This assertion requires explanation, for among other things it is contradicted by the passage quoted from *The General Theory* on p. 69.

As I pointed out earlier (p. 54), the "traditional," pre-Keynesian view of the economic world included a more or less tacit perception that, given the institutions of property, it was against the interest of owners (a) of assets, and (b) of skills and muscular powers, to waste those resources. Indeed, it was tacitly recognized that there was a universal incentive, under division of labor, not to ask values or prices for inputs or outputs *under barter,* at ratios of exchange for the outputs of others which prevented the achievement of gains from exchange; or *under a monetary system,* at prices which exceeded market-clearing values.

But the observable fact that not all resources *were* being utilized, or "fully" utilized, led to the empirically based pre-Keynesian conclusion that *there was no "automatic," "self-adjusting" mechanism which could ensure that the required relative prices of inputs and outputs would be established.* Hence the problem of designing institutions more compatible with fuller resource use had to be faced. Both within and between different sets of productive operations, it was believed, incentives to price the services of men and assets at market-clearing levels were being frustrated. Pre-Keynesian economists did not, I believe, use the thought-clarifying word "market-clearing." But it looked as though the profits from pricing all inputs and outputs at that level were being ruled out by governments (for the benefit of private interests), or overruled through governmental tolerance of private coercion. As I have already explained the situation, a condition of depression was due to a "measure of anarchy" having been superimposed upon the orderliness which the mechanism of the pricing system could otherwise have created.

The Keynesian nostrum was an attempt—an attempt which has failed—at a supposedly very simple solution, namely, centralized control of the spending of an increasing *nominal* money stock. I argue, however, that *there is no such easy solution;* that a state of discoordination *needs* coordination; and that, for "economic efficiency," reform requires the refashioning of property rights so that the crucial coordinative decision-making actions rest with those who are in a position *to act responsibly* (see below, pp. 75–76 et seq.). In a 1934 broadcast address, Keynes admitted that his economist predecessors had *not* assumed "an inherent tendency toward self-adjustment" in the economic system, although he is widely believed to have made that charge and certainly left that impression. Pre-Keynesians did, indeed, take it as indisputable that all large and sudden economic changes, whether of ends or of means, required *countless, widespread, and deliberate* entrepreneurial acts of coordination, each of which implied price adjustments. I propose to elaborate this point in Chapter 7.

I am not ignoring all the uncertainties which confront *individual* entrepreneurs when they commit resources to long-term uses. It is precisely because such uncertainties are unavoidable in the actual world, that *the decentralization of decision making* among entrepreneurs subject to market discipline, and *in proximity to the relevant details,* is essential for good administration—conducive to both efficiency and stability (the minimization of uncertainty) under economic freedom.

Pre-Keynesians like Philip Wicksteed greatly emphasized what I call the "planning aspect" of business management, that is, the conscious, purposive actions of *those entrepreneurs who can be aware of the detailed facts about changing ends and means.* They perceive people, in choosing means to ends, as disciplined under a framework of property institutions. These institutions ensure or protect the process under which *the prices of* the flow of services at all stages of production up to the final or marketing stage, can be set at market-clearing values. I repeat, *pre-Keynesian economists did not use such terms.* But they did perceive that it was through this pricing process that among other things the composition of inputs and outputs was determined, and that nonuse of assets and men was the exception, not the rule. Services were allocated—directed into each of the different kinds of outputs—up to the stage at which people's scales of preference pointed to the use of resources for other things.[29] And, in the course of this allocation process, among other things, the relative proportions of assets of short and long economic life expectancies were determined.

An important flaw in most Keynesian thinking lay, I suggest, in (a) its apparent blindness to the tremendous importance of the detailed entrepreneurial knowledge to which I have just referred; and (b) its tolerance of, indeed, in some cases, actual advocacy, of policies which involved overruling the disciplined decisions of business managements acting in the light of that detailed knowledge. Keynesians failed to view businessmen as taking calculated risks and accepting responsibility for the wisdom or good luck of their decisions.

Keynesians, like other "leftists," deceive themselves and their readers largely by the simple process of transferring the adjectives "deliberate," "purposive," and "conscious," which are the obvious attributes of free entrepreneurial action, to centrally controlled decisions *for which governments must accept responsibility, but can hardly be held responsible.* Those adjectives, "deliberate," "purposive," and "conscious" can much more validly describe individual entrepreneurial action which is subject to loss avoidance and profit reward. Government officials, in contrast, can seldom be effectively subjected to a similar social discipline. They must almost necessarily be *irresponsible* in the marketplace. Under democracy, they are legally and ultimately subject to the ballot; but they can seldom be aware of the relevant, detailed data which are required for the coordination of the resource allocation process. Nor can they be penalized for error (by losses) or rewarded for wisdom (by profits).

Moggridge thinks Keynes simply "rejected laissez-faire in its dogmatic form."[30] I cannot myself think what "its dogmatic form" is. If there is one clear, almost unchallengeable attribute of the true laissez-faire hypothesis, it is surely its *freedom* from "dogmatism." The laissez-faire advocates I envisage are economists whose insights seem to have shown them that *almost the only principle of orderliness*

---

[29] That is, as we now put it, up to the stage at which marginal prospective yields were equated with the rate of interest.

[30] Moggridge, op. cit., p. 38.

in free human action is found in the institutions of the free market.[31]

The institutions of the market have seldom been deliberately planned. They have survived, on the whole, only when they have worked satisfactorily. But their philosophical defense is derived from the perception that rational planning must rest upon entrepreneurial choice of profitableness in free markets. For then *the crucial decisions are made in the light of detailed as well as generalized knowledge, while these deliberate, conscious, purposive predictions and actions can be safely termed "responsible" only if they are rewarded when they are wise or lucky and penalized when they are unwise or unlucky.*[32] "Profits" are proof of social service. Entrepreneurial decisions are successful when they are performed in a manner of which society in its consumer role approves. This applies especially to decisions which commit resources to long-term uses—in other words, "planning" decisions.

Defensible "planning" under free enterprise is, then, deliberate, purposeful and based upon detailed, specialized, local knowledge of means to ends, as well as careful observation of ends themselves. It seems to me that all rejections of laissez-faire eventually come down to the attributes of responsible business decision makers under the free market being transferred by Keynesians or "leftist" critics to government officials. Yet *officials not only cannot have the necessary detailed awareness which market signals provide; but most important, they cannot be caused to lose property through error nor be rewarded by the acquisition of property through success.*

Moreover, on this issue, critics of the market appear to ignore the question of *disinterestedness* in decision making. *A main virtue of the property rights system* under division of labor, with its use of contractual agreements (that penalize unwise or unlucky decisions and reward wise or lucky decisions), *is that it serves as a framework of law and institutions which does not have to rely upon an assump-*

---

[31] Laissez-faire in the market certainly does not exclude a role for the state, for example, defense, enforcement of contracts, weights and measures, etc., provided a *democratic* government has been assured; for then competitive and egalitarian pressures are released or encouraged. Today, however, such pressures are being so widely restrained in the private interest that "libertarian" economists think of the "socialist" governments of the United States and Britain.

[32] Any dispassionate student of business administration perceives, I think, that in spite of the inevitability of risk-taking, the judgments of businessmen are in general responsible, and founded on sound, expert observation and experience in countless specialized fields.

tion that decision makers will act altruistically. But it has been a traditional weakness of kindhearted economists *to assume* that once initiative is transferred from entrepreneurs subject to market discipline to governments subject to voters, altruism replaces egoism.[33] The truth is, *in almost all circumstances,* exactly the reverse. Whenever we find that individual or sectional interests prevail over the people's interest, we find also that it is due to the fact that decision making has been motivated by the politicians' prospective profit, or the profit of politically powerful groups.

In the light of this explanation, we can return to consideration of the "automatic," "self-adjustment" view of the pricing system, attributed to pre-Keynesian economists. First, such a view did *not* (as Keynes alleged) rest on an "assumed fluidity of money wages."[34] It *could* be said to have rested in part on a belief that *if* such "fluidity" of wage rates *were* achieved, the system would work better and wasteful layoffs of workers *would occur less frequently.* Any *wasteful* unemployment which did emerge from time to time was thought to be due to discernible conduct that caused costs (particularly labor costs) to be priced inconsistently with market clearance of former outputs. Defective pricing in any one occupation was *diagnosed* as the cause of any withheld capacity and hence underutilization of resources attached to that occupation; and (even more important) an attenuated contribution to the source of demands for other, noncompeting inputs or outputs.

Keynes usually disparaged free enterprise generally, which he called "capitalism," although there are some passages in his writings which point the other way. But many neo-Keynesians regard his work primarily as having been beneficial in providing a method of centralizing power which ultimately supersedes the free market generally, and enables the establishment of a socialist system. Hence it may be useful to define exactly what the system envisaged by the defenders of market freedom is.

By "capitalism" is meant a society in which the prime role of governments is that of defending the institutions of the "free market" and the process of "competition" from fraud, theft, or coercive impositions. Under "capitalism" people in their entrepreneurial or planning role commit resources to long-term uses (thereby determining the composition of the assets stock), and they contract with and

---

[33] See James M. Buchanan, "Politics, Policy, and the Pigovian Margin," *Economica*, February 1962, pp. 17–28.
[34] Keynes, *The General Theory*, p. 257.

direct wage and salary earners to cooperate with those specific assets which they predict will best satisfy consumers and thus yield the highest rewards. Under "capitalism" entrepreneurs can, as we have seen, be trusted to act responsibly as decision makers, being disciplined by a democratic consumers' sovereignty in which people in their consumer role are the ultimate employers of (a) entrepreneurs (paid by results), (b) owners of assets and (c) workers.

Under "pure capitalism," that small group of people who have been elected as "governments" are clearly perceived as public *servants,* not *rulers.* But like judges and juries, they are necessarily entrusted with the right to make vital decisions. The dominant institution under which they operate is what we call the free market. Under it, the determination of values and prices is demonstrably a social and democratic process, since the uses of all resources are controlled, directly or indirectly, by consumers' commands on the one side and natural scarcities on the other.

In contrast, under "socialism," governments are clearly *rulers,* not *servants.* The most far-reaching commands and decisions are made by them—the small groups of private men and women (as we have seen, necessarily entrusted with great powers) who form governments. All too easily, their commands come to serve private ends, even when their edicts are sincerely intended to be altruistic. Such commands originate, under socialism, not with the great bulk of the people, as under capitalism, but, I repeat, with politicians or officials whom it is extraordinarily difficult or impossible (a) to subject to any discipline similar to that of market incentives, and (b) to provide with the detailed information or knowledge of the preferences and desires of people and of the particular means available for a response to those preferences. But both forms of knowledge are *relatively* easy for the ordinary businessman (the private entrepreneur) to obtain (that is, relatively cheaply although by no means free).

The Keynesians are wont to refer to the "unplanned capitalist economy." They charge that in a capitalist order there is no "self-correcting" mechanism which tends among other things to restore employment when idle capacity has developed.[35] But I myself, during a lifetime of studying and teaching business administration, have throughout believed that I have actually observed, in detail and in countless greatly differing circumstances, the continuous working of this "self-correcting process." Among other things I have been aware

---

[35] For example, Minsky, *John Maynard Keynes,* pp. 2–3.

continually of the efforts of responsible decision makers to avoid the discoordinating pressures imposed by private coercion, and by government coercion in the private interests of the politically powerful. But the market pricing or valuing mechanism, which is the un-invented apparatus through which heterogeneous resources can be allocated for the satisfaction of even more heterogeneous ends and objectives, is not only democratic in its essence but also extraordinarily efficient when attempts to coordinate are not suppressed.

In his weakest book, *The End of Laissez-Faire* (1926),[36] Keynes skillfully and irresponsibly challenged the capitalist system. He failed to recognize it as what it truly is, a system under which the most important planning decisions (and, I repeat, purposeful, deliberate, thought-out decisions) are made by *responsible* entrepreneurs, who are continually observing preferences of consumers, and discerning means to ends. They put their (or their stockholders') capital *at risk* into assets, which they administer themselves or entrust to managers.

Nor did Keynes perceive that, as I have just explained, the working of the laissez-faire system is not something which has been thought up by theorizing academics. It is a system of which the processes can be seen in persistent, actual operation. Admittedly, those who work the system seldom understand the forces within which they operate. Yet they appear in general to be remarkably efficient because of the efficiency of the social discipline to which they are subject.

We are now brought to grips with what I have come to regard as *the paramount practical problem*. It is, I suggest, essential for realistic economists to challenge the assumption, particularly common among Keynesians, that because of "the structure of the labor market," laissez-faire policies which maximize the wages flow, and the flow of complementary incomes (via market-selected wage-rate adjustments) have to be rejected from consideration. It is implied that any attention paid to such a politically inconceivable possibility would be a stupid waste of time. The vested interests and tremendous strike power of the labor unions are as much realities as the Rocky Mountains.

Yet *it can be shown* that the value adjustments required in depression would raise the value of employment outlets in general, minimize wasteful unemployment and suboptimal employment, and reduce inequalities of income as determined in the market. For

---

[36] It was a tremendous success and went to several editions.

freedom to purchase all labor where it is cheapest would release entrepreneurial opportunities for workers previously confined to suboptimal kinds of work by "the rate for the job." They will be free for the first time to accept jobs of greater productivity and value, sometimes because training for the work would then become profitable. If the prospective benefits could be communicated to electorates, might not the reforms which could ensure them be eagerly sought? *If adopted they would, I suggest, put all other conceivable anti-poverty programs into the shade.* These are my sober conclusions after four decades of disinterested observation of the facts, and study of the literature. Why should such conclusions be incommunicable?

Although there is much inconsistency, Keynes and his disciples tended to reject reliance on policies that aim at releasing free market pressures which force reductions in those prices or wage rates which have been pushed *above* market-clearing levels. I do not recall any Keynesian who has frankly admitted that such policies must *ceteris paribus* raise those wage rates which have been pushed *below* those levels.[37] They, the Keynesians, *appear* at times not even to have perceived that the overpricing must have been displacing persons employed in the occupations affected; while in each such occupation the boosted prices of constrained inputs must have been reducing the wages flow, and thereby reducing demands for the outputs of non-competing activities generally. Thus, *if the value of the money unit is maintained at a constant purchasing power, and coercively imposed wage rates are reduced, market-determined wage rates must tend to rise, unemployment of labor tend to fall,* and employment of labor in suboptimal activities also tend to fall, through the voluntary transfer of workers to more productive channels.[38]

My explanation to myself of the Keynesian blind spot on this subject includes a suspicion that, not understanding Say's law, Keynes' "circus" (see p. 34) believed that market-selected wage-rate adjustments, when productive resources had been priced into idleness,

---

[37] As I showed many years ago, each "contrived scarcity" implies an "incidental plenitude." W. H. Hutt, "Natural and Contrived Scarcities," *South African Journal of Economics,* September 1935, pp. 345–53.

[38] Under such a policy it is possible that *prospective* yields from investment in money would rise, bidding up the real value of the aggregate money stock. But under the assumption we are making here, that monetary policy is committed to the prevention of deflation, a temporary rise in MV would prevent the average of prices from falling.

implied a reduction of *"the* wage rate" (*the average* wage rate) while it actually meant the opposite—a rise in average earnings. And that was capable not only of restoring "full" employment but, far more important, of achieving stronger pressures toward "optimal" employment.[39]

Chapter 2 of *The General Theory* begins, in the first paragraph, with a complete misstatement of what I, at any rate, had always understood pre-Keynesian economic theory to be. Keynes said that most economic treatises were *"primarily concerne*d with the distribution of a *given* volume of employed resources between different uses. . . ."[40] The words "primarily concerned" (which I have italicized) are not justified; but Keynes' disciples tend to go further and to omit the qualification contained in this phrase. Even the late John H. Williams (by no means a Keynesian) referred to Keynes' great contribution in "focusing attention upon income and in challenging on monetary grounds the assumption, implicit in classical economics, of a full employment level of income automatically sustained."[41] That assumption has never been implicit in *my* mind nor have I ever read it into "classical" or pre-Keynesian teaching. I say unequivocally that economics in the "classical" tradition does not deal simply with the distribution of a given body of *employed* resources between different uses. It is concerned (a) with the causes of resources *having value,* which is the capacity to be "employed" as well as the capacity to contribute to income; (b) with the factors determining the extent to which valuable resources *are* "employed," that is, *allowed* to produce;[42] and (c) with the causes leading to savings, that is, growth in the stock of resources and hence in the flow of income. There is no assumption, explicit or implicit, about any "given volume" of employment, nor any assumption of conditions

---

[39] By "suboptimal" employment is meant a situation in which the services of men and assets have not been invested where the workers and assets-owners predict that the yields will be highest, because some man-made obstacle has banned their entry. In the case of men, "yields" are net of all costs of acquiring their inputs, including fringe benefits and conditions of service. To achieve full employment in "optimal activities," all obstacles (of which "the rate for the job" can be the most effective) must be removed.

[40] Keynes, *The General Theory*, p. 4.

[41] John H. Williams, "An Appraisal of Keynesian Economics," *American Economic Review, Papers and Proceedings,* May 1948, p. 279.

[42] For example, consider J. S. Mill, *Political Economy,* chap. 8, headed "On what depends the degree of productiveness of productive agents," which he described as "the second great question in political economy."

of "full employment."[43] This is surely true even of Ricardo (the only economist to whom Keynes referred for support of his assertion), who admittedly argued that "No law can be laid down respecting quantity" of "wealth" (that is, productivity). For Ricardo's point seems to have been simply that there were no laws of growth of productivity in general, as there *were* laws of distribution of the results of productivity.[44]

During the decade which preceded *The General Theory,* pre-Keynesian economists had been largely concerned with discovering the laws governing the relations between institutional developments and the phenomenon of scarcity. Thus, they were devoting increasing attention to the special phenomena due to structural maladjustments, monopolies, price rigidities, etc., institutional forms which were increasingly regarded as the cause of waste, idle capacity, curtailments of and fluctuations in possible income. The student learned that, in the current institutional setup, the economist had to study a world of restrained competition in the shape of sectionalist restraints on productive power, or collective restraints in the sectional interest, and that the rational study of contemporary society had to give attention to the nature of the force restrained, namely, competition.[45]

In the light of that approach, the general rate of growth of utilized productive power, and the degree of utilization of that power in the modern world, were held to result from a struggle between two sets of opposed forces:

(a) On the one side were population growth; successful prospect-

---

[43] "Full employment" as a *conceptual isolate* is employed as a methodological device in abstract analysis. See my *The Theory of Idle Resources: A Study in Definition* (2d ed.; Indianapolis: LibertyPress, 1977), pp. 52–54, 60–61, 219.

[44] In the same paragraph Keynes alleged also that "the pure theory of what determines the actual employment of the available resources" had "seldom been examined in great detail." This last charge seems to have more substance. Indeed, my *The Theory of Idle Resources,* which was partly intended to be a direct answer to the assertion (i.e., an answer in the form of a detailed statement of the causes of actual employment), is a tacit admission of the gap which formerly existed. *Yet I expressly put forward that book not as anything essentially original, but simply as an ordered statement of "pure orthodoxy."* Certainly no critic has ever suggested that it is anything else. I wrote, "The types of idleness analyzed in the pages which follow are all of a kind which are implicit—if not expressed in sufficiently clear terms—in orthodox teaching. This essay is felt to be original only in the sense that, through more careful definition, it seeks to clarify what is already known and understood. It is pure orthodoxy."

[45] See my article, "Economic Method and the Concept of Competition," *South African Journal of Economics,* March 1934, pp. 1–23.

ing; the opening up of new areas; inventions; the accumulation of technical knowledge generally and skills; the application of the inventions, technical knowledge, and skills accumulated; managerial ingenuities; and the accumulation of man-made resources. It was understood that population growth tends, *ceteris paribus,* and statically considered, to cheapen labor in terms of other services[46] (although every cheapening of one kind of labor implies an increased uninflated demand for all noncompeting labor); that every individual application of new technical knowledge (discoveries, inventions, managerial ingenuities, etc.) also tends, *ceteris paribus,* either to cheapen labor and other physical resources or, in the absence of wage-rate and price adjustment, to cause unemployment and recourse to suboptimal employment; that all economic progress is either labor-economizing or capital-economizing (and hence *unemployment-creating) in its immediate impact;* that each individual act of accumulation of productive capacity tends, *ceteris paribus,* to cheapen capital resources and (in the absence of price adjustment) to cause unemployment of some of those resources; yet that each economy or growth thus effected (although tending to cause unemployment) constitutes an increased and uninflated demand for the services of all noncompeting resources.

(b) Opposed to such economizing (and demand-creating) innovations and growth, were seen various kinds of output restrictions and scarcity-creating procedures—privately contrived or state-imposed—practices which must be viewed as *the withholding of productive capacity and the diverting of resources from relatively more demanded to relatively less demanded uses.*[47] It was understood that such practices restrain growth because, in preventing the full or most productive use of existing resources, they may—through reactions upon the propensity to save—render additions to that capacity less profitable; that they cause, in particular, rigidity of prices downward; and that they lead, therefore, to the anomaly that the growth of output in a trade due to an economy is unable to make its full potential

---

[46] It tends to cheapen labor *in terms of money* only if *M* is assumed constant.

[47] By *withheld capacity* or *withheld resources,* I mean unemployed resources which would be employed if their services were appropriately priced at market-clearing levels, that is, in relation to consumers' preferences and entrepreneurial forecasts of profitability. By *diverted capacity* (or *suboptimal employments*), I mean resources which would be employed in more productive ways if they were similarly priced. These notions are more fully explained in *The Theory of Idle Resources* (2d ed., pp. 191–288). I have further explained the importance of the "economizing-displacement process" in *The Strike-Threat System,* pp. 14–25.

contribution to real demand for the products of noncompeting industries.

Hence it seemed (in pre-Keynesian days) that, in studying the causes of the irregularity of economic expansion, we were concerned on the one hand mainly with the irregularity of savings, in the sense of provision for the future[48] (which it was understood would be influenced by irregularity of movements in the rate of interest), and on the other hand with irregularity of the withholding and release of capacity. Monetary policy was thought to be relevant because it could be shown to influence these two factors.

The most important conclusion to which orthodox economic thought was leading in this connection was that the great defect in contemporary economic organization, the ultimate source of nearly all discoordination, unemployment, fluctuations in activity, uncertainties and lack of security, was the absence (due mainly to such sectionalist restraints) of price flexibility downward. Both theoretical analysis and economic history appeared to point to this as the chief source of the economic ills of each generation.[49] It is the conclusion which I have already stated and which I am about to explain further.

Keynesian thinking, on the other hand, has been responsible for a conception of the monetary system as an instrument primarily for government use as distinct from an instrument for the use of the people; as a means of controlling "effective demand" with a view to ensuring employment instead of as a means of maintaining a money unit of defined value in terms of which contracts involving credit (government as well as private) may be concluded. I hope to show that it is utterly misleading to regard monetary or fiscal policy as determining "the level of aggregate demand." It determines the value of the money unit, and if this value *is changing,* it can influence the release of capacity which sectionalist pricing has withheld, and hence the flow of income. In this way only can what is clumsily called "the level of aggregate demand" be influenced. I hope to show, indeed, that *expenditure,* engineered through fiscal policy, is *in no intelligible sense* a generator of income. (See Chapter 11.)

But the Keynesian student is often taught that the pre-Keynesian

[48] In using the phrase "provision for the future" here, I am postponing consideration of the extent to which saving in some other possible sense may *not* imply net accumulation of productive capacity.

[49] That this represents the direction of my own teaching before 1936 can be seen from my *Economists and the Public,* written before and published immediately after the appearance of *The General Theory.*

economists believed that the world consisted of a perfectly competitive system with full employment! He seems to be taught at the same time that it is unnecessary to worry about what would happen if institutions were deliberately refashioned to break down the key rigidities.[50] When he is considering problems such as the achievement of full employment or the elimination of the trade cycle he is not led to consider the promotion of *competition, in the sense of the substitution of lower-cost methods of achieving economic ends,* as an objective worthy of study. Prices *are* rigid, he is told. Things just happen to be like that, and realists will not waste time in arguing about what might happen if things were different.

When the coordinative role of price adjustment is understood, however, all the principal Keynesian theses seem to dissolve. I propose to demonstrate in later chapters, for instance, that *under price flexibility,* it is virtually impossible to sacrifice current consumption except for net accumulation; that if the flow of productive services is not used in one way, it must be used in another;[51] that *the relative values* placed on consumption now and in the future may, *in the extreme case,* change without actual provision for the future changing and so without any *actual* sacrifice of the present; and that there are no theoretical limits to the extent to which the *value* of the flow of services entering into final products may fall without their ceasing to be fully consumed (when consumption in the future is strongly preferred to consumption in the present), although we *can* conceive of realistic limits, namely, (a) the extent to which we can imagine people *wishing* to sacrifice the present for the future and (b) the degree of versatility of resources.

I shall show also that this conclusion is unaffected even when it is assumed that the value of the money unit is rising. For all prices and all values are, under the assumption of price flexibility, assumed to be immediately and continuously adjusted to expectations of the changing value of the unit. In other words, the general scale of prices is taken always to be perfectly adjusted to all its anticipated levels at each point of time in the future. Hence the falling prices of services and of the products into which services are embodied will not prevent their consumption. If this argument is valid, it follows that the whole Keynesian case rests upon the assumption of price rigidity and the withholding of capacity which it implies.

---

[50] For the argument that it would be self-defeating, see chap. 12.

[51] Of course, part of an existing flow of valuable services may be "withheld," that is, no longer supplied.

The basic assumptions on which Keynes' rigorous analysis is constructed are, I think, stated for the first time in Chapter 18 of *The General Theory,* which he intended to be recapitulatory. But these assumptions are curiously unrealistic, in that the sorts of things which nearly all economists are led by their empirical studies to accept as changeable, are regarded as given. Speaking of some of his assumptions, he said: "This does not mean that we assume these factors to be constant; but merely that, in this place and context, we are not considering or taking into account the effects and consequences of changes in them."[52] But "in this place or context" turns out to mean virtually the whole of *The General Theory.* Keynes' models are, indeed, almost wholly static and flagrantly mechanical. Only occasionally do dynamic insights and realistic assumptions intrude and then nebulously and inconsistently. This fact will complicate exposition in every chapter of the present book.

I have here restated broadly, briefly, and in my own preferred jargon, my interpretation of ideas which Keynes so ruthlessly attacked. But some of the modern Keynesians *seem* actually to admit that the great contributions for which they hold we are indebted to Keynes, do not rest in any improvements achieved in monetary and fiscal theory or policy. The great benefits have been won, they appear to believe, through the indirect effects of attempts to apply his teachings, in quietly increasing governmental power to serve sectional interests. Yet they never see it, or at any rate they never put it, this way. Thus, Moggridge sees governments "protecting and/or compensating some of those too weak to take part in or adversely affected by the working out of economic forces. . . ."[53] But as we have seen, Buchanan demonstrated, in his famous article criticizing Pigou,[54] that it is common to *assume,* with no attempt at justification, that when decision making is transferred from the market to government, altruism will replace egoism. And Moggridge provides us with a typical example of such an assumption. Far from "the weak" being the beneficiaries of the centralization of governmental power, it is the politically strong who benefit most, and mainly at the expense of those poorer than themselves. It is this flagrant truth which needs constant emphasis.

---

[52] Keynes, *The General Theory,* p. 245.

[53] Moggridge, op. cit., pp. 166–67.

[54] Buchanan, op. cit.

4

The Academic Appeal of Keynesian Doctrine

Social institutions have not developed through the medium of rational planning. They have evolved largely out of the chance events of history. This is a precarious basis for the benefits which the peoples of Western Europe and the Americas have happened to secure—especially the connected freedoms of the mind, the spirit, and enterprise. We tend to treat the virtues of the system which we know as though they had fallen like the gentle rain from heaven. We are seldom reminded that the rights we take for granted were fought for by a long line of martyrs; and we have not consciously studied the course of history in order to perceive exactly how the accumulation of technical knowledge and the expansion of occupied area have proved conducive to the winning of liberty of thought, discussion, and decision—that security from central or sectional force which is conferred by the institution of property.

In particular, we have failed as peoples (or our teachers and elected representatives have failed) to perceive the origin of that security which emerges from the right to enter into and rely upon contract, a right which permits cooperation without coercion— cooperation under conditions of freedom. Even less do we perceive the true source of two subsidiary yet fundamental rights, equally dependent upon the institution of property: *the right to work* (in the sense of the right to acquire valuable skills, and to contract freely with those who want our skills or with those who can organize our skills to satisfy demand), and *the untrammeled right to use the accumulation of valuable resources* in the manner which we expect will be most acceptable to society in its consumer role.

It is ultimately through the failure to understand these things that mankind has not yet learned to diagnose the causes of, and to devise means of eradicating, *the evils which are expressed either as inflation or as unemployment (depression).*[1]

Generalizing boldly, it can be said that there have been two kinds of diagnosis: the pre-Keynesian[2] (which was briefly discussed in the previous chapter) and the Keynesian. The former diagnosis places the blame on a discoordination expressed through prices being fixed at levels which are inconsistent with full employment under uninflated money income,[3] and it prescribes the adjustment of prices in order to achieve full employment, more productive employment, and stability. The Keynesian diagnosis blames lack of money-spending power on lack of "effective demand," and it prescribes (in formulas which often obscure the true nature of the prescription) the *creation* of additional money-spending power which will raise final prices and thereby reduce real costs. I am arguing here that this second diagnosis diverts attention from the crucial issues and that the remedy associated with it is socially harmful.

To me, the course of the Great Depression of the 1930s had provided an empirical demonstration of the general soundness of the pre-Keynesian analysis and synthesis (not of its all-sufficiency or infallibility!). At the same time *it had demonstrated equally clearly how unacceptable, for a variety of sociopsychological reasons, disinterested teachings had become.* I was prompted by these circumstances to write my *Economists and the Public.* In it I dealt with the problem of authority in economic science, and the reasons for the current unacceptability of teaching in the pre-Keynesian tradition. It seems to me that, at the same time, others were unconsciously groping for some *politically more acceptable* substitute for the old economic teachings. Naturally, the Keynesians will not be easy to convince that the mere palatability of their theories had any influence upon them. They interpreted the Great Depression in the opposite way. To them it was the great practical refutation of the traditional system of thought or fundamental parts of it. I make this point here simply to show how diametrically my own reactions to the economic experience of the interwar period have differed. As

---

[1] The reader should notice that this paragraph is quoted unchanged from my 1963 *Keynesianism.* I have an impression that I was the first to point out this now commonly accepted truth, in my *The Theory of Idle Resources,* 1939; 2d ed., 1978.

[2] The Austrian diagnosis was the most advanced.

[3] Uninflated money income is the money valuation of income when monetary policy maintains the scale of prices constant.

I mentioned earlier, Keynes' *General Theory* appeared while my *Economists and the Public* was in the press. Since then, rightly or wrongly, I have not moved with the tide; although Keynes' confidence, eloquence, and reputation—not his reasoning, which at first left me bewildered—dealt the hardest blow to my own intellectual confidence which it has ever received.

The controversy can be well defined by the contrasted passages below. I quote first from Michael Polyani's delightful, lucid, yet independent popularization of Keynesianism, and next from Kenneth E. Boulding's most able and beautifully written *Economics of Peace*. I follow with a statement of how I see the same issues. The quoted passages represent quite fairly, I believe, the post–World War II attitude of the great bulk of economists—critical and uncritical—toward Keynes' teachings.[4] I maintain exactly the opposite.

Polyani wrote:

> The Keynesian discovery in 1936 of the mechanism by which the level of employment is determined revealed that conditions of over-production are actually quite common. . . . It is difficult to see any reason why the Keynesian mechanism should not have been recognized, say, in the year 1800—or at any time between that date and the year 1936—except for the fact that men were not clever enough to see through the puzzle which was facing them. Thinking takes time. . . . The course of past history thus appears to have been determined to a fateful degree by the slowness of human thought. . . . The Keynesian theory is really quite simple—perhaps difficult to grasp at first, but once understood quite easy to handle. . . . The blunders of governments . . . . were often emphatically supported by authoritative representatives of economic science. But since the early 1930s a new and more enlightened opinion has begun to dawn upon economic science, and through the publication in 1936 of *The General Theory of Employment, Interest and Money,* by J. M. Keynes, the light finally broke through, . . . and the general public is also rapidly modernizing its attitude to monetary affairs.[5]

Boulding wrote:

> One of the most important things that has happened in the past twenty years . . . has been the development of a body of thought on

---

[4] A physicist by profession, Polyani had a very thorough grasp of economics as it was being taught when he wrote.

[5] Michael Polyani, *Full Employment and Free Trade* (Cambridge: Cambridge University Press, 1948), pp. xi–2.

the subject of depressions which is at last commanding general acceptance among economists. . . . This is the theory that has grown up
around the name of Lord Keynes. . . . [T]here has been accomplished
a revolution in economic thought . . . that transcends in importance
anything that has happened in economics since Adam Smith. [The
revolution consists in the recognition of] a fragment of truth that had
been unrecognized by the orthodox economists, . . . that under certain circumstances there may be a deficiency of purchasing power
or of consuming power, in the sense that the public is not willing to
buy, at existing prices, the total volume of goods that are offered for
sale. . . . [M]y income is always somebody else's expenditure, and
my expenditure is somebody else's income. . . . [E]very *transfer* of
money is at the same time income to the person who receives it
and expenditure to the person who gives it. This truth is so obvious,
once it is stated, that it seems almost impossible that it could be
misunderstood; nevertheless, the Keynesian revolution in economic
thought consists essentially in the explicit recognition of this truth
and its incorporation into the body of economic thought.[6]

I maintain:

Pre-Keynesian economists had long understood the factors which
determine the rate of flow of *valuable* output (that is, the extent to
which resources are *employed*).

The Keynesian kind of thinking has existed almost from time
immemorial, but until well after World War I, it got little support
among critical thinkers in the universities. It emerged, as a powerful
academic movement, I believe, owing to a growing unwillingness of
economists to face *the implications* of existing theory. This led, I
suggest, to a groping toward ways of thinking which divert attention
from the fundamental issues. Economists came to regard income as
created by transfers of money instead of as provided in the form of a
flow of productive services *measured* in money. To such an extent
did the new methods succeed in obscuring the causes of unemployment, that absurd notions like that of general overproduction came
to be seriously discussed. The degeneration of economic teaching
appears to have been accelerated because the politicians were seeking
justifications for policies which broke with tradition but which they
had decided that it was expedient anyhow to pursue. If economic
doctrines which support some line of action are likely to be politically
useful, then undoubtedly some economists will find sincere encouragement in supplying what is wanted.

---

[6] Kenneth E. Boulding, *The Economics of Peace* (New York: Prentice-Hall,
1946), pp. 126, 132.

For more than a century, however, what we can now recognize as the Keynesian fallacies were relatively uninfluential. This does not mean that pre-Keynesian economics could ever have been described as having determined policy. Indeed, the teachings of the "classical" economists had nowhere led to the state adopting policies which were wholly based on their tenets. The reputation of orthodox economics had, however, *restrained* certain major irrationalities, such as recourse to schemes based on the notion that spending (as distinct from pricing) creates employment.

Since the death of Keynes, economists who before that time were inclined to accept Keynes' teachings, have been gradually discarding the ancient fallacies which he had resurrected. They have been slowly and clumsily feeling their way back to a scientific attitude toward monetary affairs. This has come about, I suggest, not mainly through any new theoretical insight, but chiefly through the march of world events which have obviously belied the Keynesian thesis. The retreat has taken the form not of frank admissions of earlier error—perhaps too much to expect—but rather of attempts to restate the old orthodox truths in Keynesian terminology.

Unfortunately, the old insights cannot be *well* stated in Keynesian jargon and concepts. This is because the concepts themselves have sometimes been designed (as I shall show) in such a way that vital issues are obscured. For that reason, it has been necessary for me to devote some time to reestablishing conceptual clarity, and then to treat some of the basic propositions in terms of more satisfactory concepts.

It is sometimes said that mankind has more to learn from experience than from theory. That may be true of a body of doctrine *labeled* theory; but if so, then it is very poor theory. Properly conceived, economic theory is simply the process of handling economic experience, reducing the enormous, diversified, and heterogeneous actuality of existence in a changing world into intelligible categories. The supposed *abstractness* of theory is the abstractness of a spanner or a slide rule. It is independent of the things which it handles. Hence I need hardly stress the truth that the use of unreal, abstractly conceived *premises* may be wholly legitimate and highly fruitful, provided the concepts manipulated are self-consistent and are capable of being replaced by realistic premises before conclusions are drawn. I do not therefore decry the use of highly simplified mental isolates or models; for such devices may help us to reason our way through the complex actualities of the economic system.

Now the notions on which the Keynesian exposition has been constructed, although unsatisfactory from other standpoints (as I shall show), have the virtue of being capable of precise mathematical statement (for example, in the multiplier, the accelerator, and macroeconomic concepts generally[7]); and once the rather disconnected ideas of *The General Theory* had been systematized by Keynes' disciples, they could be very easily grasped by the beginner (the more uncritical the student, the more easily). And provided the student possesses some facility in mathematics, he is able to progress rapidly to what has come to be regarded as advanced economics, with mere mathematical difficulties to overcome. In fact, his thoughts may well be diverted from the difficulties of economics to the ingenuities of mathematical manipulation. For the difficulties lie, not in the *manipulation* of concepts but in the constant testing, by reference to experience (including the recorded experience of history), of the premises on which models are constructed and the conclusions which have been drawn. When this is not understood—and some of the modern Keynesians fail to understand it—economists are capable of erecting impressive mathematical models upon conceptually confused foundations. Consider, for instance, a phrase like the following: "If investment is below its boomtime level, the level of national income generated will not be high enough to give full employment."[8] "Full employment" *means* "full national income" (whether that income is measured in actual money units or in "real" terms). Hence the phrase quoted states that the level of income generated will not be high enough to generate full income! I shall show that it can be given an intelligible meaning only in the light of Say's law, a suggestion which must shock any Keynesian. The release of withheld capacity in any field—the "generation" of additional services in that field—is likely to induce the release of capacity (the generation of additional services) in noncompeting fields.

But partly because it has become the fashion to state the Keynesian ideas in mathematical form, the ideas of *The General Theory* have served as the foundation of a multitude of studies in applied mathematics. This has created—quite unjustifiably—the impression that

---

[7] See, for instance, what I judge to be a splendid attempt—almost a pioneering effort: R. W. Garrison's *Austrian Macroeconomics* (Menlo Park, Calif.: Institute for Humane Studies, 1978).

[8] R. C. O. Matthews, "Capital Stock Adjustment Theories," in Kenneth K. Kurihara, *Post-Keynesian Economics* (New Brunswick, N.J.: Rutgers University Press, 1954), p. 173.

such studies are *scientific;* for has not mathematics been called "the language of science"?[9] And if mathematics has produced such formidable results in physics, say, why should not the same methods prove equally successful in the understanding and ordering of the economic system? Feelings of this kind have, I feel, been a not unimportant explanation of the hold which Keynesian *methods* have acquired in many universities.

Recourse to inappropriate simplifications has led also to the recognition of what is usually a quite illusory similarity between the problems of economics and those of the natural sciences. Attempts have been made to solve questions which involve the adjustment of scarce means to competing ends through methods appropriate to the sphere of physics and engineering. I do not suggest that all such attempts have been fruitless or fallacious; for it is often possible to make use of analogies and relationships so discerned in a parallel but independent study of the complex world of choice and decision.[10] But my criticisms remain valid, I believe, of a large part of the "new economics," and they are, in particular, relevant to the so-called macroeconomics which consists, as Wilhelm Röpke has put it,

> of a tendency to regard the whole economic process as something purely objective and mechanical. Hence purely mathematical and statistical methods, it seems, can be applied and the whole economic process can therefore be quantitatively determined and even predetermined. Under those circumstances an economic system readily takes on the appearance of a sort of huge waterworks, and the science which treats of that economic system quite logically assumes the appearance of a kind of engineering science, which teems with equations in ever-increasing profusion. And so oblivion threatens to engulf what, as I see it, is the actual fruit of a century and a half of intellectual effort in the field of economics, namely, the doctrine of the movement of individual prices.[11]

Economics, continues Röpke, "requires the constant application of a supreme attentiveness . . . that intuitive power which enables us to

---

[9] Keynes' own expressed attitude toward mathematical economics was by no means uncritical. But I am dealing with developments which have followed his own contributions. See *The General Theory,* pp. 297–98.

[10] A splendid example is Garrison, op. cit.

[11] Wilhelm Röpke, "The Place of Economics Among the Social Sciences," in Mary Sennholz, ed., *On Freedom and Free Enterprise: Essays in Honor of Ludwig von Mises* (Princeton: D. Van Nostrand Company, 1956), p. 121 n.

keep our eyes on all the complicated threads at once, and to emulate the juggler who never loses sight of a single one of the balls he is keeping aloft."[12] It is the vice of the concepts and models which Keynes and his disciples have chosen to use, that they have precisely the opposite effects. They turn attention away from the most vital aspects of the rational allocation of scarce means in response to competing ends. It is because the range of attention demanded is so vast that economics is a difficult science. Its complexity often baffles scientists trained in other fields when they first turn their attention to it. Attempts to confine attention to a few relevant issues only, through the use of summarizing concepts like averages, and the creation of abstract, highly simplified models, in which *constants* are substituted for *preferences, judgments, and decisions,* may greatly facilitate exposition and the mechanical part of thinking. But unless they are always accompanied by an independent consideration of the problem at issue in relation to the whole system of adapting means to ends, such concepts or the models into which they are built can be disastrously misleading. And if economists are subconsciously trying to find justifications for preconceived views—and such a possibility cannot be ignored—there must obviously be a temptation to leave analysis just when simplified models have brought it to a point at which the conclusions favor the preconceptions.[13]

"The model" is a set of simplified assumptions, particularly concerning the interdependence of different factors. But the paramount reality of the economic relationship is that, in expressing preferences for ends, and in judging the productiveness or profitableness of means, every single choice or judgment affects all others. Model making is not illegitimate in economics, but it is extremely dangerous. "The model" assumes that human action is subject to mechanical rules and hence capable of being more or less mechanically predicted from assumed autonomous stimuli. Hence its function must be that of a mere step in reasoning.

So far has the fashion of abstract model making gone, however, that Shinichi Ichimura can claim that "the standard procedure of economic theory is to consider an economic system as isolated from other factors of a noneconomic nature and ignoring the secondary

---

[12] Ibid., p. 117.

[13] In case what I have said should have left a wrong impression, I must stress that I am not attacking the use of mathematics in economics. (I return to the topic on pp. 99–103.)

effects of these factors on the economic system."[14] But such a procedure is incredibly superficial and misleading. Until three decades ago, the *standard* procedure—at least since Léon Walras—was always to bring all factors into the reckoning insofar as they have any effects (direct or indirect) upon values, and to regard all such factors as "economic." One has necessarily to resort to the use of mental isolates—imagining certain factors as remaining unchanged in order to consider the implications of one or more other factors. But before any *significant* inferences can be drawn (that is, results significant for policy), any conclusions tentatively reached have to be considered in relation to the whole complex of factors observed to be operative in the changing world.

But I believe that the most important cause of the remarkable flood of Keynesian contributions from the universities has been due to a misinterpretation of the great achievements of unanticipated inflation. Of course, neither Keynes nor his disciples thought of themselves as inflationists when *The General Theory* was published (see Chapter 9), and I certainly do not suggest that they have been blind to the tragedies of inflation.[15] Yet creeping inflation does appear always to have accompanied periods in which the kind of policies their doctrines imply has been attempted. In the era which followed Keynes' *Treatise on Money,* the Keynesian-minded economists saw the recovery of the United States, and the methods adopted seemed to them to be on the right track, in spite of the depreciation of the dollar; they saw the almost staggering recovery of Germany under Hitler which followed rearmament expenditures, but tended to view the accompanying inflation as incidental; they saw no relevance in the subjection of the labor unions under Hitler; they saw the more gradual recovery of Britain which slowly followed her departure from gold, but did not attribute this to the mild, unanticipated inflation

---

[14] Shinichi Ichimura, "Toward a General Nonlinear Macrodynamic Theory of Economic Fluctuations," in Kurihara, op. cit., p. 194.

[15] The inflationary nature of Keynes' thesis was never *explicit,* and in 1963 the majority of students, if asked whether the Keynesian system is inherently inflationary, would probably have answered no. But many passages in *The General Theory,* with which I shall in due course be dealing, *imply* recourse to inflation as the remedy for unemployment. For example, on p. 10, Keynes states that "When money-wages are rising . . . real wages are falling." Such an assertion, together with the implication that falling real wage rates will restore employment, can mean one thing only, a fall in the real value of the money unit. But as we have seen, self-styled Keynesians are today not ashamed of the appellation of inflationists.

which occurred; they saw also the enormous assistance which the abandonment of traditional monetary policy apparently rendered to the Soviet economy during the Stalinist epoch, and the rapid recovery of all nations following the monetary policies which accompanied the vicissitudes of war, yet without adequate consideration of the role of unobserved currency debasement in the prosperity observed. Moreover, they compared these almost miraculous achievements with the black years of depression when governments had tried to keep faith with those who had trusted the contract to redeem currencies in gold. The Keynesians seemed unable, originally, to bring themselves to believe that the benefits of rectifying spending whenever activity had tended to slow down, were incapable of being won side by side with the maintenance of the value of currencies;[16] while later on they were gradually led, I shall suggest, to recommend repression of the inflation which would otherwise have resulted. They came to advocate a proliferation of imposed restrictions on the price mechanism, without perceiving the full implications—economic, sociological, or political. It is, I think, largely because they have not seen the consequences of thus seeking an easy immediate solution to declining activity, that their doctrines have obtained so remarkable a hold.

A further factor may have been the unwillingness of the majority to be nonconformist or out of fashion. There was an eager claim, shortly after Keynes' death, that his doctrines were "at last . . . commanding general aceptance among economists."[17] I have already referred to the wholly predictable, infectious nature of Keynes' doctrine. But such claims have now ceased. Not only does there appear to be a growing number of Keynesian-trained economists who are uneasy about the traditions he has left,[18] and a clearly

---

[16] A post–World War II shift from this viewpoint—on the part of some at least—will be considered later.

[17] Boulding, op. cit., p. 126.

[18] In 1963 it was too early yet to speak with confidence on this point, although the late David McCord Wright and Seymour E. Harris had reported a growing reaction against Keynesian teaching in 1945 and 1947 respectively. See Wright, "The Future of Keynesian Economics," *American Economic Review*, June 1945, pp. 284–307; and Harris, ed., *The New Economics*, p. 3. (See Chapter 18.) In 1956, I asked one of Keynes' disciples who had been closest to him to be so kind as to read and criticize some memoranda which, I said, disputed the very essence of Keynesian teaching. Very courteously, he regretted his inability to assist me, but emphasized that I must not think of him as a Keynesian. A recent example is Moggridge who, although reared on *The General Theory* and obviously an admirer of Keynes (as indeed I am in some ways), can certainly be regarded as most uneasy about some of his teachings.

marked retreat (which I shall discuss in Chapter 18), but there has always been a group of eminent economists who have made it clear that they are more or less in the opposite camp.

There is a tendency today among quite a number of economists, some of whom were once regarded as among Keynes' most eminent disciples, to describe themselves as neutral. The disinclination to recant is understandable; but it is only confusing to suggest that Keynes was partly right and partly wrong. I maintain that where he was right, he was not original, and that where he was original, he was wrong.[19]

---

[19] I wrote this sentence long before I had seen Henry Hazlitt's comment on *The General Theory:* "I could not find in it a single important doctrine that was both true and original." Hazlitt, ed., *The Critics of Keynesian Economics,* p. 3.

Appendix

The Limitations of Mathematical Method in Economics

I have referred earlier (pp. 92–94) to the limitations of mathematical method in the study of economics. Here I wish briefly to develop this thesis.

It is, I believe, as a result of serious conceptual confusion that some economists appear to be bewildered by the complexities of the economic interrelationships which they perceive in the actual world. The great simplifying perception which they miss lies, I suggest, in the recognition that all expressions of human preference which are relevant to the phenomenon of scarcity have an identical status and significance in praxeological studies. Man does not always choose, and make sacrifices to get, those things which are provided in the form of physically measurable outputs. Sometimes he prefers consumption in the distant future rather than in the immediate future. Sometimes he demands leisure. Sometimes he demands the pleasures of gambling. Sometimes he demands the feeling of security which he can achieve through risk-avoidance. Sometimes he demands liquidity —all the advantages and conveniences of holding money. Through the failure to grasp the truth that each of these objectives concerns a preference which is of the very same nature as that expressed between, say, bread and cake, or shoes and shirts, or cricket bats and tennis rackets, the illusion emerges that it is essential for the "scientific" study of society to separate different kinds of human ends, or the response to these ends, into measurable categories. And this illusion has caused some economists to try to imagine *a simplified* reality in the form of ridiculously unreal "models." Instead of searching for appropriate concepts, which they could have found through a careful study of the nature of human preference and the phenomenon of scarcity, they have had recourse (especially since Keynes) to logically unacceptable constructions and abstractions which have been chosen mainly by reason of their convenience for mathematical treatment.[20] This is above all true of the field of economic fluctuations.

If simplified models and notions are to be legitimately used, an explicit replacement of unrealistic simplifications by empirically determined and realistic postulates is essential; and this means in practice that allowances must be made for (1) change in the institutional setup and (2) change in any impinging external factors. Moreover, changes in ends and changes in means must be distinguished with the utmost clarity; when they have been distinguished they must be allowed for; and when changes in expectations are factors, allowance must be made for the fact that the working of cause and effect is profoundly complicated through the expression of free will. Events become determined not merely by what *has happened* but by *purpose,* i.e., expressed preferences. For these reasons, all attempts to understand the economic world by analogies with the world of nature are highly dangerous, a truth which both Röpke[21] and Faustino Ballvé[22] have pointed out.

Some writers have suggested that the application of mathematical methods to economics has been wholly barren. Thus David Novick, in a trenchant, challenging, and courageous article (which has been belittled rather than dispassionately answered by those who have felt themselves criticized), has roundly described the use of mathematics in the social sciences as "an addition to the *esoterica* of the sciences."[23] "There is," he says, "nothing substantively different in

---

[20] As Stigler has pointed out, it is all too easy to confuse clarity with "familiarity or susceptibility to logical manipulation." *Five Lectures on Economic Problems,* p. 40. Moreover, the enthusiasm of the mathematicians may induce them to "make certain basic assumptions because they are easily treated mathematically." J. Tinbergen, "The Functions of Mathematical Treatment," *Review of Economics and Statistics,* November 1954, p. 367. They are apt to create what Champernowne has called "mere toys" because "the assumptions which are most convenient for model-building are seldom those which are most appropriate to the real world." D. G. Champernowne, "On the Use and Misuse of Mathematics in Presenting Economic Theory," in ibid., p. 369.

[21] Röpke, op. cit., pp. 121–22.

[22] Faustino Ballvé, "On Methodology in Economics," in Sennholz, op. cit., p. 129.

[23] David Novick, "Mathematics: Logic, Quantity, and Method," *Review of Economics and Statistics,* November 1954, p. 358.

the use of Greek letters arrayed in algebraic form than in the use of words combined into sentence and paragraph form."[24] Now I should be the last one to suggest that the great economies of thought which mathematics permits have been fruitless in the social sciences.[25] But I do think that *mathematicians writing on economics* have seriously harmed economic thought of recent years. It seems unfortunately to be true that, until recently, few economists of note have been mathematicians. Even more unfortunately, many mathematicians have discussed economics, and proficiency in mathematics has tended to be regarded as proficiency in economics. Yet "the ability to judge the relevance of an economic theory and its conclusions to the real world," says Champernowne, "is but rarely associated with the ability to understand advanced mathematics."[26] Obviously, it cannot be contended that training in mathematics, or an inborn gift for the subject, is *necessarily* a barrier to an understanding of the more difficult aspects of economics! But mathematicians appear remarkably inclined to confuse mathematical clarity with valid inference; at any rate, this seems to be the position when they are considering the relations of economic preferences to the means for the satisfaction of those preferences.

There is no traditional or orthodox economic theory which, provided the sort of simplifying assumptions which have become fashionable in contemporary "model-making" are made, cannot be expressed in terms of equations which satisfy the criterion that the number of unknowns does not exceed the number of equations. But the possibility of stating economic propositions in such a form is irrelevant to the truth of these propositions. It shows that, as they are enunciated, they have self-consistency, nothing more.

Hence Novick is right beyond question when he objects to the "tendency to assume that expressing these same theories in mathematical form creates absolute knowledge."[27] This truth can never be too strongly stressed. There is a propensity to assume that, once a proposition has been expressed in the brevity and elegance which

---

[24] Ibid., p. 358.

[25] On this matter I agree with Israel M. Kirzner who quotes effectively Croce's remark that "the dignity of abstract analysis" rendered a great service to an economics which had been "darkened . . . by the mass of anecdotes of the Historical School." *The Economic Point of View: An Essay in the History of Economic Thought* (Princeton, N.J.: D. Van Nostrand Company, 1960), pp. 67–70.

[26] Champernowne, op. cit., p. 369.

[27] Novick, op. cit., p. 358.

mathematics makes possible, it has been established as true. For instance, Lawrence R. Klein has recently referred to "the beauty and elegance"[28] of Ragnar Frisch's well-known article, "Propagation Problems and Impulse Problems in Dynamic Economics."[29] Yet, if my criticism of this book in my *Keynesianism* (pp. 317–19) can be accepted, this contribution has been responsible for an appalling intellectual muddle which has led many economists into whole realms of barren speculation.

Such an example illustrates the danger to which Tinbergen has referred, that when people are "too enthusiastic for the mathematics involved they may . . . somewhat neglect" what he has called the "qualitative part of research, characterized by distinguishing different categories of economic concepts and by their exact definition."[30] Mathematics is merely "shorthand logic," while the sin of many mathematical economists has been "a regrettable failure to apprehend the significance and importance of accurate definition," as E. C. Harwood has pointed out.[31] And mathematics does not, says Tinbergen, participate in the enumeration of the phenomena to be included in the analysis;[32] nor can it assist in the formulation of theories and hypotheses. In particular, the models which I have found defective fail to assist us in understanding the motives which lead to the reshaping of the production and marketing framework, for example, the factors which eventually lead to a single managerial or entrepreneurial act or several independent or connected managerial or entrepreneurial acts which cause the setting up or the breakdown of a cartel, or of a system of resale price maintenance, or of a set of trade union demarcations.

To insist upon these limitations of purely abstract analysis is not to argue for what has been called "institutional economics." Nor does it suggest that special economic theories are appropriate for different institutional assumptions (for example, that we need different economic theories for, say, a hypothetical laissez-faire economy, for existing capitalism and for the existing Soviet system). The economic

---

[28] Lawrence R. Klein, *Review of Economics and Statistics,* November 1954.

[29] This article appeared in *Economic Essays in Honour of Gustav Cassel, October 20, 1933* (London: G. Allen and Unwin, 1933), pp. 171–205.

[30] J. Tinbergen, "The Functions of Mathematical Treatment," *Review of Economics and Statistics,* November 1954, pp. 366–67.

[31] *Current Economic Delusions* (Great Barrington, Mass.: American Institute for Economic Research, 1941), p. 9.

[32] Tinbergen, op. cit., p. 367.

theory which has assisted my own empirical studies has always seemed equally relevant to all kinds of societies, indeed, to have universal applicability. My present argument simply insists that the nature of economic analysis must be determined in the light of its practical limitations.

I do not think it is unfair to say that many economists have become fascinated with the *manipulation* of concepts but impatient and bored with the really difficult part of the economist's task, namely, that of achieving perfect conceptual clarity. Indeed, they have, I feel, tended sometimes to regard careful concern with the fundamentals as mere verbiage. Having recognized that certain ideas common to all thinking about economics are capable of being expressed in mathematical form, they have come to regard form as content. I have been driven to the conclusion that the extraordinary way in which the errors of Keynes have been accepted for so long by so many economists, and uselessly elaborated, has been due very largely to the fact that they have found its mathematical statement capable of elegant development and refinement.

It is always possible to state the axioms, assumptions, and conclusions relevant to any practical economic problem in nonmathematical form, however complex the mathematics needed for the actual handling of the problem.[33] I know of no *important* case where, axioms and assumptions having been clear and acceptable, the conclusions so stated have been false as a result of *mathematical* error. It is, therefore, not in the manipulations that fallacy creeps in. It is in the course of distinguishing and defining categories and concepts that we can trace the confusions of this age. And it is at that stage in thought that Keynesian economics can be seen to have misled the students of a full generation.[34]

---

[33] Compare Champernowne, op. cit., pp. 370–71, and Stigler, op. cit., pp. 44–45, on this point.

[34] Need I repeat that this appendix is in no way an attack on the use of mathematics, either as an aid to thought or as a tool of exposition? There are economists who use and do not abuse the method. Thus, Fritz Machlup's important contributions, although often employing mathematical reasoning, have consisted largely of attempts to restore conceptual clarity in fields in which a structure of mathematical and abstract thinking has been erected on unsatisfactory economic notions. Referring to his long continued activities in this field, Machlup significantly remarks: "Serious terminological ambiguities and conceptual obscurities have been found to exist, some of them curable, others beyond hope of clarification." "Statics and Dynamics: Kaleidoscopic Words," *Southern Economic Journal,* October 1959, p. 91.

5

The Nature of the Keynesian Thesis

Both the *Treatise* and *The General Theory* found in thrift, and in the demand for liquidity, the principal causes of the idleness which policy is expected to rectify. Curiously no attempt seems to have been made to explain the most general apparent inconsistency in Keynesian thinking which is so expressed. Why should two particular expressions of preference concerning ends, namely, that between the present and the future (thrift), and that between the services of money (liquidity) and all other services, or the response to those preferences in the form of certain ways of using the scarce means available, give rise to unemployment—either as a chronic, or spasmodic, or cyclical phenomenon? Admittedly, (a) changes in the rate of savings (in either direction) and (b) changes in demand for money (hoarding or dishoarding)[1] can cause a parallel contraction of real income in the absence of price and monetary flexibility; but if accumulation of assets declines, it is because savings decline as income declines. I shall suggest that to blame saving preference, or the savings which result, is to reverse the true position.

Keynes contended that changed expectations can influence not only the *form* of output but the *amount* of output and employment.[2] No one would deny that expectations of prices provide an inducement (among all other inducements) to withhold or release productive

---

[1] The discoordinative effects of dishoarding are seen when it is not offset by credit policy *and* there is price rigidity upward. "Shortages" will develop, with queues or rationing.

[2] That is, in Keynes' words, "changing views about the future are capable of influencing the quantity of employment and not merely its direction." Keynes, *The General Theory*, p. vii.

power; but that does not justify the Keynesian thesis that only an increase in "investment" expenditure or an increase in the "propensity to consume" can counter the expectations which create that inducement. It is like saying that only (a) a particular way of using resources, namely, in making goods of long life expectancy—"producer goods"—the sort of goods which are typically produced when the rate of consumption falls short of output, or (b) a particular change in preference about the way in which resources shall be used, can bring resources into utilization. I can find no rigorous explanation of why the particular ends for which resources are actually used, or why the particular preferences expressed through saving preference (that is, time preference), can affect the extent to which demanded capacity is priced above or below market-clearing values—withheld or released. Of course, if the alternative to "investing" or "consuming" is an increase in demand for money balances, there will be a deflationary effect. But even this postulates (a) that monetary policy is aiming at a lower scale of prices and so does not offset the hoarding, and (b) that the deflationary policy is incomplete and lacking self-consistency because the necessary coordinative steps to bring prices nearer to market-clearing values are not being taken. (See pp. 132–33.) But such considerations seem never to be noticed by the Keynesians.

I shall argue that the pursuit of no economic end need result in either unemployment or depression, but that all changes in ends (that is, all changes in individually or collectively expressed preferences, or entrepreneurial judgments) must, unless they are accompanied by coordinative action with the appropriate price changes, cause the withholding or diversion of capacity into suboptimal uses. Time preference and so-called liquidity preference[3] are no different in principle or in practice from all other economic preferences.

When relative demand for final products falls (owing to a rise in saving preference), *the full employment of the resources which make them is consistent with the fall in demand but not consistent with the maintenance of the prices, either of the products themselves or of the services embodied in them.* Does it not follow that the decline in real

---

[3] The term "preference" here is not very appropriate because we are concerned rather with a choice of means than a choice of ends. But obviously, if M is constant, an increased demand for monetary services must have deflationary results.

income and the consequences upon realized growth are because of discoordination? I shall argue, therefore, that when the Keynesians blame thrift, they are turning attention away from the failure to adjust prices to changing preferences; and when they blame hoarding (liquidity preference), they are turning attention away from the failure of governments to tackle the problem of *unstable price rigidities,* that is, the unwillingness of governments to take the steps needed to permit prices continuously to reach a level at which further *general* price changes will be unexpected.

In his attempt to remedy the supposed failure of pre-Keynesian economics to explain the volume of employment, Keynes set out to write economics from an entirely new angle; and it was the defects of his new approach which, I believe, were largely responsible for his misconceptions. He asked us to consider the relations and reactions upon one another of great aggregate magnitudes, like income, employment, consumption, output, savings, and demand. If it is possible to conceive of units in terms in which such magnitudes can be *legitimately* expressed, there is no objection to such a method except that it is an extraordinarily clumsy way of reaching results. But I propose to show later on that the "macroeconomic" method, as it is called, has not in fact been applied with the use of logically defensible units, and that it has led to a host of subtle fallacies. At this stage it will suffice to deal with two aspects:

(a) *As measurable quantities,* income, output, employment (of all resources), consumption *plus* savings (or consumption *plus* investment) are identical notions and magnitudes—merely different ways of looking at the same phenomenon. For the employment of resources can be *measured,* in any intelligible sense of the term, only by some value measurement of the flow of services rendered by them; and the magnitude of the "real" value of the flow of services not only constitutes the aggregate "quantity" of output but is ultimately what we all mean when we talk of income. (See Chapter 11.) Of course all these things may be *arbitrarily defined* so as to be different magnitudes. But in the controversies with which we are concerned that has not been the position.

Moreover, aggregate demand is also identical with these magnitudes if it is carefully defined to cover the offer of some productive services (some income) for the flow of other productive services. This usage avoids confusion with what I shall show to be the basic determinants of the rate of interest—demand for assets through the offer of services or (really the same thing) demand for services with the offer of assets (demand for capital from income, or demand for income from capital).

(b) The concept of "effective demand" is defective. Consonant with their macroeconomic approach Keynesians hold that economic activity declines when "effective demand" is deficient.

The phrase itself is as old as Adam Smith[4] (he used the word "effectual") and was used by several of his successors to distinguish between mere wants—that is, what we *would* demand if we had greater means and what we *do* demand with the limited means at our disposal. Yet for over a century the term "demand," unqualified, has been used to mean the offer of services or things in return for other services or things. In these circumstances, it is fatuous now to use the adjective "effective" at all, although the writers of textbooks during the last two decades have mostly followed Keynes in this usage. The term is usually employed in the sense of "aggregate demand" *measured in terms of money*. That is, inflation (even if unaccompanied by an increase in real income) is supposed to generate an increase in "effective demand."

Keynes described effective demand as determined by the intersection of his aggregate supply function with his aggregate demand function,[5] and later he explained the notion further as "simply the aggregate income (or proceeds) which the entrepreneurs expect to receive, inclusive of the incomes which they hand on to the other factors of production. . . ."[6] In this typically tortuous explanation, he was clearly assuming that what entrepreneurs *expect* to receive from output determines their *current* demands for the flow of productive services which create output.[7] But in this explanation he seems to have forgotten the aggregate supply schedule, for what he says envisages only the entrepreneurs' offer. Equally appropriately, he could

---

[4] Adam Smith called this, very badly, "absolute demand." Keynes probably inherited *the term,* although not the connotation he gave to it, from Alfred Marshall. See Marshall's *Principles of Economics: An Introductory Volume* (8th ed.; New York: Macmillan Company, 1948), pp. 511, 699.

[5] Keynes, op. cit., p. 25.

[6] Ibid., p. 55.

[7] I am not challenging the acceptability of this statement as an explanation of the conditions necessary for the profitableness of investment, in the sense of the acquisition of *assets* or the acquisition of *services* for embodiment in assets. But what Keynes failed to state was that "the incomes which (entrepreneurs) hand out to the other factors of production" are determined according to the extent to which, at any moment, the prices of potential inputs happen to have been fixed at market-clearing values, that is, *priced* so that the entre-

have called the magnitude determined by the intersection "effective supply," meaning "aggregate supply." But if he and his disciples had always substituted the words "effective supply" where they have used the term in this sense, they would have seen all the issues in a quite different light.

It is to be my case that entrepreneurs are intermediaries and merely interpreters (as distinct from creators) of the demands they express. I shall argue that their offer[8] is a demand determinant of neither the real nor the money value of output as a whole; that it merely determines (a) the relative values of different outputs of varying life expectancies, and (b) the rate of interest; that it is irrelevant to the magnitude or value of output (apart from its possible repercussions upon the rate of realized savings); and that only the determinants of the number of money units and the demand for monetary services can influence the *money valuation* of a given flow of productive services.

Certainly entrepreneurs demand the productive services which are embodied into assets to replace or add to inventories of products being sold, or agents of production being used or used up. But as I shall be explaining, *in their entrepreneurial role,* the extent of their bidding against one another for such services does not determine the "quantity" or value of output; it determines only *the form* taken by income (in particular, the life expectancies of outputs in general); while the particular products they demand, and the proportions in which they cause output to be appropriate for mere replacement of, or net accumulation of productive power, are a response to demands expressed by income receivers in their capacity as consumers and savers. The composition of output is, then, influenced among other things by the extent to which income receivers (via entrepreneurial interpretations and predictions) demand goods of relatively short economic life expectancies (consumer goods and services) and goods of relatively long economic life expectancies (producer goods). In Chapter 13, I shall suggest that the origin of the fallacy expressed in Keynes' effective demand notion is exposed as soon as we have

---

preneur will judge investment in them to be profitable. Had Keynes said "effective demand" is that part of the *potential* aggregate supply of productive services (including the services of entrepreneurs) which is valued for market clearance, it would have been meaningful.

[8] The entrepreneurs' offer is variously described as "prospective yields," "predicted return over cost," "the marginal efficiency of capital," "anticipated profits," "investment demand."

obtained conceptual clarity (a) on the nature of the entrepreneurial function, and (b) on the distinction between the offer of assets for services (and vice versa) and the offer of services for services.

Without realizing it Keynes was, I suggest, actually trying, in his aggregate supply and demand functions, to represent Say's law! But such an aim is impossible under any macroeconomic construction; and his fallacious method led him to think of demand in general (his aggregate demand function) as somehow originating, not in supply in general, but in entrepreneurial expectations.

But let us return to the elusive concept of "demand in general." Carelessly or mechanically handled it can lead to quite untenable conclusions. When I use the term "demand" in contexts in which it obviously means "demand in general," I shall really mean *"demands in general"* and *not a measurable aggregate*. Because the supply of one thing is the demand for another (some noncompeting thing) and because services may be offered for other services or for assets (or assets offered for services or other assets[9]), all that can be meant when we talk of "an increase of demand in general" is that *services* are being priced so as to permit their exchange to a greater extent, up to the point at which they are fully absorbed, or that the flow of services is increasing because productive capacity is increasing and is being utilized. The exchange of *assets* for one another is a quite different matter. But when services are priced for full consumption or full absorption into the next stage of production, there is always an "effective" demand for all raw materials, work in progress, intermediate products, and final products as additional services are embodied into them. Reserves—inventories performing the productive service of availability[10]—constitute only an *apparent* exception. Demand in general becomes "effective" therefore according to the degree in which services are appropriately priced; and this implies the appropriate pricing also of the products into which they are embodied.

I shall sometimes use the term "uninflated demand" when I discuss demand in this sense; I shall then mean that the "demands" I am describing have not been accompanied by any contraction of the

---

[9] The offer of services for assets and *vice versa* does not, I repeat, affect the scale of prices. It determines the rate of interest.

[10] This includes inventories in the shops and in the home. Such inventories are productive assets and the services of these assets are being demanded.

measuring rod of value;[11] and I shall show that the Keynesian "effective demand" is simply the sum of money demands, inflated in the measure necessary to bring relative prices into better coordination, *in the circumstances in which inflation can have that effect.*[12]

It was partly through the clumsiness of the macroeconomic approach that Keynes came to believe that the idleness of valuable productive resources (he stressed labor) is caused by factors other than the mispricing of the flow of services and products. For instance, the clumsy concept of *the* price of labor, conceived of as *the* hourly money wage (a sort of average wage rate of labor of all kinds),[13] is, in a large part of the argument, taken as constant. And when Keynes did think in terms of this "price" having a crucial task, he seemed to assume that the adjustment required to induce full employment is an equal percentage reduction in all wage rates and secondly to assume that rises or falls in the general level of wage rates correspond to rises or falls in the general flow of wage receipts. Neither assumption is acceptable.

The macroeconomic approach makes abstraction of the vital and continuous process of competition. Pre-Keynesian theory, however, always focused attention on the ongoing process of substitution of lower cost methods of achieving ends. Hardly ignoring the importance of aggregates for certain purposes, economists in the classical tradition stress rather the importance of increments and margins as the determinants which operate the system; and these ultimately determine "employment" and "output," even when cheap money has facilitated the required changes in relative values.[14]

It was through his speculations about the demands which express time and liquidity preference that Keynes arrived at his revolutionary idea of interest. He claimed that the determinants of the rate of interest are the supply of and demand for money ("liquidity"). Now, the intelligent novice in economics jumps quite naturally to this kind of conclusion, which Keynes obviously thought he could make the

---

[11] When I use the term "money demand," this will imply that the money unit *may* have changed in value.

[12] That is, when the inflation or the actual rate of inflation is unexpected by a sufficient number of people, and the money illusion is a material factor.

[13] Different actual units of labor are supposed to be weighted in proportion to their skill, which can only be measured in terms of value. *The Theory of Idle Resources,* 1st ed., pp. 32–34; 2d ed., pp. 50–52.

[14] The actual working of this process is discussed in Chapter 4.

keystone of his system. For instance, Boswell records how Samuel Johnson, referring to a question which had always puzzled him as a young man, remarked:

> Why is it that the interest of money is lower when money is plentiful; for five pounds has the same proportion of value to a hundred pounds when money is plentiful as when it is scarce? A lady explained to me, "It is (said she) because when money is plentiful there are so many more who have money to lend that they bid down one another."[15]

It is not surprising that an idea which has so immediate a plausibility should have had a powerful attraction when enunciated by a prominent pundit. Yet as I shall demonstrate, it is wholly wrong. What is true is that *an increasing* number of money units (as distinct from *an increased* number) in relation to the aggregate real value of money will be accompanied by a market rate of interest below the natural level[16] and, the determinants of the natural level being given, a reduced market rate. (See Chapter 7.) But this is the pure orthodoxy which Keynes belittled.

Today, I believe, nearly all economists recognize that, in dealing with this topic, Keynes dismissed the basic and ultimate determinants of interest altogether and emphasized factors which previous economists had rightly recognized as short-term influences. But because Keynes' concepts and methods minimized consideration of the possibility of *costs and prices* moving at levels which are chronically fixed too high (absolutely, or in relation to expectations) to permit full employment, he eventually concluded that it is the rate of interest which might "fluctuate for decades about a level which is chronically too high for full employment. . . ."[17] That the value of the rate of interest which is consistent with "full employment" is simply a rate sufficiently below the natural to effect the inflationary increase in "expenditure" needed to induce the release of withheld capacity was subtly (I do not say purposely) hidden.[18]

---

[15] James Boswell, *The Life of Samuel Johnson,* Newnes ed., II, p. 295.

[16] By "the natural level" here I mean (as I shall explain) the noninflationary, nondeflationary level. This is but one possible meaning of the term "natural" as Wicksell (who introduced the term) used it.

[17] Keynes, op. cit., p. 204.

[18] It is doubtful, however, whether Keynes was indeed envisaging such a divergence. (See below pp. 116–17 n. 27.)

Keynes' belief that he had found a single, universal solvent for price disharmonies dominated all his thinking. In throwing over not only the classical theory of interest, but the Wicksellian refinement of it, he contended that, if we must talk about the ideal rate of interest, we should conceive of it as the rate which guarantees full employment.[19] He called it "the optimum rate." But how could any *single* value-relationship, even so crucial a value-ratio as the rate of interest, guarantee or ensure full employment? If the right to price services above market-clearing values (which enables the absorption of their full potential supply) is permitted, how can any rate of interest put things right? For instance, if the maintenance of interest at a rate below the natural for a while is used to raise final prices relative to costs, what is to prevent costs being raised again? This is, of course, what has almost universally happened when such policies have been followed. If the answer is, "But we ought not to have allowed that to happen," my point has been admitted. Keynes and his disciples often appear to be expecting one value—the rate of interest— to rectify all the disharmonies caused by sectionalist pricing, which result in general underemployment; although at other times it is the *expenditure* engendered by "the optimum rate" which is stressed.

Again, it was the sheer cumbersomeness of macroeconomics which led to the cardinal error that monetary or fiscal policy or the rate of interest through "effective demand" determines the "volumes" of "real income," or "employment," or "output." In fact, the "volume of employment" is determined, in any given state of knowledge and accumulated resources, by the extent to which valuable resources are permitted—by relative prices and direct withholdings—to be fully utilized. Changes in the value of the money unit (caused by changes in the relations of market interest to natural interest) have an influence only insofar as they affect the relations of prices (at each stage of production) to money income.

Although reduction of the value of the money unit is one way of inducing an expansion of output or inducing increased savings (and hence increased future output) when productive capacity has been withheld from use, it, however, does not justify the formulation of a *monetary demand theory of output or employment*. There are conditions in which monetary policy and output are not unconnected; but even in those conditions monetary policy is only *one* factor in output-determination. A virtue of the pre-Keynesian theory was that it took

---

[19] Keynes, op. cit., p. 243.

all such factors into account and was therefore a general theory. A vice of the Keynesian theory is that it is a special theory. It has often been said that the pre-Keynesian economists overlooked the connection between monetary policy and income.[20] That is false. There never have been any doubts about the possibility of inducing the release of capacity through an unanticipated inflationary increase in M or V.[21] However, it has been recognized that the coordination is achieved in exactly the same way as when it is brought about by price and cost adjustment.[22] It is Keynesianism which draws attention away from the crucial determinants in which monetary policy is merely one factor.

Hence, the stress in *The General Theory* on the monetary or expenditure determinants of income and demand, misdirects attention from the relevant truths (a) that monetary factors are an influence upon the *size* of real income (as distinct from its *measurement* in money units) solely through their influence upon relative prices at different stages of production, and (b) that coordinative changes in prices are equally *possible* (I do not say *"equally easy"*) if the money unit (in which income and other economic magnitudes are measured) is of constant or other defined value.

If the distinction between ends and means is clearly perceived, we can think of the people expressing preferences respecting ends for which the means are scarce (by buying or refraining from buying different quantities of different things in the market) as exercising "consumers' sovereignty." But in his justification of Keynesian doctrine, Dillard says that "it is pure euphemism to say that consumption is the ultimate purpose of production." Conversely, it is "the expectation of being able to convert real goods into money at a profit" which "is the significant motivation."[23] Yet the entrepreneur who (1) predicts successfully the nature and scale of the demands of those who exercise consumer preference, and (2) achieves low-cost methods of responding to those preferences, is aways in the last resort an interpreter of consumers' preference. And he is rewarded by

---

[20] See, for example, Dudley Dillard, "The Theory of a Monetary Economy," in Kurihara, ed., *Post-Keynesian Economics,* p. 3.

[21] An "inflationary" increase in V is one which is deliberately not offset by monetary policy, or inadvertently not offset.

[22] For example, see Edwin Cannan, *An Economist's Protest* (London: P. S. King and Son, 1927), p. 397.

[23] Dillard, "Theory of a Monetary Economy," in Kurihara, op. cit., p. 27. Of course, ignoring the "money illusion" is being unrealistic, but dismissing concern with the "real world" is being even more so.

profits when his interpretation proves wise or lucky (just as he is penalized by losses when it proves unwise or unlucky). Is it not obvious that, merely because entrepreneurial predictions and calculations are made in terms of money values, we are not forced to a monetary demand theory of output?

Curiously enough, Dillard's use of the words "at a profit" ought to have led him to see that conversion into money has nothing to do with the matter. It is almost always possible to convert any product into money *at some price.* As I have explained more fully in my *A Rehabilitation of Say's Law,* all assets have "money's worth," although their owners will not actually release them at their money's worth when they judge it to be more profitable to carry them through time. Moreover, the ability to liquidate outputs does not mean that the type of good produced has been a profitable choice. It is, however, the profit, not the acquisition of money, which is the proof of successful prediction. In other words, profit-seeking (or loss-avoidance) provides the motivation, not the fact that economic calculation usually takes place in money terms and transactions normally require the transfer of money.

However, Dillard is led to the conclusion that, because firms think and calculate in terms of money, "money is genuine wealth and real goods are an artificial and transitory embodiment of hoped-for values to be realized by their conversion into money."[24] To him, money is "the socially recognized *form* of wealth." Hence mercantilism, "based on the realistic view that money is wealth (to the individual merchant)," is correct.[25] Of course, what he should have said is, "money is the socially recognized *measure* of wealth (value)." The liquid assets of firms are not "wealth" in a greater degree than any other of their assets. They are productive in the same sort of way. And when I say this, I am not unmindful of the fact that in practice the functioning of every business entity demands the continuous replacement of the bank balance and the cash in the till, in the same manner that it requires the replacement of all other inventories and equipment.

It may be objected that not all Keynesians hold views as extreme as Dillard's. But I know of no renunciation of his interpretation of Keynes by any Keynesian of eminence, and Dillard obviously regarded himself as a faithful disciple and expositor.

Not only have the Keynesians succeeded in diverting attention

---

[24] Ibid., p. 28.
[25] Ibid., pp. 28–29.

from the possibility of achieving full employment through price adjustment, but on the rare occasions on which they feel obliged to refer to the issue, they seem to argue (a) that it is a politically impracticable remedy (meaning politically *unacceptable*) and (b) that in any case it would be a self-defeating remedy. They have made (b) a convenient second line of defense. It was first erected with any pretense to rigorous argument in *The General Theory*. (See Chapter 12.) It is based not only on the assumption that politics or other institutional factors make *difficult* or impossible the adjustments necessary for full employment, but on an argument which has had several quite different—but all wholly fallacious—attempted justifications. "It cannot be done," they seem to say, "and in any case it is a waste of time trying to show that it can be done, because we can produce even more fundamental arguments to show that it must necessarily be self-defeating." The most plausible of such arguments are to the effect that the reduction of those wage rates or prices which have caused wasteful idleness is a futile method of bringing back resources into use because it must inevitably result in a shrinkage of income. The chief *originality* in Keynesian teaching rests in this thesis. What is new is the argument that price and cost adjustments must *aggravate* the situation (Again, see Chapter 12.) Harrod has well stated the Keynesian position as follows: "If a certain level of interest is established, which is inconsistent with full activity, *no flexibility or mobility in other parts of the system will get the system to move to full activity*"[26] (my italics). It is obvious that, in this passage, Harrod is thinking, as was Keynes himself, of the absolute level of market interest and not of its relation to the natural level.[27]

---

[26] Roy F. Harrod, "Keynes, the Economist," in Harris, ed., *The New Economics,* p. 69. The tiny element of truth in Harrod's rather subtle statement rests in the power of generally unperceived deviations of interest from the natural level to coordinate. But the rate of interest proper is simply a ratio. It is something which *results from* economic choice and activity, not something which can be said to influence the volume (as distinct from the form) of activity. It is determined, like all other manifestations of value, by preferences on the one side and scarcities on the other. And the action needed to cause the money or market rate of interest to diverge from the noninflationary or nondeflationary level (the natural level) can be regarded as a determinant of the volume of activity, only insofar as, not being anticipated, it indirectly brings about coordinative adjustments in relative values. That is the tiny element of truth.

[27] This is equally obvious in Keynes' reference to a rate of interest which might "fluctuate for decades about a level which is chronically too high for full

In one of the approaches which has proved to be most influential, the Keynesian doctrine is based on the notion that the community may wish to consume *plus* accumulate net ("invest") an "amount" which is less than the full flow of valuable (that is, scarce) productive services. But this notion has always seemed to me to be self-contradictory. Productive services have value (that is, they are scarce) solely (a) because people *want* to consume them, or the products into which they can be embodied (or the products which such products can in turn provide), either in the *immediate future or the more distant future,* and (b) because people not only *want* these services but have something valuable to offer for them. It seems to follow that demands in general can be deficient only in the sense that supply is withheld.

It is appropriate to conclude this brief statement of the nature of Keynesianism by insisting that because pre-Keynesian theory rejected the mercantilist view of money, it did not overlook or segregate the monetary factor, as the Keynesians like to assert. On the contrary, monetary theory was more of an integral part of economic theory as a whole in the pre-Keynesian analysis than it was in the Keynesian. Indeed, in the traditional treatment, monetary theory was so intimately woven into the general texture of theory that superficial economists failed to perceive the implications of money in every line, paragraph, page, and chapter, and explicitly in every reference to price. It would be less unfair to say that the Keynesians (and some of the post-Wicksellian Swedish economists) have tended to think of—or at any rate to treat—monetary theory as something quite apart from economic theory as a whole. Then, having fallen into all the logical traps to which so indefensible a procedure has led them, they try to marry the creature of their misunderstanding—monetary theory—to "real theory" in order to explain income or employment, and to decry pre-Keynesian theory for attempting to be fruitful without such a marriage. And this seems to have led the new Keynesians, like the old, to the belief that monetary or fiscal policy, through the control of spending, can act as a universal solvent of all price disharmonies and, like an invisible hand, make unnecessary, or less necessary, the difficult task of overhauling the institutions which make up the price system.

---

employment." Keynes, *The General Theory,* p. 204. For had he meant the noncoincidence of market and natural levels, he would certainly have said, "with the scale of prices falling for several decades," or "with the value of the money unit rising," or words to the same effect.

I find it increasingly difficult to judge exactly how much of Keynes' basic teachings are still held by those who originally accepted them; for many of those who seem unprepared to defend reasoning of the kind to which I have been referring continue to use the defective concepts which emerged out of it. *Keynes established, I suggest, a fashion of subtle equivocation in monetary discussion, a fashion which, through habit and domination, has become almost a convention. This comes out in countless different forms to which I shall have to be constantly referring.* An example is found in the modern tendency to attribute inflation to "excess demand" instead of to monetary and fiscal policy. It is all very well to answer, "But we all know that is what is meant!" The fact is that this manner of expression and a host of others divert attention from the deliberateness or weakness of action which results in every depreciation or loss of parity of a currency.

So firm is Keynesianism's grip, however, that it is now common to talk of checking expansion when what is meant is curbing inflation. Everything is looked at in terms of the government, through the monetary authority, controlling the rate of activity by determining the rate of expenditure. But if governments are to be regarded as responsible for *economic progress,* they can play their part in two ways: (a) by providing and administering a framework conducive to security of contract (and a defined value of the money unit is crucial here) and flexibility (and this includes price flexibility); and (b) by encouraging or compelling thrift. And if they are expected to control the "level of economic activity," then, as I shall show, they can do no more than influence or regulate the release of productive capacity which has been withheld from use by pricing at above market-clearing values, or mitigate control of output (perhaps imposed by the government itself). And this they may do through unanticipated inflation, or by means of policies designed to induce direct coordination.

In the assumption that monetary control of activity is the means to economic health, hesitant lip service is quite often paid to the ideal of stability of prices. But the student is not told that, under the gold standard, the objective of a stable real value of the money unit was implied by the very choice of the standard; that, under wise administration of the system (when the ability to convert was never subjected to strain), the real value of the money unit was expected to vary very little from year to year; and that although monetary policy was not regarded as in any way concerned with objectives like full employment and steady growth, the monetary authority was recognized as having its part to play in a stable and progressive economy (especially in the scrupulous avoidance of cheap money, so as to eliminate the necessity for eventual deflationary rectification).

Admittedly, the notion that any defensible monetary or fiscal policy could ensure the pricing of goods and services so that people are always able and willing to buy them, would have been generally regarded as absurd by pre-Keynesian economists. But it *is* absurd! The Keynesians have merely introduced involved ways of saying things which have made such a notion appear plausible.

Yet so attractive has the Keynesian teaching proved that most modern governments seem to be motivated by the conviction that a coordinated economy requires collective action to ensure a "balance" between "savings" and "investment," government revenues and expenditures, and imports and exports. In subsequent chapters, I shall pursue more deeply the origins of these notions, which I shall trace in part to the fallacy that expenditure generates money income and "effective demand" (discussed in Chapter 11), a fallacy which is aggravated by conceptual confusion concerning the magnitudes "savings" and "investment" (discussed in Chapter 12).

6

Consequences of the Keynesian Remedy

To consider the *consequences* of Keynesian policies, one can hardly avoid discussing the phenomenon of creeping inflation. But as I have already conceded, not all Keynesians would have agreed, when *The General Theory* was published, that the tacit approval of inflation was implied by their teachings. I must therefore ask those readers who may feel that I am here misrepresenting Keynesian thought to withhold their judgment until the end of this chapter. They will readily admit that, wherever Keynesian ideas have been influential in policy, inflation has in fact been experienced; and I am now concerned with the apparent results of that policy.

Today's neo-Keynesians appear to assume that imposed restrictions or controls can effectively repress forces which would otherwise be expressed as open inflation. I hope to make it clear in due course that the repression of inflation merely reduces its crude coordinative power. Hence the reasonableness of *my assumption* in this chapter that the relatively "full employment" which some countries have witnessed from time to time since the 1930s is *attributable to less than fully anticipated inflation* (and not to other virtues of Keynesian policy).

The issue can be summarized as follows: The Keynesians have centered attention upon the possibility that, in the exchange identity $PT \equiv MV$, an increase in MV (that is, in M or in V) may cause an increase, not in P but in T (output) owing to the release of withheld capacity. Economists have always known that an increase in MV *could* result not only in an increase in P but subsequently in an increase in T. Indeed, this has been explicitly recognized at least since the days of Hume. But since Hume and before Keynes, it was almost always tacitly accepted that that was a very bad way of increasing T (as compared with coordination through price adjustment).

In Keynes' earlier writings, the possibility of a rise in prices was ignored and stability of the scale of prices was an implied ideal. Subsequently, however, the argument *seems* to have developed that, while prices will rise as increased expenditure stimulates output, the inflation is nevertheless defensible. (See Chapter 10.) In other words, it is assumed that, up to the point of full employment, output will increase in sufficient measure to make inflation a lesser evil than withheld capacity.[1] Had the assumption been unambiguously enunciated in these terms, subsequent controversies would have been more fruitful. The main issue would have boiled down to the effectiveness and justice of inflation as a means of bringing prices nearer to market-clearing values, in comparison with other means available.

The Keynesians seem often to be claiming that their remedy in some way creates stability. Yet as we have seen, if convertibility or a tolerable scale of prices is to be preserved, the "maintenance of effective demand" seems inevitably to lead to a boom; and hence either to the necessity for a period of drastic general downward price adjustments or to a period of depression. For just as cost rigidity downward is the main cause of the *persistence* of depression (in the absence of unanticipated inflation), so is the very much less marked cost rigidity upward which is experienced during an unanticipated inflation, the main cause which prolongs a boom. The lag of cost increases below revenue increases explains why inflation succeeds in stimulating outputs—the *real boom;* and the fact that the flow of residual incomes (generally speaking, entrepreneurial incomes) increases relatively to the flow of wage and other contractual incomes and contains an illusory element (resulting from capital gains—caused by interest below the natural—tending to be treated as income), explains in part why inflation can so easily induce a *speculative boom* (through causing exaggerated predictions of yields).

Obviously, then, we are unable to draw a common (and politically very popular) Keynesian conclusion: if wage receipts rise as rapidly as residual receipts, the boom can be prolonged. What *is* true, and this is the truth which is often missed, is that if wage rates and other costs were perfectly flexible upward, it would not pay to indulge in

---

[1] See p. 83 n. 47.

inflation. Inflation would then be purposeless, ceasing to have any coordinative tendency (although it might certainly continue through mere habit, like continuance with a drug which has been known to give relief in the past). For the public's expectations tend to force the scale of prices toward the level to which it is believed that policy is aiming (drift being regarded as one policy). Anticipated inflation becomes pointless; and the use of the monetary system as an instrument of "national policy" is practicable only as long as the public does not understand or can be deceived about objectives.

Indeed, the degree of inflation needed (in any given situation with unemployment) to bring relative prices into coordination increases in proportion to the extent to which the inflation can be forecast. In the absence of "controls," which, if politically tolerable, would make the inflationary remedy redundant, the "maintenance of effective demand" can succeed only when the majority of people can be misled into thinking that the expansion of credit is about to cease or that it will be much more moderate than it is destined to be. Unless this deception is possible, those who are in a position to raise prices and wage rates will do so in advance of the declining value of the money unit so that the original degree of withheld capacity will tend to be perpetuated.

Inflation once commenced appears, indeed, to be self-perpetuating and, in the Keynesian atmosphere, inevitable. Theoretically there is no limit to the extent to which V can rise for this reason. But if M does not increase, and the monetary authority does not in fact intend to increase it, it seems likely that wrong expectations will soon be corrected. For as prices rise (through an *increasing V*), more money units will be required for the same real volume of transactions and more demanded therefore. In the present age, however, monetary authorities nearly always remove this deflationary barrier to the private reinforcement of their policy. For by this time they have all forgotten the simple lessons which economists learned in the days of the British pre-1844 currency controversies, and it appears to be their unmistakable duty to respond to the "obviously legitimate" demand for money. Moreover, it has been noticed that, insofar as any inflation is initiated or enforced by way of budget deficits, each deficit tends to generate an inflation of government expenditure in anticipation of revenue, thereby causing a succession of deficits.

In practice, it is seldom possible to resort to inflation merely as a transition from an era in which prices are widely in excess of market-clearing values but are being reduced to restore the real wages and income flow, or from an era of dislocating rigidity to an era of price flexibility. Raising the general scale of prices can hardly serve as a stepping stone to a regime in which it will be possible to establish a defined measuring rod of value as well as maintain full employment. For the institutional setup which permits the rigidities evaded by the inflation will remain unreformed. Withheld capacity will return and further inflation will be demanded on the same old grounds.

It is, I think, for this reason that, even during the practice of inflation itself, some concrete recognition of the true remedy seems often to be discernible; for while depreciation of the money unit is in progress, it is almost universally accompanied by measures to prevent, or at least to discourage direct discoordination of the price system. It is recognized that antisocial sectionalist action to force up wage rates and prices, unless checked, would cause *runaway* inflation. But the required checks are usually imposed, not in the form of strict antimonopoly control or action to prevent labor unions from reducing aggregate uninflated wages, but by "incomes policies"— the crude expedients of price control, moral exhortations to industry, commerce and organized labor, and very occasionally, wage ceilings.

Perhaps the strongest objection to the attempt to maintain coordination by "maintaining effective demand" is, then, that it removes (a) pressures to coordinating adjustments within the existing framework of institutions and (b) the incentive to fundamental reform of the framework. *The politicians may feel that far-reaching reforms are needed. But cheap money eases things for the time being and enables them to procrastinate.* For this reason it permits the survival of distortions in the price structure or concomitant distortions in the form taken by production functions. This is partly because it *obscures* the inherent contradictions and inconsistencies in the functioning of economic institutions due to sectionalist pricing, but partly because it *destroys the collective incentive* to refashion institutions. Perpetual recourse to the line of least resistance results in unplanned institutional modifications which stand as powerful, temporary obstacles to a more efficient, just, and stable social order.

It is because the inflationary method is so easy that the great nations since the 1930s have been able, sometimes for long periods, superficially to eradicate virtually all signs of the "trade cycle"— beyond minor recessions and upswings—without any attempts at major institutional reform. What "sound finance" *did* do in the pre-Keynesian era was to create every incentive to reprice services and products the sale of which was being held up, as well as to create a strong social motive to eradicate practices which reduced the flow of uninflated income. In the private sphere, the pressures were fairly successful, and had it not been for contrary action by the government, they could, I believe, have rescued the British economy—without inflation—from the Great Depression. But the reaction of governments was, typically enough, to impose further discoordination. For instance, the multitude of relatively small-scale withholdings of capacity throughout the world which had developed during the 1920s had caused so serious a contraction in uninflated demands that large-scale state-imposed output and trade restrictions were resorted to (at that time mainly "valorization" schemes and tariffs). The repercussions of the situation caused by these measures aggravated the decline in uninflated world incomes. There was then an enhanced incentive for cheap money. But the degree of inflation which was possible before the general abandonment of convertibility in the 1930s could not, as B. H. Beckhart has pointed out, "bring about that readjustment of retail and wholesale prices, wages, and costs, on the basis of which any substantial improvement in business must be founded."[2] It is precisely because there could have been no other way out that, if there had been perseverance with "sound finance," insistence upon a return to market-directed coordination and institutional reform may well have become irresistible (especially if the bulk of the economists had recognized the necessity and pressed for the reforms required).

The actual working of the mechanism of value determination certainly needed redesigning. Difficult institutional changes were called for—not simple "expenditure" panaceas, but carefully planned structural adjustments based on patient, painstaking studies of the psychological, sociological, and political resistances likely to be encountered. No attempts whatsoever have been made at such replanning.

A stable currency is possible without the general problem of economic coordination having been successfully solved. But if so, it must be at the expense of less burdensome but *more conspicuous forms* of waste, including unemployment of labor. Only when the problems of inflation and discoordination are tackled simultaneously

---

[2] Quoted in William Adams Brown, Jr., *The International Gold Standard Reinterpreted, 1914–1934* (New York: National Bureau of Economic Research, 1940), 2:977.

can "sound money" accompany "full employment." *Hence, the cessation of inflation requires far-reaching reforms of a nonmonetary kind.* Wise monetary policy *demands* nonmonetary coordination. In practice that means reforms to achieve such flexibility of values and prices as permits a more free allocation of means to ends (whether those ends are expressed individually or collectively).

The arbitrariness of the inflationary remedy should be obvious; for is not the extent of the withholding of capacity in different sections of the economy (which it is intended to offset) wholly arbitrary? *Keynesians who admit the inflationary nature of their proposals often claim that only a "moderate" measure of inflation is needed (see pp. 227–30), just sufficient to reduce real wage rates by the required amount.* But can we say that inflation is "moderate" if it no more than keeps pace with the rate of withholding—in the sense that the rate of release of the flow of productive services is equated with the rate of withholding? The notion is preposterous. *Yet I have found no attempt to define that crucial word "moderate" in this context!*

Moreover, recourse to the maintenance of "effective demand" as a means of countering withheld capacity discourages mobility of resources in response to change and leads to misdirection of resources and effort in many forms. For instance (especially when devaluation is needed in order to permit its continuance), inflation assists export industries at the expense of a not necessarily unfair burden on the sheltered industries, and an unfair burden upon industries using imported materials and upon consumers of imported goods. And the relief obtained by devaluation is the result of a particularly short-sighted type of adjustment. Prices are adjusted for foreign purchasers but not for the benefit of domestic purchasers. Is it not a stupidly crude way, in a civilized society, of bringing resources in the export industries into full utilization and international values into equilibrium?

As I have said, many Keynesians claim that their policy creates stability in some sense. Actually, the inflationary policy implied gives rise to a relatively painless, yet for that reason a more insidious, form of uncertainty. One of the weaknesses of *deliberate deflations* (such as that by means of which Britain returned to gold, from 1920 to 1925, and then maintained parity until 1931) is the difficulty of estimating the extent to which prices will ultimately fall (a weakness due to the existence of price and wage-rate rigidities believed to be unstable. See pp. 148, 192–94). But with *inflation,* where convertibility obligations no longer exist, or where for other reasons such obligations are accepted on an insufficiently wide scale,[3] it is never possible to forecast its duration, or the rate at which it is to occur, or the currency value which will ultimately be established; and if it were possible to predict its future course with certainty, the inflation would, for the reasons to which I have just referred (pp. 124–25), lose its ability to release withheld capacity.

Hence, in the absence of convertibility (and I include an obligation to maintain the scale of prices constant as a form of convertibility) or fixed exchanges (which imply some other kind of convertibility), an inflationary policy may prove to be far too discoordinating to be tolerated without exchange equalization or exchange control. Unless such controls are employed, exchange rates may fluctuate with speculative predictions, and wide-sweeping fluctuations tend to destroy all sense of entrepreneurial security. Ah! my Keynesian friends will say, "you are admitting the deficiencies of the price mechanism." But it is folly to suggest that exchange control is required during inflation *because of the deficiencies of the "unassisted market mechanism."* When a market is dealing in packets of commodities, the amount of the contents of which is constantly changing in an unpredictable manner, we can hardly expect the market to do more than reflect current guesses of speculators about what the packets will prove to contain at different future times. And when monetary authorities everywhere are trying to "create confidence" by statements, gestures, and procedures which are intended to mislead or at least to mask the true situation, no wonder the forecasts of speculators generate disconcerting fluctuations. In such circumstances, exchange equalization or control is inevitable. But it can provide security only against short-run fluctuations. It cannot, of itself, guarantee long-term stability. It is by no means a substitute for the security of convertibility. And it is hardly coordinative machinery in international dealings.[4]

---

[3] For example, as under the temporary convertibility of the dollar into gold after 1934 and until 1971, and the maintenance for long periods (buttressed by exchange and trade controls) of many other currencies at parity with the dollar.

[4] Once obligations to redeem currencies have again been undertaken, and once the willingness and ability of the authorities to maintain those obligations have been accepted, the money markets of the world will be fully capable of recreating the pre-1914 measure of orderliness and economy in international monetary relations. True, in 1945 the International Monetary Fund brought some order in the relations between currencies but that was not because it had provided a superior mechanism to the gold standard: it was because it provided *some* limi-

Not only does the Keynesian system require arbitrary controls, but the particular form of inflation which Keynes recommended—the "socialization" of investment, which he thought would facilitate the spending of income—means, as I have explained already, the transfer of power to determine ends from the market to the government, from the people to the politicians, from society to a group, from the many to the few. Some will welcome such a transfer; others will deplore it. The tragedy is that many of those whose ethical convictions cause them to abhor totalitarianism, fail to perceive that the transfer of power from society to the politician is a step from social to private control, a step toward the destruction of the ideally free society.

One of the most serious of the consequences of having abandoned the policy of "sound money" has been adverse sociological reactions. Almost all inflations have some of the features of *repressed* inflation. And where "controls" intended to curb the effects of an increase in deposits and currency in circulation exist, enterprise tends to be diverted into black-market operations, and to lobbying for licenses or dealing in them. We all know that, as the necessary "controls" increase, opportunities for corruption multiply and the temptations to corruption are fostered. For this reason also, the incentives to the investment of time, effort, and money in skill acquisition are dampened through the resultant narrowing of the gap between the remuneration of skilled and unskilled work. But most important of all, cheap money tends to weaken the process of what Bresciani-Turroni has called "the natural selection of firms."[5] The cessation of bankruptcies, which is so often and so easily hailed as evidence of "prosperity," is properly seen, according to Bresciani-Turroni, as "a symptom of the *malaise* of the economic system."[6] It means that the incentives of both rewards for efficiency or success and penalties for

---

tation or brake on the autonomy of individual monetary authorities (although it was never effective against inflation of the dollar). But many countries have had to rely on exchange controls in order to carry out their agreements. And other contracts between nations have had to be concluded in order to curb monetary nationalism. Is it not significant that the virtues of all these agreements are those which are found in the fullest measure when currencies are based on clear-cut iron-clad contracts to maintain some defined value for the money unit, as they were in the gold standard days?

[5] Costantino Bresciani-Turroni, *The Economics of Inflation: A Study of Currency Depreciation in Post-War Germany,* trans. Millicent E. Sayers (London: George Allen and Unwin, 1937), p. 219.

[6] Ibid.

inefficiency or failure of entrepreneurial activity are weakened.[7] Nor can we be blind to the distributive injustices associated with inflation; its merciless treatment of the politically weak;[8] its tendency to reward those responsible for the discoordinations which it so crudely rectifies; its penalization of those whose actions have in no sense been responsible (those classes which loathe the idea of striking or threatening to strike—the salaried middle classes, the thrifty *rentiers,* the learned and charitable institutions which have relied upon interest on endowments, the pensioners, and so forth); its encouragement of a sordid scramble on the part of each organized group to get more for itself out of the common pool; its destruction of the motive to give of one's best in the common social task, particularly at the entrepreneurial level; its weakening of the rewards for ingenuity, enterprise and effort; its sapping of the incentive to thrift and growth; its discouragement of individual responsibility toward one's own future and that of one's dependents; its creation of resignation toward a taxation system which robs the community of capital for the financing of innovations; its encouragement of acquiescence in the squandering of the community's capital; its need, in practice, for a multitude of officials and controllers with delegated judicial and legislative powers, able to make or destroy fortunes and subject therefore to the temptations of corruption; and the tendency it serves toward the degeneration of representative government into a system of vote buying.

I want my Keynesian friends to consider whether it is not fair to claim that, as it has in fact worked out, the policy of maintaining "effective demand" has amounted to *the buying off* of antisocial pricing. Thus, when credit expansion is accompanied by an expansion of output *plus* some inflation, then the inflationary part of the expansion of money income can be defined as that part of the increase in MV which is not accompanied by an equivalent increase in T. This inflationary part of money income may be regarded as *the*

---

[7] I have not included among these consequences the tendency of cheap money to bring about reduced real earnings. This has often been the consequence of inflations, but the effect need not follow. When authoritarian redistribution is resorted to, and when the future progress of a community is sacrificed for the purpose, the artisan and laboring classes may gain *in the short run,* at the expense of a reduction in the rate of supply of the assets and tools which multiply the yield to labor.

[8] Keynes' cynical reference to the *"euthanasia of the rentier"* is hardly appropriate. In many countries, his policies have borne *cruelly* upon the rentiers in the middle classes, who, deserted by the politicians in whom they had put their trust, have had largely to suffer the grossest injustices in silence.

cost incurred by the community to persuade those who are withholding capacity, by pricing it above its market-clearing value, to release it; and in general, the withholding to be bought off is not that due to the money illusion or to those price rigidities which are caused by mere inertia. *It is that withholding which is attributable to the attempt by certain sections to draw more for themselves out of the common pool, by collusive action, which the Keynesian remedy seeks to buy off.* Is it now a satisfactory solution that society should be forced to pay ransom, so to speak, to those who would otherwise throw the whole economic system out of coordination?

That since the widespread adoption of Keynesian policies the Western world has progressed in productive capacity and standards of living for the masses is obvious. But this advance has been mainly the continued outcome of great developments in technology and management, and (in the United States at least) an enormous entry of married women into the labor force.[9] On the other hand, monetary policy and the inevitable "controls" which accompany creeping inflation have braked the process. The political support of labor generally, and agriculture in many parts, has been bought by means which are parasitic on technological advance. Even when "full employment" has been enjoyed, it has been achieved at the expense of a serious divergence from ideal resource allocation, the forcing of men and assets into suboptimal activities; and it has caused the gravest injustices. In particular, the clumsy ways in which labor scarcity has been perpetuated have undoubtedly caused distortion in capital structure and production arrangements. The tragic irony of the situation is that virtually no one benefits in the long run.

Since World War II, Keynesian policies have not explicitly aimed at maintaining full employment, simply because prices have tended, gradually but increasingly, to be forced up as rapidly as, or ahead of, wage rates and costs.[10] The burden of the maintenance of peace (which, in face of the Soviet threat, has involved an enormous cost in armaments and armies) at first appeared to make the chief problem that of confining demands for normal consumption and develop-

---

[9] The number of multiearner families has increased by 10 percent since 1970; that is, the number of working wives has risen by 24 percent (or 4.4 million) so that by 1978 nearly half of American wives were earning pecuniary income.

[10] After 1958, growing general awareness of the phenomenon of anticipated inflation seemed for a time to force action to protect the nominal gold value of the dollar, and to have induced price restraint as well as (to a markedly lesser extent) wage-rate restraint in the United States. But since the middle 1960s, we have seen a gradual relinquishment of a moral commitment on the part of governments to reject currency debasement.

ment to a degree dictated by defense needs. But instead of this objective being rationally sought, through the price mechanism, it soon became expedient for governments not only to finance the necessary measures through inflation instead of through overt taxation, but to employ a rising proportion of the funds so easily raised for the purchase of political popularity. And governments have quite easily pursued such policies because Keynesian escape clauses undermine attempts to establish a stable international monetary policy. Each country has been able to blame world inflation for its own contribution to that inflation; and provided it has no more than kept pace with the general rate of currency depreciation, it has had the implied unqualified blessing of the IMF.

Ludwig von Mises' contention that "inflation is the fiscal complement of statism and arbitrary government . . . a cog in the complex of policies and institutions which gradually lead toward totalitarianism"[11] has been confirmed by one who might be wrongly interpreted as welcoming this result. Martin Bronfenbrenner has argued that through the Keynesian influence upon policy—through the consequent secular inflation—the "peaceful acceptance" of Marxian aims has been secured. Where the drastic measures which Marx himself contemplated would have failed, Keynesian methods have quietly succeeded.[12] "Secular inflation" has, in fact, proved to be the "principal weapon for extortion of surplus value,"[13] and has had "the net effect of permitting all 'active' pressure groups to gain at the expense of the 'dead hands' of the salariat, the *rentier,* and the pensioner."[14] Bronfenbrenner describes inflation as a "social mollifier" which permits the politically dominant goups, like the labor union movement and organized agriculture, to increase their share of the real national income "without decreasing the money income of anyone else, and therefore without arousing the volume and vehemence of opposition which might be expected."[15] This triumph of Marxian

---

[11] Ludwig von Mises, *Theory of Money and Credit,* trans. H. E. Batson (New Haven: Yale University Press, 1953), p. 428.

[12] Martin Bronfenbrenner, "Some Neglected Implications of Secular Inflation," in Kurihara, ed., *Post-Keynesian Economics,* p. 54.

[13] Ibid., p. 50.

[14] Ibid., p. 36.

[15] Ibid., pp. 35–36. He discusses the "ethical convictions" of the agricultural and labor sections, noting that they have the "normal voting strength necessary to backing up these convictions." The words "ethical convictions" are an interesting description of the realistic avarice of organized agriculture and organized labor. The sole ethical principle is that of might is right.

aims by more subtle methods than Marx's own, this gradual process which we are currently witnessing of the euthanasia of the politically weak classes, is, according to Bronfenbrenner, to be preferred to what he apparently regards as the inevitable alternative, expropriation on orthodox Marxian lines.[16] When totalitarianism in one form or another has triumphed, he thinks, inflation will probably "grind gradually to a halt!"[17] Although he claims that Keynesian policy "may with little exaggeration be credited with having saved capitalism in the 1930s,"[18] it was presumably saved from a sudden death in order to experience the only conceivable alternative, slow death by strangulation. "Inflation was always a terrible instrument for the redistribution of wealth," wrote Bresciani-Turroni, discussing the great German inflation which followed World War I.[19] But the great British inflation following World War II redistributed income just as "terribly" and cruelly, but quite differently. The intensity of cruelty is not to be judged by the intensity of squeals.

I am not questioning Bronfenbrenner's realism. It is true that Keynesianism "has been tried and found good by those potent bodies, the farm and the labor votes."[20] It is true also that it is likely to be politically disastrous if politicians "use their monetary authority deliberately to chastise inflationists with unemployment."[21] And one can agree also that, for this reason, economic conflicts have had to be resolved "by giving higher money incomes to all the combatants at the consumers' expense."[22] But this means at everybody's expense and to nobody's advantage except those who, mainly through political influence, are permitted to exploit the rest.

Bronfenbrenner talks of all the combatants demanding gains "at the consumers' expense." He does not consider the possibility of new combatants. May not "defense groups" arise to fight the pressure groups? Is it beyond the bounds of the conceivable that schoolteachers and the "white-collared" generally, independently of the AFL-CIO, should get together and threaten to strike for exorbitantly

---

[16] Ibid., p. 52.
[17] Ibid., p. 53. I think Bronfenbrenner is wrong here. Inflation has certainly helped to rectify the discoordinations of the totalitarian regime in Soviet Russia.
[18] Ibid., p. 49.
[19] Bresciani-Turroni, op. cit., p. 286.
[20] Bronfenbrenner, op. cit., p. 38.
[21] Ibid.
[22] Ibid., p. 39.

higher salaries, or *alternatively for a solemn pledge on the part of the government* (a) *to take effective action against the pressure groups— if necessary by declaring strikes illegal,*[23] and (b) to issue index bonds (securities bearing interest, at a special rate, but with a guarantee that their real value shall be maintained)? A nationwide organization which would lead to bank clerks, office employees, professional engineers, and others withdrawing their labor *en bloc* could have the effect of a war to end war—the eradication of a type of economic warfare in which one side has been aggressive while the other has so far been passively submitting to gradual dispossession.[24]

But what of the role of academic teaching? Is the situation which Bronfenbrenner so realistically describes one which the economist as teacher should represent to his students as unchangeable? Is not this situation itself largely due to the fact that, for many years, in hardly any university have the students been taught that it was the possibility of this very situation developing which largely motivated the economists' protests against Keynesian nationalism in the 1920s? Is not the use of monetary policy as "an instrument of national policy" (that is, political policy) at least in part a result of academic acquiescence? How many students have their attention drawn to the pertinent debate with Frank D. Graham in the *Economic Journal,* where Keynes tacitly but strikingly refrained from facing the surrender to "rackets" (as Graham described the chief vested interests) which the approach in *The General Theory* implies? If university teaching had been explaining the nature of the nauseating fight for higher *money* incomes which Keynesian policy renders inevitable, an incalculable impetus would have been given to the reactions I have been describing.

---

[23] I mention the banning of strikes particularly, simply because they have been the chief, not the only, coercive weapon responsible for restricting the flow of uninflated wages and income.

[24] The reader must remember that stockholders in industries known to be strike vulnerable are *not* among those dispossessed, if they have acquired their shares at prices which have already been depressed by fear of future strikes.

7

The Nature of Coordination Through the Price System

It has been said that pre-Keynesian economists were prepared to leave the fate of the economy to the price mechanism—that they placed full reliance on mythical "automatic" stabilizers. Those who make such assertions do not understand that the price mechanism[1] was regarded as a vast system of disciplined decision making which, because it relates every individual decision to every other economic decision, acts as the supreme coordinator of the economic system. As I have shown, the pre-Keynesian economists believed that, *properly administered,* with the government performing *its* appropriate role in that administration, the price system could maintain values and prices in harmonious relationship with one another. And they believed also that, if resources became unemployed, so that the flow of uninflated income contracted, it was due to a remediable defect in the administration of the system. Scarcities (that is, values) were expressed in prices as market signals—essential data for self-consistent, rational action, whether of the normal coordinative action guided by the entrepreneur or of any remedial coordinative action taken collectively when the whole economy has got seriously out of gear and depression has descended.

In this respect, the older economists had deeper insights regarding the price system than those of the Keynesian generation. Keynes diagnosed wrongly the source of fluctuations in employment. He thought he could find it in monetary, banking, and fiscal institutions, and in propensities to consume or spend, and not in any malfunctions

---

[1] By the "price mechanism" or the "price system" is meant the framework of institutions through which the values of services and assets are expressed in terms of the value of a unit known as *the money unit.*

of the price mechanism as a whole. In his early contributions he was brushing aside with the most scant references the purpose of changes in *relative* values, their consequences upon aggregate income, and the task of facilitating the movement of versatile resources in response to such changes, as well as to changes in the money valuation of given real incomes.[2]

Yet I have maintained above that the apparent success of Keynesian policy is attributable to its serving as a crude (although cruel and unjust) method of bringing the economic system into coordination; that it can, on the whole, merely *offset* coordination failures; and that it cannot remedy the ultimate causes of discoordination. What is usually needed is *not a blanket change in relative price-cost relationships such as is achieved through unanticipated inflation, but a mass of individual adjustments.* (See pp. 273–77.)

This chapter is concerned with the process of such coordination and the possibility of achieving the required objective by means of price adjustments and without resorting to Keynesian expedients.

An economic system is well coordinated when (a) *the rates of flow* of all productive services, materials (and other semifinished goods), and final products through the different stages of production and into consumption are such that, while there are reserves (inventories) at different points, there are no gluts or bottlenecks, and (b) the needed synchronization is achieved in such a way that each good flowing into consumption is produced at least cost.[3] Because we are here interested in the conditions which secure the continuous utilization of productive capacity ("full employment"), our concern will be centered principally on this question of *synchronization*.

The rates of flow of final products into consumption are determined by the prices charged. Prices are "market signals." As Benjamin M. Anderson wrote, "Prices have work to do. Prices are to guide and direct the economic activities of the people. . . . Prices must be

---

[2] In his earlier writings he had suggested that what matters is the relationship between various subsidiary price levels, prosperity depending upon these price levels being adjusted to one another. But he failed to see or to stress the *general* problem of coordination to a changed situation, through the diversion of marginal capital and labor to new employments, in response to changing values expressed as changing prices.

[3] The term "cost" here covers among other things the cost of remunerating the entrepreneur. "Least cost" is achieved in this respect when there is no "contrived scarcity" element. (See below, pp. 141–42.)

free to tell the truth."[4] But the Keynesians have enormous difficulty, I think, in recognizing this essential function of prices which Anderson so effectively stated.[5]

Insofar as Keynes himself recognized price and wage-rate adjustment as a means of restoring activity, he seems to have thought of it almost entirely in terms of its effects upon profit expectations— changes in the marginal efficiency of capital which make "investment" profitable. That is sound enough if it is recognized that it is the pricing of services to permit the employment of the assets which (or the people who) provide them that can be said to make their employment "profitable."[6]

If the rate of production[7] of any particular final commodity is perfectly coordinated with the system as a whole, the market price will be such that consumers are *able to* buy and *willing to* buy the full flow coming forward. *Ability* to buy is determined by what people can afford and by the extent to which they prefer the product in question (at its current price) to all other valuable things. *Willingness* to buy is determined by people's expectations about future prices[8] and the current necessity for the services provided by commodities in general. If, at any stage, the price of a material or intermediate product is reduced, the rate of flow at that stage will, *ceteris paribus,* tend to increase because, demand remaining the same, *final output is likely to increase;* and if the price is raised, the

---

[4] Benjamin M. Anderson, *Economics and the Public Welfare: Financial and Economic History of the United States, 1914–1946* (New York: D. Van Nostrand Company, 1949), p. 550.

[5] Polyani, for instance, appeared to approve of the frequently heard view that "while unemployment prevails it is not far from the truth to call pounds, shillings and pence 'meaningless symbols.' " See his *Full Employment and Free Trade,* p. 123. Yet unemployment itself may be regarded as a consequence of the meaning of these "symbols" *not* having been perceived.

[6] But the *proportion* of the aggregate flow of income which accrues or is expected to accrue as remuneration of entrepreneurial effort (profits) does not determine *the "volume" of activity* (although—as we shall see—it may certainly influence *the form of activity*). Moreover, the decisions of entrepreneurs are motivated as much by the wish to avoid further losses as by the wish to achieve profits on the *original* value of services invested in the activity.

[7] "Production" includes the marketing function, covering "the creation of value" in all forms, whether purposely or passively. "Consumption" here means the "extermination of value," again whether purposely or passively. These are J. B. Say's inspired definitions.

[8] Abstraction is made here (for simplicity) of the services rendered by money as part of the assets stock.

rate of flow will tend to decline. (Here also, of course, expectations must be brought into the picture.) It follows that the rate of flow of directly consumed services and work in progress, through all the stages of production and into consumption as final products, is determined by the prices asked being fixed at market-clearing levels.[9] Keynesian teaching is really a challenge to this sort of assertion. But if every particular price is adjusted to all other current and expected prices, and provided services offered are not for any reason *valueless,* the rate of flow of any one needed thing *can* be synchronized, through pricing, with the rates of flow of all complementary things. The exceptions which it is possible to imagine are only apparent exceptions. For unless services *are* valueless there must be a demand for them and, in the absence of restraint, the potential products into which they are embodied will move through the stages of production toward and into consumption.

When prices are coordinatively determined, then, not only are final prices fixed in relation to money income and consumer preference, but the prices of services and intermediate products at all stages of production are fixed in relation to expectations of demand at the next stage.[10] Prospective prices at the next stage of demand are in turn derived from predictions of demand at subsequent stages, including the ultimate demand for the final product.

In a state of barter there is never any reason why any commodity which one individual produces should not be exchanged if the producer wishes to exchange it, while others regard it as valuable. The Keynesian objection at times resolves itself into the idea that people may cease demanding nonmoney services and goods because they demand (with what they are producing) the services of money.

The *wasteful* form of idleness in resources arises when their services are priced above their market-clearing values, so that people are unable or (in the light of expectations) unwilling to purchase the full flow. It then becomes unprofitable for entrepreneurs to direct the full flow of services into the replacement or net accumulation of inventories or agents of production.

---

[9] Strictly speaking, I should say *by the values* asked. Services are acquired for direct consumption, or for embodiment into resources at the next stage of production, when the owner of the resources values the services so as to permit this. (See above, pp. 135–36, and below, pp. 272–75.)

[10] If "work in progress" moves to the next stage (that is, if further services are embodied into the semifinished product) within a firm, it will be because the present discounted value of the prospective sale value makes that profitable.

The prices which are too high to permit full utilization may occur at any stage in the productive process. But the *critical* price is that of the final product, for that price is, in a sense, the sum of the prices of all the services (including the marketing and entrepreneurial services) which have been embodied into it.

It is unnecessary to discuss all the circumstances in which a price change at one stage of production will not immediately affect prices (and hence rates of flow) at other stages. It is merely essential to show the relationship and to show that predicted or actual price changes tend to influence rates of flow. Hence unless some subtle fallacy vitiates the above reasoning, the system can be brought into synchronization if the right prices are fixed at the appropriate stages. How can such pricing be achieved?

The answer is reliance on pressures due to the loss-avoidance, profit-seeking incentive which I discussed above, an incentive which is *dependent upon* the power of substitution which we all possess to some extent when we act as consumers or entrepreneurs in the economic sphere. In the less appropriate language which is usually used, the incentive is called "the profit motive." When both the power of substitution and this incentive are present, the synchronization tends to be "automatic." For entrepreneurs, who *direct* the rendering of productive services (labor and skill or the services of capital resources), will try so to use these services that their prospective marginal return on the value of services or resources devoted to any use will not fall below the rate of interest. I define "loss" as a realized yield on any increment of investment which falls short of interest, and "profit" as a realized yield on any increment of investment which exceeds interest.

It is important that what is called the profit motive (the loss-avoidance, profit-seeking incentive) shall not be confused with *acquisitiveness* (that is, private thrift, the worthy motive of the individual to replace and accumulate). The urge to use resources "profitably" or rationally has nothing to do with acquisitiveness. Yet these two conceptually distinct motives are nearly always confused. The profit incentive we are discussing is merely the rational use of productive power in response to ends—ends being expressed by the people in their consumer role. For if the power of substitution to which I have referred is effective, there is an inducement for people as entrepreneurs to treat consumers' preferences as paramount. By consumers I mean those people in the community who make the effective decisions about the form and amount of consumption.

("Consumers" in this sense may be income receivers in general—as in democratic societies, or commissars—as in totalitarian communities.) Hence "consumers" in this context refers to those individuals who possess "consumers' sovereignty."[11] The essential condition is that this power of substitution, or "competition," shall be effective. If the argument which follows is accepted, this will be seen to be another way of saying that *the market mechanism shall be allowed to function freely.*

For many years now, I have defined the process of competition as the substitution of prospectively lower cost methods of achieving objectives, including the production and marketing of any product, or the substitution of a preferred product, a definition which corresponds, I think, to what economists have always *ultimately* meant by the term. As all economic ends are expressed by people in their consumer aspect, this always means substitution for the consumers' benefit. Such a definition may appear at first not to conform to the notion of "perfect competition," which has become conventional in the last three decades. But the term "perfect competition" (which I have always maintained is an inappropriate one)[12] merely refers to the equilibrium condition which is brought about when each producer can provide only a very small part of the aggregate supply of any commodity. It is a static description of a particular situation, whereas competition realistically conceived is of a dynamic nature and demands a dynamic definition.

I call the achievement of a lower cost method "competition" no matter what institutional setup may be necessary to release or protect incentives for the required substitutions. In a very crude way the same result can be achieved under central planning. The difference is that, in a "private enterprise economy," this result is achieved, as someone has said, "not by the whip (direction) but by the carrot (incentives)."

Just how effective can this process of substitution be when reliance is placed upon the carrot? Even in the most flexible economic system

---

[11] All who express economic ends (whether or not those ends are influenced by advertising, or propaganda) are expressing "consumers' sovereignty." See my *Economists and the Public,* Chapter 16, and my article "The Concept of Consumers' Sovereignty," *Economic Journal,* March 1940, pp. 66–77.

[12] See my criticism of Joan Robinson's *Economics of Imperfect Competition:* "Economic Method and the Concept of Competition," *South African Journal of Economics,* March 1934, pp. 1–23. We do not talk of "perfect" or "imperfect" gravity because there are such things as balloons.

imaginable, there would be hardly any producer or dealer who had no *short-term* monopoly power. But this does not mean that, in respect of the price which it will pay him to charge for any output, a "price searcher"—taking into account the long-term repercussions he can predict—may not be as helpless as a "price taker," a hypothetical producer who is confronted with a horizontal demand schedule (the case of "perfect competition"). It can be shown, I think, that when the economic framework of society has been appropriately planned and government is performing its "classical" role, that will be the approximate position.

Keynes' terminology, concepts, and models appear to cloak the *withholding of capacity,* especially when this occurs in the field of labor. That it is the pricing of the services of men or of assets at above their market-clearing values which causes some of them to be idle or idling is not kept effectively in mind. Keynes' only use of the term *withholding* that I can recall in *The General Theory* concerns leisure preference, which he seems to assume covers all motives for the withholding of *effort.* "[E]very kind of reason which might lead a man, or a body of men, to withhold their labor," he classes under "disutility."[13] That the purpose of a body of men in collusively withholding labor (or the services of other resources) may not be "disutility" in any imaginable sense but the "exploitation"[14] of consumers, or investors, or fellow workers (laid off and forced into, or kept in suboptimal employments), is not considered.

I have felt it to be desirable persistently to reiterate—almost *ad nauseam,* some readers may feel—the very points which the Keynesian models and "macro" concepts persistently obscure. I shall

---

[13] Keynes, *The General Theory,* p. 6. His phrase continues, "rather than accept a wage which had to them a utility below a certain minimum." Having mentioned "disutility," this seems a mere tautology to me.

[14] I have defined "exploitation" as follows: "Any action taken, whether or not through discernible private coercion (collusion) or governmental coercion, or whether through monopolistic or monopsonistic power, which, under a given availability of resources (including the stock of knowledge and skills), reduces the value of the property or income of another person or group of persons, or prevents that value from rising as rapidly as it otherwise would, *unless this effect is brought about through* (a) the dissolution of some monopolistic or monopsonistic privilege; or (b) the substitution of some cheaper method (labor-saving or capital-saving) of achieving any objective (including the production and marketing of any output); or (c) the expression of a change in consumers' preference; or (d) through taxation authorized by explicit legislation accepted as legitimate in any context." (Hutt, *A Rehabilitation of Say's Law,* p. 23.)

be constantly reminding the reader that downward price adjustments in fields in which prices exceed market-clearing levels (that is, in which scarcities have been contrived) can restore (and, indeed, are the only means of restoring) *uninflated* income; and uninflated income is uninflated power to purchase the full flow of productive services without net decumulation of productive power.

The practices which hinder the economizing-substitution process (including the economizing-displacement process[15]) occur with varying degrees of deliberateness. They range from organized restriction of output at one extreme to a mere failure to reduce prices in response to a fall in demand at the other extreme.[16] They occur whenever resources which (through the loss-avoidance, profit-seeking incentive) would otherwise be devoted to the production of a particular commodity are prevented from being so used. *The effect of such a contrivance may be that certain resources become unemployed* (through collusive action or natural monopoly), *but the more usual result is that the resources excluded from the most productive uses are gradually diverted to less productive uses.* The consequence in practice of restraint of the market mechanism is, indeed, less frequently "withheld capacity" than the much less conspicuous form of waste which I have called "diverted capacity" or "suboptimal employment,"[17] in which the *composition* of replacement and accumulation of assets is adversely affected.

For various reasons (connected I sometimes think with the desire to stress the politically fruitful slogan of "full employment"), the Keynesians have stressed "unemployment," particularly of labor. But insofar as there is any content in their claims to be concerned with human well-being at all, it is not merely "withheld capacity" (idle resources) which they want to be released for employment, through the forms of expenditure which they recommend, but *already employed resources* which are capable of being much more productively used. The Keynesians could say that they do bring "suboptimal employment" into the reckoning as unemployment of the kind that Mrs. Robinson has termed "disguised unemployment." But I cannot recall their having made use of that concept since she gave a name to it.

The relative burden on the community of "withheld capacity"

---

[15] For a full explanation of the term "economizing displacement," see my *The Strike-Threat System,* pp. 19–20.

[16] This concerns the case which was much discussed about thirty years ago under the term "administered prices."

[17] See definitions in my *The Theory of Idle Resources,* 2d ed., pp. 254–63.

(wastefully unemployed resources) and resources confined to suboptimal activities is a matter of great importance. *Men and assets diverted to less urgently preferred kinds of production are probably responsible for far more waste than unemployed men or underemployed assets.* Idleness of resources is, in other words, by no means the only or the most important aspect of waste. But in practice idleness—"unemployment"—is the most obvious objective expression of *the first stage* in the continuous fight against expanding productive power and expanding income. When assets are excluded from employment in a particular field, in the long run they are either scrapped or they seek other employments, while further services are no longer embodied into assets-forms which are specialized for that field. Hence actual unemployment may ultimately disappear although the waste persists.[18]

For simplicity of exposition, however, *I propose henceforth usually to refer simply to the withholding and release of capacity, when strictly speaking I should always draw attention to the full consequences of productive factors which have been diverted from more profitable to suboptimal, less profitable employments.*

Some critics are likely to object that I have not given sufficient weight to the reality that the coordinative function of the pricing system is restrained not only through the use of governmental power for private benefit or the tolerance by governments of the private use of coercive power, but through sheer entrepreneurial inertia. If the demand for a particular product falls, the price may be maintained. Some part of the resources employed must then either fall idle or be diverted to suboptimal uses.[19] It is my considered opinion that withholdings or diversions *due to mere inertia* are not of great practical importance, although I do not propose to assume this. (I shall deal with some possibilities of this kind later.)[20]

Of the incipient discoordinative factors which I have specified

---

[18] "Waste" may be defined as useless consumption.

[19] If the resources are specific, they will be forced into idleness. If they are versatile, they may be freed to accept suboptimal employments.

[20] Thomas Atwood and Henry Thornton had drawn the attention of the early classical economists to the rigidities (particularly in respect of the price of labor) which existed at the end of the eighteenth and early nineteenth centuries, referring to the same kind of phenomena we face today. In the judgment of their contemporaries, however, these phenomena were not important. But we now know that trade union organization in Britain at the time was powerful in certain of the emerging industries (the Combination Acts were leniently enforced) and that monopolistic collusion in other forms was more effective than the contemporary economists believed it to be.

above, the most difficult to explain, although in my opinion the least important, is what may be called "irrational reaction to costs incurred." I have in mind here producers' behavior in relation to what are called (very misleadingly) "fixed costs" or "overhead costs," and to contractually fixed prices.

In the first place it must be made quite clear that "fixed costs," "overheads," and contractually fixed prices (or contractually fixed rates of interest) are, in themselves, in no sense price rigidities.[21] They concern agreements about the division of the value of output. True prices are market prices which, in any case, may exceed or fall short of contractual prices being paid, the difference being made up of an element of speculative gain to the one party and speculative loss to the other. Only if producers can be assumed, in the presence of such gains or losses, to act irrationally or be subject to a *special* inducement to act collusively in respect of output and prices, through the existence of "fixed" or "overhead" costs and contractually fixed prices, can they be blamed for impeding the coordination process.

The irrationality to which I have referred may, however, *conceivably* be highly important as a cause of price rigidity. Resembling the "money illusion," which some economists deem so important in the pricing of labor, it has probably been aggravated by conventional cost accounting practice. But unless it influences collusive action (as it may well have done at times), I think it can have only a negligible force, just as the "money illusion" would probably have an inappreciable effect if it were not for collusive labor organization. In my judgment, the almost universal reluctance of managements in nonunionized activities to cut wage rates in recession, so as to avoid layoffs, constitutes a serious example of harmful irrationality; for their reluctance works to the detriment of the very workers for whose intended well-being managements refrain from the necessary coordinative action[22] needed to restore the income flow.

The condition which I call "price flexibility" must be thought of as being achieved according to the wisdom with which economic institutions have been planned and are being operated. *As an abstractly conceived ideal,* it presupposes a system in which as a result

---

[21] For an example of an influential discussion which is undermined by a failure to face this point, see U.S., Congress, Joint Economic Committee, *Recent Inflation in the United States,* by Charles L. Schultze, Study Paper No. 1, 86th Cong., 1st sess., 1959, p. 2.

[22] It is, of course, difficult to distinguish *that* reluctance from the conceptually separate managerial reluctance to avoid layoffs when the required wage adjustments would arouse enduring resentment.

of all the forces at work—government, entrepreneurs, and consumers—prices are adjusted in a manner consonant with attempts to achieve *all* economic objectives and ideals at least cost with no potential productive services being allowed to run to waste. And the price adjustments needed in response to change must always be fully adapted to the relevant expected prices. Such prices are "market-clearing."[23]

How different is the world of reality! The institutional pattern of contemporary society is ultimately responsible for myriad price rigidities. Cartels, output restrictions, price rings, divisions of territory, predatory selling through price discrimination, resale price maintenance, labor union standard rates, demarcations, restrictions of entry—these practices which sometimes "freeze" wage and price adjustments are in no sense inherent in the nature of a free economic system. In saying this, I do not imply that "perfect price flexibility" is attainable. (See below, pp. 146–47.)

The attempt to bring prices into coordination directly, by fixing maximum prices, may be merely correcting a symptom rather than the disease. Thus, unless the reduction of wage rates (in a trade in which they have been fixed at a level which is inconsistent with market clearance of the output, so that some labor is unemployed) is accompanied by the unemployed workers being *permitted* to return to employment, there is no reason why *the price of the product* should fall to a level consistent with full employment of the resources which can make it; and unless that occurs, an effective step toward re-coordination of the economy may not have been achieved. The aim must be twofold: restoring the right to accept employment (for men and other resources) at market-clearing wage rates or prices, so that all resources make their greatest possible contribution to real income and demand *in their existing employments;* and restoring the right of men and other resources to move to *new occupations* when they judge their contribution to income will be thereby increased. Price fixing by edict can be successful only when it is a device for setting such reactions going.[24] Thus, during the course of *a transition* to a noninflationary full employment situation, prices and wage rates

---

[23] For a fuller discussion of the "market-clearing" concept, see my *A Rehabilitation of Say's Law,* pp. 19–20, 89–102.

[24] The same considerations apply to all attempts to get the economy going by deliberately fixing any particular variables. Thus, attempts to work through influencing "investment" or "consumption" are fatuous unless accompanied by unanticipated inflation. Again, they are treating the symptom, not the disease.

generally might have to be reduced with the same frequency and severity as they had previously been raised during the inflation. The appropriate method of achieving this result with the minimum of friction could conceivably be through the medium of *temporary* "incomes policies" (see pp. 166 et seq.). The success of such policies would be judged, however, by the speed at which the controls could be removed (through the consequent recovery or expansion of the flow of uninflated wages and income). And unless the aim could be forthrightly explained as that of raising profit prospects (minimizing loss prospects), it would be likely to create all the disincentives, injustices, and impoverishment which have always resulted from wage and price controls.

Achieving a less imperfect coordination of economic activity (and, especially, eliminating the succession of boom and slump) requires an institutional reorganization to allow costs and prices to be as flexible downward as they are upward. "What!" self-styled realists will shout. "Don't you see that human nature alone makes your ideas impossible to apply?" Well, there have been many examples of wage cuts being voluntarily accepted in emergency, in order to avoid layoffs. *But do I have to rely upon empirical refutation of the proposition that workers will universally refuse to take the steps essential to their own well-being?* Suppose they are participating in a system of "shared entrepreneurship" under which they have contracted to put at risk (out of agreed compulsory savings and future earnings) a sum which will eventually equal half the capital of the undertaking, in return for an ultimate right to share equally in management and enjoy half the profits. In such a situation, I suggest, the workers would hardly hesitate to accept remuneration consistent with the continued maintenance and sale of the output.

Hence frank recognition of the obvious political and sociological difficulties which reforms to secure more sensitive price adjustments must encounter should not *cause economists to inhibit consideration of such reforms.* Admittedly, the reforms needed demand a reversal of the tendency of the last century. We do now have a long tradition of governments acting in the sectional interest and refraining from acting in the collective interest, for fear of offending powerful groups.

But even under the existing economic order, and over a wide range of activities, the coordinating machinery can be seen to be operating; for *the fundamental incentive* still exists, and adjustments result. Competition is a hardy process. Coordination is much more clumsy, sporadic, and inefficient than it need be, but it does occur, even though considerable withheld or suboptimally utilized capacity exists. If the synchronizing functions of the price system were clearly understood, it would be possible so to plan institutions that the prices of products and services in all fields could be adjusted in an orderly way, not only in response to changes of preference (including time preference) but also to meet moderate changes in the value of the money unit (such as occasionally occurred in the gold standard era), or even to meet large changes in the price index (which might have to be brought about after inflation in order to honor obligations). Changes in preference and economizing innovations also demand changes in those established routines and habits which enable the "automatic" working of an exchange economy. But when prices are flexible, society can easily adapt its routines to both sets of changes. There may perhaps be greater problems in discarding routines and customs than there is in discarding obsolete equipment.

It is important, however, to distinguish between "perfect price flexibility" and "effective price flexibility." "Perfect price flexibility" implies the existence of incentives to price not only for the full absorption of particular outputs but for the full absorption of outputs in general *when the value of the money unit changes*. This means, in other words, the absence of the money illusion. When I think of *perfect* price flexibility, I suppose first that people regard the money unit as a measuring rod which expands or contracts without affecting the size of the things measured, and second that people are in-different to experienced, current, or anticipated appreciations or depreciations of the money unit. If, for any reason, MV has changed, is changing, or is expected to change in relation to T, people will always adjust the prices of everything to market-clearing levels, so that (a) the full flow of productive services is absorbed; (b) no "shortages" emerge; and (c) no speculative demand for money is induced, because all prices are immediately adjusted to expectations.

In practice, admittedly, *perfect price flexibility* has never existed and may never exist. Indeed, in order to understand certain aspects of monetary theory, it is important to accept *as a realistic assumption* the existence *of unstable price rigidities* (which give rise to a speculative influence in the demand for money).

Hence, when I talk of price flexibility, unqualified, I shall mean "effective price flexibility"—the sort of flexibility which is empirically observable under appropriate conditions; that is, *under suitable economic policies*—given the sort of institutions with which the student of business administration and business practices is familiar.

In depression, of course, much more drastic adjustments are demanded in order to bring the system into coordination. Thus, *to restore the wages flow and raise demands for labor most rapidly, wage rates are needed which are very much lower than those which are destined to be forced by the market when the wheels of productive activity begin to turn faster.* For the increased outputs achieved through reduced costs in any one productive activity are raising demands for the inputs and outputs in noncompeting fields generally.

As far as wage-rate flexibility is concerned, we find that labor and skills are, on the whole, naturally highly versatile and can (in the absence of labor union restrictions such as demarcations) be transferred (not always without cost) from the production of one commodity to another, as preferences or supply conditions change.[25] There are, however, special institutional and sociological restraints in this field, and the history of adjustment in the modern world has usually been that of powerful opposition to the required revaluations. Strikes, bitterness, and lingering resentments have normally accompanied action by means of which the flow of uninflated wages and income revives or increases. Perhaps the major economic problem (or perhaps *political* problem) of this age is how society can overcome the labor union fight against the means to an increased flow of real wages, better working conditions, and stability of employment. The elimination of private force in the determination of the price of labor could certainly achieve this.

Keynes himself placed chief emphasis on the *inflexibility of wage rates* when he did refer to prices as a cause of discoordination. I prefer myself to discuss *price rigidity*—regarding wage-rate rigidity as a special case—because the problem is a quite general one and because I do not wish to place all the blame on unions for policies which force down the flow of wages and income. Yet on empirical grounds, Keynes' emphasis does appear to be justified here. While unions are the chief impoverishers, they are not the only ones.

In Bronfenbrenner's opinion, the "Austrian" remedy for industrial depressions "will no longer be permitted to work for any length of time in a democratic society, despite such spectacular instances of success as the depression and recovery of 1920–22 in the United States."[26] But the pre-Keynesian or "Austrian" policy was more one

---

[25] There are some important exceptions, for example, musicians and professional athletes.

[26] Bronfenbrenner, "Some Neglected Implications of Secular Inflation," Kurihara, ed., *Post-Keynesian Economics,* p. 48.

of *avoiding* depressions than curing them. Had that policy been adopted, quite different reforms would have been encouraged. It is impossible to be dogmatic about what the results would have been. *Certainly the benefits would not have been spectacular. For social institutions which work well are taken for granted, seldom discerned or recognized, and rarely accorded the credit they deserve.*

While there is a great deal of evidence of downward wage-rate adjustments *forced by depression* being followed by recovery, no deliberate attempt to increase uninflated income (including the flow of wages) by reducing all prices (including wage rates) which appear to be above the market-clearing level has ever been purposely pursued.[27] For decades, actual policies have been based upon the politically attractive rule, justified by appeal to Keynesian teaching, that disharmony in the wage-rate structure must not be tackled but offset; while the current tendency is to assume dogmatically, with no adequate examination of the institutional and sociological factors involved, that to advocate a return to market-selected wage and price adjustments is to recommend the conquest of the moon.[28]

Part of the pre-Keynesian remedy for a discoordinated economy relied upon the achievement of greater price flexibility. In such a solution, an increase of uninflated money income accompanied and facilitated, rather than effected, improved synchronization. In the Keynesian solution, the increase of money income is regarded as the cause of the recoordination.

It can be said that effective price flexibility is secured when a large measure of free access to markets has been guaranteed. Curiously

---

[27] In my *Keynesianism* I referred to "reducing all prices which appear to be above the natural scarcity level (including wage rates)." Such a policy would appear to be more drastic than my own suggestion (pp. 168–75). Yet it would tend to release labor and complementary assets not only from unemployment but from suboptimal employments; and it would cause, therefore, a rise in the remuneration of men and assets profitably transferred to more productive work. It would also raise the natural scarcity value and hence remuneration of workers generally who are employed in less productive and lower paid (not necessarily suboptimal) jobs.

[28] See, for instance, Schultze, op. cit., p. 68. Schultze abandons rigorous analysis and resorts to sheer irony when he refers to the policy of achieving price coordination without the assistance of creeping inflation. He mocks as "pulverizers" those "who would attempt to solve the problem by strengthening the various antitrust laws, applying them, in modified form perhaps, to labor as well as business" (ibid., p. 41). One cannot help wondering how far his attitude is due to his apparent acceptance as an inexorable law of nature, to be treated with due reverence, that "wage increases do, and price cuts do not, win union elections" (ibid., p. 68).

enough, the Keynesian thesis sometimes takes the form of an argument which seems to be to this effect. We are told that it should be the object of economic policy to "assure markets" which are not assured "automatically."[29] But the policy implied by non-Keynesian teaching is exactly this, although the word "automatically" is usually vague and ambiguous. What is essential in a coordinated economy is the *right of access* to markets for all resources and services; and in a money economy, this requires *pricing* to satisfy both buyer and seller. "Markets" can be "assured" *for producers as a whole* in no other way. All other methods are essentially either protectionist—assuring markets for some by excluding others from them—or inflationary. And the inflationary method itself operates by bringing relative prices closer to market-clearing levels. Lavington perceived the true principle when, asking why entrepreneurs operate resources at low pressure during depression, he answered that the absence of reasonable expectation of being able to sell additional output was due to consumers failing to purchase *"because they themselves are not producing."* The consumers' proper name is, he says, "other producers."[30] Moreover, in depression "the individual firm is working at low pressure because other firms are working at low pressure. Each is inactive because the general power to consume has fallen; and the general power to consume has fallen because of and in proportion to the general decline in the activity of production. The inactivity of all is the cause of the inactivity of each. No entrepreneur can fully expand his output until other entrepreneurs expand their output."[31]

It has not been recognized, I think, that successful strategy to bring formerly rigid prices into coordination (or to effect the elimination of contrived scarcities generally) may be viewed as *an act of innovation.*[32] In particular, the constant search by managers for lower cost methods of achieving ends should be regarded as the most

---

[29] The word "automatic" has been used of the continuous and conscious entrepreneurial decision making needed for this purpose. But that term can be justified only in the sense that *discretion* in the vital predictions and decisions is limited by rule and not by whim, the ultimate controlling forces being social in origin (expressed in markets) and not political in origin. But the Keynesians customarily use the term "automatic" in a manner which ridicules and misrepresents their critics. They suggest, indeed, the kind of system in which the coordinative functions of the government are blindly neglected.

[30] Lavington, *The Trade Cycle,* p. 23.

[31] Ibid., p. 24.

[32] Innovation is only a stimulus to "prosperity" and growth when it is of an economizing nature and hence increases income *and* savings. Otherwise, it merely changes the form of replacement and net accumulation.

important kind of innovation activity which can lead to a rise in the marginal efficiency of capital. Indeed, every act of competition, every substitution of an economizing method of production for the consumers' benefit, *every breach of a price rigidity, is an act of expansive innovation,* because it brings about a more productive use of scarce resources.[33] Far from the cutting of rigid prices bringing about a fall in the marginal efficiency of capital, it is conducive to its rise. *But—and this is the point on which the Keynesians appear to be most undiscerning—such innovations do not always mean that prospective yields are bound to rise in any industry in which an economy is introduced. Yields will tend to rise for all noncompeting industries.* The innovator—including the price cutter—will usually find that it pays him to increase the stock of resources which he is using; but unless the demand for the product is highly elastic, or unless general expansion elsewhere in the economy happens to be raising the demand schedule that confronts him, the expansion which his decisions effect will cause loss of profits to his competitors or even make it profitable for some of them to disinvest.

The apparent Keynesian failure to appreciate the process through which the heterogeneous economic aims which people are seeking are brought into consistency, and through which a synchronized cooperation in response to those aims is achieved, can be attributed, I think, to that unawareness of the social purpose of price changes which I alleged and discussed on pages 135 et seq. Such changes (both *individual price changes* and changes in the *scale of prices*)[34] being socially purposive, the more "violent" the changes, the more serious the discoordinations which are being rectified, the greater the magnitude of the changes called for, and the greater the social benefit to be realized from the changes. But Keynesians tend to regard price fluctuations as an evil in themselves. Their attitude causes pressure to coordination to be diagnosed as the origin of disorder. The distortion in question is typical not only of Keynesian thinking but of "leftist" thinking as a whole. The essentially stabilizing nature of the pressures which are expressed through the price mechanism, and which perform a major part of its coordinative task, tends to be ignored, overlooked, or misinterpreted.

Admittedly, the price mechanism will perform its coordinative

---

[33] It was, perhaps, Joseph Schumpeter's most serious blind spot that, in his perception of the enormous importance of innovation, he failed to perceive—or at least to *stress*—this reality.

[34] The full meaning of this assertion will become clear later. Fluctuations in the scale of prices may be evidence that monetary coordination is needed.

task defectively if the data tend, either at particular crucial times or generally, to be misinterpreted by entrepreneurs. If the environment created by current prices and current price trends induces the wrong reactions, discoordination will ensue. But entrepreneurial decision making is continuous and subject to perpetual adjustment, while individual errors of interpretation incur increasingly heavy penalties the longer the period before they are rectified. Only if there are, so to speak, *infectious* errors of prediction can it be argued that reliance upon the mechanism of price adjustment has inherent defects.

In my judgment, entrepreneurs are seldom *unwisely* optimistic or pessimistic when they observe the growth or decline in economic activity and judge the profitableness of expanding or curtailing their own activity accordingly. Where apparently contagious errors in forecasting with cumulative results can be observed, it seems to me that this is almost entirely due to general uncertainty about future governmental policy as a whole (and the results of that policy). The situations envisaged by those who fear *infectious* misinterpretation of prices and price trends nearly all arise—as I shall show—*because the objectives of monetary policy are vague.* That is why I place such great stress on the desirability of the monetary authority being committed to *the maintenance of a money unit of some defined value.* If most entrepreneurs have faith in the willingness and ability of treasuries and central banks to achieve the objective of a *defined* money unit, *most* of the self-perpetuating cumulative movements of prices will be eliminated. (See below, pp. 198–99.)

To the Keynesian mind, however, depressions occur as a result of *the unwillingness of people to buy goods,* or the *inability to sell goods,* both of which may be brought under the idea of *absence of markets.* The truth is the contrary. Depressions occur as a result of an increasing *unwillingness to sell* things at prices consistent with the maintenance of noninflated money income and a consequent increasing *inability to buy* at the prices fixed. For the failure to buy all the *valuable productive services* potentially available (including goods into which they have been embodied) cannot be due to the failure to demand them but to the *failure to release them.* The fact that they have value is proof that they are demanded; and they have value if they would be purchased at any price above zero. Failure to sell (that is, failure to price at market-clearing values[35]) is

---

[35] As we have seen, investment in the accumulation of inventories of an output is not "frustration of the buyer" when that investment promises a marginal prospective yield that exceeds the rate of interest on the capital value so invested (see my *A Rehabilitation of Say's Law,* Chapter 3). Thus, the market-clearing

frustration of the buyer, not the seller. If consumption declines, while no services normally devoted to making final products fall *valueless*,[36] it is impossible to attribute any idleness of resources to some inherent propensity of consumers. The factors responsible for the slowing down of activity cannot be expressed in any "consumption function" derived from some "psychological law." *The responsibility lies wholly in policies which ignore the social purpose of prices.*

What is essentially the same issue can be expressed from another aspect. When investments generally have proved to be less remunerative than had been predicted, although a distortion in the structure of the stock of assets has occurred, there is no reason why the greater part of that stock should be unable to supply valuable services to replace the value of consumption or provide for the net accumulation of assets. For there is always complete absorptive capacity for all *potential productive services which have value,* and for many which have not. Price rigidity because of government or private coercion, or due to mere inertia, may prevent absorption, so that the final stage in production, namely, sale for consumption, is not completed. But such a situation ought to be described as *underproduction* through discoordinative pricing.

The view that the income and spending power of consumers should be sufficient to clear the market of goods is a cart-before-the-horse arrangement. I say, prices should be fixed so that, in the light of expectations, the money income and spending power of consumers can always clear the market. Depression develops when the failure of one set of interests to price in the collective interest motivates or reinforces the unwillingness of another. This sets up a chain reaction which can lead to panic repercussions and so aggravate the cumulative withholding, leading to privately disastrous declines in the values of certain kinds of inventories.

A more radical cleavage of opinion could hardly exist. Is it "unwillingness to buy" or "unwillingness to sell" at coordinated, market-clearing prices which leads to valuable resources falling into disuse? Keynesians fail to see that the cutting of prices in any field is simply the creation of additional demand for noncompeting goods, because power to purchase is released for other purposes. Indeed, as we have already noticed, Keynesians tend to regard such price adjustments as the cause, not the cure of crises and depression. The

---

price for any inventory of physically completed products is that which liquidates the inventory at a rate that is predicted to maximize the profit.

[36] See my *The Theory of Idle Resources,* 1st ed., pp. 41–56; 2d ed., pp. 63–75.

adjustment of prices early in the process, as prices have been getting out of the range of consumer income, appears to them as *a likely initiating cause* of a cumulative decline (as distinct from *an aborting factor*). Thus, Dillard contends categorically that "slight provocation may set up a cumulative wave of liquidation. . . . Every business transaction on the selling side involves an embryo crisis."[37] How hopelessly wrong it all is!

Dillard sums up Keynes' position on the issue as follows: "Elasticity in the supply of output and in the size of inactive balances provides the basis of flexibility whereby the economic system adapts itself to the shocks which orthodox theory assumed *could and would be absorbed by flexibility of prices*"[38] (my italics). The pre-Keynesian position is misrepresented of course. Had Dillard expressed the case he was attacking fairly and accurately, he would have said "could and *should*" instead of "could and *would*." Insofar as the pre-Keynesians believed that the economic system *could* adjust itself, through price adjustment, to the shocks of demand changes, their view was founded upon observation. And when they assumed that institutions were such that the condition of full employment, once departed from, would tend to be restored, this was *on the assumption that policy would aim at, or not destroy, the incentives for the required adjustments.*

It must be emphasized again that the Keynesian remedy itself relies tacitly upon the price mechanism and the same fundamental incentive. The restraints imposed in practice upon the substitution of lower cost methods (competition), and serious errors of judgment or prediction, may upset the reactions upon which the Keynesian remedy relies, just as they may frustrate attempts to coordinate through price adjustments. But very broadly, Keynesian policy seeks to restore coordination by making it possible for people to *afford to buy,* not by enabling them directly to increase their contribution to real income, but by increasing the money valuation of their income in the expectation that this will cause an increase in the contribution of others to real income. The Keynesians admit that price rigidity perverts the market mechanism, but they seldom explain clearly that the increase of money income they recommend merely *circumvents* the discoordinating rigidities by inflating income to meet inflated prices. Moreover, their admissions on this point are obscured by the

---

[37] Dillard, "Theory of a Monetary Economy," Kurihara, op. cit., p. 29.
[38] Ibid., p. 24.

assumption that, even in the absence of price rigidities, it is essential to preserve the flow of services and products by maintaining expenditure (or certain categories of expenditure) by means other than that of adjusting prices in harmony with current income and expectations. (See Chapter 12.)

The confused thinking which arises through the use of such unsatisfactory notions as "lack of markets" has, I think, had most seriously adverse results upon the coordination of international trade relations. The Great Depression records two kinds of pricing reactions to the situation created: discoordinative, those which tended to aggravate the chaos; coordinative, those which tended to mitigate the depression. Now, *by no means the least cause of the persistence of the depression was the tendency in influential circles to class these opposites together,* as though they were of the same nature. For instance, in a discussion of international trade, Alexander Loveday (by no means a Keynesian in later years!) wrote (in 1937):

> Prices on world markets were forced down by import restrictions imposed by this or that country to improve its balance of payments. Each country tried to obtain a larger share in the melting snowball of international trade by reducing costs; each undercut the other. This competitive attempt to achieve a common objective failed. The universal attempt by each country to arrest the depression on its frontiers by stopping *the germ carriers, the low-priced foreign goods,* failed no less inevitably.[39] [My italics.]

Like so many of his contemporaries and subsequent economists, *Loveday did not perceive that cost reduction and price cutting reflected increases of uninflated demands, for which the world was languishing,* while import restrictions reflected the eradication of some of those demands. The producers of the goods which were offered at cut prices were demanding goods in exchange, whereas the exclusion of goods by import restrictions was exterminating demand. Had the arrival of cheap foreign goods in any country been followed by similar price adjustments internally, or had the nations of the world been successfully encouraged by their international advisers to cut tariffs and mitigate restrictions, a rapid world recovery *with a great expansion of real and money demands would have eventuated.* It is dodging the whole issue to object that the price

---

[39] Alexander Loveday, "Collective Behavior and Monetary Policy," in Arthur D. Gayer, ed., *Lessons of Monetary Experience: Essays in Honor of Irving Fisher* (New York: Farrar and Rinehart, 1937), p. 428.

cutters were demanding not goods but money. *The pricing of services so as to keep inventories cleared and the full flow of services absorbed is the very condition which brings about a noninflationary expansion of credit, and hence the revival of moneyed demands.* The international economic tragedy of 1929–31 occurred more because of the failure to use the monetary mechanism than because of any of the mechanism's defects. The various countries adjusted to the shrinking world demands by restricting output instead of adjusting prices, thereby causing a further shrinkage.[40] In place of each country adapting its prices and costs so that there was a new balance between internal and external demands for its products, the tendency was for each country to seek a way out through a further insulation of its economy. Both exports and home-consumed products should have been sold at prices which fully reflected the cheaper materials which were being incorporated into them. But too many employed sectors of labor and capital tried, with disastrous results, to retain the benefit for themselves. Naturally, the world flow of services which was compatible with convertibility into gold was bound to contract. Governments everywhere acted as though in complete unawareness of the social purpose of pricing, creating new rigidities rather than breaking down those which had already developed. Insofar as recovery resulted from direct (as distinct from inflationary) adjustments it was—with few exceptions—*in spite of government policy*. (See pp. 269–70.)

At this stage I repeat my charge that one of the most serious consequences for which Keynesian doctrine and influence must accept blame is that they have helped to prevent a clear insight into the inherent contradictions and consequent inefficiencies of the economic institutions of the contemporary "capitalist" world. In stressing the notion of *lack of purchasing power* or *lack of "effective demand,"* instead of the less easily grasped, but realistic, notion of *defective coordination,* Keynesianism has hindered the emergence of a fuller understanding of why unanticipated inflation so often activates previously idle resources. The apparent successes of inflation could have assisted us in diagnosing the defects of the coordinative mechanism. Inflation has, when unanticipated, been successful in stimulating production in peace and war solely because it has brought prices into better relations with one another. *Its "successes" are, in*

---

[40] See Milton Gilbert, *Currency Depreciation and Monetary Policy* (Philadelphia: University of Pennsylvania Press, 1939), pp. 12 et seq., where Britain's reaction is described. It is just as applicable to other countries.

effect, proof of what noninflationary coordination can achieve with incomparably greater efficiency and lower cost, provided *political institutions render that possible.*

Inflation has coordinated also (in the same indirect and crude manner) in reducing entrepreneurial fears of exploitation by organized labor following investment in specific, capital-intensive forms.[41] For instance, in Britain during the interwar period, the danger of strikes subsequent to such investment discouraged modernization in many vital industries, probably most seriously in coal mining. During the post-1945 period, however, the expectation that aggressive union action to force increases in wage rates could be met out of continuously inflating demands for output, seems to have provided the required inducement for investment in labor-economizing and capital-economizing equipment. Yet how much more beneficial would have been legislation to prohibit the private use of coercive power! If trade union action calculated to destroy entrepreneurial incentives (and hence to hold back a growing flow of wages and income) could have been outlawed, productive power would have expanded in the most economic forms.[42]

Once the lesson has been clearly learned and taught by economists, it will appear to be intolerable that society should allow discoordination to be rectified only through the deceptions of inflation—*a remedy which leaves the genesis of the disease undisturbed,* or even aggravates the disease. And most economists have taken so long to learn the lesson because, at the moment when world events were proclaiming the answer, Keynes came forth with an answer that was more compatible with the thinking of politicians and businessmen— that the idleness of valuable resources resulted from insufficient spending.

I deny that money has any function or power to "promote" or "stimulate" economic life, or production, or the "development" of the economic system, except (a) in the sense that any efficient technical mechanism plays its part in the productive process (for example, the transport system), or (b) in the sense that the multiplication of money units may (when expectations are not adjusted to

---

[41] In general, entrepreneurs avoid specific forms of investment which they anticipate are likely to be exploited by trade union action subsequent to the investment. (See my *The Theory of Collective Bargaining,* 2d ed., pp. 62–63, and *The Strike-Threat System,* pp. 4–6, 9.)

[42] Productive power *in all forms* would then *be likely to* expand through the stimulus to savings via the interest offer. (See Chapters 13 and 14.)

such a policy) be used as an alternative to the direct coordination of prices.[43] There is no other manner in which money can be said to "stimulate" the economic system.[44] The word "lubrication" (which has been chosen to describe the role of money in trade since the seventeenth century) can, however, certainly be appropriately so used. It *is* the essential function of money to overcome the absence of "double coincidence of wants" under barter. *But you cannot run a car on a lubricant.*

I have used the phrase "crude coordination" of policies which aim at achieving full employment through the manipulation of expenditures (effective demand). But such policies not only coordinate, they remove other pressures to coordination, and they create inducements to discoordinate. For instance, if organized labor knows that full employment of labor is guaranteed, demands for wage-rate increases will be relatively uninhibited. And if "employers" know that inflation will follow in order to enable them to pay the higher rates, they will tend to lose sight of their social duty to resist the fixing of wage rates by the threat of private force. Indeed, for such reasons, when inflation is generally anticipated, its coordinative effects are completely destroyed.

For instance, in 1949 Lionel Robbins warned of the outcome of assuring the labor unions that, however high they pushed up wage rates, governments would validate the situation by reducing the purchasing power of the money unit. Nevertheless, he adhered then to the opinion that wise monetary policy would among other things aim at maintaining high levels of employment.[45] But no argument I have read or heard has convinced me that the sole contribution that *monetary* policy can *wisely* make toward the achievement of a high level of employment (which *means,* incidentally, a high real income)

---

[43] Similarly, the multiplication of money units may be used as a means of temporarily restricting consumption and forcing "real saving." It is equally true that deflation (resorted to in order to honor agreements) is not discoordinative, except in the sense that other factors cause it to be so.

[44] The term "stimulation" applied to economic activity can be rightly applied, as I have shown, only to output (the source of real demands) or anticipated output. Economizing inventions "stimulate" because they permit greater output. *All* additional output, priced for absorption at home or abroad, has an expansive effect on the whole economy. It makes no difference whether that output is to be sold for home use or sold in the form of exports. What is essential is its pricing for market clearance, in which event it adds to uninflated income.

[45] Lionel C. Robbins, *The Economist in the Twentieth Century, and Other Lectures in Political Economy* (New York: St. Martin's Press, 1954).

is that of maintaining a money unit of defined value, removed by iron-clad rules from the discretion of vote-hungry politicians. It was precisely because British monetary policy *did* aim at maintaining "high levels of employment" that she *experienced* the outcome against which Robbins warned.

Keynesian doctrine sometimes rests on the assumption of wage-rate rigidity (and sometimes on price rigidity generally). And the Keynesians might claim that their doctrine does allow for unemployment caused by wage rates and prices being fixed too high. But they show an obvious reluctance to explain actual depression phenomena in terms of costs or prices having been forced above market-clearing levels or maintained there through sheer inertia.[46]

In referring to the retreat from Keynesian teaching observable about two decades ago, William Fellner contends that Keynesianism "by-passes the question of the consequences of money wage and price adjustment with an answer that is *evasive*." Nevertheless, he maintains that the Keynesian answer is not *"meaningless"* because "we frequently wish to proceed as if a self-adjustment mechanism . . . did not exist." For even in a free market, he rightly says, it is "a very sluggish mechanism, operating with lags and detours and impeded by institutional obstacles"[47] (my italics). He continues, "Keynesianism favors policies that work toward restoration of the balance without reliance on significant changes in the general level of money wages and prices. These policies include countercyclical regulation of the relationship between fiscal revenues and fiscal expenditures as well as central bank techniques."[48] But pre-Keynesian policy did *not* rely on changes in "the general level" of money wage rates and prices. Fellner's treatment actually amounts to a virtually unqualified acceptance of non-Keynesian criticisms, with the suggestion that, for the reasons stated, the Keynesians still adhere to the policy of coordination otherwise than through price adjust-

---

[46] They might contend of course that the advocacy of a return to noninflationary coordination under current political conditions is mere nostalgia, a visionary's dream. *But that is to argue that it is hopeless to expect mankind to profit from past blunders.* And if that is really the Keynesians' conviction, they should say so in explicit, unequivocal language, and face the controversy which will follow. See pp. 40–41, 43–44, 65–66, and my *Politically Impossible . . . ?* pp. 22–27 and 54–71.

[47] William Fellner, "What Is Surviving? An Appraisal of Keynesian Economics on Its Twentieth Anniversary," *American Economic Review,* Papers and Proceedings, May 1957, p. 68.

[48] Ibid., pp. 68–69.

ment. But that must mean through some measure of inflation. As a just representation of Keynesianism, the passage *seems to imply* that stability of the scale of prices is envisaged. In fact, the word "significant" is the loophole which leaves the way open to advocacy of creeping inflation.

Controversy is thus brought to the following position. Non-Keynesians, on the one hand, advocate the deliberate planning of the institutional framework to eliminate lags and general sluggishness so as to permit the more effective coordination of the economic system without changes in the general level of prices. Keynesians, on the other hand, believe that institutional defects cannot be effectively tackled, and that the crude coordination achievable through the *gradual* depreciation of the money unit (not sufficiently rapid to cause "significant" changes in the level of prices) must therefore be adopted. Thus they commit themselves to the persistent deception of the public regarding monetary intentions or to disguised totalitarianism; these are the inevitable alternatives under continuous inflation.

When unemployment exists, then, the recovery in real income and employment can come about only as a direct result of (a) the release of withheld capacity by pricing productive services nearer to market-clearing levels, or (b) net accumulation of productive capacity[49] through thrift (which adds to the capacity to demand). Now the recognition of this reality does not guarantee a parallel recognition of the effects of pricing at market-clearing values upon the *dynamics* of the situation. We also must always keep in mind the *indirect or time* results of the release of capacity. Say's law (in the broad sense of the principle that the demand for any commodity is a function of the supply of noncompeting commodities) implies that thrift constitutes the most potent dynamic element in the determination of the development *tempo*. In a world of coordinated prices, it would not be the mere current absence of withheld capacity which would stimulate the simultaneous growth of productive capacity and consumption power. The stimulus would come from the knowledge that capacity would not be withheld in the future, through the collusive fixing of prices and wage rates, with the result that thrift and growth would be generated. (See Chapters 13 and 14.) The enormous importance of the elimination of the arbitrariness of sectionalist pricing and output control can hardly be exaggerated. And the resulting stimulus to

---

[49] Net accumulation of productive capacity is intended to include the capital value of discoveries and inventions. (See Chapter 13.)

inventiveness in techniques and management due to the consequent elevation of risk taking to a new level has also to be brought into the reckoning.

In particular, the reactions of wages upon wages seem to me to have been seriously neglected. Under conditions of unemployment, it is certainly not essential, as Keynes assumed, for average real wage rates to fall in order that recovery may occur. For instance, during the downward wage-rate and price adjustments which occurred in the United States during 1920–22, *per capita* real earnings rose substantially, the previously unemployed being regarded as having had zero earnings.

The dynamics of contraction are no less important. When the mechanism of price adjustment is defective, a wave of self-perpetuating and self-aggravating withholding of capacity may be created by any factors which lead to an initial decline in real income. We have, for example, disturbances such as bad harvests, or external changes which reduce the aggregate value of imports which a given volume of exports is able to earn. The phenomenon can be illustrated by a reduction in the real profitableness of foreign trade. A clear instance is to be found in the United States in the early 1930s. It was the cessation of demand for American agricultural products due to the cessation of American lending to Europe, and the fact that the Fordney-McCumber and Hawley-Smoot tariffs made it impossible for Europe to buy the previous value of American products with earned income, which depressed first the earnings of United States agriculture and, in turn, the earnings of industry. Then, in reaction to the situation so created, both sectors of the economy attempted in vain to preserve money earnings by trying to curb the fall of prices rather than by adjusting prices to the new situation. In this attempt, they reduced still further their mutual demands for one another's products. The general depression was inevitably intensified.[50]

But the *initiating* cause of cumulative withholding may arise not from natural or external events but through internal action which results in discoordination. Thus, "wage-push," a wave of union-enforced increases in wage rates, may be responsible.[51] Moreover,

---

[50] In this case, price and cost adjustment in both fields ultimately reversed the cumulative withholding into a cumulative release of capacity from about the middle of 1932. This recovery would, I believe, have persisted had a policy of encouraging further adjustment been adopted. But NRA policy prolonged the depression.

[51] See my *The Theory of Collective Bargaining,* 2d ed., pp. 107–8, 110–13.

oligopoly is a possibility. Businessmen are confronted with large "overheads"; and the widespread existence of withheld capacity causes them to become aware that they are producing under decreasing average cost.[52] They perceive that, in the existing recession, it will not pay them to cut prices, although price cutting would be to the advantage of any individual firm if it could rely upon the others in the same industry failing to follow suit. The *likelihood* of oligopolistic phenomena being an important factor is, however, small. Even collusive monopolies are subject to internal stresses and strains through divergences of interest, and often exploitation of the consumer can be effective only through iron-clad agreements involving sanctions against members who do not toe the line. But to the extent to which firms can evade antimonopoly laws and arrange for price maintenance, it does have a cumulatively depressing effect.

When capacity begins to be generally withheld, complete price adjustment at any one stage of production in a particular industry may still not prevent *some part of the capacity* from becoming *temporarily valueless* (especially if the resources employed lack versatility). This condition implies that it will be unprofitable for any entrepreneur to use that capacity *even if offered at a hire value sufficient only to cover depreciation.*[53] Such a condition is, I think, less frequent than is usually assumed, even in the most disastrous depression. What in fact happens most often when businessmen generally become apprehensive is that the normal intensity of utilization of their assets appears to be disadvantageous. They are justifiably pessimistic, faced with low *prospective* yields. Hence the market-clearing prices of potentially profitable inputs are very much lower at that moment than they are destined ultimately to be. (See above, pp. 55–56, 147–48.)

Then, the cumulative effects of each such contraction of output on demands for other kinds of outputs seem often to give rise to a situation in which there is a sudden catastrophic *general* fall in the prospective profitableness of replacement and growth. This is the origin of what Keynes regarded as the collapse of the marginal efficiency of capital and the disappearance of "investment opportunities." It was this which led him to insist that we must "set investment going" again. But he did not perceive that to do this without

---

[52] I have suggested above that there *may* also be an element of irrationality present owing to the psychological consequences of overhead costs. (See pp. 181–83.)

[53] See my *The Theory of Idle Resources,* 2d ed., chap. 2.

inflation, it would be necessary to restore prospective demands for the product of each industry through cost and price adjustments *in the industries which had not been competing with that industry.*

Against this background, we can consider the belief of many Keynesians that we can find in the condition of specificity and durability of resources in the construction industries the origin of a situation in which (to use my own terminology) an initial withholding of capacity is induced by a change in time preference, which sets going a chain reaction of further withholdings. The resulting decline in real income is believed, in turn, to dry up part of the source of savings, which in turn dries up also the prospective profitableness of net accumulation, which in turn further reduces the incentive to save, and so on. The crucial initial withholdings are supposed to occur in the consumers' goods industries (although this is not always made clear) or in the marketing stage (the failure to replace inventories) because, owing to an increase in savings, demand for consumers' goods declines. (This argument is discussed at length in Chapters 13 and 14.)

Our discussion above suggests, however, an explanation along the following lines. When productive services and products in the "consumer goods" industries (producing goods of short life expectancy) have been generally priced too high in relation to (a) current preferences, (b) the size of current incomes, and (c) anticipated prices, it will undoubtedly appear unprofitable to add to or even to replace full productive capacity. The inability of entrepreneurs in one field of activity to acquire productive services at prices which are consistent with *a prospective yield in excess of interest* on the inventories or other assets acquired tends to be aggravated through further cumulative withholding in noncompeting fields, thus generating a general decline of the economic system. Because labor, manufacturers, and merchants are unwilling to sell at prices which can keep inventories turning over and other assets employed, it *looks* as though people are unwilling to buy. In such circumstances, the deflationary action necessary to preserve the value, convertibility, or parity of a currency can well *appear* as an aggravation of a depression initiated by a burst of thrift; and the deflation might well, as some Keynesians suggest, affect the constructional industries differentially at first, causing the withdrawal of part of their contribution to aggregate real demands (through the withholding of capacity or through some capacity falling temporarily valueless). This might in turn require further withholdings in many fields, thus making still further monetary contraction essential in order to maintain the value, convertibility, or parity of the currency.

Such an analysis is sometimes not without plausibility as an explanation of "the chain reaction" in withholding capacity. But time preference merely expresses *ends,* and when monetary policy maintains the purchasing power of the money unit constant, *credit contraction is not a cause but an effect of unrectified discoordination in the system and consequent idleness.* Admittedly, changes in saving preference—in either direction—may cause disturbing value changes, just like all other major changes in preference or changes in supply conditions; and as we have seen, in a badly coordinated economy, withheld capacity may result. But the reactions described are not attributable to defects in noninflationary *monetary or fiscal* policy.

Thus, in recommending recourse to additional spending in order to restore the "effective demand" needed to employ idle resources, Keynesians tend to blame, not discoordination due to errors in pricing, but changes in freely expressed preferences—including time and liquidity preference—and changes in entrepreneurial predictions.[54] It is all too easy to assume, when policy has *permitted* major inconsistencies to arise in the economic system (or when it has itself *created* such inconsistencies), that the cause lies in "collective behavior"—the choice of certain *ends* (such as provision for the future) or the choice of certain *means* (such as investment in money, when prices are regarded as *unstably* rigid in a downward direction). (See Chapters 8 and 13.) The origin of such "economic disturbances" must be attributed, I suggest, solely to the factors which prevent the value system from performing its coordinative task. For *there are no economic ends, and no entrepreneurially chosen means which are incompatible with "full employment."* Entrepreneurs will never fail to use the full flow of productive services if the price mechanism is allowed to work or made to work. *The only "collective behavior" to be set right is that of the propensity to resist price adjustment.* The weakness of the Keynesian nostrum is, as we have seen, that it tries, not *to correct* that behavior, but *to offset it.* Keynesians never discuss the *general* problem of why *particular* shifts in social preferences, propensities, and predictions should cause discoordination; they do not plead for the organization of a more flexible and more sensitive adjustment to the particular shifts of demand which are alleged to be

---

[54] See Keynes' reference to expectations affecting "the quantity of employment and not merely its direction." Op. cit., p. vii.

responsible; and they do not suggest, as far as I know, any system of overt taxation of or discouragement of demand for those things to which "too much" demand is supposed to be transferred in order to force people to continue to demand as before. Instead, they recommend, as we know, the inflation of money demand for those things which the community wants less, but without reducing demand for those things which the community wants more.

The supposed effect of changes in liquidity preference upon the market rate of interest plays an important role in Keynes' system. But he completely missed, I suggest, the *coordinative* role of interest. That is, he failed to recognize that the market rate is the most vital value ratio in the whole economic system, bringing consistency of values between the immediate and distant futures; that when the monetary authority functions efficiently, the market rate set (determined in the same way as all other market prices) permits the measuring rod of value—the money unit—to be almost as satisfactory over time as it is over space; and that because entrepreneurial decision making is dominated by perpetual forecasting—the cautious extrapolation of present trends into the future—market interest (in relation to the natural level) becomes the one value to which all other values are adjusted.

The fact that, under the *unrealistic* assumption that the number of actual money units is constant, changes in liquidity preference (i.e., changes in $\frac{1}{V}$) will affect the relation of market interest to the natural level(i.e., causes change in P), does not cause changes in liquidity preference to upset the coordinative functions of interest. But owing to the common confusion of time preference with liquidity preference, Keynesians seem to have difficulty perceiving this. They usually confuse the issue by tacitly attributing to saving preference the disturbances which accompany changes in the demand for money (the exercise of liquidity preference).[55] But it is wrong to blame speculative changes in the demand for money, still less autonomous changes in it, for the strains which as yet uncoordinated major value changes create in the economy; for to do so is to confuse *a response to a disturbing condition* with the disturbing condition itself. People bid up M_r, the aggregate real value of money, not because they become miserly, or in my opinion (in the absence of *repressed* inflation) because they demand more money through sheer inertia

---

[55] This point is developed below, particularly in Chapters 11 and 13.

when the magnitude M (the number of money units) happens to be increasing, but because economic policy has brought about serious anomalies in the value system which cause the prospective yield from money held to incease relatively to that from other assets.[56]

There was at one time some discussion about whether the Great Depression of the 1930s was or was not a monetary phenomenon. The answer is simple: the fall of prices obviously *was;* the unemployment and the fall in real income *were not* appropriately so described. The Macmillan Report said that the British depression of the thirties *could* be regarded as a monetary phenomenon because monetary policy had failed to solve the problems caused by "a conjunction of highly intractable nonmonetary phenomena."[57] But we are now brought back to the question, *Why should monetary policy be expected to solve such problems?* We are abusing any monetary system if we try to use it to rectify nonmonetary discoordination. There was, I maintain, no conceivable response on the part of individual *monetary* systems (or by a world *monetary* institution had one then existed) to the depression situation of 1931, which could have eliminated unemployment and waste without unanticipated inflation; but it is just that which Keynesians of the pre-1932 world were expecting monetary policy to achieve.

Admittedly, in the disorder which five years of attempting to persevere with the tolerance of (a) the private use of coercive power in wage-rate determination, (b) cheap money, and (c) convertibility had produced in Britain, in 1931, it could have been seriously argued that the situation was remediable with least resistance by a response to the panic demand for liquidity which had arisen— through credit expansion, in whatever form seemed most expedient from the political angle. The defensible case for such a policy (which in the climate of expectations then ruling would have meant the temporary abandonment of convertibility) supposed, however, the

---

[56] The bidding up of M_r (the purchasing power of M) which is sometimes experienced during an inflation (especially when it is accompanied by rationing and other "controls") is not, I think, attributable to inertia. In the latent inflation caused, *present* opportunities for consumption and replacement or net accumulation of nonmoney assets are less promising than predicted later opportunities. Thus, in this case also, it is anomalies in pricing policy which induce the holding of a greater real value of money as an accompaniment of increased savings. The rise in real money balances does not itself create the anomalies.

[57] *Committee on Finance and Industry, Report,* Presented to Parliament by the Financial Secretary to the Treasury by Command of His Majesty, June 1931.

enforcement of a drastic reduction of wage rates which had been imposed under duress in the sheltered industries, in order to restore the flow of wages in the unsheltered industries and suboptimal occupations. But if Keynes had candidly enunciated a *special theory* based on special assumptions of this kind, it would not have been necessary to write this book. As things are, he turned what *might* have been accepted as the wisdom of expediency in a difficult situation into an article of faith.

The justification for such a "special theory" would have been, then, that it was part and parcel of a complete or "general theory" concerning the coordination of the economic system. That is, it would have had to cover the whole sphere of economic institutions and not merely the province of money, interest, and credit. It would have had to envisage, as a concomitant of the relief to be afforded by cheap money, efforts being made to design a society in which it was no longer possible, through private coercion or government action for private advantage, to price a large part of the flow of goods and services beyond the reach of uninflated income or out of harmony with expectations.

It is a *dangerous* policy that I am here contemplating. For although moratoria or incomes policies to permit cheap money *might* assist government action to evade man-made obstacles to an increased flow of wages, such policies must tend, in themselves, to weaken market pressures to the basic adjustments needed. Only if the government proposes to act powerfully in ending the economic anarchy which the appeasement of sectional protectionist pressures has created, can a case be made out for any temporary abandonment of convertibility, on the principle of, as the French say, *reculer pour mieux sauter* ("stepping back in order to jump better"). But *The General Theory* was virtually blind to this aspect of reform; and until recent years, it seldom, if ever, surfaced in the writings of the Keynesians.

In the light of this background, I should again refer to a practical question which I feel many readers will be asking, namely, What do *you* recommend should be done about the restoration of "general activity" in a depression? My answer is first that whatever governmental policy does happen to be chosen, it should be based on an explicit acceptance of the Lavington diagnosis, Say's law, and other relevant considerations which I have explained in the above pages.[58]

---

[58] The discussion of this topic in my *A Rehabilitation of Say's Law* is relevant.

One such method involves a particular form of "incomes policy" which, as I insisted above, *might serve the community as an emergency procedure for a very short, limited period.* In this chapter I outline a possible scheme.

But is such a remedy possible? In a recent article of great interest, Robert Skidelsky, criticizing Max Beloff,[59] asks categorically, "Does he claim that there was some non-Keynesian way of overcoming the slump of the 1930s, or preventing future slumps arising, which would have served capitalist democracy better?"[60] My own answer is a confident, but qualified, yes.

This is also the answer that Allan H. Meltzer gives in a brilliant article in *Fortune.*[61] Effectively refuting Keynes of *The General Theory,* but adhering to the Keynesian form of analysis, he puts forward a plan with which "we can reach zero inflation, a balanced budget, high employment, and satisfactory growth rates *within about five years.*" (My italics.) He envisages this objective being accomplished through a gradual reduction of the nominal money supply. But Meltzer is handicapped by the apparatus he employs, although he is at home with it. He perceives, just as I do, that "high employment" must be a concurrent objective, but he is silent on the question of future wage-push. He recognizes the true problem as that of a price-discoordinated society; that many wage rates and prices have been forced above market-clearing values; yet he still argues as though he regards unemployment as a demand phenomenon and not as a pricing phenomenon. Had he approached the problem as I have done, he would have perceived that the problem of inflation could be immediately solved by stabilizing an existing average of prices, and the problem of full employment could be relatively rapidly solved along the lines that I am about to suggest.

Let me rephrase the question. Can the recoordination of a discoordinated and hence depressed economy be achieved through the application of broad non-Keynesian principles? What we call "politics" is involved, and that is a field in which I do not pretend to have any special expertise. In the remainder of this chapter, therefore, I shall be writing with great humility. Moreover, a scheme which could have had a very good chance of succeeding in the middle

---

[59] Max Beloff was professor of government at Oxford until 1974. He is now principal of University College, Buckinghamshire.

[60] Robert Skidelsky, *Spectator,* August 7, 1976, p. 8.

[61] "It Takes Long-Range Planning to Lick Inflation," *Fortune,* December 1977, pp. 96 et seq.

1930s might be held to be out of the question today; for both in Britain and in the United States the sabotage power of organized labor has grown frighteningly, and successive governments seem to have been more and more inclined to capitulate to the most preposterous abuses of purely private power. I shall, however, describe in the present tense a reform which, by greatly increasing the wages flow, could eradicate depression, as though I thought that a government had somehow emerged whose members were concerned more with the victims of the strike-threat system (that is, on the whole, the least affluent income classes) than with retaining the support of the AFL-CIO, or the TUC, or similar organizations in other countries.

The most formidable aspect of the institutional changes required for the plan I imagine would be that of *communication*. An inevitably suspicious electorate about the purposes of a quite revolutionary operation would need to be courageously faced. Not only the form of the actual operation but the manner in which it is carried out will require the most careful consideration.

All previous attempts at incomes policies have failed abysmally. Yet here am I actually *defending* wage control as a collective transition procedure. This makes it imperative that the announcement of the scheme shall make it obvious, with unchallengeable sincerity, that the whole intention of the proposals is that, at the very earliest possible moment, a free labor market will again resume sway. In other words, the objective is to substitute the order, security, and justice of wage rates determined through social forces—through the free market—for the discrimination, arbitrariness, and injustice of politically enacted wage rates.

Skidelsky, thinking of Britain in the middle 1930s, repeats the charge that "the chief fault of individualistic capitalism was . . . that no one was responsible for keeping demand as a whole sufficiently high to provide employment for all those seeking work."[62] But the labor of all able-bodied persons *was* demanded throughout the depression years. *It was not supplied.* This is not barren semantics. Labor was withheld on a wide scale, by reason of many groups holding out for wage rates which, while already depressed, had yet remained higher than market-clearing values *as they were then;* and so, by not producing its normal full potential output, each such group was exterminating a source of demands for the outputs of noncompeting groups. The market-clearing value of labor all over

---

[62] Skidelsky, op. cit., p. 8.

the economy was depressed because workers everywhere had ceased to contribute normally to uninflated income. This was the very point that Lavington so clearly explained. (See p. 150.)

The long-term objective of the reforms I am about to suggest will be the eradication of any surviving poverty resulting from the confinement of men and assets to wage-induced unemployment and suboptimal employments. The success of the plan will mean the maximization of market-determined equality of economic condition.

Now if (which I certainly do not expect) the recommendations I am about to sketch were tried, they would soon be observed to be achieving their goal. Demands for outputs would rise almost immediately. Taking the case of the United States, for reasons I am about to explain, the Federal Reserve Board would concurrently raise the nominal money supply to prevent any deflationary reaction. These success signals would, I think, prove to be the critical point. For they may be expected to provoke tremendous opposition and misrepresentation from union officials and from the left generally, which will first oppose and then count on the failure of the initiative. Hence the *immediate* exposure of predictable misrepresentations would have to be planned in advance.

The initial, frankly proclaimed aim will be to raise prospective profits and hence raise demand for labor; *but built conspicuously into the scheme will be, first, a guarantee that each additional dollar or pound accruing in the form of interest plus net profits will create rather more than twice as much additional income in the form of an enhanced wages flow;* and, second, machinery for the scheme's automatic dissolution in the event of its failure.

As I have said, the utmost candor and patent honesty will be crucial if the scheme is to survive its initial accomplishments. The attention of the electorate must be drawn to the following aspects of the scheme: (a) it will operate over a limited, prescribed period of only, say, five years; (b) its continuance, even within that period, will be subject to defined achievements by certain dates; (c) if aggregate dividends—that is, interest *plus* profits or *minus* losses—should, at the conclusion of any year, be found to have increased more rapidly than the flow of other incomes, a tax on dividends will be levied on corporations and other businesses and redistributed by some governmental agency. (In the United States, for example, the Social Security Administration or the Internal Revenue Service could undertake this task.) The sum redistributed will take the form of money bonuses, varying in proportion to earnings (in order not to weaken incentives); *but such redistribution is likely to be unnecessary because the initial consequences will almost certainly favor the flow of wages and salaries.*

For the particular scheme I am suggesting, a *Special Authority* will have to be appointed to administer the dissolution of the initial wage control. *Its function would be to apply a rule, not exercise discretion.* I envisage the scheme being announced by a solemn governmental proclamation along the following lines:

> We are to pursue, consciously and deliberately, the objective of "full employment" at uninflated prices. With this end in mind, we have constituted a *Special Authority* which we have instructed *to keep the flow of output going* during a maximum period of five years, by removing existing obstacles to the pricing of products at market-clearing values. As top priority, the Federal Reserve Board has been instructed to take such steps as it calculates will maintain the purchasing power of the dollar as closely as possible to a constant value, for the period of five years.
>
> To assist the Board in this aim, the private monetization of gold is to be authorized, so that contracts may be concluded in terms of dollars valued in gold, when preferred by the parties. The two currencies (the private gold dollar and the Fed dollar) will be completely independent of one another. We do not expect their values to be identical.
>
> During this five-year period, all private use of the power to disrupt the normal workings of a corporation or firm, that is, all strikes, strike threats, or boycotts will be forbidden. Workers' grievances which allege a breach of contractually agreed conditions of service, if not satisfactorily resolved by collective-bargaining decisions, will be reportable to the *Authority,* which will appoint arbitrators to adjudicate the issue. The arbitrators' recommendations will be binding until the objectives of the plan are achieved or until the lapse of five years from the inception of the plan, whichever period is the shorter.
>
> Accompanying the pursuit of this objective, steps will be taken to increase the total wages flow and total profits by calling upon the managements of firms where wage rates have risen in terms of dollars, under collective bargaining *during the previous decade,* to reduce those wage rates by deductions of five percent per quarter of the amount by which they had been raised during the previous decade. This process will continue (a) until, in the extreme case, the wage rates in a firm, occupation, or industry have fallen to the level at which they were at the beginning of the decade, or (b) until managements can notify the *Authority* that the wage rates they are paying have reached market-clearing levels, and that, unless they

refrain from making the next scheduled deduction of five percent, they will lose workers who can obtain higher wage rates or better prospects elsewhere.

As soon as the *Special Authority* is in a position to declare a satisfactory measure of "full employment" to have been adequately achieved for the community as a whole, its responsibility in this respect will cease.

But the Federal Reserve's obligation to maintain constant the long-term purchasing power of the money unit could well continue after wage-rate control was abandoned. Indeed, I am inclined to predict that the policy will be so successful that public opinion will strongly approve of the continuation of the Fed's instructions. Even so, I strongly advise that it should be instructed to plan for an eventual return to a gold standard, *thereby relieving future governments of any discretion in determining the value of the money unit.* It is unnecessary here to go further into the mechanics of the restoration. It will suffice to draw the reader's attention to the fact that there is some evidence that there will be an acceptable stability of value of the dollar in terms of gold, if it were again accepted as the basis of a major currency. From 1717 (when Britain first *officially* adopted the gold standard), the recently constructed wholesale commodity price index (by R. W. Jastram) crossed 100 again and again, several times between 1821 and 1860, in 1874–75, and again in 1914–15. (One hundred was its original value in 1717.) But the private monetization of gold, *encouraged as a parallel monetary standard,* operating independently of the official price-indexed money unit, could greatly assist a judgment about an acceptable gold value equivalent for the money unit, a value which might then be judged likely to endure. If the electorate, in the light of, say, ten years' experience, preferred the aim of price stability, then the Fed, or a nongovernmental institution bound only by solemn contract, could take over the function.

However, I repeat that whatever scheme was accepted, it could always be framed in the light of an understanding of the Lavington analysis (see p. 150) and Say's law. The transparent objective should be not to dictate to the market what its valuation of labor ought to be but, on the contrary, to release the market from restraints which are preventing it from freely determining the remuneration of different forms of effort and skill.

If the reader fears that the kind of policies I have envisaged imply drastic downward valuations of costs and prices on all sides, he has failed to understand my thesis. The average of all prices would oscillate about a zero trend. That is, by reason of the Federal Reserve's obligation to maintain a dollar of constant purchasing power, widespread *general* downward cost adjustments would be ruled out. But as the indirect objective would be to foster the competitive process, my plan would subsequently *minimize the likelihood of drastic downward price adjustments becoming necessary at all.* The reader should not jump to the conclusion that large price adjustments (to large changes of preference or supply) can ever be totally *avoided.* In certain occupations, it is true, quite drastic changes might be necessary. Yet in the light of expectations created under faith in the integrity of the Authority and the Fed, I predict that the increase in real income would be rapid.

The enhanced flow of productive services would all be immediately consumed or embodied into the assets stock, whether that part of the stock which is destined for early consumption, or that part (including money) which is expected to cooperate with labor in the production of additional income. While statesmanship demands compromise—wisdom in the recognition of the contemporaneous—it never requires the abandonment of principle.[63]

Ceteris paribus all market-selected downward movements of costs and prices toward market-clearing levels cause an increase in real income. We can say therefore that the adjustments I recommend mean an increasing demand for the services of the aggregate money stock, thus raising the magnitude, M_r (the aggregate value of money in real terms). This will in turn *permit a* noninflationary increase in M,[64] to which the scheme itself is committed. (The concept of M_r is fully explained in Chapter 8, p. 183, and in Appendix C, pp. 211–12.)

Under "monetary rigidity"[65] a general and purposeless deflation

---

[63] See my *Politically Impossible. . . ?* especially Part 2.

[64] Keynes *seemed* to assume, however, that the only way in which wage cuts could raise "aggregate demand" was through such an increase in M, which he *seemed* to think will somehow be automatically forced when it is noninflationary (as it would in fact if the money unit had some official, constant, defined value). But the lowering of the rate of interest which must follow in those circumstances is due to *real* factors—a growth in the flow of services from a given assets stock.

[65] By "monetary rigidity," I mean a policy under which the "nominal money supply," M, is prevented from varying or not caused to vary in proportion to the estimated flow of inputs and outputs, and in proportion to other changes in the demand for monetary services which determine M_r. (See pp. 197–202.)

would occur as the expansion of real income was experienced. But if the value of the money unit *is* to be maintained at a *defined and constant value,* monetary policy will *have* to be flexible and the nominal money supply must rise in proportion to the flow of services. Certainly, while *abnormal* provision for the future is in progress, a bidding down of the relative prices of goods of short life expectancy, in relation to the prices of goods of long life expectancy, will occur (the impact upon prices varying in proportion to the life expectancies of assets and the degree of versatility in the assets stock and in labor's efforts and skills). But, as I have already insisted, *all* large autonomous changes in human preferences require far-reaching coordinative adjustments and hence large changes in relative prices.

It has not really been my purpose, however, to recommend a political solution. The self-dissolving transition policy I have sketched is certainly not the only means of tackling the problem of poverty eradication and the achievement of greater equality in income distribution.[66] I *can* claim with confidence, however, that it is economically sound and practicable. That is, although its objectives are revolutionary, they are within our grasp. But in respect of political acceptability, I have, as I have stated, much less confidence. These issues I have discussed elsewhere.[67] *My plan is, however, the only concrete suggestion which (at least as far as my reading has gone), while designed in the light of political realities, is built on a demonstration that the stranglehold of the strike-threat system can be eradicated.*

Most important, however, is the principle on which the scheme I have asked the reader to contemplate is based. It does not seek to create demand for labor out of thin air, by increasing the community's *spending power,* which is the Keynesian solution. It aims at creating *purchasing power* by removing obstacles to the pricing of productive services at current market-clearing values. And it does so through tackling the price of labor in activities covering less than one quarter of the total number of employees outside agriculture in the United States, while the real earnings of a large proportion of those within this group are likely soon to improve as a result of the scheme.

---

[66] Incidentally, I believe that a policy such as I have suggested *could* also establish a long period of greater income stability, a cheapening of the product that we call "security" of employment, as well as the greatest possible measure of equality of condition that is compatible with human freedom.

[67] *Politically Impossible. . . ?*

But antitrust vigilance could supplement the provision of temporary income transfers to labor where interest *plus* profits and *minus* losses happens to expand more rapidly than wages *plus* salaries.

The exact role of government in the process of non-Keynesian recoordination of a depressed economy has long been a matter of controversy. I have just sketched a conceivable role in concrete terms. But one thing *is* clear. There has never been a case for a government *to overrule* the market. Yet there is a case for the collective overruling of a privately contrived overruling!

Moreover, there *is* an uneasy case for suppressing certain demands—certain private objectives sought through the market—hard drugs, sedition, subversion, prostitution, pornography, and the like. The market mechanism simply enables persons, corporations, and governments rationally to aim at satisfying *all* objectives, *individual or collective,* good or bad, wise or unwise, with the minimum sacrifice of other objectives. And above all, the market permits nonmaterial but costly objectives, individually or collectively sought, to be achieved at least cost in terms of competing ends. It is seldom perceived that the ethical, or aesthetic, or spiritual aims of mankind can be most sensitively achieved through the market. For example, the sacrifice people wish to make of other things for each expression of what the press has called (very inappropriately) "ecological" aims, is determinable if it is sought through purchase out of the proceeds of *proportional* taxation. Otherwise, it is extraordinarily difficult to assess, through "cost-benefit analysis,"[68] how much food, clothing, footwear, shelter, leisure, and so forth, should be sacrificed to objectives which we can feel certain the wealthy will welcome, but for which we can hardly expect the poorer classes to express the same preferences. The ideal solution is, however, always open bidding to secure the desired objective. The community as such has the right to insist on value for money. Government action is, however, inevitably involved.

Again, a government must act when "externalities" or "social costs" hinder or prevent the *private* expression of demands. Otherwise its primary role ought ideally to be limited explicitly to the prevention of the countless private restraints, which society has come

---

[68] Unfortunately, in many fields, lack of, or indifference to, common humanity dominates most so-called ecological initiatives today. The cost of achieving each objective tends to be highly regressive, bearing disproportionately on the poorest classes.

to tolerate, on the achievement of greater affluence and maximum equality of condition.[69]

A government may, indeed sometimes *must,* itself use the market for collective ends. For instance, as we have seen, it must *purchase* the objective of peace or national security at a huge cost in today's world. But while peace must be treated as the top priority, the armaments needed should still be acquired in the cheapest markets.

At this stage, I should refer to the fact that it is very easy for politicians to represent market pressures as "cruel." As I explained in 1934,[70] however, the process of competition is like gravity. If you defy it, you may fall and get hurt. If you have been operating under a competitive regime from the beginning, you will have no monopoly gains which can be seized by interlopers who may break into your privileged field.

When I remarked above that there is never any case for governments *overruling* the market, I insisted that there may at times be a case for their *temporarily* overruling the values determined by private constraints on the free market.[71] I sometimes think that the urge of the *"pseudo*-Keynesians" today to recommend incomes policies in part falls into this category. As I remarked above (pp. 167 et seq.), I can appreciate a government which understands the argument I have presented, resorting to edicts calling for input prices forced above market-clearing values to be reduced, so as to restore "profits" or "prospective yields." Restoration of "profits" was, of course, always *ultimately* Keynes' objective. And it is equally the aim of my own tentative suggestions. But the ultimate aim is that of multiplying the wages flow by raising the profitableness of employing additional labor in the aggregate.

And Keynesian critics *should* be reminded, again and again, that Keynes himself was throughout seeking higher prospective yields— higher profits—as the chief means for achieving fuller employment

---

[69] Above all, in the ideal, governments should be forced to abandon what often seems to be their present major purpose, which is that of exploiting the politically weak for the benefit of the politically strong (in terms of votes, favors, or finance). It is easy to decry this approach as hopelessly naive. I have treated the problems at some length in my *Politically Impossible. . . ?*

[70] "Economic Method and the Concept of Competition," in *South African Journal of Economics,* March 1934, pp. 1–23.

[71] I should be most wary of any recommendation to control any prices. The role of government is to remove constraints, not to fix what governments believe prices would be under competition. But the strategy of reform may require the occasional but open suspension of normal principles.

of labor. If there is initially much unemployment and (in the actual world, an even greater burden) much suboptimal employment, governments could honestly tell the people that *for every one dollar increase resulting in the form of aggregate dividends (interest + profits), plus profits plowed back, they could count on an increase of at least two dollars in the aggregate wages flow.*[72] Why, then, should we naively assume that an enormous mitigation of poverty is politically impossible?

---

[72] Possibly *via* taxation and a bonus handout.

Appendix

The Attitude of the Cohen Council

In spite of all the wisdom reflected in the 1960 Report of the Cohen Council ("The British Council on Prices, Productivity, and Incomes," 1957–60), the Council failed, I think, sufficiently to focus attention on the fundamental role of price adjustment. Thus it wrote: "It is important to be candid about the fact that" a check to the growth of production "is to be expected and tolerated" if inflation is to be brought to an end.[73] "Excessive demand" (meaning inflation)[74] "cannot be restrained if at the same time it is sought to wring the last ounce of output out of a given constellation of human and material resources."[75] "In our opinion," the report said later, "it is impossible that a free and flexible economic system can work efficiently without a perceptible (although emphatically not catastrophic) margin of unemployment."[76] The Council felt that it was essential to reduce prospective yields so that employers would offer stiffened resistance to wage demands.[77] But this *assumes* that deliberate accompanying action to allow a restoration of the flow of wages and income has to be ruled out. Such a reliance upon the pressure of unemployed or underemployed resources can be defended only on grounds of political ex-

---

[73] Cohen Report (first report of the Council on Prices, Productivity, and Incomes), 1957–60, para. 117.
[74] The words "excessive demand" (for "inflation") quite subtly suggest that demands in general are responsible for inflation and not persons—governments.
[75] Cohen Report, para. 117.
[76] Ibid., para. 135.
[77] Ibid., para. 137.

pediency.[78] But to restore the employment of wastefully idle resources in any occupation, it is essential to *increase* prospective yields from the incorporation of the services of men, or existing assets (materials, etc.), into the product of that occupation.

The Council recognized the importance of governments taking the required action in the sectors of the economy to which the Monopolies and Restrictive Practices Act applied, especially in its recommendation that consideration should be given to the suppression of resale price maintenance, even when enforced by individual manufacturers.[79] If it could have assumed not only that the government would not shirk its duty in this field but that it would act with similar disinterestedness in the fields of labor and agriculture, the Council could have avoided the dismal conclusion that only the pressure of idle resources is capable of bringing the economy into coordination. Its phrase "wring the last ounce of output out of the system" merely means using resources with the maximum economy; and I fail to see how *this* process can ever be "overextended." Indeed, it is the only way in which demands for outputs generally can be raised. It is solely the multiplication of money-spending power more rapidly than the multiplication of purchasing power which can be "overextended" and manifested as inflation.

The cessation of inflation need have no tendency to "dampen demand," which is the Council's phrase.[80] Private reactions to such a policy may perhaps do so. But if the government is allowed to perform its planning and coordinative functions, private interests will not be permitted to cause any contraction of the source of demand. Market discipline alone will see to that. Far from leading to a situation in which competition for labor is likely to decline, we should then be more likely to witness an increase in "poaching" by managements, higher overtime offers, and the offer of employment to pensioners (that is, increased bidding against the demand for leisure), as well as increased inducements as a form of bidding against less

---

[78] To ask managements to act as the defenders of the flow of wages and full employment against labor union attacks, is to call upon private people to fight private coercion because the politicians wish to avoid the unpopularity of doing so. But only expediency can justify any failure to proclaim and enforce the principles that all private use of coercive power should be outlawed and all deliberate contrivance of scarcity should be forbidden.

[79] Cohen Report, para. 155.

[80] The Council's approach was weakened by the Council's failure throughout to make explicit the distinction between inflated and uninflated income and "demand." See pp. 318–19.

well remunerated occupations, like those of housewives, or against suboptimal occupations generally.

Of course, it would have been perfectly legitimate for the Council to say that, *given the existing institutional setup,* any tendency for the rate of inflation to slow down must mean some decline in prospective yields, in realized profits, and in employment; and that this may be expected in the long run to lead to reasonableness of labor's demands in the fixing of wage rates and prices. My criticism is that the Council placed insufficient stress on its vital assumption of a defective framework of institutions. It failed to emphasize *the source* of the dampening effect. I have the feeling that the Council *perceived* the source, but saw no way of effectively describing it.

A far more deplorable example is to be found in the United States in the 1962 *Report of the President's Council of Economic Advisers.* In an apparently frank support of the principle of private enterprise, the Council recommended that there should be no interference with union-negotiated wage bargains! At the same time it referred with approval to the discipline of antitrust in the business and industrial sectors of the pricing system. Why, then, did the Council not advise a similar discipline in *all* sectors of the pricing system? The need for an explanation was glaring.

8

The Nature of Money

Some Keynesian authors have belittled pre-Keynesian economics by suggesting that those whose thinking relied upon it did not perceive its limitations. Critics have quite rightly insisted that the concept of the "quantity of money," even with the adjective "nominal," is by no means a simple notion. It may indeed be true that not all pre-Keynesians appreciated this. But I fail to see that their thinking went seriously astray for this reason. My own treatment of money in the present chapter is primarily an attempt to simplify and clarify exposition. But incidentally I shall clash with some Keynesian notions.

Actually, the concept I have introduced—namely, the "aggregate value of money in real terms," that is, in terms of purchasing power, which I represent by M_r—is much more easily comprehensible than is M, "the nominal quantity of money," or "the number of money units," or "the number of containers of purchasing power," as I find it convenient to explain the symbol. For not only must what I shall call "the pure money equivalent of hybrid money" ("near money" or "money substitutes") be included, but the student must recognize that the magnitude M is influenced by all credit, or lending and borrowing, whether it occurs within the banking system or not, or whether it is influenced by the use of credit cards, or whether simply by producers or merchants finding it profitable to give longer (or shorter) credit to purchasers without themselves increasing (or curtailing) their own borrowing.

Among other matters, I propose to show that complicated realities do not permit the inference that pre-Keynesian (or monetarist) attempts to explain the role of "the quantity of money" in the operation of a free society are invalidated because of an alleged "vagueness" of the concept—a weakness which, it has been suggested, Keynes perceived while his predecessors did not.

Let us begin by considering the usefulness of the "Fisher exchange identity" ($MV \equiv PT$). This formula can be retained as a clarifying expositional device when an increase in the factor V represents a fall in the demand for money, not correlated with changes in aggregate output, rather than an increase in "velocity." V is a factor a rise in which, unless offset by a reduction in M, reduces the market value of the money unit—the measuring rod of value.

The point is important because the distinction between "*simple* velocity of circulation" of money and "*income* velocity of circulation" is a false one. If prices generally rise, we must all, on balance, pay a larger number of money units to acquire a given *quantum* of non-money; and we must all do so because the value (purchasing power) of the money unit has been reduced through "*money-spending power*" having been allowed or caused to increase more rapidly than "*purchasing power.*"

Let us consider next Keynes' apparent respect for the concept of the "circular flow of money." In Chapter 11 I argue that the transfer of money ownership—the passage of money from hand to hand or from account to account—does not *generate* "real income" (in the sense of maintaining or increasing the flow of productive services) unless, in a discoordinated economy, it has an *unexpected* inflationary effect. I suggest further that *the process does not even influence the money valuation of a constant real income*. No economist has yet challenged this conclusion, either in print or verbally.

It is important to explain that the term "monetary policy," as I use it, embraces "fiscal policy"; for virtually the only difference between the two is that the latter has a certain political advantage —it puts what Keynesians sometimes call "newly created money" (that is, an addition to the number of money units) initially into the hands of government instead of into the hands of those individual borrowers who, being confronted with the concurrent entrepreneurial search for the highest prospective yields to investment, outbid others for the increased money-spending power. In a free market, borrowers have to compete for any additional *money-spending power* (not necessarily additional *purchasing power*) that is made available. Under "fiscal policy" the politicians have discretion about who shall gain and who shall lose; for when demands for one part of the flow of services are increased, demands for another part are reduced.

The beneficiaries of fiscal policies are either arbitrarily or corruptly (though legally) chosen. Hence "fiscal policy" is simply one device in the government's armory for controlling the magnitude M in relation to the demand for money, and must therefore be regarded as one method of maintaining the value $\dfrac{M_r}{M}$ constant, or increasing or decreasing it in accordance with any convertibility obligation or contract, or according to "the national interest" (which in practice generally means the private interests of the men who form governments and their supporters).

Pure monetary policy can be defined as so operating the monetary and credit system of an area that the value of the money unit is caused to change or be maintained at a desired level. An important instance of the principle of "separation of powers" is relevant here. It is, I suggest, highly undesirable that any authority which undermines the desired value of the money unit (constant, falling, or rising) shall be the same authority as that which operates any central bank to achieve that value. That is, the powers of any central bank ought, in my judgment, to be strictly limited to the carrying out of clear (secret or open) instructions. For instance, if government policy is to use the monetary system with a view to the achievement of "full employment," Congress or Parliament, or some nonmonetary authority such as, say, the Department of Labor, should proclaim from time to time a certain speed at which a given price index is to change. It would then be the task of the central bank to cause the measuring rod of value to shrink, to be preserved, or to increase. In other words, it would be the central bank's task to reduce, maintain, or add to the money unit's value. The efficiency of the central bank in this respect would depend upon the magnitude of the oscillations of the price index in relation to the standard. For instance, suppose that the instructions communicated to the central bank are to maintain a constant free market magnitude of the price index. The bank would have to cause the magnitude M to change in relation to changes in M_r. Its power to do this is complete, in spite of the magnitude M_r being beyond its ability to influence. Fluctuations about a zero trend in a constant price index would be inevitable. But speculative factors would reduce the amplitude of oscillations if the central bank were efficient in inspiring confidence in the persistence of the objective.

Thus, if the price index at any moment deviates from 100, then *ceteris paribus* the further the deviation, the greater will be the probability that it will move in the opposite direction. At any rate, this will be the position if the objective is trusted. The method of controlling M through which this effect will be achieved, is of a feedback type, and there is a theoretical possibility therefore of antidamped fluctuations to be set up. But if there is faith in the sincerity of the objective, that is, in the willingness of the central bank to reduce M immediately it is observed that the price index is rising, speculative influences of an arbitrage kind will work toward the achievement of a general stability of prices.

For all its defects, pre-Keynesian monetary theory had certain clear-cut virtues. It was conceived of as an essential and integral part of the theory of value (price) and production. The study of monetary phenomena was woven realistically into the study of economic theory as a whole.[1] Economists were trained to think simultaneously in terms of money prices and in real terms—to be continuously aware of the reality under the veil (the very real veil) of money. The monetary system and monetary policy were viewed in their relation to the expression of preferences, entrepreneurial responses and their effects upon values and the money expression of values. I regard it as a misrepresentation to say (I quote Roy Harrod) that "those who discussed general economic theory, namely the supply of and demand for commodities and factors of production . . . were living in a different world from those who discussed banking policy and the general level of prices."[2] But Harrod was simply echoing a common conviction.

As incipient *praxeologists,* the early economists had perceived the inherent homogeneity of all economic relationships.[3] In one respect only did the classical economists and their pre-Keynesian successors fail, it seems to me, to bring monetary policy sufficiently closely into relation with the general body of their science. They did not understand *clearly* enough that money assets are productive, that they provide services in exactly the same manner as other assets, and that they (money assets) are invested in for the same reasons. Economists tended to speak, wholly unjustifiably, of money having *a yield of nil.* It was in this respect, I think, that the pre-Keynesian

---

[1] Arthur W. Marget, in particular, has demonstrated this. See his *The Theory of Prices: A Re-Examination of the Central Problems of Monetary Theory* (New York: Prentice-Hall, 1938, 1942), 2 vols.

[2] Harrod, *The Life of John Maynard Keynes,* p. 460.

[3] This was clearly *implicit* in the remarkable insight, possibly inspired by James Mill, of J. B. Say. It was ultimately clearly *explicit* in the developments for which Wicksteed was responsible.

treatment of money was most defective—its inadequate generality, its assumption (often inconsistently held) that pecuniary yields are the only yields, and therefore that money is "barren," "dead stock."[4]

But Keynes, both in the *Treatise* and *The General Theory,* tried to find in the factors determining the value of the money unit the genesis of output and income (although *he* would not have described his aim in such words). He linked monetary theory to the economic world only through unsatisfactory concepts such as employment, income, and effective demand.[5]

In macroeconomic models and formulae, he drew attention away from the crucial phenomena of pricing (discussed in the previous chapter), the revision of entrepreneurial plans which are implied in every price change, and the nature of resistances to coordinating price adjustments. Moreover, his approach here replaced the formerly realistic treatment of the functioning of the credit system with an analysis developed on the assumption, for ease of model construction, of a constant number of money units.

Hence Keynes did not, as some have supposed, *assimilate* monetary theory to the general theory of value and production. Rather he attributed to monetary and fiscal policy coordinative functions which are normally performed in a quite different way. Hence it was Keynes himself who *segregated* the monetary factor from other factors; and in doing so, he showed that he misunderstood the classical tradition. He stated that, before he began writing *The Treatise,* he was still "moving along the traditional lines of regarding the influence of money as something so to speak separate from the general theory of supply and demand."[6] But this was not "traditional." It was merely *the form* which Marshallian exposition had taken; and it seems to have encouraged Keynes to jump to the opposite standpoint, to try to invent a monetary *demand* theory which would provide a full explanation of "income" or "employment." That monetary and interest policy was *relevant to* the use of resources (employment and output) was never denied by the economists whom Keynes belittled; nor was the denial ever implicit. Consider, for instance, Part 3, Chapter 5 of Mises' *Theory of Money and Credit.* Section 4 of this chapter is headed "The Influence of the Interest Policy of

---

[4] I have dealt with this issue in my article "The Yield from Money Held," in Sennholz, ed., *On Freedom and Free Enterprise,* p. 460.

[5] See Keynes, *The General Theory,* pp. 25 et seq.; pp. 205–6. See also my *The Theory of Idle Resources,* pp. 31–35; 2d ed., pp. 43–48.

[6] Keynes, op cit., p. vi.

the Credit-Issuing Banks on Production." That is, however, a quite different thing from alleging a monetary demand explanation of production.

Keynes' treatment was in no sense progress. Even in matters of detail, it is difficult to find valid originalities. The erudite Marget's *Theory of Prices* abounds with examples of how supposed originalities in the *Treatise* and *The General Theory* were part of the common heritage. The truth is, rather, that Keynes' chief originality lay in his ironic attack on previous thinking about money and other things. And his attack created, I believe, so much confusion in the minds of the young economists of subsequent generations, that it has, as I suggested above, set back progress right down to this day.

Although attempts to defend the roots of Keynesian thinking have now been long abandoned, the models and conceptual apparatus that he and his disciples introduced still clutter up the textbooks, even the elementary ones, enormously multiplying the difficulties of achieving conceptual clarity. For any textbook which fails to pretend to be neutral between the Keynesian and non-Keynesian approaches still takes the risk of excluding itself from the greater part of the market.

I do not propose in this contribution to attempt a new treatment of the fundamentals of money and credit. But I think it will help exposition if I make use of a few unfamiliar although quite simple concepts which have assisted my own thinking. I shall distinguish between "pure money" and what I find it convenient to call "hybrid money," meaning by the latter assets which are partly money and partly nonmoney, that is, assets which have "moneyness" ("money substitutes," "near money," "secondary liquidities," etc.), providing not only monetary services but other satisfactions or output as well.

I shall use the conventional quantity theory identity, $MV \equiv PT$, as follows:[7] M stands for the valuation of the aggregate money stock in terms of actual money units; V for what is called "velocity," or the rate at which money units are exchanged for nonmoney;[8] P for the scale of prices (an index number of the prices of productive

---

[7] The identity shows necessary relationships, not causes. It is a useful tautology, that is all.

[8] I use the term V because, if so defined, it causes the identity $MV \equiv PT$ to be very useful. The *term* "velocity" has, however, proved to be not only inappropriate but misleading. The more rigorous economists have, in fact, used the term "income velocity" where the use of the term V, as I have defined it, would make no difference to their reasoning.

services); T is that demand for money which tends to vary with output (that is, with the flow of productive services).

T and $\frac{1}{V}$ represent the expression of demand for monetary services derived from (a) preferences concerning ends (subjective valuations of monetary services) and (b) choice of means to ends. It is convenient to distinguish between those elements in the demand expressed for money which are a function of the output of services (income), which I call T, and *all the other elements in demand for money,* which I call $\frac{1}{V}$. These "other elements" make up what Marshall represented as K and Keynes called "liquidity preference," a decline in V meaning a rise in liquidity preference, and vice versa. But both equally represent demand for monetary services (through the offer of nonmoney).

In the presence of convertibility, the magnitude M is always a question of policy in the short run and the value of the commodities or currencies into which the money unit is convertible in the long run; and in the absence of convertibility, it is a question of policy in both the short run and the long run.

But because the quantity theory which I believe to be both valid and useful is a simple tautology (and my subsequent argument tries to justify this point of view), a change in any factor, while it implies an offsetting change in one or more of the other factors, does not itself record any causal connection. Thus, if an increase in M is not accompanied by an increase in P, a decline in V or an increase in T is implied. But in facilitating conceptual clarity, the identity does not permit mere mechanical thinking. For example, the factors which may cause an increase in P, otherwise than through an increase in M or V, must imply a contraction in T; while (in a society in which many inputs or outputs have been priced above market-clearing values) if the increase in P does imply an unanticipated increase in M or V, it is likely to exert a coordinative effect and cause a rise in T.

"Money" may be defined as that which produces monetary services. It cannot be usefully restricted, as is commonly done, to "deposits *plus* currency in circulation" (the chief forms of "pure money"). It covers the "pure money equivalent" of "hybrid money" also[9]—every commodity, token, document, or claim which can serve the purposes of a medium of exchange, etc., and which is demanded

---

[9] See following page.

for those purposes, irrespective of whether these commodities, tokens, documents, or claims are performing other economic functions also. The test is whether the value of such assets is raised by reason of their being demanded for the monetary services they provide. If they are so demanded, I call them "money" or "money assets."

To measure the quantity of money we must have a unit. The pound, the dollar, the florin, and the franc are money units—what I shall call "actual" money units. We can, however, conceive of an *abstract money unit of constant purchasing power,* an index number concept. Actual money units may have a defined value (for example, in terms of constant purchasing power, such as we have just mentioned; or in terms of a metal or a combination of metals; or in terms of some foreign currency; or in terms of a unit the value of which is market-determined; or the aggregate number of money units increasing by a fixed percentage annually; or they may have no defined value). If money units have no defined value, there must be some legal tender provision or some custom which causes certain documents or tokens to be accepted as the yardstick of value.

When I refer to the number of money units, M, I shall mean the aggregate value of money assets (pure *plus* the pure money equivalent of hybrid) *in terms of some actual money unit,* for example, in terms of pounds, dollars, etc.

"Hybrid money" is an original term which I have found useful. It is normally referred to as "near money," "money substitutes," etc. It refers to assets which are partly money and partly nonmoney, like treasury bills. An investment in "pure money" brings a nonpecuniary yield in the form of "liquidity," the value of which tends to equality with the market rate of interest. In a business the value of liquidity services is embodied in the value of the product, just as is the value of electricity used. But an investment in "hybrid money" brings a yield in liquidity *plus* a pecuniary yield, the value of the latter being reduced by the value of the yield in liquidity.

The "pure money equivalent" of a "hybrid" investment allows for that; it can be determined by the ratio between (a) what the yield would be if the investment of a given sum had been in the form of a perpetual bond (such as British "consols") and (b) the actual yield to the same sum invested in a hybrid security. Thus, if the yield to a perpetual bond is six percent and the yield to a hybrid investment is four percent, then two thirds of the yield to an investment in hybrid money is pecuniary and one third nonpecuniary, a yield in liquidity. Hence two thirds of that hybrid security is a nonmoney investment, offering a yield of four percent, and one third an investment in money, offering a yield in liquidity only.[10]

My very useful concept, M_r, the "aggregate value of money in 'real terms,' " has greatly assisted my own thinking.[11] There is no *physical* measurement of the "amount" of money, as there is for individual commodities. It is no more measurable in physical terms than is output in general. It is a value measurement of the volume of abstract units of constant "real value." Its only relation to physical measurement is through the physical quantity factors in the weights of the index numbers which are chosen to define the price index or "deflator." I represent it by the symbol M_r. M and M_r represent the same aggregate value, but measured with a different yardstick. The *ideal* price index is one which theoretically gives equal weight to every component of the flow of productive services (into direct consumption or into replacement of consumption and net accumulation of assets) which constitutes real income.[12]

Attacking what he called "the fetish of liquidity" as one of the "maxims of orthodox finance," Keynes insisted that there is "no such thing as liquidity of investment for the community as a whole."[13] How wrong he was! Society can become more liquid just as an individual may, simply by using its resources in a different manner and bidding up the value of money assets in the aggregate by offering more nonmoney for money.

The magnitude M_r increases when monetary services come to be more highly valued in terms of nonmoney services; and this can occur (a) owing to an increase in T (T varying with the flow of services as a whole, that is, "output," in which the aggregate value of

---

[10] Keynes was of course curiously blind to the essential productiveness of the liquidity condition, especially when its origin is what he called the "speculative motive." He regarded liquidity preference in times of general uncertainty as peculiarly deleterious. But in a world of unstable price rigidities, no one is able to avoid speculation. Indeed, to remain passive in respect of the liquidity composition of one's assets is merely one form of speculation, a stupid form!

[11] This notion has had surprisingly little influence in economics. See Appendix C to this chapter.

[12] The purchasing power contained in money units consists of rights to obtain assets of relatively long life expectancy, or of relatively short life expectancy, or of zero life expectancy (services consumed as they are rendered). But the value of which I conceive in the notion of "constant purchasing power" is uninfluenced by *relative* changes in the values of these categories. Such valuations influence (as I shall later show) only the rate of interest. The *practical problem* of constructing such an *ideal* index is a big one.

[13] Keynes, op. cit., p. 155.

monetary services forms a very small proportion) or (b) owing to a decline in V (V varying with all the factors apart from output which affect the demand for monetary services). This demand will tend to vary with changes in business institutions and procedures,[14] habits, and *expectations* about the future value of the money unit and about changes in the market rate of interest.

Given the part of the demand for monetary services which (in the conventional quantity theory identity) is represented by $\frac{1}{V}$, it is the productive system which "creates" the money contained in money units (that is, M_r) and not the credit system. And T (a function of output, or the flow of services) being given, it is the demand for money represented by $\frac{1}{V}$ which determines the magnitude M_r. The expansion of credit merely reduces the content of each money unit, unless society is currently producing additional productive services (an increase of income) out of which additional monetary services are demanded, or for other reasons placing a greater value on money in relation to nonmoney.

An increase in T and a decrease in V both imply an increase in M_r, but for different reasons. In the case of an increase in T, the additional content of M_r is supplied by an increased flow of services for which, or for the products of which, money units are exchangeable. In the case of a decline in V, a rise in the value of M_r is implied because money and monetary services become valued more highly *for other reasons,* that is, in spite of real income not having changed.

The number of money units, M, is determined, as I am about to explain, by the issue or withdrawal of credit; and this process has no influence on M_r unless it happens to influence the wantedness or prospective productiveness of money, or induces the release or withholding of capacity. That is, while changes in M or in V or in T influence P, changes in V and T do so through influencing M_r while, statically considered, changes in M do not. Only if changes in M influence expectations or encounter the "money illusion" will they influence V and hence M_r. If the Keynesians had merely placed explicit stress on the possibility of a rise in M causing the release of overpriced capacity, they would have precipitated much less controversy in the theoretical field.

---

[14] Monetary institutions (for example, clearing machinery) are included under this heading.

I have always had the strongest objection to the idea of banks "manufacturing money,"[15] or even of the state doing so. When the credit expansion is inflationary they can "manufacture" it only in the sense that forgers manufacture it; and when the expansion is noninflationary they *respond to* an increasing M_r. Banks (that is, the banking system, including any central bank) dilute money, so to speak, when they "advance credit" to an extent or in a manner which must involve (a) depreciation of the money unit in terms of a convertibility obligation, or (b) depreciation in terms of scarce things in general. Banks may increase the real value of the money *unit* (and cause appreciation, again in either of the two senses) when they "withdraw credit." But when they "expand credit" in circumstances which do *not* spell depreciation (in either sense), their action is merely a response to something which has happened in the economic system as a whole. The aggregate value of money assets in terms of purchasing power is not "created" or "destroyed" by the banking or credit system. It expands or contracts, as we have seen, with the community's decision to hold (that is, to use) assets for the monetary services they can perform; and *ceteris paribus* the community's demand for this purpose will vary with the flow of productive services in general (that is, the flow of products).

The number of money units may change as a result of the deliberate expansion or contraction of credit by some monetary authority with an unfettered or limited discretion, or as a result of the "automatic" working[16] of economic institutions *under given convertibility obligations.* Thus, the factors which determine the demand for or supply of any monetary metal, or any commodity or commodities forming the standard, are *among* the determinants of M.[17] But monetary authorities like central banks and treasuries are

---

[15] R. S. Sayers, *Banking* (1938): "Banks are not merely *purveyors* of money but also in an important sense manufacturers of money." Hartley Withers was, I think, responsible for introducing this seriously fallacious notion, in his *Meaning of Money,* chap. 5, "The Manufacture of Money" (1909).

[16] By "automatic" working is meant responsible entrepreneurial decision making within the framework of a contract-limited discretion.

[17] The commodity or commodities may of course be chosen in the first place, or accepted over the years, because, working together with the credit system and other factors, the effects of this demand and supply can be expected to result in a stable scale of prices. In practice, it seems to me, a high degree of price stability was so achieved through the gold standard system when it was judiciously administered; and this was, I think, responsible for its long survival, under the relatively more effectively planned and coordinated economies which existed before 1914. (See p. 172.)

merely intermediaries in the exchange of debts. *The ultimate issuers of bank credit are those holders of deposits and notes who are not themselves indebted to the banking system,* and they can, in the absence of restraint, withdraw credit at any time, preferring notes, or deposits in another bank, or foreign exchange, or a monetary metal, or "hybrid money," or nonmoney.

It should be noticed that I do regard the expansion or curtailment of credit not as accelerating or retarding the "virtual" velocity of circulation of money units (as some important writers, notably Knut Wicksell,[18] envisaging metallic currency, have suggested), but as changing the magnitude M. The difference is important. While an increase in M and an increase in V imply the same effects upon P, a change in V means a change in M_r, while a change in M does not. And one of the factors which may influence V is anticipation of changes in P, which means changes in the purchasing power of money units.[19]

The credit system is operated through all actions which, a noninflationary level of interest being given, influence the market rate of interest. Such actions cover not only rediscount operations, open market operations, note issue, enacted reserve ratios, treasury bill transactions, and fiscal policy, but various other actions. If they influence the value of the money unit, they are credit or monetary measures, whether they are in the form of "free banking" with convertibility, conventional central bank action, treasury action, or "direct controls." The tendency to confine the notion of monetary operations to central bank activity has caused much confusion. Thus, reserve ratios; credit rationing (restriction of bank advances otherwise than by a common, nondiscriminatory market rate of interest); restriction of installment selling or of interest payable by savings and loan association operations; the limitation of private capital issues; these and all similar controls are crude—and usually discriminatory—efforts at credit contraction. They may have some deflationary effect, but all too often they tend to act rather like shutting one door and leaving another (a privileged door) open. Insofar as they are effective, they raise the market rate of interest or

---

[18] Knut Wicksell, *Lectures on Political Economy,* ed. and introd. Lionel C. Robbins (London: Routledge and Kegan Paul, 1935), 2:65–67.

[19] Successful forgeries have the same effect as credit expansion, except that when M contracts through the eventual refusal to honor the forged notes, an innocent holder is penalized. In the case of noninflationary credit, no one is robbed when the volume of deposits and notes in circulation contracts or expands.

lower the noninflationary level. Obviously, then, they are monetary measures and are intended to be such.

When the money unit has a defined value (and that implies convertibility in some sense) the market rate of interest is set by the judgment of the monetary authority reacting to the demand for monetary services. The market rate coincides with the natural rate when M is caused to vary in direct proportion to M_r; but the market rate may always be set with a view to maintaining any defined value of the money unit, *even a changing one.*

For when M is determined by the issue or withdrawal of credit, an increase in the number of money units does not mean a permanent addition to an "existing stock." It means that the number of units, M, *may* expand or contract flexibly according to all the other factors which influence M_r. Whenever there is any use made of the credit device, there is *some* flexibility of this kind. The measure in which it in fact works this way depends upon monetary policy. But *when this policy embraces the convertibility of a currency, it provides incentives which, to the extent to which the defined value or standard is noninflationary, tend to prevent the credit system from causing the depreciation or appreciation of money units.* The policy may then be said to be neutral.

By "monetary policy" I mean the policy adopted by "the monetary authority." And by "monetary authority" I mean the central bank or other note-issuing authority[20] and a treasury.

It is a convenient simplification to think of the monetary authority as consisting of the central bank and the treasury. The "monetary authority" *so defined* is solely responsible for the magnitude M. I am afraid, however, that this simple assertion is likely to provoke resistance. For instance, the typical discussion of monetary policy seems *to assume* that the failure to balance budgets is inflationary or deflationary, according to whether there is a deficit or surplus. But fiscal policy as such *may* be neutral. Governments *may* borrow to meet deficits. It is when governments incur or settle debts on such terms that they influence the relation of market interest to the natural level that credit is extended or withdrawn. The fact that deficits create an incentive for governments to call upon monetary authorities to inflate by lending at rates below the natural, while surpluses facilitate monetary policies which lead to the cessation of inflation (or conceivably even to a rectifying deflation), must not be allowed to confuse the issue.

---

[20] Even if there is no "central" or "reserve" bank, treasuries may issue notes.

Similarly, it is nearly always taken for granted that an increased or abnormal demand for monetary services is deflationary and a decline in that demand inflationary. But the former is deflationary only in the sense that economizing inventions or the release of capacity are deflationary! When M remains constant and T rises, P must decline! We must beware of assuming away monetary policy. Because the value of the money unit is either laid down by convertibility obligations or a matter of government or treasury expediency (acquiesced in by a central bank), we have to recognize that a rise in the demand for money does not create deflation and vice versa. It creates a condition in which the avoidance of open deflation causes latent inflation, or in which latent inflation is prevented from becoming open (because demands for larger money balances happen to accompany an increase in M). *Latent inflation* means a condition in which the withdrawal of credit will become necessary, in order to avoid open inflation, at some future date, when people begin liquidating their money balances.

I do not suggest that it must necessarily be misleading to treat increases in T and decreases in V as *deflationary tendencies,* and decreases in T and increases in V as *inflationary tendencies,* to be *offset* by the monetary authority in a degree determined by the nature of the defined money unit value. It is indeed natural that the officials of a central bank should regard their task as that of *rectifying such tendencies as do not accord with the objectives to which they are committed by treasuries or governments.* Hence, the term "monetary policy" as I shall use it refers solely to the function of so operating the credit system that *a defined or a desired value of the money unit* shall be achieved. (The word "desired" here has reference to the desires of the state.)

If banking were conducted by pure private enterprise, it would be difficult to conceive of a monetary *authority.* There would simply be the contractual or legal obligations accepted by the banks to pay out deposits on demand and redeem notes on demand (supported, possibly, by reserve ratio requirements).

I am not suggesting of course that, under central banking, the policies of the private banks have no effect upon the value of the money unit. But the commercial banks themselves are not then called upon to maintain or change that value. This obligation is taken off their shoulders. They act only *within the limits* set by note issue, discount policy, open market policy, reserve requirements, or other action taken by the central bank, or the treasury, etc., to influence M in relation to M_r. But if my interpretation of the situation is correct, although the commercial banks play an important part in *operating* the system which causes changes in M (relative to M_r), they may only be said to *determine* that policy to the extent to which they submit to pressure or exhortation to exercise credit restraint or the reverse. And when they do so act, they virtually become part of the central banking system. (That is, their position then resembles in some measure that of the Bank of England when, for a long time before it was nationalized, it submitted to Treasury hints or pressure.)

It is difficult to discuss monetary policy unless we assume that the authority has some clear-cut objective. Thus, if we are concerned with the situation in which the treasury is prepared to take the risk of being faced with the subsequent dilemma of the alternatives of deflation or devaluation, we can realistically assume that it wants to postpone the necessity to face this dilemma for as long as possible. Such a postponement must then be regarded as the objective. Ought not the treasury, therefore, to make clear from time to time the rate at which it regards it as expedient that inflation shall proceed? But if there is no ultimate defined goal of this sort, there is a frustrating void in any policy discussion. I shall accordingly use the term "inflationary policy" or "deflationary policy" to mean monetary policy with an inflationary or deflationary objective, even when the treasury tolerates or dictates mere drift, week to week pragmatism, hoping that inflation will not occur but not being prepared to authorize or require the only steps which can effectively prevent it.

As it is within the power of the monetary authority to maintain or change any long-term value of the money unit, *I shall regard all such changes as due to policy*—that is, as ascribable either to the aims pursued or to the degree of success in achieving those aims. For instance, if V increases and M does not contract, that is due to policy.

It is always a matter of discretion, or of judgment, about exactly how an obligation to maintain a particular value of the money unit may best be achieved. Thus, if M_r changes (owing to the growth or decline of output, or institutional changes, or through various speculative reactions) and M does not change, market interest, i, will diverge from the natural level, r. Whenever $i \neq r$ the divergence must be regarded as caused wholly by the failure of the monetary authority (whether by aim or erroneous judgment) to adjust M in proportion to changes in M_r. Presumably any passivity of the monetary authority is deliberate. If so, the resulting depreciation or appreciation of the money unit must express policy; and in particular there seems to be no reason why M should not be allowed fully to respond to that determinant of M_r which Keynes termed "speculative" (caused by predictions of capital loss from a rise in interest rates), provided that the monetary authority remains willing and able to compensate any subsequent decline in M_r (as the rate of interest rises) by an immediate contraction of M.

Nothing could be more confusing than to imagine depreciations or appreciations of currencies as phenomena which may be beyond the full control of the monetary authority. The notion of treasuries "fighting inflation" without success, for instance, is absurd (unless all that is meant is that they are—necessarily unavailingly—trying to keep internal prices stable, while another currency to which their money unit is tied by fixed exchange rates is depreciating). But if there are convertibility obligations (or if fixed exchange rates have to be maintained, or if a rising scale of prices is regarded as politically inexpedient) and latent inflation is inadvertently allowed to emerge, it is certainly beyond the control of the monetary authority to fulfill its obligations without recourse to rectifying action. The postwar inflations of Western Europe and the United States were due to policy weaknesses, weaknesses which, in my judgment, were dictated by treasuries motivated by political considerations, rather than by the technical requirements of a stable monetary system.

It is because governments are so often trying to use the administration of the monetary system in order to achieve other ends than the simple one of providing an efficient mechanism of exchange that we so often hear it argued that mere monetary action is ineffective. But, I repeat, there is never any obstacle to the effective use of measures which determine the volume of bank deposits *plus* currency in circulation (in the light of hybrid money and the factors which determine the demand for monetary services), so as to maintain a money unit at *any* enacted or desired (constant or changing) value.

In modern controversies, for instance, we often meet the contention that bank rate action is ineffectual. The truth is that, used with sufficient boldness, it can never fail,[21] however clumsily it operates in relation to, say, open-market operations. Of course, when latent inflation is verging toward open inflation, far more drastic action of this kind may be needed than in a more normal situation. But obviously, if monetary stability is to be achieved while the government's

---

[21] In my opinion, this is amply demonstrated by British experience in 1957. But bank rate merely determines broad limits, within which there is a wide range for discretion in credit policy, for example, open-market operations.

power to borrow from the central bank on its own terms remains unchecked, the *restriction* of credit offered *to the private sector* may have to be severe.

Although the task of a monetary authority is a professional, technical matter, the nature of that task is simply enough *defined*. Ideally, the aim is undoubtedly that of ensuring that the operation of the credit system permits debts to be settled in units of the same *defined value as those in which they were contracted*. But a wise aim, sincerely pursued, may not necessarily be wisely administered. The test of the soundness of the *administration* of a monetary system lies in two things.

First, its ability to maintain the defined value without recourse to exchange control, or control of capital issues, or credit squeezing (or other rationing), or other limitations on speculation, flight capital, and so forth. For if monetary institutions have been wisely designed and their administration is being wisely executed, any speculation which does not *assist* policy objectives will subject the speculator to the penalty of pecuniary losses. All "controls" ("exchange," "import," etc.) other than those imposed entrepreneurially in order to fulfill *contractual* obligations, frustrate the coordinative mechanism of the price system.

Second, administration is sound when it maintains the defined value of the money unit in the short run as well as in the long run, that is, *together with stability.*[22] This aim may be said to be achieved when any deviation from the defined value encounters, or itself brings into operation, forces (including "automatic" or routine policy reactions) which *tend* to press the value of the unit in the direction of the defined value. In the best imaginable economic system, the process of recovery from an initially uncompensated disturbance is bound to be affected by innumerable chance influences, some assisting, others hindering the achievement of objectives. All sorts of unstable rigidities, resistances of unpredictable duration, rebounds, elasticities and inelasticities are to be expected. But the essential stability will have been accomplished if (a) the pressures toward the defined value build up continuously and cumulatively, and (b) the

---

[22] Short-term variations in the productivity of money (and hence in the value M_r) due to the periodic concentration of tax payments, transactions in government securities, etc., may be responded to by various methods of changing the normal ratio (dictated by prudence, convention or rule) of liquid assets to liabilities in the banking system as a whole. In this way M can be maintained in that relation to M_r at which monetary policy is aiming *in the short run as well as the long run.*

milieu in which they operate tends to iron out the inevitable fluctuating tendency. And the *milieu* will exert this stabilizing effect when there is faith in the intentions and ability of the monetary authority. It will, of course, be impossible to eliminate the "too much—too little" reaction; but fluctuating divergences from the defined scale set up by any single disturbance will tend always toward a narrowing amplitude.

Wicksell realized that credit *could* act simply "as a corrective to an occasional shortage of the medium of exchange," so that there would be an automatic and self-regulating canceling out of "fluctuations in the amount of money."[23] "But," he said, "as everybody knows, this does not happen."[24] If my interpretation of the situation is correct, the reason why it does not happen is that, in practice, policy in respect of convertibility (or the maintenance of the value of the money unit), and the expectations created by that policy, are inconsistent with the objective of convertibility. And they are inconsistent, I believe, partly because the problem has not been perceived with sufficient clarity, but mainly because monetary stability has conflicted with the desire to avoid the consequences of price discoordination in the easy way—through supplementing aggregate purchasing power with additional money spending power.

Given a stable measure of value, depression is the penalty of such a cheap money policy, in the sense that it is the inevitable outcome of the rectification of the inflationary consequences, and perhaps even of the mere cessation or braking of an open inflation. Only in the absence of a stable money unit can cheap money persist for any length of time without a deflationary reaction. Serious depression has been avoided in most countries since the 1930s, simply because cheap money has been accompanied by a money unit of no defined value, with creeping inflation. *Indeed, chronic or creeping inflation is nothing else than an alternative form of the disease we call "depression"* —a far more serious and debilitating form, because (as we have seen) it permits continuous procrastination and postponement of efforts to rehabilitate the machinery of economic coordination.

I can turn now to the Keynesian objection to a money unit of defined value. In general terms the Keynesians feel that mankind should be free from the "tyranny" of a rigid yardstick, and the

---

[23] Wicksell regarded credit as affecting velocity of circulation and not as influencing the number of money units. (See above, pp. 193–94.)
[24] Wicksell, op. cit., 2:66.

"balanced budgets" which that "tyranny" in general makes expedient. Their attitude on this point seems to derive from their conviction (which we have already noticed)[25] that certain economic preferences, judgments, or values can throw the economy out of coordination, causing "effective demand" to contract; and hence that the results of such preferences, judgments, and values need rectifying, by state edict, in the field of monetary or fiscal action.[26]

Keynes himself never understood that these preferences and judgments, when concerned with the time factor, are *the sole cause* of that market rate of interest which is neither reduced by inflation nor raised by deflation. Hence he failed to perceive the true determinants of *M* in a credit system.

In the pre-Keynesian tradition, the theory of interest, *paraphrased in a manner which relates to my own exposition,* has been to the effect that, on the one side, the desire to provide for the future, and on the other side, the search by entrepreneurs for the most productive and profitable ways of combining and changing the form of the assets stock,[27] replaced or accumulated by savers, are brought into equilibrium by market interest. In order to show that this is not so, and that interest somehow influences *expenditure* and effective demand, Keynes appealed to liquidity preference and maintained that interest is "the 'price' which equilibrates the desire to hold wealth in the form of cash with the available quantity of cash."[28] This tantalizing, confusing definition[29] turns out to mean that it is the demand for and supply of money (liquidity) which determines interest; and even so Keynes failed to make it clear that he was concerned with a judgment about the relative profitableness of holding money and

---

[25] See pp. 105–6, 164–65.

[26] Keynes never explicitly considered in this context the general truth which Wicksteed had helped to clarify, that in a rational, self-consistent order the productive system must *accept commands from expressed preferences* about how the community's resources are to be utilized (whether the government, politicians, and officials, or the people—that is, the "free" market—have the right to express those preferences).

[27] This stock may be growing or contracting according to the strength of positive or negative saving preference and the elasticities of response to that preference by the *productive* system.

[28] Keynes, op. cit., p. 167. The theory has been riddled with criticism; but Keynesians who no longer defend it have not always abandoned the doctrines in which it is an essential link.

[29] Had he said something like the following, it would have been *clear* enough: "The rate of interest equilibrates the marginal utility of money, held as an end or as a means to ends, with the marginal utility of nonmoney assets in general."

nonmoney. Keynes was, in fact, thinking solely of market interest, and pushing aside the determinants of the natural level. He explicitly denied that saving was relevant although, curiously enough, he regarded it as important in determining what he called "investment," and although he continued, in discussing interest, quite inconsistently, to bring in the notions of discounting and the propensity to consume. In reality, liquidity preference can affect the relation of market interest to the natural only under the unrealistic assumption of monetary rigidity (a constant M, which Keynes did not *always* realize he was postulating).[30]

Not only did Keynes hold that *changes in* the volume of money (meaning *changes in M*, but not clearly distinguished from a *changing M* or a *changing MV* in relation to T) can affect interest, he went further and claimed that it is a weakness of private enterprise that, whereas it can produce everything else, it cannot produce money.[31] Accordingly, he thought, private enterprise is prevented from bringing the marginal efficiency of money into relation with the marginal efficiencies of other assets; the production of nonmoney things is slowed down; and the marginal efficiencies of the two categories of assets are thus brought into equilibrium.[32] This is one of the chief grounds for his contention that unemployment is a monetary phenomenon, a phenomenon which, he thought, was inevitable under laissez-faire.

He was implying here, of course, that "private enterprise" cannot cause a change in M. But if by "private enterprise" we mean institutions which include note-issuing, credit-issuing commercial banks, bound by obligations to maintain a defined value of the money unit

---

[30] Such monetary regidity is, however, the general assumption of *The General Theory* in rigorous exposition. It is justified only as a mental isolate for a stage in reasoning. More generally defined, "monetary rigidity" means the condition in which M remains constant or varies less than proportionally to changes in M_r. It could be regarded as a particular form of monetary policy.

[31] Keynes attributed to pre-Keynesian economists the view that the marginal efficiency of money differs fundamentally from that of other assets, in that changes in its volume affect merely prices and not interest. What pre-Keynesian economists did believe is that a changing M in relation to T, V being constant, affects both market interest and P, but that a changed M having eventuated, the change will have affected not interest (V being unchanged) but merely P. Similarly, they believed that a changing V in relation to T (M being constant) must influence market interest. (I should remind the reader that by V, I mean all factors other than those represented by T which influence the demand for monetary services.)

[32] John Maynard Keynes, "The Theory of the Rate of Interest," in Gayer, ed., *Lessons of Monetary Experience*, p. 147.

(that is, bound to convertibility in some sense), "private enterprise" certainly *is* in a position to cause M to change and it has in fact always done so.[33]

The level of the rate of interest which is consistent with the convertibility of any money unit of defined value is unaffected by monetary policy. It works in exactly the opposite way. But monetary policy *is* concerned with the continuous achievement of that consistency. Thus, when the defined value is indicated by a constant value in terms of purchasing power, measured by a certain price index, the monetary authority *must* react to changes in the natural level according to the nature of the obligations undertaken by the monetary authority. Keynes diverted attention from these vital issues. Both he and his successors have written as though the value ratio established by time preference and prospective yields (the noninflationary rate of interest) *needs correction*. They have treated interest as a value which *should be determined by authority* or, as Seymour Harris has put it, "according to the requirements of the domestic economy"—as a value which should be regarded as "the handmaid of industry."[34] Such phrases are found ultimately to mean nothing more than (a) inflation which is not fully expected, while (b) the market rate is set sufficiently below the noninflationary level to be consistent with full employment when many input and output prices initially exceed market-clearing values.[35]

I have already argued that Keynes confused time preference and liquidity preference. It was this confusion, I think, which led him to the conclusion that intended saving can exceed planned investment.[36] He thought that liquidity preference could drive the rate of

---

[33] Thus, if privately owned central banks, or other privately owned banks, issue notes convertible into gold, and the value of gold happens to be more or less constant in real terms under that system, they will obviously have to operate credit so as to cause M to vary in direct proportion to M_r (whether the latter changes through changes in T or V).

[34] Harris, "Keynes' Influence on Public Policy," in Harris, ed., *The New Economics,* p. 13.

[35] As a corollary, it follows that contractual relations between national currencies (fixed exchanges) should be abandoned in the interests of the inflationary method of bringing each individual national economy into coordination. The reader should notice that these words appear in my *Keynesianism* (1963), i.e., I used them well before the emergence of *widespread* advocacy of "floating exchange rates"—that is, "benign neglect" in respect of defined ("fixed") exchange rates between different currencies.

[36] It is true that an increased desire to provide for the future will, under the extreme assumption of absolute specificity of men and assets, result in no increase in either the net accumulation of assets or an increased proportion of

interest up to a level at which it is unprofitable to employ resources to the full. He was, I suggest, misinterpreting a hypothetical situation envisaged by those pre-Keynesian economists who had read Wicksell. They understood that, in the course of *a declining* magnitude of *MV* in relation to *T,* there will be a rise in market interest above the natural; that if we make the unrealistic assumption that *M* is constant, the value of the money unit will be rising or falling as the demand for monetary services (through a changing *T* or *V*) is rising or falling; that this will cause the market rate of interest to be above or below the natural level respectively; and that if we are thinking of the market level, then we are tacitly taking the natural level as given.

If Keynes had merely been objecting to a *purposeless* deflation,[37] we should have known where we stood. But he was (in *The General Theory,* at least, and in his controversy with Frank Graham)[38] clearly opposed to *any* monetary policy which aims at maintaining a money unit of *any* defined value, whether the gold standard, a commodity reserve standard, or any other. Possibly because of his obsession on this point, he thought he perceived the origin of the alleged fallacy in traditional teaching that money as such is irrelevant to employment and output. Yet as we have seen, traditional economics does not regard monetary policy as *irrelevant* to output and employment. It has a different view of its relevance. It simply makes it clear that, if cheap money is to be accepted as a method of restoring employment, the implications should be faced unequivocally.

The popularity of Keynesianism has been due to its having focused attention on the "stimulus" of an increase in *MV* (brought about by interest or fiscal policy) in relation to *T,* while diverting attention from the essentially temporary nature of the stimulus and the condition necessary for the "stimulus"—"withheld capacity" or "suboptimal employment" of men or assets. The Keynesians have spread the alluring notion that monetary and fiscal policy can somehow make nations prosperous or wealthy, not by providing an efficient but otherwise neutral price mechanism, but by creating "effective

---

productive services being embodied into assets of relatively long life expectancy and a smaller proportion consumed directly or incorporated into assets of relatively short life expectancy.

[37] For example, as some would allege occurred in the United States from 1930 to 1933.

[38] Keynes, "The Objective of International Price Stability," *Economic Journal,* 1943, pp. 185–87, and "A Rejoinder," ibid., 1944, pp. 629–30.

demand." Believing originally that their recommendations were non-inflationary and compatible with a money unit of stable value, they later came to recognize that a depreciation of the money unit *was* implied, while insisting that it should not be called "true inflation" if the release of any withheld capacity was induced by it. (See Chapter 10.) But I suggest that monetary policy is inherently unsuitable as a means of coordinative adjustment to (a) changes of preference (including time preference) other than changes in liquidity preference, or (b) changes in the conditions of supply which make profitable the devotion of services to new kinds of uses, or (c) changes in entrepreneurial optimism or pessimism, unless these things are judged to be causing a change in M_r and so, M remaining unchanged, tending to cause the value of the money unit to diverge from any contractual value.

Appendix A

The Use of the Term "Neutral"

When monetary policy maintains a money unit of defined value, it seems to me to be the most appropriate use of terms *to call that policy "neutral,"* and if the defined value is constant in terms of purchasing power, *to call the monetary standard "neutral."* The neutrality rests merely in the fact that *the yardstick of value can be relied upon in the formulation of entrepreneurial plans,* in the sense that other weights and measures may be relied upon. The money unit is neutral as yards, ounces, pints, and amperes are neutral.

The actual standard defined is solely a matter of convenience. It *could* be, theoretically, a unit which depreciated in terms of a price index by an announced and fixed percentage per annum. What is fundamental is that the meaning of contracts made in terms of money shall be explicit. When this is the position, the monetary implications of contracts do not change.

The term "neutral" in connection with money has often been used in quite different connotations.

Appendix B

The Irrelevance of the Noninflationary
Level of Interest to the Demand
for Money

It is important to insist that the demand for money is not, as the Keynesians teach, a function of the absolute level of the rate of interest. It may be held to be a function of the relation of current market interest to expected market interest (or a function of the relation between the current and expected price indices,[39] or between current and expected prospective yields); for these relations may induce a speculative demand for money (positive or negative). And a speculative demand, unless offset by a change in *M,* will cause a divergence between the market rate and the noninflationary level. But this has nothing to do with the *absolute* height of that level of interest. The extent to which people will sacrifice *pecuniary* interest in order to hold money is completely uninfluenced by the absolute level of that rate; *for a similar sacrifice has to be made in order to acquire or retain all other assets.* Obviously, we shall not acquire or retain them unless we expect the yield (in some sense) on their current value to exceed interest!

Keynes' treatment of interest is, indeed, hopelessly wrong and muddled (although to many economists it seemed at first to be the keystone of the Keynesian arch). The confusions for which it was responsible have obscured both the crucial role of interest and the task of monetary policy in the coordination of the economy. (See pp. 164–65.)

---

[39] Such a speculative demand will emerge when prices are in some measure *unstably inflexible,* and it will last until the scale of prices has become adjusted to the new situation. This is another way of saying that speculative demand will cease when the money unit has reached its expected value. The market rate of interest will exceed or fall short of the natural level while this equilibrium is being attained—while the scale of prices is *falling or rising.*

Appendix C

The Concept of the Aggregate "Real" Value of Money

Hume seems to have had the germ of the idea of the nonmoney *content* of money. He said, "Money is nothing but the representation of labor and commodities, and serves only as a method of rating or estimating them."[40] Greidanus[41] and Patinkin [42] are among the few economists who have perceived that the concept of the *real value of money assets* is useful and used the notion explicitly. (It is largely because of his perception of the relevance of the concept that the latter's view of latent inflation is similar to that which I myself have formed). There was some suggestion of the notion in Wicksell's reference to the possibility of money being regarded as "an abstract symbol, a mere quantity of value."[43] But somehow Wicksell failed to use the distinction I have made between money assets as a whole measured in real terms and actual money units. He was therefore led to the conclusion that "the laws governing the general level of concrete commodity prices and its changes, are quite different from the laws determining the exchange value of the commodities themselves . . . simply because money is not a commodity like other commodities."[44] This view is clearly due to a confusion between *money* measured in terms of purchasing power, which is not a commodity, and

---

[40] David Hume, *Essays,* Chapter 25.

[41] Greidanus talks of "the quantity of money in terms of goods." See Tjardus Greidanus, *The Development of Keynes' Economic Theory* (Staple Press, 1950), p. 36.

[42] Patinkin, "Keynesian Economics and the Quantity Theory," in Kurihara, ed., *Post-Keynesian Economics,* p. 136.

[43] Wicksell, op. cit., 2:19.

[44] Ibid., p. 20.

actual *money units,* which act like commodities, and the value of which is determined in a manner which is identical with that of the determination of the value of all commodities.

Many economists have, of course, made good use of the concept of the real value of cash balances.

9

The Concepts of Inflation and Deflation

I have at times referred to the significance of *anticipated* inflation. But in the present chapter, I propose, except for the middle paragraph on p. 214, to make the preposterous assumption that neither inflation nor deflation is expected to continue. By the terms "inflation" and "deflation," unqualified, I mean one thing only: a fall or rise respectively in the "purchasing power" of the money unit.

Under an international gold standard, in which a large proportion of the countries of the world have adopted currencies based on gold, there would of course be advantages *in normal times* in accepting gold as the criterion for inflation. So conceived, inflation would occur only when inconvertibility led to loss of parity. *When there is no money unit of defined value,* which I must now assume as a normal condition,[1] it is possible to use these terms only in relation to some abstractly conceived money unit of constant value. But as in practice any *defined* value (monetary standard) fixed is likely to have been chosen by reason of its expected long-term stability of value, when I talk of "inflation," I shall be implying, for most practical purposes, that MV has increased in relation to T (M in relation to M_r).

Moreover, it is important for some periods or some purposes to consider the significance of rising or falling prices in terms of gold itself; for there may be a fall or a rise in the exchange value of gold in terms of goods and services in general.[2] This is particularly likely

---

[1] When my *Keynesianism* was published, this could not have been a realistic assumption because, in the United States, it was still possible to obtain gold from the banking system at $35 an ounce for the settlement of international debts and for certain other purposes.

[2] There have been occasions when adherence to the gold standard would have meant serious inflation in terms of money units of constant purchasing power

if only one or only a few countries adhere to a gold standard. It will then be possible for their money units to change very greatly in terms of goods as a whole without the gold value of the currency being influenced or convertibility threatened.

The notion of a money unit of "constant purchasing power" is a purely abstract conception. When I use the term, I envisage (as I have explained) an index which is devised to give, as far as practicable, equal weight to all the elements which make up the flow of productive services in the country concerned. This notion will become clearer, I think, when the reader has considered the concepts of income, consumption, and savings, which I discuss in Chapters 11 and 13. Used as the criterion of "inflation," such an abstract unit of value amounts to the same thing as a measure conceived in terms of the value of *final goods and services*. That is, my definition does not think of the value of the money unit as accurately reflected in the value of consumers' goods and services or the "cost of living." For instance, in the early stages of an "inflation" as I conceive of it, a "cost of living" index may be expected to exaggerate the extent of the depreciation (that is, in terms of the value of *all* services currently flowing into direct replacement and net accumulation). Moreover, the money unit may retain its value in terms of the internal prices of a country but lose value in terms of external prices.

But apparently intractable problems of this kind merely serve to remind us of the inherent limitations of concepts which are based on measurement through averages, such as index numbers. When I talk of a unit of "constant purchasing power," however, *I am thinking of the internal prices of a country*.

It is both purposeless and misleading to confine the term "inflation" to large, exceptional, inordinate, or catastrophic rises in the scale of prices, as some writers have done. There may be small as well as big inflations. My usage does not exclude the use of special terms to describe the extent or speed of inflations. Thus, we may perhaps talk of "hyperinflation" or "creeping inflation" to describe, say, the depreciation of British and other currencies achieved since 1945 according to whether we are thinking of the scale or the tactics employed; or use the term "runaway inflation" to describe the policies resorted to in Germany, Russia, Hungary, etc., after World

---

(for example, as in Sweden during World War I when, in order to prevent inflation *in this sense,* they allowed gold to rise to a premium).

War I; or refer to "secondary inflation" to describe a typical phase in many inflations, namely, the stage at which a rising P, due to an increasing M, induces (through expectations) an increase in V.

We sometimes talk of "repressed inflation" to mean an inflationary condition in which, owing to various kinds of rationing, price controls, etc., the actual scale of prices as indicated in some official price index does not rise (although if these controls were removed a fall in the value of the money unit—as defined by such an index—would occur without material changes in M); or we may talk of "latent inflation" (a broader, more general term which covers "repressed inflation") to mean a situation in which V is abnormally low for a wider variety of reasons. Hence, conditions or situations in which it is probable that open inflation in the unqualified sense will sooner or later occur, or for conditions or situations which make it essential to reduce M in order to prevent the emergence of expressed or open inflation, may be termed "latent inflation." When F. W. Paish says that a rise in prices is not "the essential characteristic of an inflation, although it is normally a symptom of it,"[3] he is defining as "inflation" what I call "latent inflation."[4] This condition does not necessarily spell inflation as I have defined it. Just as a substance may be explosive without an explosion actually occurring, so may a situation threaten inflation without inflation actually resulting. In general terms, if an increase in M is accompanied by a decline in V so that the value of the money unit remains unchanged, inflation is likely to be latent, simply because it can be assumed that V will probably regain some "normal" value. In the meantime, the money valuation of income may not have risen. But under the "controls" which are essential for repressed inflation, the meaning of such an assertion is by no means simple. What is important in the present context, however, is that the possibility and probability of subsequent open inflation may well be there.

Nothing could be more misleading than the description of latent inflation (by the modern Keynesians) as "excessive liquidity"; for

---

[3] F. W. Paish, "Open and Repressed Inflation," *Economic Journal,* September 1953, p. 528.

[4] Paish's definition is the result of his thinking of money income as a certain kind of money receipts, instead of the money valuation of the flow of services. He talks of "a rise in money incomes rather than in prices," while real income is not increasing as rapidly. Ibid. This notion of money income, which at one time I also thought was *serviceable,* I can now see to be defective. (See Chapter 11.)

when M is increasing relatively to T, it is only the abnormal demand for liquidity—the fact that for some reason people want to be more liquid than normally—which prevents open inflation. If the term "excessive" is to be used at all in this connection, it ought to refer to the continued issue of credit on an undiminished scale *as demands for money tend to fall.* For when ultimately V increases, M can be reduced as fast as debts are settled, with no deflationary effect. Keynesians are apt to write of the condition in which latent inflation is breaking into open inflation as though it were something for which current monetary policy can renounce responsibility. There is no foundation for such a view.

Again, it is possible to talk without ambiguity of "wage inflation," or "cost inflation"; and, indeed, any disproportionate and disequilibrating growth *of one set of incomes* could be similarly described by an appropriate adjective.[5] It is important, however, that if such terms as "cost inflation" or "wage inflation" are used to describe portions of the community's money income which may be held to have risen "unduly" in some defined sense, thus causing other money incomes to have fallen (in the absence of inflation), with consequent strains or distortions of the economy as a whole, we are not led to the notion that the discoordinative pricing is the cause of a decline in the value of the money unit, except in the sense that the fall in T due to the discoordination will cause inflation unless M contracts proportionally. But as I have stressed, M is a policy-determined magnitude. Hence the forcing up of particular prices through government action, or through government tolerance of the private use of coercive power, or through voluntary private collusion, does not cause inflation unless all that is meant is that the situation may render inflation politically expedient. As I have constantly stressed, it is frequently because relative values and sectional incomes are permitted to get out of harmony with one another (in the sense that the price mechanism would have disclosed a different social valuation) that resort is had to inflation (although the reverse may sometimes be true, inflation itself appearing as the cause of such distortions).

Equally misleading are the related terms "price-induced," "cost-induced," and "wage-induced" inflation. For although the fixing of

---

[5] Although such conditions are usually *likely* to be "inflationary," they *need* not be. The increase of one set of incomes may be accompanied by the decrease of another; and unless there is a change in the relations of MV and T, this result *must* follow.

certain prices, costs, and wage rates at levels which must cause the cumulative withholding of capacity, *in the absence of countervailing price reductions elsewhere in the economy,* may be said to "induce" governments to resort to the inflationary remedy, this use of words inevitably leaves the false impression that in some sort of automatic way the process of fixing the prices of certain products *causes MV* to increase relatively to *T*. The value of the money unit is, I repeat, a matter either of contract or of discretion—policy. For the same reasons we ought, I suggest, to reject the common distinction between what have been called "cost-push" and "demand-pull" inflations. All such "wage-price spiral" theories, as Walter Morton has put it, mistake "the instrumentality by which inflation occurs for its causes"[6] and lead to the fallacy that wage rates and profit margins determine the price index. Of course, governments find comfort in this fallacy because, as Morton points out, they prefer to exhort or threaten labor and business rather than take straightforward monetary action. He does not deny that action to discourage monopolistic price enforcement may render noninflationary monetary aims more acceptable politically. But he holds that antimonopoly action to meet a threat of unemployment should be undertaken "for its own sake; it need not be done in order to control the general price level."[7]

We often hear of "imported" inflation or deflation, or of inflationary and deflationary "impulses" from abroad. Such influences may be regarded as affecting the situation in two ways. They may tend to change the magnitude of M_r or of M, although changes in M due to influences from abroad do not affect the general principle that the magnitude M is policy-determined; for such external influences can always be offset by the monetary authority, just as that authority can always prevent latent inflation from becoming open.

Let us first consider the situation in which M_r is caused to rise. This will be brought about according to the extent to which the profitableness of foreign trade rises. If T increases because of increasingly profitable trading of domestic goods and services for foreign goods and services, M_r will increase and there will be an "imported" deflationary influence unless M increases. Similarly, an "imported" inflationary influence will arise when there is a contrac-

---

[6] Walter A. Morton, "Trade Unionism, Full Employment, and Inflation," *American Economic Review,* May 1950, pp.15–16.

[7] Ibid., p. 38.

tion in that part of aggregate output which is due to trade with those abroad. But whether inflation or deflation will actually occur remains purely a matter of the monetary standard or monetary policy.

Turning to the situation in which M is influenced by external conditions, we see that when a currency is tied to a foreign currency by fixed exchange rates, and the foreign currency depreciates, the currency in question will be subject to what is usually *called* "imported inflation." But actually a type of deflationary pressure is exerted, in the sense that an increase in M or V relatively to T will become essential to prevent the domestic currency from appreciating *relatively to the foreign currency*. The modern tendency to call any inflation which thereby results "imported inflation" is a loose and— I sometimes think—a reprehensible use of terms. Revaluation is always possible.

10

Keynes' Notion of True Inflation

It is sometimes claimed that Keynes was not an inflationist. The well-known passage in his *Economic Consequences of the Peace* (1919), in which he attacked the process of secret and arbitrary confiscation which is the essence of inflation, has been quoted in support of this claim. Debauching the currency, he said, was a subtle and sure means of "overturning the existing basis of society."[1]

Moreover, his argument in his *Tract on Monetary Reform* (1923) had been for *stability* of prices. Indeed, before 1925, although his idea that government spending could always put things right seemed already to be in process of formation, he was *suggesting* that convertibility obligations could be safely abandoned and the internal value of a currency left under the control of a monetary authority responsible to the state. He apparently believed that governments would not abuse the power entrusted to them.[2] The monetary authority would, he suggested, allow only such an expansion of credit or of the note issue as would not allow a rise in the scale of prices

---

[1] The putting into practice of Keynes' doctrines has, in fact, been performing the sinister role which Lenin is supposed to have attributed to inflation—and with greater subtlety by reason of the very gradualness with which it has spread, and the succession of emergencies to which appeal has been made to discourage or stifle criticism. The consequences were quite clearly perceived, I believe, by some of the shrewd and influential leftists among Keynes' supporters; but they have been totally unobserved by the majority of those who have acquiesced. (See pp. 131–32.)

[2] Roy Harrod assures us that this was his conviction, and describes as a "bogy" the fears of Keynes' critics in 1923–24 that under such conditions an inflation would be likely. *Life of John Maynard Keynes,* p. 345. But continuous inflation *has* actually followed the entrusting of such powers to governments.

(for in 1924, a stable internal value of the money unit was still his expressed ideal).[3] But this plea for stability seems to have been used as a casuistic strategy in his campaign for the abandonment of the gold standard. He found it expedient to stress, in his *Monetary Reform,* not the danger of depression, but the danger of the gold standard forcing a period of rapidly *rising prices* which, he argued, was being prevented only by the current deflationary action of the Federal Reserve Board in gold buying. In *The Treatise on Money,* he contended that "inflation is unjust, deflation is inexpedient." And when, previously, it had been regarded as a matter of honor (as well as a question of creating long-term monetary confidence) to restore the contractually agreed gold value of the pound sterling—when he *should* have said, "to avoid deflation is unjust"—he had argued (on grounds of expediency) for stability of the price level.

In his early writings, however, he appeared to be denying that cheap money would mean inflation either in the sense of a straining of the ability to convert or in the sense of causing an actual loss of parity or a decline in the real value of the money unit. He seemed to have had a deep, though never explicitly expressed, conviction that cheap money was not the cause of rising prices. Although they had opposed the return to gold, Keynes and his disciples still *seemed* to believe, between 1925 and 1931,[4] that cheap money (without rectifying deflation later) and convertibility were compatible. They advocated what they called a "managed gold standard." But if that had meant cheap money, it would have demanded not only the management of the standard but permanent reliance on trade and exchange restrictions, indeed, the sort of system which has, in fact, been built up since that time in many countries.

---

[3] This notion of using monetary and fiscal policy to achieve "full employment at a stable price level," involves an inherent contradiction, unless all that is meant is that a money unit of constant value assists the process of pricing for market clearance. The bogus results obtained under repressed inflation are in practice short-lived achievements.

The power of a sound, stable, and *trusted* currency to bring about recovery, provided there is some collective attempt to recoordinate an economy through price adjustment, is very great. But Keynes was the last person to see or stress the importance of that point. In 1923, Edwin Cannan declared that the "introduction of trustworthy currency" was more important for the salvation of Germany than any "abatement or settlement of reparations or even the evacuation of the Ruhr." It was he who forecast correctly, as early as 1923, that the Germans would in fact return to gold before the British. See his *An Economist's Protest,* pp. 347–49, 359–62.

[4] Keynes' position on this point seems, however, to have been changing *during* 1931.

Now when (a few years later) Keynes wrote *The General Theory,* when he spoke of the euthanasia of the *rentier,* he seemed to have forgotten about the advantages of a stable scale of prices. At any rate, he made no attempt to reconcile his change of front. Already, when the American president had inaugurated the long inflation which grew upon the devaluation of the dollar, not only had Keynes declared Roosevelt to have been "magnificently right," but had described this action as a challenge to the world.[5] Clearly, he was then pressing for the *abandonment* of the ideal of stability of real value. But he always avoided stating this in unequivocal terms. Whereas in the *Treatise* he had made use of Wicksell's indispensable concept of the natural rate of interest, in *The General Theory* he dismissed it with the comment that it is "merely the rate of interest which will preserve the *status quo;* and, in general, we have no predominant interest in the *status quo* as such."[6] But a money unit of constant or defined value has no more tendency to preserve the status quo than a constant pint, ounce, yard, or ampère.[7] Keynes was, in fact, inhibiting explicit thought about the value of the money unit, and at the crucial point at which the issue of the compatibility of cheap money with the maintenance of a defined value for the money unit ought to have been faced, it was evaded. The obscure implication is that any rate of depreciation of the money unit, however rapid, is not to be termed "true inflation" provided it brings *any* idle resources, however insignificant in amount, into activity.[8] He rejected the view (his words) that "any increase in the quantity of money is inflationary (unless we mean by *inflationary* merely that prices are rising)."[9] These vital phrases are almost casually expressed, as though they were referring to some minor side issue. It has been alleged that he was here defending "reflation," not inflation. But this could only have been justly contended if he had specifically and unequivocally argued (in 1936) for the restoration of some previously existing scale of prices, and demanded other means of maintaining employment when that scale had been attained. This, he conspicuously

---

[5] Harrod, op. cit., p. 445.

[6] Keynes, *The General Theory,* p. 243.

[7] Henry Hazlitt remarks that "it is hard to call" the passage I have quoted "anything else than a deliberate misrepresentation." *The Failure of the "New Economics": An Analysis of the Keynesian Fallacies* (Princeton, N.J.: D. Van Nostrand Company, 1959), p. 248.

[8] Keynes, op. cit., pp. 119, 303.

[9] Ibid., p. 304.

failed to do. Others have asserted that he did not advocate inflation but merely removed inhibitions against its use. But if you conduct propaganda to remove inhibitions about using heroin, are you not in fact *advocating* its use? That some measure of inflation is always tacitly implied in the Keynesian proposals is clear from the fact that the admitted purpose is that of reducing real wage rates (to be accomplished not through direct coordination of values but through the depreciation of the money unit). There is, however, usually a lack of frankness on this issue.[10]

"[I]n his later days," admits Harrod, Keynes came "to be regarded as something of an inflationist—whether truly so depends on the definition of that term."[11] It is a pity that on this point Harrod refrains from giving a definition of "inflation" under which Keynes could *not* be regarded as an inflationist. Keynes himself defined "true inflation" as a condition in which "a further increase in the quantity of effective demand . . . entirely spends itself on an increase in the cost-unit fully proportionate to the increase in effective demand."[12] In the light of the context in which this definition appears, it can be paraphrased, quite fairly, as follows: "Rising prices do not constitute inflation. Only a rising scale of prices which is more than sufficient to bring into operation productive capacity the services of which have been priced above market-clearing levels can be properly called *inflation*. Thus, inflation has nothing to do with the rapidity at which prices are forced up. What *is* relevant is the degree to which that process fails to bring into utilization resources which society could not previously afford to employ." The popular appeal of Keynes' teachings has rested largely upon his failure to state this proposition in frank and clear language of this kind.

It has been claimed also, in defense of these passages, that he was opposed both to inflation and deflation, but that he regarded the latter as the greater evil. Yet I know of no economist who has ever *advocated* deflation except as a correction for inflation, and even then only on grounds of distributive justice and the moral necessity for honoring contractual obligations. Pre-Keynesian economic teach-

---

[10] James Edward Meade, Michael Polyani, and Abba P. Lerner are among the exceptions who are quite frank on the point.

[11] Harrod, op. cit., p. 272.

[12] Keynes, op. cit., p. 303. Keynes did not adhere rigidly to this definition in subsequent writing. Already in 1937 he was warning against "inflation," in spite of the existence of much unemployment of labor. (See *The Times,* London, March 11, 1937.)

ings may be said to have defended deflation only in the sense that a surgeon may defend the amputation of a gangrenous limb.

Keynes was obsessed by his conviction that monetary and fiscal policy, freed from any obligation to maintain convertibility or a defined value of the money unit, can always maintain full employment. (He did not consider what the effect would be if any depreciation of the money unit could be forecast. *Paraphrased in the terms which I prefer to use,* he contended that monetary policy can draw idle resources into activity by increasing the number of money units in relation to the demand for monetary services (a demand mainly correlated with the size of real income) through maintaining an interest rate below the natural; or, *as he would have preferred to put it,* through maintaining such an interest rate as will stimulate sufficient "investment" to absorb "savings"—that being the rate consistent with full activity.

No economist would have challenged the reality that, when many input and output prices have come to be fixed above market-clearing levels, so that there exists much withheld capacity or suboptimal employment, recovery can be brought about by a successful policy of restoring expected yields to investment. But it is the incorporation of a certain value of income into capital ("income" in the sense of the flow of productive services, of men and assets) which constitutes "investment."[13] If we *are* to use the word "investment" to *mean a magnitude,* we must recognize that any other meaning is distressingly arbitrary.

Keynes, of course, meant by "investment" the acquisition of "nonliquid assets," *presumably* either through an acquisition of additional nonmoney by reducing money stocks,[14] causing an increase in V, and bidding down the value M_r, or with no change in the demand for money out of money income—that is, out of the flow of productive services, but simply through a relatively larger proportion of that flow being incorporated into assets of long life expectancy ("investment goods" or "producer goods") and a relatively smaller proportion into assets of short life expectancies ("consumer goods"). But the reality is that *all* income, that is, *all* productive services, is either consumed as it is rendered or incorporated into the stock of assets, of which a small proportion *may* be retained as *additional*

---

[13] "Capital" in this context is best envisaged as a stock of assets of varying life expectancies.

[14] As I would put it, "reducing aggregate investment in money."

money (a decline in V bidding up the value M_r) or vice versa. And, of course, nonmoney assets may be sold and the proceeds invested in money. But *the process of saving* consists of incorporating into assets (irrespective of their prospective economic lives[15]) the *whole* of that part of the flow of productive services which is not consumed directly. And the flow of services is used partly to replace (wholly or partially) the value of "consumption" (services and assets of which the value is exterminated) and partly to add to the value magnitude of the assets stock, irrespective of its composition. Keynes sometimes thought of any such *addition* as the magnitude of "investment." But at other times he seemed to be thinking of growth in the aggregate magnitude of the stock of "nonliquid" assets, while at other times he envisaged growth in the stock of "investment goods," presumably assets of relatively long life expectancies, with the concepts of "long" and "short" left vague. The conceptual fuzziness is remarkable.

However, as I remarked above, all economists agree that the recuperation of a run-down economy can be achieved only *via* improved prospects of yields to investment in inputs generally. The controversies center on the *method* of restoring profit expectations, not on the desirability of so doing. Keynes thought that the method required was the fixing of a market rate of interest at that level which, through ensuring the absorption of savings (which he thought of as not investing them in money), was consistent with full activity. Yet there are two ways in which that can be done. Let us ignore at this stage the most fundamental issue, the release of *withheld demands* for inputs and outputs, caused in each case by *withheld supplies* of *noncompeting* inputs and outputs. Then, the encouragement of positive saving preference (thrift) which *ceteris paribus* will reduce the noninflationary level of interest and cause contributions to the assets stock to be transferred from products of relatively short life expectancy ("consumer goods") to products of relatively long life expectancy ("producer goods" or "investment goods"), will be one way of raising demands for labor, through the accumulation of a greater stock of wage-multiplying assets.

Keynes' convictions on this point led him, however, to the idea that these results could be achieved more directly than through overt monetary policy, namely, through governmental action via budget

---

[15] Services consumed as they are rendered may be regarded as products of zero life expectancy.

deficits (a) "to maintain investment" by expenditure on public works, in which case the inflation needed to permit the expenditure was regarded rather as a subsidiary policy of a neutral nature; or (b) to maintain expenditure on consumption, a remedy which had the great political advantage of implying the desirability of income redistribution from the thrifty to the less thrifty or from the more productive to the less productive members of the community, or from the "haves" to the "have nots." These ideas were expounded without any emphasis on the effects upon the price index.

It was, then, subsequent to the *Treatise* that Keynes appears to have realized that the benefits of cheap money can be won solely through a rise in final prices with lagging costs (or through depreciated exchanges which cause prices in foreign currencies to fall, without a fall in domestic prices). He appears accordingly to have quietly changed his conception of inflation as his convictions gained in realism. After Britain's departure from gold, he treated it as something which it was best not to mention, or as something which at any rate ought not to be *called* "inflation" as long as it was performing the beneficent role he attributed to it. The tradition persists. For instance, there have been Keynesians, such as Harrod, who have held that, in spite of creeping price increases in terms of almost all currencies, there was at one time a shortage of international liquidity which was having a deflationary influence. Because they expected a worldwide increase in M to stimulate economic growth and international trade, they thought it appropriate to regard the current rate of inflation as deflationary![16]

And other Keynesians have tended to follow their master in thus fogging the issue. Quite often they have argued that expenditure (or certain kinds of expenditure, or money income, or the circulation of money, etc.) ought to be sufficient to prevent the emergence of unemployment and to secure the fullest utilization of resources, but not high enough to "endanger the currency," or to "threaten financial stability," or some other equally inexplicit notion. They have never asked unequivocally, *Are these aims compatible? Is cheap money in any form compatible with any kind of contractual or de-*

---

[16] See Fritz Machlup's reference to Harrod and others on the point in his *Plans for Reform of the International Monetary System* (Princeton, N.J.: International Finance Section, Department of Economics, Princeton University, 1962), pp. 8–10. This penetrating essay was published while the type of my *Keynesianism* was being set.

fined value of the money unit? The truth is that these objectives *are* absolutely incompatible.[17]

The attempt of the "moderate" Keynesians to follow their master's tactic of refusing to call a "mere" rise of prices "inflation," had led them into a dilemma in the early sixties. Alarmed at the results, they were beginning to refer to the mounting cost of living as "inflation." But there was no consistency in their so describing the rise in prices since 1946, especially as they were inclined to talk of "wage-induced inflation." For, costs *in certain fields* having been forced up, under strike threat or other coercion, *every rise of prices has been an essential concomitant of the maintenance of full employment through the maintenance of "effective demand," and so ought not, in terms of Keynes' definition, to be regarded as "inflationary."*

When typical Keynesians *have* deigned to consider the evils of inflation they have been infuriatingly vague. For instance, Harrod, in his *The Trade Cycle,* tried to distinguish between good and bad depreciation of a currency. He approved of it if it "occurs as the natural and inevitable result of strenuous internal measures undertaken by a country to secure higher activity and greater employment at home"; but his approval was withheld if it is "artificially engineered as a means of stimulating [economic] activity." It is "impossible to lay too much emphasis" on this distinction, he says.[18] But where is the distinction? Under "full employment" the Keynesians admit that there can be no stimulation of activity. At what point, then, do "strenuous measures" to cause depreciation (as a means of inducing the release of capacity) become "artificial"? And in what sense is depreciation up to that point "natural"?

The Keynesians have no criteria at all. They feel that they cannot defend runaway inflations, but they have enunciated no standards to tell us just what rate of inflation is beneficial and what rate harmful. The term "artificial" is meaningless.

This unwillingness to face frankly and unequivocally the issue of inflation and reemployment is, I believe, common to almost all the

---

[17] Under price flexibility (which could deprive the Keynesian case for inflation of all its content) cheap money *could* create latent inflation, which could persist for some time without convertibility being threatened. But it would have to be followed by credit contraction with nondeflationary consequences.

[18] Roy F. Harrod, *The Trade Cycle: An Essay* (New York: Augustus M. Kelley, 1961), p. 188.

Keynesians. They tend usually to dodge the issue in theoretical analysis by *assuming* (tacitly or explicitly) perfect elasticity in the flow of output up to the point of "full employment." In the words of *The General Theory,* "so long as there is unemployment, *employment* will change in the same proportion as the quantity of money."[19] The qualification of the principle by the explanation that, for various reasons, "we have in fact a condition of prices rising gradually as employment increases,"[20] is treated as though it were a minor qualification!

A host of other factors can prevent the price stability which the Keynesians assume, *in theoretical discussions,* will be maintained (up to full employment) as expenditure increases. The most important, as I see things, is that while there are some fields in which there is much withheld capacity (increased demands may cause the release of much of this capacity without significant further price increases), there will be other fields in which *anticipated* yields may be raised through spreading liquidation of present inventories over longer periods. That appears to me to be the most that can be reasonably claimed.[21] The notion that the supply of productive services is elastic up to the point of full employment, and inelastic beyond that, has therefore this measure of validity, that the greater the extent of withheld capacity, the more elastic will the release of capacity tend to be. But the cumulative effects of the release must necessarily *slow down* as any remaining withheld capacity is coaxed into operation. Hence credit expansion is likely to be less inflationary during the earlier part of an inflation-engineered recovery from depression than it is as the point of full utilization of resources begins to be approached or after it has been achieved.

Let us consider the case of wage rates which remain stationary *in a certain trade* while demand is directed to other things, with resulting unemployment. It may then happen that a return to the former level of money demand for *the product of that trade* will result in the full restoration of employment. There may be a very high elasticity of supply of labor (and complementary services) in this sense. But it is impossible, I suggest, for this to be the position *in general.* For in the absence of deflation, why should there have been a decline in money demands for most things? Only because the

---

[19] Keynes, op. cit., p. 296.
[20] Ibid.
[21] Ibid., et seq.

prices of certain services have been pushed to, or maintained, above the market-clearing level compatible with the full employment of the resources which make them.[22] *A nondeflationary decline in demands in general* (measured in money) can occur only as a reaction to a decline in the flow of services as a whole, however caused. Hence, *the idle capacity which Keynes seemed to think would be released under maintained monetary demands must in fact require inflated monetary demands to induce its release.* It is solely in the case of a purposeless deflation (that is, one which is not rectifying a previous inflation) that Keynes' argument could hold. In that case, but in that case only, is the term "reflation" admissible. It has to be stressed, however, that each release of capacity induced by increased expenditure is contributing to increased uninflated demands for whatever noncompeting things (services or assets) it is destined to be exchanged for. Here we have the dynamic factor toward which Keynes seems to have been groping—what I shall call "the true multiplier," but which is actually nothing more than Say's law—the law which Keynes had summarily rejected without stating it or quoting Say.[23]

I argued on pages 216–17 that the notions of "price-induced inflation" and "wage-induced inflation" are inherently defective concepts, although the phenomenon which has come to be called "wage-push" is certainly a major cause of the political expediency of inflation. But in the *absence* of inflation, pushing up some prices above market-clearing values either pushes other market-clearing price levels down, or sets in motion a cumulative decline in aggregate purchasing power. Now this process might *appear* to be inflationary if it is accompanied by monetary rigidity. But as I have insisted, the magnitude M ought to be accepted as policy-determined. Hence, unless the response to the repression of the flow of purchasing power is responded to by a contraction in M, then inflation must occur. It follows that monetary policy is solely to blame for the inflation, just as monetary rigidity is to blame for deflation when an increased demand for money (whether due to a rise in T, or in

---

[22] *Ceteris paribus* the market-clearing level will be higher in any trade the more rapidly prices are falling to market-clearing levels in noncompeting trades.

[23] Keynes *thought* he had stated the law in a phrase which, as far as I have been able to trace, had never been used before he used it in *The General Theory*. Interestingly enough, that phrase seems to have been accepted and repeated by virtually every other economist who has since referred to that law. See my *A Rehabilitation of Say's Law*, p. 3 n.

$\frac{1}{V}$) is accompanied by a constant *M*. It follows that if capacity has been priced out of employment in the absence of deflation, that is, if any credit contraction has merely been that required to prevent inflation, it will be impossible to bring about the release of capacity by any form of noninflationary credit expansion. *It is no more true to say that, in general, all unemployment is induced by deflation than it is to say that inflation must always restore employment.*

In the purely imaginary case in which an expansion of *MV* merely reverses a former *purposeless deflation,* it may *restore prices* in the industries which did not withhold capacity and *restore outputs* in the industries which did withhold capacity. But it is a matter of some doubt whether a *purposeless* deflation (that is, deflation which is not a deliberately chosen means to an end, such as rectifying injustices in the distribution of income, or a determination to fulfill contractual convertibility obligations) has, in fact, ever occurred except inadvertently.[24] At the same time, I cannot think of any non-Keynesian economist who would deny the possibility that there have been times in which deflations have been misconceived or ill-advised.[25]

In my judgment it is in those rare circumstances in which deflation has been unintended, that credit expansion may be justified solely by the release of capacity which it may be expected to induce. And only insofar as it fails to call forth a proportionate increase in output is credit expansion "inflationary" in my sense.[26] What the Keynesians must contend is that the only way to achieve the noninflationary element in credit expansion—given what they

---

[24] The world *has* witnessed a *purposeful* deflation which has not been a *rectifying* deflation. For instance, during the two years preceding World War I, the French, Germans, and Russians were *deliberately* pursuing austere deflationary policies with a view to building up strength for war. Their abnormal attraction to gold at this time seems to have forced some deflationary action and mild recession in other parts of the world.

[25] There are several non-Keynesian economists (notably Milton Friedman and Clark Warburton) who interpret the United States deflation of 1930 to 1933 in this light. Even so staunch an anti-inflationist as Benjamin M. Anderson recognized the defects of Germany's policy a year after her return to gold. (See his *Economics and the Public Welfare,* pp. 149–50.) In 1925 she was maintaining plentiful funds in the short-term money market but starving her industries and the business world of working capital.

[26] Beyond the point of full employment, the speed of noninflationary credit expansion will obviously be dependent upon the extent to which the community prefers to sacrifice consumption in the immediate future for consumption in the more distant future (in the light of current technological progress and demand for leisure).

regard as inevitable rigidities—is to endure the inflationary element. But few Keynesians would like their case to be put as clearly as this!

Now *if, owing to a high elasticity of release of withheld capacity, a small measure of inflation will result in a rapid transition to full employment, the chief objection to the achievement of this result through direct coordination falls away.* For in the light of such assumptions, it can be cogently argued that a relatively small measure of reasonableness in respect of the adjustment of wage rates and prices may be expected to call forth the output reactions which justify a large expansion in noninflationary credit and a rapid recovery of demands in terms of money.

This argument appears never to occur to the Keynesians. Polyani's excellent popularization of *The General Theory,* for instance, is explicit that the benefits which a "moderate" rise in prices brings about are due to the effect it has of reducing real wage rates. "Expansion," he says, "will cause (real) wage rates to decline and contraction will cause them to rise."[27] Obviously, he believes that moderate reductions of real wage rates will be sufficient to bring about full employment. Then why does he not ask, "If moderate adjustments of real wage rates can cause a material increase in activity and prosperity, why should we not seek these moderate adjustments directly, and so avoid all the difficulties and restrictions which are the inevitable concomitant of inflation in practice? Because just a *little* reasonableness and public spirit on the part of the labor unions could produce a great increase in the flow of wages, and in employment, surely it is better for us to plead for that public spirit and, if our plea fails, to enforce it." It is strange that he is not led to any such suggestion; for a solution of that kind would be much more conducive to the avoidance of the disaster which, he warns us, must inevitably result from "any serious attempt to raise the level of wage rates and salaries to compensate for rising prices."[28]

Today the distinction between "true inflation" and "inflation" is seldom made; but the securing of a rise in the scale of prices is still not regarded as inflationary when it is a method of bringing withheld capacity into utilization. Polyani is, I think, the most explicit of the Keynesian popularizers in admitting that an expansion of the circulation may be expected always to affect the price level[29] if it is to

---

[27] Polyani, *Full Employment and Free Trade,* p. 88.
[28] Ibid.
[29] Ibid., pp. 87–88.

have any employment-restoring effects. And he brings in a criterion which is not to be found in *The General Theory*. He advocates (without defining) "a moderate increase of prices."[30] He adds that governments should "clearly recognize the implications of an expansion policy for the price level" and refrain from "anti-inflationary regulations."[31] But what does he mean by these words, "clearly recognize the implications"? He is clearly telling governments that they must rid themselves of the idea which earlier Keynesian propaganda had spread, and *The General Theory* had not clearly renounced, that cheap money is consistent with stability of the money unit.[32] Is he not suggesting that governments should proclaim their position as follows: "We stand for a policy of inflation—*moderate* inflation. We are striving to achieve an increase, a *gradual increase,* in the cost of living"? But what would be the repercussions of an honestly adopted and confessed policy of inflation in a free society? (I discuss this question in Chapter 11.) Polyani does not ask this question, although he comes very near to asking it. "Wage adjustments will follow on rising or falling prices," he says, "but will never quite catch up with these changes. . . ." But "the power of the workers to exercise pressure for an advance in wages increases rapidly with the approach of full employment."[33] What sort of reaction, then, can be expected from the labor unions when they come to understand such a policy?

It is only since World War II that *some* Keynesians began openly recommending continuous depreciation of the money unit. Because of the inherent weakness of the Keynesian method of bringing relative prices into coordination—because that method leaves the causes of economic discoordination unremedied—Keynesians of this school feel that they are forced to argue that whenever activity declines (that is, whenever prices forced above market-clearing levels have

---

[30] Ibid., p. 89.

[31] Ibid.

[32] According to Harrod, Keynes himself had earlier favored a "gentle upward trend of prices" but, "in view of the difficulty of getting any good policy adopted and of the need for having definite rules of action for the various authorities concerned, he deemed it better to keep to the clear objective of a stable price level." *The Life of John Maynard Keynes,* p. 410. But an objective of a "gentle upward trend" of say 1 percent per month, or 12 percent per annum is an equally clear objective, and equally prescribes a "definite rule of action." Should not Harrod have said that people would have been too shocked if Keynes had advocated such gentle inflation? Or was it that Keynes feared that if a "gentle inflation" became the declared objective, people would be so misguided as to discount the gentle rise in prices and defeat its purpose?

[33] Polyani, op. cit., p. 88.

caused a contraction of the flow of uninflated income), inflationary action must be resorted to as a matter of policy. For instance, Edward Nevin complains of the failure of the British banking system "to create the extra money supply needed" in 1937. This was at a time when the index of wholesale prices (which increased by 34 percent in the period 1933 to 1937) was rising at an accelerating pace. He describes the hesitation on the part of the Treasury as "a curious development . . . in the light of the repeated official affirmations of adherence to a cheap money policy. . . . Credit was not," he says, "subsequently expanded *pari passu* with the rise in demand for active balances so as to maintain the level of interest rates which had been achieved by the conversion operation of 1932."[34] The attitude may be not unfairly summed up as: "Maintain gilt-edged interest low and don't worry about prices." But those who once took this line are now gradually finding themselves confronted with the dilemma—to which I have already referred—that confessed inflation is anticipated inflation; while anticipated inflation can bring none of the beneficial effects which have accompanied inflation in the past—not at least unless it is accompanied by controls to maintain a continuous lag in wage rates and costs in relation to final product prices.[35] And "controls" to keep wage rates and costs in a coordinated relationship to final prices are so obviously equally possible in the absence of inflation that, when resort to such measures has to be advocated, it seems that the very essence of theoretical Keynesianism is being abandoned.

The Keynesians like to praise the "cranks" such as Hobson, Gesell, Townsend, Douglas, Foster, and Catchings on the grounds that they at least recognized the defects of the system which (it is alleged) pre-Keynesian theory had created. At the same time the Keynesians insist upon differentiating themselves from the naive reasoning and naive panaceas of the "cranks." They would be ashamed to hold, as the "cranks" in effect did, that merely to dole out additional money is the cure for unemployment. Yet are not the identical ideas in all their naiveté at the root of Keynes' teachings, obscured in a mass of impressive but conceptually unsatisfactory theoretical

---

[34] Edward Nevin, *The Mechanism of Cheap Money: A Study of British Monetary Policy, 1931–1939* (Cardiff: University of Wales Press, 1955), p. 118.

[35] For when the classes who suffer grow too conscious of what is happening, they demand compensation, or start a scramble for higher incomes, or become disinclined to lend at current interest rates.

paraphernalia? And when it is suggested that it is expenditure on "investment" which essentially creates the employment (because the propensity to save, in the form of accumulating money balances,[36] would otherwise cause expenditure on "investment" to contract, income to shrink, and savings subsequently to fall in a like manner), the Keynesians are merely expressing their faith in the beneficence of an increase in MV in relation to T through a formula which, by reason of the tortuous route through which it leads the student's mind, creates an illusion of a profound train of thought.

Polyani has referred to the absence of principle in schemes such as James Edward Meade once advocated for doling out money to consumers.[37] But the state could distribute the additions to M with at least as much principle as it deals with income transfers. Thus, if one has agreed criteria for the ideal redistribution of property or income, one can presumably advocate the doling out of money to those whom the state has decided to favor. In this way the ends of full employment and "social justice" objectives may be served at one and the same time. On such grounds an attempt might be made to defend Beveridge's recommendations for the doling out of the inflated money in the first place in the form of various kinds of social security benefits. Polyani objects to the Beveridge proposals because they entail "enlargements of the public sphere of responsibilities . . . which the public would otherwise not wish to adopt," and because they generally confuse the issue by linking full employment policy with things like governmental control of investment and consumption, greater equality of incomes, etc.[38] But political control of investment, subsidization of consumption, and redistribution of income via income transfers in favor of the improvident, the indolent, the irresponsible, the incompetent, or the unlucky, *are* implied in the Keynesian thesis, even if they are regarded as, or intended primarily to serve as, its selling points. And from the standpoint of "creating employment" in the Keynesian manner, it does not matter a tinker's cuss *how M or MV* happens to be increased in relation to T if the aim is merely to bring what I have called "withheld capacity" into operation, or suboptimally employed resources into more productive uses. Polyani himself recognizes this when he asks, quite logically, "If you require a budget deficit . . . why spend only on 'construc-

---

[36] As I have shown, Keynes himself did *not* make this important qualification.

[37] James Edward Meade, *Consumers' Credit and Unemployment* (OUP, 1937).

[38] Polyani, op. cit., p. 134.

tional' and not on 'current' items?"[39] The answer is that, when it comes to inflation, the sole question is whether the disguised taxation is used for acceptable purposes. The only real advantage of inflation expressed through fiscal policy as distinct from monetary policy is political. As I have shown, it enables politically favored interests to be subsidized instead of allowing the highest bidders (entrepreneurs who, interpreting consumers' market signals, value prospective productive opportunities highest) to receive the additional credit.

There is no doubt, however, as I have continuously insisted, that provided inflation is not generally anticipated (that is, provided costs lag), it can bring about not only the release of capacity which is being withheld by being priced above the market-clearing level, but the release also of suboptimally used resources for more productive uses. The "cranks" perceived this. They failed, as the Keynesians fail, to perceive the implications.

---

[39] Ibid., p. 126.

11

Income and Its "Generation"

Since Keynes, at least, there has been a fashion for economists (the present writer included) to use the phrase "generation of income" for the phrase "production of income." The fashion has its virtues. To acquire grain, one must own or hire a fertile field in an appropriate climate, plow it, add manure, add seed, often add water, remove obnoxious weeds, and spend valuable time in supervising the process, etc. We must, that is, incur the costs of all those inputs in order to reap outputs in the form of harvests. In so doing, we have relied upon the "gifts" of nature: the atmosphere; the warmth of the earth and the sun; the light of the sun; nature's regular provision of water in the form of streams, rivers, rain, and so forth. All of these things affect the input costs we have to incur in order to purchase or rent the land profitably. It is because nature's bounty is passively given that the word "generation" has seemed to be acceptable. But for the most part even these "gifts" have scarcity. If one person claims more of one of them, someone else can have less. Moreover, effort is essential for the enjoyment of all the fruits of natural resources—the work of man multiplied by the use of assets. Hence, in spite of the analogy of the "generation" of electricity, I propose to talk of the production of income instead of its generation.

Thirty years ago Melvin Reder held that, "prior to *The General Theory,* there was no coherent theory of the level of (national) income and employment in existence," in the sense that it was "regarded as an unknown to be determined by the equilibrium conditions of the system."[1] Pre-Keynesian economists are said, indeed, to have

---

[1] Melvin W. Reder, "The Theories of John Maynard Keynes—Discussion," *American Economic Review, Papers and Proceedings,* May 1948, p. 295.

held that the magnitude of income is determined by factors irrelevant to such equilibrium, namely, (a) technical progress, (b) population, and (c) the stock of capital.

That is, I think, only a fair statement of pre-Keynesian orthodoxy if it is qualified by two further conditions, namely, (d) saving preference—the ultimate determinant of capital formation—and (e) the extent to which the potential productive services of men and assets are priced at market-clearing values, that is, for absorption into direct consumption or into the production and marketing process generally, providing the optimal composition of the assets stock. The Keynesian theory of income or employment is simply an attempt to *substitute,* through a theory in which price rigidity is not an essential assumption, something else for condition (e). In this attempt, the Keynesians are led to the view that there can be equilibrium without the "full employment" condition. But if, as I maintain in Chapter 12, this theory must be rejected, there can be no alternative *equilibrium* theory to explain the magnitude of income unless it accounts among other things for the factors which determine condition (e). And that is entirely a question of *policy*—of institutional and administrative planning, upon which no imaginable equation can throw the slightest light.

But the most seriously fallacious notion on which the typical Keynesian theory of income production rests is the role given to spending. For *spending,* as distinct from *demanding,* causes neither the *money valuation* of income nor the *size* of real income, although the whole Keynesian analysis is couched in terms which assume that it does. And the error is magnified when the relations of broad categories of expenditure (on "investment" or on "consumption" conceived of as components of "income," for instance) are also supposed to be influences. The acceptance of these infectious ideas is, of course, not confined to the Keynesian camp. I shall contend, however, that parts of the income analysis approach which has become conventional are basically defective.

The present chapter is devoted then to an attempt at rigorous examination of the theory that income is produced through expenditure; and I propose to show, by means of a careful consideration of concepts, that neither money income nor real income can be said to be created by spending, although money is an important factor of production and it is productive of income because it can ultimately be spent, and is held for that purpose.

By "money income" I mean "real income" measured in a particular way, namely, the value of the aggregate flow of people's services and the services of the resources they own, measured in terms of actual money units. "Real income" is "money income," but we call it the one thing or the other according to whether we measure it, or changes in it, in *abstract money units* of constant purchasing power or in *actual money units*.

Income is "produced" by whatever results in a flow of services. Services flow from resources in the case of assets, automatically, or in the case of people, through effort, and that effort may be either simple effort, as when a person supplies his own services without the use of assets, or effort combined with the services of assets. Now we have seen that resources (which supply services) may have their services priced so that their potential contribution runs to waste, thus causing a contraction of income. Hence, the forces which "produce" income are those which prevent, or remove, the incentive for pricing productive services above market-clearing values, or which take the form of a certain use of income, resulting in the realized replacement or realized net accumulation of assets and in an increased proportion of assets of long life expectancies and a smaller proportion of those of short life expectancies. In other words, *income is produced by whatever results in the release, or maintenance, or growth of productive power*. The concept covers men and assets.

"Money income," as I have defined it, is neither the same thing as the rate of receipt of money units from the sale of the flow of non-money products (which has often been the definition accepted as appropriate) nor the rate of expenditure of money units on that flow. In my definition, the value of the whole of the flow of services, *including* those embodied into any unsold portion of the resulting products, is measured in money units, and not merely that part of the flow which happens to be exchanged for them.

In adopting this definition, I am breaking with a convention which I have always found confusing and rejecting an assumption which is quite unacceptable.[2] "By convention," said A. C. Pigou, economists "do not reckon as real income the whole of this net flow" (the stream of goods and services), "but only a part of it—only that part which is paid for with money or is *easily represented in money*

---

[2] The fallacy that aggregate receipts (described as "money income") are the same thing as the value of real income (or output as a whole) measured in money units, has been exposed by Gottfried Haberler in his *Prosperity and Depression* (4th ed.; Cambridge, Mass.: Harvard University Press, 1958), pp. 178–79.

terms."[3] (My italics.) That may be justified, for convenience, in empirical statistical studies. But for logical purposes, the value of *all* net products can be *equally easily envisaged and valued in money,* and I can see no justification for excluding any part of the stream from the notion of "real income" and hence from the notion of "money income." The ultimate purpose of the convention I am criticizing appears to have been the desire to think of money income as a certain flow of money receipts. But I propose to argue that, when we are concerned with income, there is only one relevant "flow," and that is of services. The movement or transfer of whatever assets happen to be used as the measuring rod of value is in no sense income but something which usually but not always accompanies it. A thing does not need to be exchanged for money in order to have money value. *Whether a commodity has been exchanged for money once, or several times, or not at all does not, in itself, influence its money value.*

Moreover, although the use of money may be said to "lubricate" the process of exchanging productive services for productive services, assets for assets, or services for assets, and although the services of money inventories are therefore highly productive in economizing transactions costs, we buy with "money's worth" and not with money unless we are reducing our inventories of money. Passage of cash from hand to hand, or of deposits from account to account, has a zero time dimension and does not influence prices. The prices of particular things are determined solely by choices, mostly expressed in money terms, on the one side, and supplies, mostly expressed in money terms, on the other side. And any average of prices as a whole rises or falls because the value of the money unit falls or rises. As I have constantly stressed, that is ultimately entirely a matter of discretionary monetary policy or of an accepted monetary standard. Particular assets (whether with short or long life expectancies) may be invested in with a view to the production of "time utilities," as well as other utilities which are necessarily time-using, such as "space utilities," "assembly utilities," "availability utilities"—indeed all types of marketing services which are in-

---

[3] A. C. Pigou, *Income: An Introduction to Economics* (London: Macmillan and Company, 1948). We can trace back this usage on the part of Pigou to his *The Theory of Unemployment* (London: Macmillan and Company, 1933), pp. 192–93, where he defined "real output" quite arbitrarily, as the "net fruit of the services" for which money payments are made. He did not regard services as "economic" unless money is paid for them.

corporated into outputs—because such services are an inherent part
of the productive process. Production, we must remember, is always
the creation of value; and (whether it is measured in terms of the
value of an actual money unit, or of an abstractly conceived money
unit of constant purchasing power) we then envisage it as part of
income. It is irrelevant whether or not anyone has yet paid for it.
Some part of real income is nearly always unsold; and much of it is
consumed directly without entering into exchange via money or
barter. This applies, for example, to the income of "gratifications"
received from capital goods in households, as well as to all the
services and goods which we produce for ourselves and families, like
the flowers and vegetables we grow in our gardens, the repairs we
make to the house, etc.[4] But apart from these, as we have seen, a
portion of the flow of products *intended for ultimate sale* is always
being invested in. And money income, as I conceive of it, values the
unsold and accumulated portion of the flow of outputs (the part
which has at no time been exchanged for money) at the present
discounted value of the anticipated receipts from future sales of the
accumulated portion. In other words, the valuation (in money units)
is the entrepreneur's reserve price, expressing his demand, in each
case.

The logical difficulties encountered in a conception of income which
includes household-produced and unsold products generally[5] merely
bring out the enormous and inevitable arbitrariness in any notion
of income *as a measurable quantity,* and hence the limited usefulness of any such concept. My approach seems at any rate to *minimize* these difficulties, although not of course for the statistician.
But to the praxeologist (for example, the economist who has grasped
the principal lesson of Ludwig von Mises' *Human Action*) the
logical difficulties are unimportant. What we are trying to measure
(in the notion of income as the flow of services) is *the degree of
success* in the achievement of *the most preferred uses* of scarce

---

[4] We bid against others for our own services or the products of our services
(or the services of our assets and their products). Hence all "real income"
represents "real demand," so that "money income" (the same thing measured
differently) must represent "money demand." (But see pp. 76–78.)

If, for any reason, the accumulated stocks are valueless, there will obviously
be no contribution to income.

[5] Simon Kuznets has dealt exhaustively with these difficulties. See his *National
Income and Its Composition, 1919–1938* (New York: National Bureau of
Economic Research, 1941).

resources which are in process of decumulation, replacement, and net accumulation.

There are two important questions to be considered: (a) What determines the money valuation of the flow of services? and (b) What determines the valuation of this flow in "real terms" (that is, its "size" measured in money units of constant "purchasing power")? The second question has to do with the size of what is measured, the first having to do with the size of the yardstick also. But because in this case a *changing* yardstick can affect the absolute size of the thing measured, the two are related.

These questions are, as we have seen, usually discussed in these days under the title of "the generation of income." Discussions of the topic frequently confuse, however, the two logically separate questions covered by (a) and (b). We ought always to distinguish explicitly between any inflation of money income (a mere change in the unit of measurement) and any true "production" of income which it induces through validating prices which were formerly above market-clearing levels. Thus, if by "money income" we mean real income measured in money units of changing value, we can hardly usefully say that *the thing measured* is changing. Indeed, one cannot properly talk of "measuring" with a changing yardstick. And yet the sort of income propagation theories which have become popular since Keynes have confused reactions upon the size of the thing measured (the flow of productive services) and reactions on the size of the measuring unit.

I propose to deal first with the issues which arise under (a), the money valuation of income.

Can we say that the money valuation of income (real income being given) is determined by expenditure? It is usually held that a decline in the rate of expenditure must mean a decline in money income. Thus, the postponement of expenditure (a rise in the demand for money, or a rise in liquidity preference—however we like to put it) is regarded as taking the form of (a) receipts (from nonmoney products sold) exceeding expenditure; or (b) an increasing average interval between purchases from the flow of non-money, (a) and (b) being regarded as different ways of looking at the same phenomenon. But all it means is that the magnitude M_r is bid up.

During the first decade of the Keynesian era, I still regarded changes in the demand for money as influencing the rate of expenditure, *and hence* as influencing the average of prices. I still thought that we could distinguish between those movements of money which *do not* affect an index of prices and those which *do,* and hence influence the money value of the flow of services (money income).

I have since come to see that changes in the general rate of expenditure (the movement of money) are a *consequence* of changes in the value of the money unit and not its cause. In other words, it is the size of the yardstick of value which *determines* the expenditure necessary to obtain goods in general. *Expenditures do not determine prices. Prices determine necessary expenditures.*[6]

Under conditions of barter, the rate of exchange of one commodity for another will alter as people's subjective valuations of the things they hold, or are acquiring from output, happen to change. This being so, exchanges of products are the results and not the causes of values, values being objectively established by the acceptance of *bids or offers* to exchange. Consider the barter of nuts for apples and suppose something makes people believe that there is going to be an abnormally plentiful harvest of apples. The value of nuts in terms of apples will immediately rise. *Subsequent* transactions will be at a different ratio. We can, indeed, imagine the change in values (prices in terms of nuts) occurring during a public holiday while no transactions are taking place. Obviously, then, transactions do not *cause* the values in exchange which emerge: they are a *consequence* of changes in values; and the number of transactions is unrelated to the ratios established.

Similarly, transactions involving money are a consequence and not a cause of the prices which scales of preference, expressed in demand and supply, have brought about. It is *demand and supply expressed in terms of money,* and not the *spending* of money, which determine prices. Buying and selling involve pricing in that they imply the acceptance of a bid to buy or of an offer to sell. But it is the value of the money unit determined in the course of *the total bidding for monetary services and nonmoney products,* and neither the number of exchanges between money and nonmoney (the actual passage of currency or checks), nor the terms of individual transac-

---

[6] The Radcliffe Committee (Committee on the Working of the Monetary System Report, 1959, para. 390) appeared to be getting near to this notion when it said: "Spending is not limited by the amount of money in existence; but it is related to the amount of money people think they can get hold of." Had it substituted for the phrase "spending is not limited," the words "the value of the money unit is not determined," it would have come still nearer to hitting the nail on the head. But *all* lending and borrowing influence the magnitude M as I have defined it. (See p. 183.)

tions,[7] which brings about individual prices, and so the scale of prices, at any time.

When I buy a commodity from a shop, part of what I pay may be held to remunerate the services of the shopkeeper and the assets he owns and uses. But it is my prospective demand, of which my actual purchase is the fulfillment, which has called forth the services that are embodied in the product I acquire. And the source of my demand is not money but my money's worth—my capital and income; the income is the output of my personal services and the assets I own.

The fact that, say, a camera is one of my purchases is because its acquisition appears to me to be the best way of using the property rights I possess (a) in my stock of capital and (b) in the contribution I am making (or that which my assets are making) to the flow of productive services. My capital and income are the *source* of that demand. The capital value I wish to hold as money (which is determined by the value I place on monetary services) is one of countless influences on the price of the camera and upon the amount I bid for all other services or assets. The complexities arise because, if people want to hold a greater real aggregate value in the form of money, and M is constant, the value of the money unit rises and prices fall. But this is not *because* spending falls (in the sense that the average interval between purchases falls). If spending falls, it is *because* the value of the money unit rises and less has to be spent to get a given quantity of nonmoney, just as the seller can obtain less money for any given quantity of things in general.

It is sometimes said that it is *expectations* of expenditure which influence prices. But even that statement is inaccurately expressed. Expectations that greater or less expenditure *will be necessary* to purchase given products later on will influence the current value of the money unit. That is why expected prices influence current prices.

If the passing of money could be regarded as a determinant of prices, then selling would have to be held to have the same effect as buying! Economists could equally logically (and equally wrongly) conceive of the money valuation of income having its origin in selling, which draws money into circulation. Admittedly, when I refrain from acquiring the nonmoney product of others, I *may* reduce my

---

[7] For individual transactions represent *relative* values in money terms and only reflect the real value of the money unit in the sense that the price of each commodity reflects in part the value of all other commodities.

expenditure.[8] Yet it is equally correct to say that other people then reduce their selling (their money receipts). Both aspects have the same relevance. The actual rate of buying (and hence selling) which emerges is clearly *the result* of the valuations which influence *the desire* to buy *or* sell more or less rapidly and *not its cause.* Hence selling no more influences the money valuation of income than does spending and the value (purchasing power) of the money unit is determined solely by monetary policy (the determinants of M in relation to M_r), the market-determined value of the money stock in terms of generalized nonmoney. Of course, the *terms* of transactions *reveal* or *record* values and prices, and current values (and trends in values) are data which are considered in the process of valuation. But if one refrains from spending at the former rate because one believes that the value of the money unit is rising or is going to rise, that is *because* the present value one puts on it *has risen.*[9]

The Keynesians are not the only economists to see the origin of the money valuation of income in buying, expenditure, the passing of money. Indeed, in an earlier treatment which I have now discarded, I myself tried to distinguish between those transfers of money (which can be viewed either as receipts or as expenditures) which affect the valuation of income and those which do not. I had not then seen how misleading and question-begging is the concept of the *income velocity* of circulation of money. I held that "mere sales of capital goods (which do not affect demand for the flow of nonmoney products)" and transfers such as when "a father pays pocket money to his child, or when a government pays an unemployment dole" have no influence on the money valuation of income.[10] But I still

---

[8] I stress the word "may" because I may have been acquiring those products *without expenditure,* that is, by some barter transaction with another person or firm. Indeed, to increase my money stocks I may have to sell the goods I have previously bartered.

[9] It is not "the expectation or intention to buy more than is available" (Abba P. Lerner, "The Inflation-Process," *Review of Economics and Statistics,* August 1949, pp. 194–95) which causes people to reduce their valuation of the money unit; it is the discovery that they have *wrongly forecast* the future amount of nonmoney available (e.g., as reflected in the depletion of inventories) and/or the future magnitude of MV.

[10] The controversies (largely in discussion of "income velocity") which have taken place concerning exactly what receipts or payments do, and what do not, enter into "income" appear to have been influenced also by the fallacy that money units perform their services by circulating. In other words, the services

thought that an increase in spending on a given flow of services must *cause* an increase in the money valuation of that flow because people will be receiving more money as income. Like most economists, I failed to see that this was like saying, "increased *selling* must cause an increase in money income (through drawing more money into circulation)." It took me many years to perceive that those notions of money income which regard it as *certain* receipts of money or as caused by *certain* expenditures are subtly fallacious. (See below, pp. 248 et seq.)

When purchasers in general openly bid up or bid down the money value of nonmoney goods (by bidding higher prices than were previously paid for a given supply, or by offering to pay less than the ruling price in the case of a supply of which inventories are accumulating, or even through passively causing nonmoney inventories to accumulate, or when sellers in general raise or reduce their offers), *the value of the money unit is determined by bids and offers which precede transactions.* And the profitableness of bidding (in money terms) for inputs and pricing outputs is, T being given, determined in part by monetary policy, that is, changes in M in relation to changes and expected changes in $\frac{1}{V}$.

"T being given" means a given flow of services (real income). Now suppose the whole of this flow is purchased, and suppose that the average size of purchase is doubled. If M remains constant, the expenditure of a period will be the same. But if it is found that, with larger average purchases, the marginal value of monetary services falls in terms of nonmoney services, so that $\frac{1}{V}$ contracts, acceptable bids and offers in terms of money will rise. The real value of the money unit will then fall under the new valuation, and greater expenditure will be *required* from all who bid for the flow of services.

Let us consider the two ways in which increased "aggregate expenditure" may come about: (a) an increase in V and (b) an increase in M (T being constant in both cases).

In case (a), the changed valuation means that people have placed a lower value on the money unit. M_r contracts. At existing prices people want to reduce their money balances. The changed relative

are regarded as occurring at particular points of time separated by periods of idleness. But when A pays or gives a dollar to B, it ceases to perform services for A and begins to perform them for B.

valuations of money and nonmoney may occur slowly, but new, higher prices will emerge as consistency is established.

In case (b), M increases, while V declines at first and then slowly recovers as the implications of the situation cause basic valuations to adjust. That is, the first reaction is latent, not open inflation. At first the expenditures needed to acquire a given quantum of nonmoney may not increase at all. This will come about only as sellers and buyers perceive the new data, and different offers and bids become acceptable. The inflation remains latent until lower subjective valuations begin to be placed on the money unit; and this is usually some time after the rate of buying and selling has changed. Only then do values reach consistency and new prices begin to rule. That is, changes in M do not work mechanically. For example, the actual spending of the results of a large successful forgery (as in the great Portuguese banknotes forgery) will have no effect upon prices until the forgery gets known, in which case the value of the money unit is likely to be adjusted *before* any further expenditure follows, or until a more rapid depletion of nonmoney inventories than is normally experienced, *being recognized,* causes the value of the money unit to be reduced (that is, prices to be raised). It is not the more rapid passing of money which brings about that result; for that may have been occurring for some time previously. And when prices in general have risen (T being assumed constant), it is not our continuing to pay more for things which maintains their prices. Exactly the opposite. As I have just insisted, we must part with more money units for nonmoney *because* their prices have risen. But our ability to pay more[11] for things and the fact that we continue to do so (thus depleting inventories) *are* proof that we have more money units to spend and so a factor which influences the prospectively profitable prices of inputs and outputs.

What answer, then, can we give to the question: Output being given, does expenditure determine the average of prices or do prices determine expenditure? The answer is, I suggest: *Prices determine needed expenditures, but acts of expenditure constitute part of the data which lead to changed bids and offers becoming acceptable, thereby changing the value of the money unit.* The numbers of such expenditures, "velocity," are not an influence but a consequence.

---

[11] I mention ability to pay more (and not willingness) in this paragraph, simply because I am illustrating the case of a large forgery.

If people in general think that it will be profitable to set higher prices for what they and their assets produce, T and M remaining constant initially, yet the position of monetary services on people's scales of preference does not change, the value of the money unit as I have defined it, its purchasing power in terms of nonmoney, will fall. But there will be inconsistencies in the situation. The conditions of the identity no longer apply. If P has risen, V *must* have fallen. Producers will soon perceive that the new prices are not clearing the market, that is, that inventories of their final outputs are accumulating, and that any further investment in the inventories will be destined to prove still more unprofitable. They will then not only cease investing in, but begin disinvesting from, such inventories, thereby tending to restore the value of the money unit.

It is through the equilibrium or self-consistency between values so established that the average of prices (which determines the real value of the money unit) and hence the money valuation of income is determined. If people *do not* act consistently and they maintain the higher prices for nonmoney (while trying to hold the same real value as money assets), they will force a contraction in T and, M being constant, the value of the money unit will fall, thus bringing this value into consistency.

Let us consider the question of credit expansion. The issue of credit, when it has merely reached the form of an advance which the borrower has not yet used to buy anything, already influences his bidding, or his acceptance of offers, and hence influences prices in the field in which he purchases. Even the *belief* that credit will in fact be available will influence money valuations.

About twenty years ago, I could still write (in an unpublished draft): "Credit can only be regarded as actually issued when it is spent and enters into current circulation." I now realize that this is quite wrong.

Hence, T *being given,* the money valuation of income is determined *first* by the value which people put on money—the determinants of $\frac{1}{V}$ —and *second* by the determinants of M. But this is a mere truism, for $\frac{M_r}{M}$ is the value of the money unit, while M_r is determined by demands correlated with T and $\frac{1}{V}$. V, the "income velocity," is no *velocity* at all. It covers all the results of people's judgments and preferences as an influence upon the magnitude M_r. The statement that inflation occurs when MV increases more than in proportion to T simply means that when, through such a change, there is a fall in the value of the money unit, income measured in money increases by more than income measured in real terms. We cannot say that expenditure in excess of money income causes inflation. It is a consequence of it; but we *can* say that inflation is caused through "money spending power" being caused to increase more rapidly than "purchasing power" is increasing.

I am afraid my suggestion that an increase of expenditure in relation to the flow of output is a consequence and not a cause of the depreciation of the money unit (the rise of prices) may appear to many readers to be hairsplitting. It is not. It is fundamental. The value of the money unit is wholly a question of judgment of the productivity of money, and the number of money units. If the length of the yard is reduced by legal enactment from 3 feet to 2, so that a field which was formerly reckoned to be 100 yards long is now reckoned to be 150 yards long, it would be absurd to say that the increased size of the field has caused a fall in the length of the yard or that measuring with a smaller yard has caused the field to grow. We must similarly regard changes in the money valuation of things, including the money valuation of income, as caused by changes in the value of the money unit and not the other way round. Money affects money income because the value attached to its services by those who want to hold it affects the capital value of each unit (M being constant).[12]

But the rate at which the money is exchanged *may* vary considerably without the value placed upon it changing at all. At times, some people will be reducing their stocks of money rapidly while others will be accumulating money equally rapidly; and a little later the process may be reversed. In such circumstances, the more rapid *circulation* (increase in money transactions) results because a greater demand for monetary services by some is accompanied by a smaller demand by others. The aggregate demand for these services may well remain constant. The transfers of money are dependent upon the rate at which the *relative* productiveness of money assets to different individuals fluctuates; and because there is in general no greater demand for the services of money, if M is constant, the

---

[12] Expected changes in the value of the money unit are, as we have seen, among the factors which affect the productivity of the unit, and hence (unless they are offset by changes in M) they are a determinant of the value, M_r.

value of the money unit will not change and money income will be unaffected.

To sum up. What affects the value of the money unit and hence income measured in money terms is the value people attach to its services (its marginal productivity) and not the number of exchanges of money for nonmoney. *The ratio of exchange* of the money unit for other things in general is no more influenced by *the number of exchanges* (the rate of circulation) than the capital value of goods which are available for hire is determined by the average of the lengths of time for which they are hired.

If we cannot regard expenditure as a *determinant* of money income, still less can we regard money receipts as *constituting* money income. For it is not only the services that form income which are sold for money, but also assets. As I showed on p. 242, when I buy something from a shop, part of the money I pay remunerates services performed by the owner of the shop and by his assets. But he has already settled, or has contracted to settle, with those from whom he has acquired his inventories. Hence the rest of my payment is a mere exchange of *my* assets (money) for *his* assets (nonmoney). It is solely my purchase of retailing services which may be held *to record* (not cause) the money valuation of income.

To say that the whole of the sum I pay forms, or enters into, somebody's income is wrong. Income will already have been received by somebody for the whole of that part of my payment which does not remunerate the storekeeper. It is, I repeat, the prospective value of products which induces the purchase of valuable services, at various stages of production, for embodiment into the developing final product (including, of course, marketing and entrepreneurial services).

Admittedly, in a money economy we normally *sell* our own services and those of our assets, receiving wages, dividends, and interest. But as a rule this use of the monetary mechanism comes *after* the flow of income has accrued. Thus, the weekly wage earner's income is contributed, and accrues—as the right to wages—while his product is being received during the week by his employer. Similarly, those who enjoy income from property usually receive money for the services which their assets have contributed continuously to income, only once or twice in the course of a year. But they receive income as their claims to interest or dividends accrue.

Even in an imaginary complete money economy (that is, in which there are no transactions which resemble barter), one's income will be normally saved at first, accumulating as nonmoney assets, according to contract until the date at which wages, dividends, or interest is due; and then, in time for the due date, the assets into which income has been embodied will be converted into money. At that stage money begins to perform a service for the wage earner or investor, whoever has produced the income (as it has previously been performing—for a short time—a service for the *employer* of the worker or of the assets remunerated). Obviously, money receipts for services rendered (usually rendered some time previously) must equal *what income was at the moment when the contract to provide services was fulfilled.* But money is utilized merely for an instant *as a medium of exchange.* The payment of money does not imply a negative demand for money. It represents the cessation of demand for money by one and the beginning of such a demand by another. Hence although receipts of money *in payment for services* may be regarded as *roughly* corresponding to the money valuation of income in what I have called a "complete money economy," it is quite wrong to regard them as *representing* money income.

If there are many changes of ownership during the period in which services are being embodied into a product, more money will be needed than if all the processes are carried out within one firm. This *will* influence the demand for monetary services, and *ceteris paribus* it will have an influence upon the value of the money unit (and hence on the magnitude of the money valuation of income). But that does not justify our regarding money income as receipts.

Strictly speaking, we do not *spend* income. We *spend* assets—money, our stock of which is normally replenished by the sale of nonmoney services or assets. In the case of wage, interest, and dividend receipts from a firm, each worker, lender, or stockholder has his money inventories replenished by the firm purchasing the nonmoney contribution to output the income receiver already owns. The first stage of his income is the product (complete or incomplete) arising from the embodiment of his services and those of his capital into the assets stock.

There is, thus, no reason why money income as I have defined it should vary *in proportion* to aggregate money receipts from expenditure on the flow of nonmoney products. It will do so only when, in a complete money economy, and on balance, *no portion* of the flow of products *intended for ultimate sale,* including inventories of materials and work in progress, is being invested in or disinvested from. And the statement is then truistical. If every part of a money income of given value is being sold for money, obviously the receipts from such sales will be equal in value to money income.

Thinking of income *as money received* leads us to such apparent absurdities as the notion of the "circular flow of income." *Income does not circulate.* Income *flows* as output (the flow of services) for direct consumption or utilization in maintenance, replacement, or net accumulation of inventories of assets of varying economic life expectancies. It is money units which circulate. There *is* a flow of monetary services; and this flow, a service to the holder, ceases when he parts with money held! The confusion arises from the belief that money *renders services* (and affects money income) through its *circulation* (that is, its movement, or change of ownership). In reality, it renders services through being held.[13] Hence there is a subtle fallacy concealed in the simple statement that increased expenditure or an increase in money receipts either *causes* or *is* increased money income. But an increase in money spending power not accompanied by an equal increase in purchasing power *doe*s raise the money valuation of income.

The attempt to think of the money valuation of this flow of services as corresponding more or less to some measurable passage of money units from hand to hand has also been responsible for the idea that expenditure in different forms "generates" income because it "puts money into circulation"! The limits to a person's power to demand are fixed by his income and capital, not by his bank balance. Yet Robert Heilbroner says: "The economy does not operate to satisfy human *wants*—wants are always as large as dreams. It turns out goods to satisfy *demand*—and demand is as small as a person's pocketbook."[14] This passage summarizes beautifully the weakness of the Keynesians' thinking. They think of pocketbooks and purses, not of assets and outputs. In reality, a *person's* demands in the aggregate are as small as the value of his inputs (his own services and the services of his property) *plus* the value of that part of his property which he offers in exchange. His demands are virtually unrelated to that small part of his total assets which consists of money.

"The central characteristic of an economy," says Heilbroner, "is the flow of incomes from hand to hand. With every purchase that

---

[13] I referred above to the significance of the fact that, when we part with money, its services for us cease. See my "The Yield from Money Held," in Sennholz, ed., *On Freedom and Free Enterprise*.

[14] Robert Heilbroner, *The Great Economists* (1950), p. 222.

we make, we transfer a part of our incomes into someone else's pocket. Similarly, every penny of our incomes . . . derives from money someone else has spent. . . . Consider any portion of the income you enjoy and it will be clear that it has originated in someone else's pocket."[15] I charge that this notion is hopelessly wrong. When one purchases, one does not transfer *income* (the flow of services); one transfers capital—assets. And neither income nor assets originate in pockets: they originate in inputs which contribute to replacement of consumption or to growth. Indeed, I must repeat that we ought not to be said to buy with money unless we are reducing our investment in money. We buy out of capital, which our income normally replenishes.

I maintain, then, that the circulation of money, that is, mere payments and receipts of money, has no income-producing effects at all. The tendency to believe that expenditures must have this effect was simply but very effectively answered by J. B. Say, who wrote:

> It has been a matter of some doubt, whether the same value, which has already been received by one individual as the profit or revenue of his land, capital, or industry, can constitute the revenue of a second. For instance, a man receives 100 crowns in part of his personal revenue and lays it out into books; can this item of revenue, thus converted into books, and in that shape destined to his consumption, further contribute to form the revenue of the printer, the bookseller, and all the other concurring agents in the production of the books, and be by them consumed a second time? The difficulty may be solved thus. The value forming the revenue of the first individual, derived from his land, capital, or industry, and by him consumed in the shape of books, was not originally produced in that form. There has been a double production: (1) of corn perhaps by the land and the industry of the farmer, which has been converted into crown pieces, and paid as rent to the proprietor; (2) of books by the capital and industry of the bookseller. The two products have been subsequently exchanged one for the other, and consumed each by the producer of the others.[16]

In short, it is the production and not the expenditure which creates income.

Thus, while income may be, and usually is *measured* in terms of money units, it does not *consist* in the receipt of money units. To quote Say once more, "although the greater part of revenue, that is to

---

[15] Ibid., p. 217.
[16] J. B. Say, *Political Economy,* 4th ed., 2:82–83.

say, of value produced, is momentarily resolved into money, the money . . . is not what constitutes revenue. . . . Indeed, some portions of revenue never assume the form of money at all. . . ."[17] He specifically warned his readers against "confounding the money, into which revenue may be converted, with the revenue itself. . . ." "Property passing from one hand to another" forms, he said, no portion of annual revenue; and money he recognized as one form of property passing from hand to hand. The annual revenue consists solely of products (or as I would put it, services, usually embodied into assets), whether or not that revenue is originally received in the shape of money.[18]

To argue thus is not to miss the importance of transfers of money *as a link* in the causation of prosperity. It is to see the functioning of money in its correct relationship to the other phenomena of exchange. The heading of Chapter 16 in the fourth edition of Say's *Political Economy* reads as follows: "Of the benefits resulting from the brisk circulation of money and commodities." The benefits of rapid turnover are, he believed, of the same nature whether it is money or other assets which move. In a prosperous economy, goods (and hence money) are turning over continuously and rapidly. The process sometimes flags, Say suggested, through various "obstacles."

The confusion between *demanding,* that is, exercising preference between different ends and hence causing values to change, and the mere use of the money apparatus, that is, *spending,* has led even so rigorous an economist as Don Patinkin into quite unnecessary difficulties. He begins his book with the proposition that "money buys goods, and goods do not buy money,"[19] but he says that there is nothing logically wrong with procedures which regard goods as buying money, thus shifting "the center of emphasis from the markets for goods to the market for money. . . . The semantic liberty of saying that goods buy money and of describing, accordingly, a demand function for money" (which he thinks characterizes Keynesian and neoclassical economics) merely makes the demand function for money "the obverse of the demand function for goods."[20] I am criticizing what Patinkin *says,* not what I believe him to *mean.*

His jump from "spending" (in both senses) to "demand" is un-

---

[17] Ibid., p. 81.
[18] Ibid., p. 82.
[19] Don Patinkin, *Money, Interest, and Prices,* p. 1.
[20] Ibid.

justified. It is not merely a question of clumsiness. Both approaches are *wrong*. *Spending* on goods is not demanding them with money but demanding them with *capital* (replaced out of income) as a whole. Only if we *retain* smaller stocks of money (measured in real terms) because we are regarding nonmoney as more profitable than money, may we be said to be demanding additional nonmoney with money. Hence, an increased demand for goods (assets) from the offer of money (assets) occurs only when the aggregate real value of money is bid down (and M being constant, the purchasing power of the money unit is reduced). Similarly *selling goods is not demanding money*. But selling goods and *retaining* the money proceeds to add to one's existing stock of money *is* demanding additional money.

In short, the aggregate flow of nonmonetary services is not a *demand* for monetary services—it is simply the source out of which monetary services are demanded,[21] just as it is the *source* also out of which the demand for all other productive services is derived. Nor is the aggregate stock of nonmoney assets a *demand* for money. The proportion of the aggregate flow of nonmoney services (which together with monetary services constitutes income) which will be exchanged for monetary services is determined by preferences and entrepreneurial judgment, just as is the proportion of the aggregate flow which will be exchanged for the services which go into producing, say, wheat or plows. Moreover, as far as the stock of assets is concerned, through changing ends or changing judgments about the profitability of different means, the relative values of money and nonmoney assets may alter. *Ceteris paribus* a fall in the money value of peanuts is certainly a *contribution* to the source of demand for all *assets* which do not compete with peanuts (including money), and a fall in the value of the services devoted to producing peanuts is similarly a contribution to the source of demand for all *services* which are not devoted to producing peanuts (including monetary services in general). We cannot say more than this.

Patinkin is misled by his method. In order to make the simplified assumptions necessary for mathematical analysis, he asks us to assume that the only nonmoney goods which exist are provided miraculously and free, like manna from heaven,[22] with a fixed amount of money in the system of which each individual has a certain sum

---

[21] This does not of course prevent us from assuming, as I have indeed myself assumed (pp. 188–90), that the most important element in the demand for monetary services tends to vary in proportion to T.

[22] Patinkin, op. cit., p. 8.

carried over from the previous period.[23] Assuming then that the individual "will find it convenient and agreeable to hold a certain average real value of money," Patinkin argues that "if the individual's initial balances are for some reason increased above the level which he considers necessary, he will seek to remedy this situation by increasing his amounts demanded of the various commodities, thereby increasing his planned expenditures, and thereby drawing down his balances." The discovery by individuals generally that they have more money than needed causes an increase in demand for the nonmoney. Under his assumptions there certainly *is* such an increase with a consequential fall in the value of the money unit; and this is the only sense in which we can then talk of an increase in demand for nonmoney as a whole (if we assume also that the flow of the miraculously provided supplies of commodities remains constant).

If M is constant, the *desire* to disinvest from money *does* imply an increase in demand for nonmoney assets in money terms. But theoretically that can happen simply by a rise in prices without any money actually passing, that is, *without any spending*. What I have called M_r will contract under the new valuation. There will be inflation with M constant.

The notion that spending is a determinant of the money valuation of income or the actual origin of income lies at the root of one of the most subtle and serious fallacies in the Keynesian system, namely, the *multiplier*. The effects of an increase in M upon the money valuation of income are in no way multiplied simply as a result of the *passing on* of the increased units in successive purchases. Only (a) if *the relative demand* for monetary services falls (which is what is really meant by the phrase "an increase in the income velocity of circulation") or (b) if monetary policy is such that a secondary increase in M is induced, will there be any "multiplication." For M is policy determined and V is determined by valuations in the light of individual forecasts of the productivity or usefulness of money.

All the factors which the Keynesians are trying to understand or explain when they discuss the "multiplier," may be included, then, under V or M in the identity $MV \equiv PT$. If an initial increase in M ("newly created money") or in V ("newly activated money") must somehow result in a further increase in V or M (whether or not it is accompanied by an increase in T—which will mitigate any tendency for the value of the money unit to depreciate), that is the multiplier.

---

[23] Ibid., p. 16.

And any increase in V is simply an expression of the fact that money is being regarded as less productive or that monetary services are falling lower on people's scales of preference. The sole reason for short-term changes in such valuations (as far as I can imagine) must be either predictions about the intentions or consequences of monetary policy, which the initial increase in expenditure may have influenced, or the money illusion. Any increase in "velocity of circulation," in the conventional sense of the actual passage of currency or deposits from the ownership from one person to another, is a mere reaction to the changed value of the unit. If capacity is released by the initiating increase in V or M, a policy-induced increase in M may occur in the form of a noninflationary credit expansion.[24] (I return in Chapter 16 to possible repercussions upon M.)

The initial increase in expenditure, which the theory of the multiplier assumes, is the consequence of one of two circumstances which must be brought about: a reduced valuation is placed on the money unit (through reaction to an increase in M, or autonomously, or speculatively), MV increasing therefore in relation to T; or the valuation of the money unit does not change because, although MV increases, so does M_r (through an increase in T and/or in I).

$$\overline{V}$$

In the first case, when the reduced value placed on the money unit is a reaction to "newly created money" (an increase in M), the new valuation will emerge in the same way that, in the barter of apples for nuts, *either the fact or the prospect* of an exceptionally good harvest of apples will cause the value of apples to fall in terms of nuts. But it is *theoretically* possible that the money illusion will strongly influence the new valuation (that is, that people will desire to hold the same *nominal* value instead of the same *real* value in the form of money), forcing the value of the unit still lower. Most probably, however, as we have seen (pp. 244–45), the reaction to an increase in M, T being constant, will be a temporary decline in V. The changed real value of the money unit will only gradually become apparent, as people begin to reduce to the normal the real value of the money they wish to hold. As David Hume put it in the eighteenth century (in discussing an increase in the quantity of specie), "at first, no alteration is perceived; by degrees the price rises, first of one commodity, then of another; till the whole at last

---

[24] If this is what Keynes meant, he failed to make it clear.

reaches a just proportion with the new quantity of specie."[25] I shall develop this argument in Chapter 16 on the multiplier.

The rather subtle fallacy that expenditure produces money income would have done little harm if it had not been for the fact that, in the Keynesian treatment, it is merged into the theory that expenditure also produces real income, that is, output or employment (through inducing the release of capacity initially withheld by the pricing of inputs or outputs above market-clearing levels). Such an approach effectively hides the fact that real income is created—in the case assumed—not by spending (buying and selling) but by coordination through pricing, or by thrift—the net accumulation of productive power.

Even if it can be argued that circumstances are such that any tendency for the value of the money unit to fall will result in a release of capacity which has multiplied effects, it will still be misleading to say that increased *spending* multiplies income. An increase in uninflated demand is then occurring because the release of capacity in one field is inducing a similar release in some noncompeting field. And as I have already stressed, if capacity is being released, each rectifying expansion of credit implies an increase in both real and money income; for the additional services purchased had previously been allowed to run to waste.

In every case the creation of income has its origin in production. For instance, if the value of my services increases owing to a rise in the real demand for them, that permits me to produce the same income (measured in terms of what my services can command) with less effort or a greater income with the same effort. But the "generation" of income originates in each case in the production of output.[26] The increased real demand for my services will, of course, have had its origin either in a transfer of demand from the services of others, in which case no increase in *society's* real income will have been "generated," or in an increase of aggregate output in noncompeting fields, in which case the increased aggregate income will have been "generated" by the expansion of output elsewhere.

These are the only circumstances in which it can be argued that monetary factors *can* produce income without inflation. But as we

[25] Quoted in Gary S. Becker and William J. Baumol, "The Classical Monetary Theory: The Outcome of the Discussion," *Economica*, November 1952, p. 369.
[26] The rise in the real value of certain assets in such circumstances, the rate of interest being constant, I treat as a contribution to the flow of services, that is, as production. See p. 299.

have already noticed, if *all prices* are imagined as being absolutely rigid—upward as well as downward—then an increase in *MV* will, up to the point of full employment,[27] seem to determine the rate of flow of services, which will vary in proportion to the rate of expenditure. Expenditure will apparently produce real income *through releasing withheld capacity* as it produces money income. This is the situation which I discussed earlier (in connection with the Keynesian concept of "true inflation"), in which an initial deficiency in *MV* is tacitly assumed to have been caused by a purposeless deflation. But except as a rectification for *purposeless* deflation, noninflationary credit expansion cannot *induce* the release of capacity. It can merely *respond* to it.

We can perceive the effects of the bad Keynesian tradition upon non-Keynesian thinking in an attempt by F. W. Paish, 25 years ago, to persevere with the notion of money income as money receipts and yet to bring his concepts into consistency. In using this attempt as an illustration, I want to repeat that, until that time, I was trying to think along virtually the same lines myself. In July 1953 I discussed verbally some of the difficulties with Paish, and he showed me the script of his forthcoming article, "Open and Repressed Inflation." I thought then that his efforts to resolve the anomalies, and the efforts which I was making did not substantially diverge. I had already discerned at that time the great importance of recognizing the productiveness of money held; although in our discussion I criticized the concept of "idle balances," yet I had not seen how completely untenable are the notions of "income velocity" and income envisaged as a certain category of money receipts. I accordingly thought that his endeavor to trace through the history of a money unit via its various expenditures from its "creation" to its "cancellation" would provide a sort of clarification which was urgently needed. I believed that an analysis of that kind could show how the unit performed, in turn, valuable services for all who held it for different periods. I can now see that it ought to have led me to challenge the idea that any part of *expenditure* (as distinct from demand with "money's worth") creates income, either its money valuation or its "real" content.

In order to take account of *all* expenditures, which Paish realistically regards as essential in any study of the value of the money unit,

---

[27] Beyond the point of full employment, of course, an increase in *MV* must involve rationing or shortages (under the assumption of price rigidity upward).

he defines the cause of inflation as "an excess of total money payments over total money receipts."[28] Then, recognizing that receipts and payments must always be equal, he says: "I think, however, that we can overcome this conceptual difficulty if we think of receipts as occurring, not quite simultaneously with payments, but an instant later. We then get a lack of identity between payments and *previous* receipts."[29] But that assumption is invalid and dodges rather than solves the difficulty.

What he is really saying is that, having received money, we may (for instance) value its services more than we did the moment previously, so that we are then prepared to part with it (for non-money) only at lower prices. Yet this would still mean a decline in both payments *and* receipts in the future. Thus, while *individuals* may spend more money units than they are receiving (that is, run down their money inventories), society cannot do this. Society can merely change its judgment about the productivity of money, and hence *increase or decrease together* its rate of *receiving and paying* money for given *quanta* of other things in general. Of course, Paish understands this as well as I do. His difficulties arise solely because he is trying to make sense of a wholly fallacious concept of income. And this fallacy prevents him, I think, from perceiving the important truth that when, M being constant, society receives and spends money more rapidly, that it is the consequence of and not the cause of the fall in the "commodity value" people place on the money unit.

Throughout, while Paish believes that he is discussing the movement of money in the purchase of services (which is what I also originally thought could be termed the "income velocity of circulation"), he is in fact discussing (a) the value of services measured in terms of money (the magnitude of income being what it is and the value of the money unit being what it is), and (b) the factors which determine the measuring rod, the value of the money unit.

There is no logical way of distinguishing, in transactions which involve the use of money, those which affect the money valuation of income and those which do not. All transactions, *in the expectation of having to make which* we acquire money, influence the value M_r in the same sort of way, whether these prospective transactions are the purchase of services (income) or the purchase of assets (capital).

---

[28] F. W. Paish, "Open and Repressed Inflation," *Economic Journal,* 1953, p. 530.
[29] Ibid.

And, T and M being given, the determinants of M_r are also the determinants of money income. No fallacy can send our thinking astray more than the idea that it is possible to make a distinction between income-creating expenditure and other expenditure.

The very real harm to clarity of thought which can be traced to the conception of income as receipts, and its production as in some way due to decisions to spend, may be further illustrated by a consideration of the first report of the British Council on Prices, Productivity, and Incomes. The wisdom of Dennis Robertson shines through this report, which I regard as strongly anti-Keynesian. Yet the thinking on which it is based, as well as the exposition, has, I suggest, been vitiated by Keynesian notions. The Council said that "if prices rise in a country, *it must mean* that money paid out for all goods produced and imported has risen faster than the actual quantities of home-produced goods and services and imports."[30] (My italics.) This is quite correct and yet quite misleading! What it would have said, I suggest, in pre-Keynesian days is: "If prices rise in a country, so that people *are obliged to pay* more for the flow of goods and services, including those obtained in exchange from abroad. . . ." This would have removed the notion that the *payment* of money is one of the factors determining the value of the money unit. The Council said further that "it is clear that the relationship between the rise in real production and the rise in money incomes . . . is central to the problem of rising prices."[31] But the rise in the money valuation of income (real production being given) *is* the problem of rising prices. I must repeat that, in making this point, I run the risk of appearing hypercritical. But I am not hairsplitting. I believe that the Council's way of stating this proposition (in 1959) would never have been used by economists forty years previously; and it illustrates to me the manner in which *the modes of thinking* of nearly all modern economists, even those who are far removed from the Keynesian camp, have been handicapped by the Keynesian trend. Of course, during an inflation, people's income measured in actual money will increase more than in proportion to output measured in money units of constant purchasing power. But that *is* inflation. It is not its *cause*.

Through its wrong approach to the question, the Council was

---

[30] Cohen Council (Council on Prices, Productivity, and Incomes), Report 1, 1959, para. 24.

[31] Ibid., para. 33.

led to the conclusion that the cause of inflation is to be found in the pursuit of "a number of objectives arising naturally from the circumstances of the time, and in themselves desirable, but making in the aggregate a greater demand on the industry and thrift of its citizens than they have had the power or the will fully to satisfy."[32] But the pursuit of objectives—whatever the enthusiasms which may accompany it—is merely the choice of ends. The search for incompatible ends can never have any inflationary effect unless inflation is chosen as the means.

It is only fair to state that the passage just quoted is immediately followed by references to the postwar transition from latent to open inflation and the official policy of cheap money. But the Council still referred to the "full employment" policy as inflationary through encouraging businessmen "to maintain a high level of capital expenditure,"[33] which suggests to me that the Council confused the form taken by purchases—"expenditure"—under inflation with the causes of inflation itself. The fact that, during unanticipated inflations, wage rates and prices tend to be below their equilibrium values, so that there are a large number of vacancies for employment, is not, as the Council claimed, support for the view that "the level of demand" is an important factor in inflation.[34] Similarly, because the Council's approach stressed "excessive demand" rather than the determinants of the value of the money unit as the cause of inflation, it was lured into the "imported inflation" fallacy—the idea that a rise in the prices of imported goods and materials can be regarded as *the cause* of a rise in the general scale of prices. But if certain materials and products (those imported) increase in price and hence absorb a larger proportion of uninflated income and demand, other materials and products will be able to command correspondingly less, *in the absence of inflation.* (And, of course, in the absence of cumulative withholding of capacity.) If the Council had meant that, in the situation it envisaged, a further measure of inflation was likely to be regarded as politically expedient, the members ought to have expressed it that way. They argued as though a "sharp rise" in the prices of imports of food and raw materials justified an exception to their general advocacy of a stable general scale of prices.[35] Yet the

---

32 Ibid., para. 78.
33 Ibid., para. 80.
34 Ibid., para. 81.
35 Ibid., para. 105.

only case which can be made for such an exception is on the grounds that it is politically difficult to permit or enforce coordination through the price mechanism, so that resort must be had to the inflationary alternative. Curiously enough, the corollary of their suggestion, namely, that the average of prices should be allowed to fall in the case of a sharp fall in the world prices of food and materials, is not mentioned. Moreover, the same fallacy leads also to the notion that the removal of rent control could, in itself, cause a rise in the scale of prices.[36] But if rents rise on decontrol, and monetary policy is noninflationary, the prices of other constituents of the flow of services must decline or a cumulative withholding of capacity elsewhere must eventuate. The Council could certainly claim that influences in the United States were a factor in the British inflation; yet only on the grounds that, like most other currencies (apart, of course, from the devaluations of 1949), sterling was being kept, partly by controls but partly by market forces, at a fixed rate of exchange with a dollar which was depreciating in terms of purchasing power.

Finally, the same fallacious notion was responsible for the way in which the Council stated the argument of a certain "school of thought" to which they refer. It did so in the following confusing phrase: "If wages and other incomes are pushed up, the level of money expenditure will tend naturally to rise with them."[37] But if *certain* wage rates and prices are pushed up, in the absence of inflation other wage rates and prices will *fall,* or a cumulative withholding of capacity elsewhere must follow. If "wages and other incomes are pushed up," it may well make inflation expedient.

When the notion that spending creates or determines income is combined with the confusion of saving preference with liquidity preference (that is, when "saving" is defined as failing to spend all money income received), confusion becomes confounded. A good example of the extraordinary reversal of cause and effect which can result is to be found in R. G. Hawtrey's statement of a main thesis in his excellent study, *Towards the Rescue of Sterling.* He says: "Inflation and an adverse balance of payments are both attributable to *excessive spending*"[38] (my italics), by which he means "spending in excess of income"; and he believes that this is a phenomenon

---

[36] Ibid., para. 107.

[37] Ibid., para. 88.

[38] Ralph G. Hawtrey, *Towards the Rescue of Sterling* (London: Longmans, Green, 1954), p. vi.

which can be rectified by thrift. But spending in excess of *money* income is not *dissaving,* and attempts to curb inflation by appealing to the people *not to spend but to save* are hopelessly confusing to those to whom the appeals are made. *Spending and consuming are unrelated.* What *can* be legitimately contended is that an increased rate of saving will permit the maintenance of relatively low rates of interest and plentiful credit without inflation. For the individual, "spending in excess of money income" is simply raising the value of nonmoney assets in terms of money; such a valuation *need* not be accompanied by dissaving; and even if dissaving does accompany it, neither the spending nor the dissaving can be blamed for inflation. The dissaving *can* be blamed for raising noninflationary interest; for the situation means that a higher market rate of interest (that is, a contraction of credit) is essential in order to *avoid* inflation.

Admittedly, the phrase "spending in excess of money income" may be intended to mean that today's money income is larger than yesterday's although real income is constant, while the excess is not invested in an addition to money stocks. If so, what is implied is that inflation is "caused" by people not "hoarding" money as M increases! *Is it not remarkable how the phrases I am criticizing divert attention from the monetary and credit policy which is solely responsible for inflation?*

Of course, Hawtrey would not have wished to do this. I am criticizing the tools he has used rather than the use to which he has put these tools or the product which has emerged. He has in fact reached conclusions in respect of *policy* similar to those which I myself am urging. He recognizes that "excess spending" (in his sense) is "only possible if people have the *money* to spend, or facilities to procure it."[39] "Spending in excess of income presupposes a supply of money in excess of that received by way of income. If the supply of money is cut short, the spending becomes impossible."[40] That is the crucial reality which makes the spending itself merely incidental and robs the term "excess spending" of meaning. Hawtrey ends by recommending a severe contraction of credit and government borrowing, and the imposition of heavy taxation to *curtail private expenditure.*

Even so, his view of inflation caused by overspending disturbs his view of the responsibility for it; for he wants *government* spending to

---

[39] Ibid.

[40] Ibid., p. 40. The point is not rigorously expressed. The rate of spending is influenced by changes in M only insofar as they affect the value of the money unit. (See above, pp. 245–46.)

continue unchecked, and it seems to him that if this is to be achieved *without inflation,* private expenditure must be cut.[41] Hence, he appears to imply, private expenditure has to bear the blame for inflation. Of course the argument could be put, with equally challengeable logic, exactly the other way around. It could be said that state expenditure is responsible for inflation, which would be just as wrong.[42] What Hawtrey could have said is that the desire of the state to spend may be *an incentive to inflation;* but so equally may be the desire not to withhold from the people the *cheap money* which they have been encouraged to expect. The source of his error lies, I suggest, in the belief that "underlying the rise of prices, and preceding it, is the excess spending,"[43] as distinct from an excessive M (in relation to M_r).

If monetary policy ceased making inflated credit available, overt taxation and unprivileged government borrowing would be the only sources of state expenditure.[44] Once monetary policy is concerned solely with the maintenance of a defined value for the money unit, governments and private people may spend to their hearts' content, possibly not without disaster *if the spending is incidental to capital consumption,* but certainly without inflation.

There is one further point relevant to income production which needs to be noticed. All assets, however short their economic life expectancies, are prospective income producers; for unless they offer a predictable income stream, they will be valueless. All valuable things apart from services which are not embodied into valuable things but consumed as they are rendered are income-producing. There are some cases in which many economists have difficulty in perceiving this. For instance, the income derived from unsold inventories in a store or warehouse is an example. In this case, the valuable services provided are in the form of time utilities, availability utilities, assembly utilities, storage utilities, preservation utilities (for example, refrigeration), and so forth. As in all cases of production, the provision of such marketing services requires fixed assets (the site of the store, the store itself); inventories of goods offered for sale, etc.; all these services, including those of shop assistants, ac-

---

41 Ibid., p. vii.

42 Of course, *the way in which* the state obtains funds for expenditures *is* often responsible for inflation!

43 Ibid., p. 13.

44 Apart from the revenues of nationalized industries.

countants, "buyers," and the like; and all "transactions costs"[45] are paid for out of the "margins of mark-up." Hence the production of what are sometimes called "consumer services," but more often and better called "marketing services," contributes to income in the same sort of way that the machines in a factory and the artisans who work in it create income. The production of any commodity is incomplete until the value of every one of these services has been incorporated into it. (The value of entrepreneurial services may of course be negative.)

Income is produced by the factors which determine output—the flow of productive services. And the money valuation of income is, in turn, determined by the factors which are responsible for the value of the money unit, in short, by monetary policy.

---

[45] The concept of "transactions costs" is important but rather elusive. The term has by no means a standard connotation in the literature. It could refer to the costs of defining and registering ownership rights, for example, as in real estate transactions. Sometimes it is the same thing as "selling costs." Sometimes it refers to "marketing costs." Sometimes it covers the costs of information, and sometimes it refers to the costs of being persuaded.

12

Are Price Adjustments
Self-Frustrating?

In Chapter 5 I placed great stress on Benjamin M. Anderson's phrase, "Prices have work to do. Prices should be free to tell the truth." It is curious that I should have thought this to be necessary, or that there could be any object in my explaining the social purpose of price changes. For there has been no controversy among serious economists about the desirability of a system which tends to ensure that different kinds of prices shall stand in a certain optimal relation to one another, or about the desirability, in a changing world, of continuous *relative* price adjustment in order to bring about some conformance to the ideal relation. From the "socialist economists" of the Lange-Lerner type to the "individualist economists" of the Mises-Röpke type, there had been, prior to *The General Theory,* almost universal agreement that the price system had important equilibrating and coordinative functions. There was growing recognition, I think, that changes, and especially those changes effected by entrepreneurial planning (that is, economizing in committing resources to long-term uses), normally entailed the unemployment of certain marginal resources *especially in their existing uses.* There would have been a gap in my exposition for many readers if I had not dealt explicitly with the need for coordination to dissolve, by price changes, the continuously caused unemployment which is the inevitable attribute of any society in which demands are changing and income is growing. Nevertheless, until the appearance of Keynes' *General Theory,* in 1936, the measure of agreement about the *aims* of institutional reform for the better working of the price system seemed to be slowly but definitely growing. There was not the same marked tendency toward agreement about *methods.* Some thought that improved pricing could be achieved through a greater centralization or sectionalization of economic power, with the final voice to decide both preferences (choice of ends) and productive policy (choice of means) entrusted to elected representatives or syndicates. Others thought that the required reforms involved exactly the reverse —the breaking up and diffusion of economic authority so that the final voice about ends rested with the people as consumers, while the final voice about the choice of means rested with those who stood to gain or lose according to the success with which they allocated scarce resources in accordance with consumer-determined ends. But in spite of this apparently basic clash, as soon as explicit plans for the devising of a workable economic system were attempted, even the divergence of opinion about methods appeared to be narrowing. The "socialist economists" were clearly attempting to restore *the market* and the *power of substitution*. So much was this so, that I believed the results of their labors would ultimately be the rebuilding of laissez-faire institutions, in elaborate disguises of name and superficial form, the result being regarded as the perfect socialist pricing system.[1]

This interesting trend toward unanimity of opinion in several fields was overlapped by and rudely broken by *The General Theory*. Since 1936, the economists have become sharply divided about the nature of the price changes which ought, in the interests of "full employment," to take place in any given situation.[2] Consider labor union or government-enforced wage rates. At one extreme, we have the Keynesians who argued initially that, in maintaining wage rates, we were maintaining consumer demand, creating a justification for new investment, and so preventing the emergence of depression. At the other extreme, we have those who argue that each successive increase of wage rates so brought about renders essential a further element of inflation in order to maintain "full employment"—a development which tends permanently to dilute the purchasing power of the money unit.

---

[1] In a discussion with Abba P. Lerner about 1933, I pointed out to him that, however opposed our approaches might seem superficially to be, the institutions which we were seeking would, in the end, turn out to be exactly the same things. He refers to this conversation in the preface to his *Economics of Control: Principles of Welfare Economics* (New York: Macmillan, 1944).

[2] Today, says Jacob Viner, different groups of economists "give diametrically opposite advice as to policy when unemployment prevails or is anticipated." See Jacob Viner, "The Role of Costs in a System of Economic Liberalism," in *Wage Determination and the Economics of Liberalism* (Washington: Chamber of Commerce of the United States), p. 31.

The Keynesian theory on this point proved enormously attractive. The idea as such was not novel; but before *The General Theory* it had enjoyed a negligible following in respectable economic circles. After 1936, it gave many economists what they seemed to have been waiting for, a noncasuistic argument for the tolerance of the collusive enforcement or government fixation of standard or minimum wage rates.

Curiously enough, Keynes' challenge was based on a sort of admission of the evils of collective bargaining and a further admission (by no means explicit, but an inevitable inference)[3] that labor in general was unable to benefit in real terms, at the expense of investors, by forcing a rise in the price of labor. Gains achieved by individual groups of organized workers were paid out of the pockets of other workers.[4] At the same time, Keynes' new teachings seemed to support strongly those who cried, "Hands off the unions!" Although his thesis was accompanied by the charge—not wholly without foundation—that other economists had closed their eyes to the consequences of the wage rigidity caused by labor union action, he always seemed to range himself on the side of the unions in their resistance to wage-rate adjustments. The reasons for his views on this question were twofold.

First, he argued that the price of labor had to be regarded as *inevitably* rigid.[5] This empirical judgment about economic reality is, of course, not confined to the Keynesians. Where Keynes was original was in *the weight* he placed on the subsidiary and supporting assumption that what other economists have called "the money illusion" is a basic cause of the rigidity.[6]

---

[3] Compare Arthur Smithies' statement of the implications of *The General Theory:* "Concerted action by the whole labor movement to increase money wages will leave real wages unchanged. Real wage gains by a single union are won at the expense of real wages elsewhere." "Effective Demand and Employment," in Harris, ed., *The New Economics*, p. 561.

[4] This theory is a counterpart of the theory that organized labor is unable to *reduce* the real price of labor. I return to this suggestion shortly (p. 271).

[5] A subsidiary argument seems to imply that such rigidity is justifiable on *ethical* grounds. "A *relative* reduction in real wages" on the part of a group, said Keynes, "is a sufficient justification for them to resist it." (*The General Theory,* p. 14.) Because of the absurdity of the implications, we should perhaps assume that Keynes meant, "the unions in fact regard it as a sufficient justification."

[6] Earlier economists were certainly aware of the illusion. Cannan once put it this way: "The ordinary person's feelings are outraged by any change in prices which tells against him more than they are gratified by a change in his favor. If his wages are doubled at the same time as the prices of the things he has been accustomed to buy rise by one-half, he will not be thankful for the actual

Second, he argued that, in any case, wage-rate flexibility downward, even if other prices are flexible, will aggravate and not alleviate depression. For even under perfect wage-rate flexibility and perfect price flexibility generally, the equilibrium achieved would not be inconsistent with unemployment. He would have preferred to rely wholly upon the second argument. But he kept the first, as Schumpeter has put it, "on reserve."

These two propositions are very much confused in his exposition and it is usually difficult to know, at any point, on which proposition he was relying. The exceptions are in passages which are rather puzzling when related to the rest of his argument, as on pages 191 and 267 of *The General Theory.* One is never quite certain when wage-rate rigidity or price rigidity is assumed and when it is not. Even before *The General Theory,* he often wrote as though his propositions would apply under the most perfect price adjustment (although he made no explicit attempt to justify such a position), whereas at other times he was clearly relying upon the failure of the price coordinating mechanism. The same applies to his disciples.

Now it is one thing to argue that wage-rate flexibility does not exist. It is another thing to argue that we should not tackle the problem of creating it. On this point the Keynesians seem often to be either silent or dogmatic. When they touch on the subject, they usually do so briefly, or in passages of great obscurity.[7]

Keynes himself had expressed the idea—almost as though it were self-evident—for some time before he provided the sophisticated theoretical justification to be found in *The General Theory.* Thus, in 1931, in a report to the British prime minister on the United States slump, Keynes reported (according to Harrod) that "wage rates had not been much reduced—this was a satisfactory point"[8] (Harrod's words). Satisfactory to whom? To the British, whose fear of United States competition would be mitigated and who would be under a reduced compulsion therefore to tackle their problem of labor costs? Or satisfactory to the people of the United States? Most pre-

---

rise in his real wages, but will be infuriated by the belief that somebody has cheated him out of part of his rights." Cannan, *An Economist's Protest,* p. 136.

[7] The *policy implications* have never been obscure. Thus, Leon Keyserling (then a member of the Council of Economic Advisers) actually urged labor unions in the United States, during 1949, to press for increased wage rates in order to boost effective demand and prevent unemployment.

[8] Harrod, *The Life of John Maynard Keynes,* p. 438.

Keynesian teaching would, I think, have answered without hesitation: "It is against the advantage of both. Readjustment of labor costs in the U.S. economy will restore the real contribution of American demands to world demands, which are so much needed today. In the current resistance to wage-rate adjustment in the United States, encouraged by Herbert Hoover and Franklin Roosevelt, we have the principal reason for the failure of the flow of uninflated dollar income rapidly to recover."

Keynes' influence (whether great or small at that time) was, I suggest, thrown in on the side of the continuance of depression in the United States itself and indirectly in the world.

The lines along which he was thinking emerge a little more clearly in the argument which he put before the Macmillan Committee to the effect that wage-rate adjustment in one country might force similar adjustments in other countries and lead to a "vicious circle of competitive wage-rate reductions."[9] Such a policy would, he contended, enable the country making the wage cut to capture a larger proportion of world trade, but that country would simply gain at the expense of the rest. In fact, his fear of the "disastrous process of competitive international wage-cutting" was not accompanied by any clear explanation of why openly obtained reductions of money wage rates should have any worse international effects than the disguised undercutting brought about by inflation, or by protection with dumping.

Was he not expressing here fears of *a vicious circle of increasing world demands,* that is, of world output? And is it not typical of the underlying idea in so much of Keynes' teachings—his *fear of plenty?*[10] In the passage just quoted, it is in the form of the notion that there is only a fixed lump of international trade in the world, so that if one country gets more, some other country will have to be content with less. The fallacy rests on the failure (which I have discussed at length in my *A Rehabilitation of Say's Law*) to recognize that every rise in an output is adding to the source of demands for noncompeting outputs. The truly vicious circle is that produced through the attempt to adjust to change by the withdrawal of outputs and therefore of real demands. And in the international sphere this is seen in the pushing up of tariff protection, or the enactment of quotas or exchange controls in response to or in retaliation against

---

[9] Quoted in ibid., p. 425.
[10] I discuss this fear of Keynes in Chapter 14.

tariff protection, import quotas, exchange controls, etc., imposed by other countries.[11] (See above, pp. 155–57.)

I cannot help feeling that these ideas of Keynes in some way had a considerable influence in the United States at the time. Indeed, the NRA episode appears almost as though it was an attempt to test in practice what Keynes had been teaching on this specific point. It was the most deliberate and clear-cut experiment at increasing business activity by the raising of labor costs. This policy was inherited from Hoover and developed by Roosevelt in the middle of 1933. What was the result? The Federal Reserve Index of Industrial Production dropped from 100 in July to 72 in November![12] NRA had, in fact, reversed the rapid credit-fed recovery which had lasted from March until July of that year; and the resumption of recovery had to wait until the Supreme Court had ruled the NRA unconstitutional, in May 1935. It seems probable that, had the NRA codes been strictly enforced, the adverse effects upon business activity would have been even worse.[13] And far from the constructional industries having benefited, as Keynesian theory would have supposed, they were exceptionally heavily hit.[14]

Of course it will be argued that Roosevelt went much *too far* with perfectly sound policies. But if a policy is sound it ought to be possible to define just how far it should go. If costs can constitute demand in any sense, there ought to be a clear answer to the question: To exactly what extent, or under what conditions, ought labor costs to be raised in order to create additional demand (presumably for noncompeting things) when resources are not being fully utilized? One seeks in vain for an answer to this question in the Keynesian literature; and it is truly astonishing that Keynes learned nothing from the bitter experience of NRA.

Keynes does seem, however, to have recognized that his earlier

---

[11] These are all developments which Keynes failed to foresee in advising the Macmillan Committee, developments the importance of which he subsequently tended to minimize or actually to defend.

[12] Anderson, *Economics and the Public Welfare,* p. 334.

[13] In fighting for survival, large numbers of small firms completely disregarded the codes. This took place on so wide a scale in many districts that it was impossible to take effective action against them. The result was that those firms and districts which showed an old-fashioned respect for the law often suffered huge losses and insolvencies; whereas those firms and districts which treated the law with contempt managed to survive and even prosper.

[14] Ibid., pp. 338–39 (citing Charles Frederick Roos, who was formerly director of research of the NRA).

explanations were unsatisfactory; yet he could not get rid of his hunch; and in *The General Theory*—in difficult and obscure passages—he enunciated a number of subtle objections to attempts to secure coordination with price adjustment.

The chief argument to this effect is that wage-rate cuts must in any case be ineffective, as a means of restoring employment in labor, because it is possible to cut money rates only and not real wage rates. Reduced money wage rates, he argued, bring reduced prices, reduced money income, reduced wages in the aggregate, and reduced effective demand. Hence the wage-rate rigidity which former economists had been inclined to criticize ought, in his opinion, to be regarded as a virtue in times of depression. Cuts in wage rates, through causing prices to fall, reduce prospective profits and cause the profitability of offering employment to decline. Exposition on the point is far from clear. Burrows interpreted Keynes' position—quite fairly, I think—as follows: "Since lower money wages would reduce marginal costs, competing producers would reduce prices. Thus real wages and profits would not be changed and employers would not be encouraged to offer any additional employment."[15]

At three points, Keynes appeared to have some misgivings about this thesis. He admitted, first, that if the real price of labor *could* be flexible, things would be different; that is, if it were "always open to labor to reduce its real wage by accepting a reduction in its money wage. . . ." This condition assumed, he said, "free competition amongst employers and *no restrictive combinations amongst workers.*"[16] (My italics.) And he explicitly admitted later that, if there were competition between unemployed workers, "there might be no position of stable equilibrium except in conditions consistent with full employment. . . ."[17] But he did not attempt to reconcile these passages with apparently contradictory passages. Here it looks almost as though, after all, he was admitting that restrictions on price adjustment must be held responsible. Finally (but this he meant as a special case), he thought that in some circumstances wage-rate cuts could create a *psychological* boost favorable for recovery.[18]

We are left, then, with the principal contention, namely, that changes in wage rates are "double-edged," affecting both individual

---

[15] H. R. Burrows, *South African Journal of Economics,* September 1952, p. 249.
[16] Keynes, op. cit., p. 11.
[17] Ibid., p. 253.
[18] Ibid., pp. 264–65.

outputs and general demand.[19] As this infectious doctrine was developed by Keynes' disciples, costs as a whole were no longer regarded as merely *limiting* output, but as *calling forth* output through demand. But it is *the flow of services priced, at all stages of the production process, for full market-clearance; (a) for absorption into direct consumption, (b) for embodiment in assets of varying life expectancy, each replacing (partially or fully) the value of concurrent consumption, or adding to the aggregate real value of assets which is the source of all demands for noncompeting outputs.*

Moreover, there is no reason why *prices in general* should fall, through downward price adjustments toward values consistent with market clearance. This will happen only if T increases in relation to MV.[20] Price adjustment cannot cause a decline in the scale of prices for any other reason. And because M is policy-determined, in the absence of a purposeful deflation, there is no reason why M should not rise so as to maintain T. It must be remembered that the only downward cost adjustments which defenders of price flexibility advocate are those which are market-selected and hence must always (a) increase real income, and (b) increase money income under any system in which the purchasing power of the money unit is maintained constant.

It is because the Keynesians have failed to perceive the meaning of *coordination* through price adjustment (treated in Chapter 7) that they think of price cutting as income cutting.[21] *But far from this*

---

[19] What seems to be a variant of this proposition is a wholly contradictory assumption in *The General Theory,* namely, that reductions of wage rates will not restore employment because marginal costs *will rise* with increasing outputs. But if real wage rates have been fixed too high for full employment (which is ultimately Keynes' assumption), then presumably the cooperant resources which the unemployed labor previously used must also have been left idle. Keynes was *assuming* relatively full employment of other resources. In fact, such an assumption can be maintained only with the support of a mass of other unrealistic assumptions. As, however, this line of reasoning in support of the proposition appears to have been finally abandoned by Keynes in his 1939 retreat in the *Economic Journal, it is unnecessary to deal further with it.* See his "Relative Movements of Real Wages and Output," *Economic Journal,* March 1939, pp. 34–51.

[20] Very early in my thinking about the nature of economic coordination, I realized that "every contrived scarcity involves an incidental plenitude." This implies that *ceteris paribus* every reduction of a "contrived scarcity price" causes some "incidental plenitude prices" to rise.

[21] This must not be confused with a much more sophisticated argument, attributed to Paul Douglas, to the effect that if higher rates are forced, employers will be able to demand inflation successfully (alleged by Frank H. Knight in his essay, "Economics and Ethics of the Wage Problem," in David

price cutting defeating the process of restoring the flow of income, it is an essential link in its restoration. If we concentrate attention upon wages, it can be said that the reductions of money wage rates needed are such as are likely to increase the flow of uninflated wages, although *statically considered,* not necessarily (or even probably) in any industry making the adjustment. (See pp. 274–76.) For, on the reasonable assumption that the growth of real income will not mean a large redistribution against the *relative* advantage of the wage earners, the effect of the wage-rate reductions which are advocated must always mean an *absolute* increase and not a decrease in aggregate wages received, and increasing demands for wage goods.[22]

Let us now return to the notion of *the* price of labor. In reality, we are concerned with the prices of different kinds of labor, while the index-number concept of "the wage level" screens off from scrutiny all the issues which seem to me to be important.[23] Throughout Chapter 19 of *The General Theory,* Keynes talked simply of "reduction of money wages." And he discussed the pre-Keynesian view of the desirability of price adjustments as though it were based on a "demand schedule for labor in industry as a whole relating the quantity of employment to different levels of wages."[24]

Through thus thinking rather uncritically about aggregates, Keynes appears to have *assumed* that wage-rate reductions imply reduction of aggregate earnings,[25] irrespective of whether the labor price which

---

McCord Wright, ed., *The Impact of the Union: Eight Economic Theorists Evaluate the Labor Union Movement* (New York: Harcourt, Brace, and Company, 1951), pp. 80–110.

[22] The attempt to handle the problem (a) in terms of *income conceived as money receipts* (see Chapter 11), instead of as the money valuation of the flow of services, and (b) in terms of the crude concept of *"the* price of labor" (see pp. 111–12) was, I am inclined to think, partly responsible for Keynes' confusions.

[23] Compare criticisms of "the wage level" concept by Robert A. Gordon, who refers to "the concentration of attention upon aggregates and upon distressingly broad and vaguely defined index-number concepts—with insufficient attention being paid to those interrelationships among components which may throw light on the behavior of these aggregates. . . ." *American Economic Review, Papers and Proceedings,* May 1948, p. 354.

[24] Keynes, *The General Theory,* p. 259.

[25] It is an interesting commentary on the uncritical nature of current assumptions that Jacob Viner felt it necessary to remind economists at one time that it does not necessarily follow, "and I think that many economists have taken that step without further argument," that an increase of wage rates at a time of unemployment will increase the payroll. "An increase of wage rates may quite conceivably reduce the payroll." Op. cit., p. 32.

is cut is that of workers in an exclusive, well-paid trade, or that of workers in suboptimal pursuits, doing poorly paid work because they are excluded from well-paid opportunities.[26]

When the Keynesians *do* think of adjustments in individual wage rates, then, they usually think of blanket changes. At one point Keynes objected to price flexibility as a remedy for idleness in labor on the grounds that "there is, as a rule, no means of securing a simultaneous and equal reduction of money wages in all industries."[27] But it is not *uniform* reductions which are wanted; it is selective reductions, the appropriate selection of which can be entrusted to markets when nonmarket *minima have* been adjusted.[28] The most depressive influences upon the source of demands in general are caused by wage rates forced above market-clearing levels; nearly always this occurs in a minority of occupations in which the demand for labor is highly inelastic. Hence equal percentage wage-rate reductions, or standard ceilings imposed by edict, or policies which in any way have a similar effect, are not only unjust, penalizing the innocent as well as the guilty, but merely crudely coordinative in their aggregate effects. Market-selected adjustments, on the other hand, tend to benefit the innocent and penalize the guilty.

Even if equiproportional wage cuts *were* enacted, however, in a regime in which there was much unemployment, uninflated aggregate and average earnings might still tend to increase, owing to the redistribution of workers over the different wage-rate groups. If it were not for union exclusiveness, it would become profitable to employ more in the higher-paid types of work, while in the lower-paid types there would have to be rationing.[29] Keynes' static, short-term methods exclude consideration of these reactions.[30] Clarity will not

---

[26] *Average* real wage rates may be expected to rise during a recovery brought about by downward adjustment of nominal wage rates. Several economists have referred to empirical evidence that demand for labor is highly elastic under conditions of unemployment. Unless that evidence is for some reason misleading, average real earnings must, under depression conditions, rise through market-selected downward wage-rate adjustments.

[27] Keynes, op. cit., pp. 264, 269. It was partly this which led Keynes to argue that wage-rate adjustment would be possible only in a communist or fascist state.

[28] Actually, Pigou has shown that equiproportional wage cuts, even under Keynes' other assumptions, must mean increased employment of labor if the reaction is a reduction of the rate of interest. Pigou suggested that this reaction is "fairly likely." See his "Money Wages in Relation to Unemployment," *Economic Journal*, March 1938, p. 137.

[29] For simplicity, I am assuming that *maxima* are enacted.

[30] The possibilities of transfers of workers from low-paid to high-paid work are

be gained while we try to think in terms of "wage levels." We have to think in terms of changing frequency distributions. This is important enough for the consideration of employment in individual industries, but still more important in relation to employment as a whole.

The Keynesian argument is that it is no use cutting the wage rates of say, carpenters, if there is unemployment among them because, even if *their* employment fully recovers, their incomes and expenditure will fall and so cause the demand for the labor of other workers to fall.[31] But the case for price flexibility by no means assumes that a moderate fall in carpenters' wage rates, together with a corresponding fall in the price of the product, will, in itself, greatly increase the employment—still less the money income—of *carpenters.* Such a reaction, although *possible,* is unlikely. Moreover, while wage-rate and price adjustments are required to dissolve withheld capacity among carpenters, to adopt that remedy *in individual trades* and on a small scale would bring severe distributive injustices in its train. Indeed, the aggregate wage receipts of the larger number employed in any trade *might* be smaller than before the increased employment.

The correct proposition can be put this way. Under conditions of widespread unemployment through general pricing of labor and outputs above market-clearing levels, *increased employment among carpenters can be most easily induced as the result of wage-rate and price reductions on the part of those persons who ultimately buy the carpenters' services.* The assumption is that the reductions raise real market-clearing wage-rate levels in the industries which do not compete with carpenters, while the increasing flow of products contributes to the source of (a) real demands and (b) money demands through concurrent noninflationary monetary expansion. *This* is the argument which the Keynesians should answer.

In all this discussion, however, the simple truth that the magnitude *M* ("the nominal money supply") is policy-determined ought always to be regarded as the crucial reality. The fear that reductions of input prices or output prices in the market-clearing direction would exert a deflationary influence is based on the assumption that the increase in real income is confronted with monetary rigidity. But why *should* we always assume monetary rigidity? Monetary expansion ought of course always to be cautious, even in deflationary conditions, but

---

magnified in the long run, because it will be possible to train for the well-paid employment opportunities which are brought within reach of income.

[31] Boulding has used this actual example and argument. See his *Economics of Peace,* pp. 141–42.

caution does not mean inactivity. The acceptance of the obligation to maintain a money unit of defined value would mean that M would tend always to change in proportion to M_r in sufficient measure to reduce to a minimum those market-enforced wage-rate and price adjustments required for the honoring of that obligation. For no monetary standard would ever be adopted that did not offer reasonable prospective stability of purchasing power in the money unit. But the significance of this simple truth will never influence policy until it is generally perceived that the phenomena of unemployment and depression are pricing, not demand phenomena.[32]

But pre-Keynesian economics (as I understand it) did not overlook what was later called "the income effect." The tacit assumption[33] was that the monetary system was of such a nature that the increased real income due to the release of productive power in individual trades (through the acceptance of lower wage rates) would result not in a reduction but in an increase of money income. No one suggested that the monetary system *had* necessarily to be like that; but from the actual working of the credit system (when previous inflation had not made a rectifying deflation necessary), it seemed to be unnecessary to consider the case in which an expansion of production would not be accompanied by an increase in money income induced by this expansion. The assumption on which Keynes built his rigorous analysis, namely, that M (the number of money units) is constant, would have seemed absurd to most pre-Keynesian economists, unless they were considering the economics of a community so primitive that a fixed number of tokens (shells, for instance) served as the sole medium of exchange, while no lending or credit of any kind existed.

In a credit economy, it was believed, there could never be any difficulty, due to the mere fact that outputs had increased, about purchasing the full flow of production at ruling prices. That is, expanding real income could not, in itself, have any price-depressing tendencies. Only monetary policy was believed to be able to explain

---

[32] This is not, of course, a denial that unanticipated inflation can, though crudely and unjustly, facilitate the required price adjustments, and that deflation can hinder the required adjustments and cause them to be more painful. See pp. 124–25.

[33] Some economists in the pre-Keynesian era, in attempting to deal with the relations of employment and wage rates, made *explicit,* highly simplified assumptions consistent with the assumption as I have worded it, for purposes of abstract analysis. But I do not know of any economist who has stated the fundamental assumption as I have done. Quite possibly the point was made.

that. But given any monetary policy, they believed that unemployment of any type of labor was due primarily to wage rates being wrongly related to demand for the product of that labor. It followed that downward adjustments of wage rates and prices which had been imposed by private or governmental coercion could never *aggravate* —on the contrary would always *mitigate*—the consequences of any inadvertent deflationary tendency caused by monetary policy.

Hence, the wage-rate adjustments needed to restore employment (when overpricing of labor in certain sectors is the cause of current unemployment) do not mean a continuing decline in the average of prices, as the Keynesians so often assume. Not only do such cost and price reductions bring a larger flow of products within reach of existing money income, thus permitting noninflationary credit expansion, but every reduction in one price releases purchasing power for noncompeting purposes. In short, far from reduced wage rates causing a contraction in the flow of real or money wages, the effect is to *increase* the uninflated earnings of labor.

At this stage the objection can be expected that I am ignoring the need for a rectifying deflation following a period of inadvertently cheap money. I am not. Nor am I denying that a *primary* deflation may induce a *secondary* deflation. But as we have seen, speculative demand for money—"postponement of demand" for nonmoney with self-perpetuating consequences—arises when current costs or prices are higher than anticipated costs or prices, while *the speculation assists correctly discerned policy.*

In more general terms, expected changes in costs or prices, unaccompanied by immediate cost and price coordination to meet expectations, lead to "secondary" reactions. A *cut in costs* docs not induce demand postponement; nor, indeed, do *falling costs* necessarily have this effect. Postponements arise because it is judged that a cut in costs (or other prices) is less than will eventually have to take place, or because the rate of fall of costs (or other prices) is insufficiently rapid. It follows that "secondary" deflations are attributable to *the unstable rigidities* which prevent the continuous adjustment of the scale of prices to the level at which policy is believed to be aiming.[34] If speculative demand for money accompanies the downward adjustment of wage rates and it is not offset by credit expansion, a rectifying

---

[34] Although Keynes never got near to perceiving this broad generalization, he appeared at one point, in a passage which it is difficult to reconcile with most of his argument, to recognize it. See his reference to the restoration of a depressed economy by drastic wage-rate cuts, in *The General Theory,* pp. 265–66.

deflation must be in progress. (See pp. 106–7, 126–27, 148, 200.)

Now when, for any reason, a change in the value of the money unit becomes the declared object of policy, or the expected consequence of policy, *the whole price system is immediately thrown out of coordination*. Thus, if the value of the money unit is expected to rise, then until the necessary adjustments have all taken place, "willingness to buy" must necessarily fall off—most seriously where values of services and materials in the investment goods industries[35] do not at once respond.[36] It is really superfluous, I feel, to have given as much attention as I have to so crude and wasteful a method of curbing secondary inflation; for a rectifying credit expansion is always possible. There is never any good reason why central banks cannot control the magnitude M so that MV is in constant relation to T, even though the most formidable and dangerous *latent* inflation might, theoretically, be built up. But defensible policy would then require recognition of, and hence powerful warnings of, the danger, with insistence upon the highest measure of liquidity in the investment portfolios of the banking system. That being so, as V returned to normal, each successive increase in V could be offset by concomitant contractions of M, yet deflationary pressures ("credit shortage") avoided, just as open inflation had been previously avoided.

I turn now to a variant of the theory that price adjustment induces a speculative decline in V, namely, the suggestion that, in certain circumstances, there exists an infinitely elastic demand for money. The emergence of this notion appears to reflect the realignment of Keynesian ideas on this topic following attempts of disciples like Lange, Smithies, Tobin, Samuelson, Modigliani,[37] and Patinkin to defend or strengthen the new creed. Successive refinements which they have introduced have gradually paved the way for the ultimate abandonment, by would-be Keynesians, of the view that wage-rate

---

[35] That is, industries producing assets of relatively long life expectancies.

[36] This is no conclusive argument against policies seeking to increase the value of the money unit, as tardy rectifications of the distributive injustices of inflations. Nor is it a good argument against rectifying price disharmonies which have been allowed to develop and strain the ability to honor convertibility obligations.

[37] It may be unfair to describe Modigliani as a Keynesian, and Patinkin has moved still further from Keynesian teaching since 1948. Indeed, the implications of the latter's treatment are devastating. It is difficult to pick out the other non-Keynesian economists who have been most influential on the point at issue; but Marget, Knight, Friedman, Haberler, Machlup, Viner, Simons, F. A. Lutz, and Clark Warburton must take much of the credit.

and price adjustments are powerless to secure full employment. The contributions of some of these very friendly critics, said Joseph Schumpeter, "might have been turned into serious criticisms" if they had been "less in sympathy with the spirit of Keynesian economics."[38] He added that this is particularly true of Modigliani's contribution. Schumpeter could have made the same remark about a contribution of Patinkin on the same issue, which appeared two years later. But the criticisms of these writers *were* very serious in any case. The apparent reluctance of some of them to abandon standpoints which their own logic was urging them to reject, clouded their exposition; but it did not weaken the implications of their reasoning.

Modigliani (whose article[39] quietly caused more harm to the Keynesian thesis than any other single previous contribution) seems, almost unintentionally, to reduce to the absurd the notion of the coexistence of wastefully idle resources and price flexibility. He does this by showing that its validity is limited to the position which exists when there is an *infinitely elastic* demand for money ("the Keynesian case"). Modigliani does not regard this extreme case as absurd, and, indeed, declares that interest in such a possibility is "not purely theoretical."[40] Pigou regarded the contemplation of this possibility as a mere academic exercise. He described the situation envisaged (although he was not criticizing Modigliani) as extremely improbable, and he added, "Thus, the puzzles we have been considering . . . are academic exercises, of some slight use perhaps for clarifying thought, but with very little chance of ever being posed on the checkerboard of actual life."[41] And Keynes himself, in dealing explicitly with this case, described it as a "possibility" of which he knew of no example, but which "might become practically important in the future."[42] Yet there are many passages in *The General Theory* which (as Haberler has pointed out)[43] rely tacitly upon the assumption of an infinitely elastic demand for money. "The new Keynesians" appear to be trying to substitute a "special theory" (Hicks' description) for the "general

---

[38] Joseph A. Schumpeter, "Keynes, the Economist," in Harris, ed., *The New Economics,* p. 92 n.

[39] Franco Modigliani, "Liquidity Preference and the Theory of Interest and Money," *Econometrica,* January 1944, pp. 45–88.

[40] Ibid., p. 75.

[41] A. C. Pigou, "Economic Progress in a Stable Environment," *Economica,* August 1947, pp. 187–88.

[42] Keynes, *The General Theory,* p. 207.

[43] Haberler, *Prosperity and Depression,* p. 221 n.

theory," which they admit must be abandoned. If an infinitely elastic demand for money *did* exist, there would, of course, truly be a "bottomless pit for purchasing power." Every increase in M would be accompanied by a parallel decline in V. But it is my present view that any attempt to envisage the "special theory" operating in the concrete realities of the world we know—even under depression conditions—must bring out its inherent absurdity. No condition which even distantly resembles infinite elasticity of demand for money assets has ever been recognized, I believe, because general expectations have always envisaged either (a) the attainment in the not too distant future of some definite scale of prices, or (b) so gradual a decline of prices that no cumulative, general postponement of expenditure has seemed profitable. General expectations appear to have erected the possibility of a scale of prices which sags without limit, because of such things as convertibility obligations, or the necessity to maintain exchanges, or the political inexpediency of permitting prices to continue to fall.

But let us keep the discussion to the theoretical plane. The most plausible suggestion in explanation of the idea that there may exist an infinitely elastic demand for money is that, at very low rates of interest, such as will accompany thrift when prospective yields are very low, the cost of investment (in nonmoney assets) will exceed interest. Hence, the argument continues, there is a flight from nonmoney into money.

The most plausible form of this notion has already been discussed. It rests on the idea that, at very low interest rates, people will invest more in money because the interest cost of so doing will be low. But the rate of interest is equally a cost of holding nonmoney assets! In the 1970s, for instance, the true rate of interest on bonds in the United States, adjusted to the decline in the purchasing power of the dollar, has been negative, but the aggregate real value of money in relation to the aggregate value of nonmoney has not risen, and there is no reason why it should have risen.

Now if one can seriously imagine a situation in which a strong desire to save—an attempt to provide liberally for the future—persists in spite of its being judged unprofitable to acquire additional non-money assets, with the aggregate real value of money being inflated, M_r growing more rapidly than a growing M, and prices being driven down catastrophically, then one may equally legitimately (and equally extravagantly) imagine continuous price coordination accompanying the emergence of such a position. We can conceive, that is, of prices falling rapidly, keeping pace with expectations of price changes, but never reaching zero, with full utilization of resources persisting all the way.[44] We do not really need the answer which first Haberler, and then Pigou, gave on this point, namely, that the increase in the real value of cash balances is inversely related to the extent to which the individual (or for that matter the business firm) prefers to save, while the rate of saving is a diminishing function of the accumulation of assets which the individual holds.[45]

One able critic of Keynes, Patinkin, has attempted to confer some sort of validity upon what Keynes had in mind when he spoke of unemployment equilibrium under price flexibility, although he admits that Keynes' own analysis (essentially static) cannot be defended.

Writing in 1948 Patinkin says it should now "be definitely recognized that this is an indefensible position."[46] That is because "flexibility means that the money wage falls with excess supply, and rises with excess demand; and equilibrium means that the system can continue through time without change. Hence, *by definition,* a system with price flexibility cannot be in equilibrium if there is any unemployment." Yet Keynes' errors on this point, and the similar errors of his manifold enthusiastic supporters over the period 1936–46, are represented by Patinkin as quite unimportant. The truth which the early critics of *The General Theory* fought so hard to establish (against stubborn opposition at almost every point),[47] namely, that price flexibility is inconsistent with unemployment, he describes as "uninteresting, unimportant and uninformative about the real problems of economic policy."[48] In spite of the mistakes which led Keynes to his conclusions, he did stumble upon certain truths of importance.

Let us consider, then, the conclusions concerning price flexibility of what Patinkin continues to describe as "Keynesian economics"

---

[44] Compare Pigou, op. cit., pp. 183–84, and Haberler, op. cit., pp. 499–500, on this point.

[45] In any case, this argument is no answer to the case in which the saving is accompanied by speculative hoarding. For this reason Haberler claims only that there is a "strong probability" and no "absolute certainty" of there being a lower limit to MV so caused. Haberler, op. cit., p. 390.

[46] Don Patinkin, "Price Flexibility and Full Employment," *American Economic Review,* September 1948, pp. 543–64.

[47] For an example of the stubbornness, see Keynes' reply to criticisms in his "Relative Movements of Real Wages and Output," *Economic Journal,* March 1939, pp. 34–51.

[48] Patinkin, op. cit.

(meaning by that an economics which rejects the logic but retains the conclusions of *The General Theory*). This version of "the new Keynesianism" contends—again in Patinkin's words—"that the economic system may be in a position of underemployment *dis*equilibrium (in the sense that wages, prices, and the amount of unemployment are continuously changing over time) for long, or even indefinite, periods of time"[49] (Patinkin's italics). "In a dynamic world of uncertainty and adverse anticipations, even if we were to allow an infinite adjustment period, there is no certainty that full employment will be generated. That is, we may remain indefinitely in a position of underemployment disequilibrium."[50]

This sounds like pure orthodoxy. Indeed, the use of the word "*dis*equilibrium" implies that some Keynesians have now completely retreated. And the reference to "uncertainty and adverse anticipations" seems to refer to hypothetical situations which, using my own terminology, can be described as follows: *Given price rigidities regarded as unstable,* deflation will cause the emergence of withheld capacity. Three cases arise: (a) general expectations (that is, typical or average expectations) envisage a fall of prices toward a definite ultimate average which is regarded as most probable; or (b) general expectations are constantly changing so that the generally expected ultimate average of prices becomes continuously lower; or (c) general expectations envisage a certain rate of decline of the average of prices in perpetuity. In case (a), the withholding of capacity will last over a period which will be longer the more slowly the predicted price adjustments come about. In cases (b) and (c), the withholding of capacity will last over an indefinite period, *unless downward price adjustments take place as rapidly as, or more rapidly than, the changes in expectations, or the generally expected rate of decline,* in which case full employment will persist throughout. In short, when the scale of prices is moving or is expected to move in any direction, the notion of perfect price flexibility must envisage current prices being adjusted sufficiently rapidly in the same direction, if the full utilization of all productive capacity is sought. This means that, if my definition of price flexibility is accepted (see pp. 148–49) wasteful idleness of resources is incompatible with it.

In admitting that Keynes cannot be said "to have demonstrated the coexistence of unemployment equilibrium and flexible prices,"

---

49 Ibid., p. 280.
50 Ibid., p. 281.

Patinkin seems not to perceive that *it remains true, equally "by definition" (see p. 281 above), that price flexibility is inconsistent with wasteful idleness, even when we take into account the full dynamic reactions to price rigidities regarded as unstable.* For price flexibility then requires that all prices shall be continuously adjusted so as to bring the spot and future values of the money unit into consistency; in other words, to establish harmony between current and expected prices. Under such adjustments, even unemployment *dis*equilibrium is ruled out.

Do not the words "adjustment period" in the passage quoted above, p. 282, show that Patinkin, in using the term *"dis*equilibrium," is in fact still envisaging some price rigidity? What other adjustments, apart from changes in prices and effective exchange values, can he be envisaging? How else can the terms "uncertainty" and "adverse expectations" be explained, unless in relation to unstable price rigidities? And the same tacit assumption of rigidity is present in his statement of what he terms "the Keynesian position, closest to the 'classics.' " In this position, he says, although price flexibility would eventually "generate" full employment, "the length of time that might be necessary for the adjustment makes the policy impractical." He tells us that this statement (like that in the previous quotation) is *not* "dependent upon the assumption of wage rigidities."[51] But what "adjustments" other than tardy cuts in rigid wage rates has he in mind? He must be thinking of unstable price rigidities *somewhere* in the system.[52]

Since my *Keynesianism* was published, the notion that the existence

---

[51] Ibid., p. 282.

[52] A critic writes that this argument seems to overlook *inevitable* rigidities. In practice, he says, contracts cannot be varied constantly, so that costs tend to follow prices with some interval. Thus, copper miners' wages can hardly change every time the price of copper changes. But I do not think that this is Patinkin's case. As we have seen, contracts are not rigidities. They are distributive agreements (see p. 144); and collective agreements with labor unions merely cover the price of labor and virtually never guarantee employment at the agreed rates. It is when the unions insist upon adherence to any such "contracts" that they condemn many of their members to unemployment and throw the system out of coordination. Thus, if the wage rates of the miners are maintained when actual or expected copper prices have fallen to such an extent that formerly marginal seams become unworkable at current costs, the disequilibrium is clearly due to a rigidity. The most complete measure of price flexibility practically attainable involves discontinuities at both the cost and the final product ends. But periodic adjustments through recontract (as idleness threatens) can meet that situation. (Sliding scales can render the need for recontract less frequent.)

of rigidities, uncertainties, and adverse anticipations in the economic system confers *some* relevance on Keynesian thinking, survives in the works of other important critics of Keynes, for example, Leijonhufvud, Clower, and Yeager. I have explained why I cannot accept all the ideas of these scholars in my *A Rehabilitation of Say's Law*.[53] I can illustrate by Leijonhufvud's treatment. He explains the chronic unemployment of depression on the grounds that, under the condition of entrepreneurial pessimism, "individual firms . . . not perceiving that more output is called for," will turn down unemployed labor which offers itself at reduced wage rates, "even if no more than labor's marginal product (evaluated at going prices) is being asked for." That is, "even if no more than the money wage that the system would have in equilibrium is being asked for." But I have argued that if, instead of "labor's marginal product," Leijonhufvud had written "labor's marginal *prospective* product," he would have realized that, at wage rates equal to the "marginal *prospective* product," all labor is immediately employable. And I argued further that the reemployment of labor (through pricing for market clearance) in any particular sector "will set in operation the required 'groping' process; this process will lead, in subsequent periods, to a rise in labor scarcity; and that scarcity will, in turn, result in entrepreneurs being forced to offer real wage rates which correspond to labor's rising *realized* marginal product."

Returning now to Don Patinkin's development of this idea in his important and influential *Money, Interest, and Prices,* his treatment here did not lead him to discard the "unemployment *dis*equilibrium" fallacy.[54] In answering Hicks' attempts to defend Keynes' position in respect of unemployment equilibrium, he still maintains that, even when due consideration is given to the "real-balance effect," and price flexibility is "supplemented by monetary policy," the restoration of full employment demands more than "automatic" price adjustments.[55] But the only noninflationary steps on the part of the state to aid full employment of which I can conceive are in the form of inducements to or enforcements of price adjustments; and Keynes' argument was directed as much against such adjustments as against adjustments which might be more conventionally termed "automatic." In any case, it is on "expectations" that Patinkin

---

[53] All these have been influenced by Patinkin's analysis.

[54] Don Patinkin, *Money, Interest, and Prices,* pp. 233 et seq.

[55] Don Patinkin, "Keynesian Economics Rehabilitated: A Rejoinder to Professor Hicks," *Economic Journal,* September 1959, pp. 582–87.

bases his thesis, and not on imperfect price flexibility. He has, I respectfully suggest, not perceived the truth on which I have laid so much stress, that expectations can have a disequilibrating effect solely in the presence of price rigidities *which are regarded as unstable.*

That he has adhered to his former views on this issue is surprising to me because of the use he makes of the concept of the "real-balance effect." For as we have seen, expectations (whether justified or unjustified) about the aims or results of monetary policy are (under price rigidities regarded as unstable) determinants of the productivity and real value of money; while under any kind of monetary system in which the money unit has a defined value, M would tend to vary in direct proportion to M_r.

In the light of these considerations, I have been led to the conclusion that the only kind of price flexibility for which we can reasonably hope is, in practice, what I have called (p. 147 above) "effective price flexibility," a situation in which the price inconsistencies which must exist at any point of time *are never in process of material or cumulative worsening* and always in process of rectification at about the same rate that they arise. That need not mean unemployment. Contract covers the short run. And inconsistencies need not accumulate. Hence, "the dynamic approach" does not, as Patinkin maintains, obviate the necessity for the assumption of rigidities and revalidate the Keynesian fallacies. On the contrary, it was largely Keynes' neglect of the dynamic coordinative consequences of price adjustment which led him into the error that wage-rate and price adjustments are no remedy for unemployment.[56]

The theory of unemployment equilibrium which I have been discussing has, I think, been made plausible through a misinterpretation of the phenomenon of chronic unemployment. Such a condition existed in a particularly serious form in Britain while Keynes' ideas were emerging. It was largely due to the nature of the unemployment insurance system.

To discern the real causes of chronic *idleness* of productive capacity, we must first remember that the waste of productive power in a rigid system takes the form of *actual idleness* (withheld capacity) only temporarily. (See pp. 142–43.) The idleness is merely an initial condition. It dissolves gradually into "suboptimal employment": (a) in the case of labor, by the failure to recruit for trades in which

---

[56] The confusion in this field ultimately stems, I feel, from a failure to achieve conceptual clarity, and is particularly owing to the absence of a sufficiently rigorous definition of price flexibility.

the price of labor is kept above that which would induce the most productive investment in and utilization of human resources, and (b) in the case of capital equipment, through the disinvestment of those resources which become redundant and not profitably replaceable when scarcities are being contrived. Insofar as labor is concerned, the resources excluded by discoordinative pricing are always sufficiently versatile, in the absence of imposed specificities, to be devoted to *some* other uses, in which they can at once be fully employed, in spite of the waste. It follows that, if withheld capacity continues to exist as *idle but valuable* resources, it must be in some way subsidized, and fall into the category "participating idleness,"[57] or be "preferred idleness." Hence it is wrong to think of disequilibrium with enduring unemployment of the withheld capacity type; and although there could well be an equilibrium in the case of labor, in respect of what I have called "preferred idleness,"[58] this is not the sort of unemployment which the Keynesians envisage.

I conclude that the chronic unemployment in Britain which Keynes was trying to explain was the result of a combination of three elements: it was subsidized through the so-called unemployment insurance benefits; the subsidy aggravated the preferred idleness element; while a participating idleness element (*plus* the expectation that there would be a revival of demand in the trades to which the unemployed workers had a prior right to employment) was an additional influence.[59]

No economist who observed and contemplated the continued

---

[57] *Withheld capacity* in physical equipment is in *participating idleness* when its scrap value remains unrealized, not solely because of an expected revival of demand (although in some cases this may be a necessary condition), but because the physical maintenance of the idle capacity permits a contractual or prospective share in the increased revenues achieved through some collusively arranged contrived scarcity. Withheld capacity in labor is in participating idleness when it remains "attached to" the industry or occupation in which it has become unemployed and refuses other available work, because it thereby maintains a claim to be first employed in that trade (in which contrived scarcity has enhanced the earnings of those who retain employment) if demand revives or if employment is ultimately restored by a wage-rate cut. For a further explanation of this term (as well as "preferred idleness") see my *The Theory of Idle Resources,* 2d ed., pp. 145–74.

[58] The term "preferred idleness" does not imply blame. It may well be held that the pride which prevents the skilled man from accepting unskilled or menial work, or work at very much lower rates of pay than the rates to which his expectations have become adjusted, is not to be condemned; but his unemployment is not "involuntary" in any realistic sense.

[59] Actually "job search" is an important form of entrepreneurial employment and it *need* not encourage preferred idleness.

unemployment in Britain during the period 1925 to 1929 could have had any doubts about the possibility of unemployment persisting even in times of boom. It seemed obvious that almost every market pressure which could have eliminated unemployment was being effectively frustrated. I see no justification for T. Wilson's suggestion that Keynes' teachings enlighten our understanding of such a "weak boom," as he termed it,[60] or for his belief that the facts in some way refute the old orthodox view that depressions can be avoided by preventing the inflationary booms which deflations rectify. Earlier economists had realistically assumed the existence of the institutions of the age in which they wrote; while the period during which Keynes' influence was growing witnessed a new and rapid degeneration of the institutions of the price system in Britain. There was nothing in pre-Keynesian teaching which implied that it was impossible more or less permanently to price resources out of full utilization and to keep the displaced labor in subsidized idleness.

Similarly, it seems to me unjustifiable to call the chronic unemployment which characterized the long drawn-out depression in the United States and Europe, which followed 1929, "unemployment *dis*equilibrium" and to claim that Keynes' theories supply an acceptable explanation of the phenomenon, or even that they throw light upon it. Admittedly the position was generally regarded as unstable. During the depression, entrepreneurs felt that it was unprofitable, with the means at their disposal, to purchase the full potential flow of services at *the wage rates and other costs which* were being demanded. Insofar as liquid assets appeared to offer greater prospective yields than the replacement or net accumulation of nonmoney assets, that must have been due to the expectation of lower costs later on. It was the slowness with which *polic*y permitted the required cost adjustments to occur which frustrated recovery.

The truth is that, during the twenties and thirties, economists were facing an entirely novel situation owing to what I have just called the degeneration of the price system. We can hardly blame them for having failed to adapt their teachings in detail to phenomena which they had never previously experienced.[61] But Keynes' sophisticated theory

---

[60] Wilson thinks that, on this topic, we find the "essential content" of Keynes' thought. See his "Professor Robertson on Effective Demand," *Economic Journal,* 1953, p. 568.

[61] Nor is it defensible to give Keynes credit for having brought these phenomena into discussion. Contemporary economists were, I know, convinced that the apparently chronic unemployment which existed in the early thirties was eradicable, *but for politics.* Economists like Cannan did not stress more per-

of unemployment equilibrium set the greater part of the academic world of economists on a false trail.

I have, I think, exposed the fallacy in the theory that there is an inherent defect in the price mechanism, price adjustments being self-frustrating. Yet this fallacy was the foundation on which the "new economics" (or the "Keynesian revolution") was built.

We are now forced back to the stark truth that the elimination of *wasteful idleness* in productive capacity, and the avoidance of the even more wasteful condition of suboptimal activity, are attainable only through the continuous adjustment of prices *or* the continuous, unanticipated depreciation of the money unit—that is, at a speed the majority of people do not expect.

---

sistently the barriers which were preventing the full employment of resources simply because they felt, I think, that it would be superfluous to reiterate the obvious to their fellow economists and futile to make any attempt directly to influence the politicians.

13

The Nature of Consumption and Saving

In a review of my recent book, *A Rehabilitation of Say's Law,* Thomas Sowell refers to my use of "idiosyncratic definitions." I have written a greal deal about definitions[1] because I judge that the major errors in economics have arisen almost entirely from loose definition and conflicting use of terms and hardly ever from defects in the manipulation of clearly envisaged and rigorously defined concepts.

In the present chapter, especially, I have found the choice of terminology difficult. Economics as a whole abounds with tendentious and inappropriate terms. Think, for instance, of how many euphemisms there are for "inflation"! That word has, indeed, come to be regarded at times either as if it were a sacred word or as a dirty word for which some euphemism or genteelism has to be substituted!

Current jargon has been so affected by the political exigencies which, I feel, economists have all too often been subconsciously serving that, when a writer begins to use language neutrally, solely in the interests of clarity of thought, he is likely to be accused of writing emotively.[2] I should have liked to avoid altogether the euphemisms and emotively toned expressions which have infiltrated into conventional theory. But that has not seemed to be practicable. If I attempted to use terms too differently, few readers would remember

---

[1] My chief contribution on this topic is in my *The Theory of Idle Resources* (Indianapolis: Liberty Fund, 1977).

[2] See, for instance, Lindley M. Fraser's objection to my use of the term "consumers' sovereignty" and my reply. Fraser, "The Doctrine of Consumers' Sovereignty," *Economic Journal*, September 1939, pp. 544–48; Hutt, "The Concept of Consumers' Sovereignty," ibid., March 1940, pp. 66–79.

that I was using words in their literal sense and not in their acquired conventional sense. But when terms have been conventionally used so *loosely* as to cover categories which exclude like or identical things or actions, or are ambiguous in other respects, I have felt it to be imperative to break with current usage. Here I must ask the indulgence of the reader. He may for instance be irritated by my talking of "accumulated assets" where he would have used the word "investment." But he will see that, on other occasions, I use the word "investment" where he also would have used it, but where it means something completely different. I have introduced new terms, however, only where they seem to me to be essential to bring out *vital* distinctions. And as I have just alleged that the root errors of Keynesianism are to be found in the concepts employed, the redefinition of central notions like consumption, saving, investment, the entrepreneur, etc., will form a considerable part of my contribution.

Some time ago, in criticizing an unpublished essay which I had sent to him, Gottfried Haberler wrote to me:

> There has been a lot of confusion in the literature on the definition of investment, consumption, etc., and there may be still cases where people get enmeshed in contradictions; but on the whole, in my opinion, this phase of the discussion can be regarded as closed. The best discussion of these matters of definition I know of is to be found in Irving Fisher's book *The Nature of Capital and Income.* It is a pity that the Keynesian literature which abounds with confusions had no firm grounding in Irving Fisher's writings.

I agree with this appraisal of Fisher's and Keynes' work. But far from agreeing that the fruitful discussion of these concepts can be regarded as closed, I hold that some of the basic ideas need reexamination and refinement. The concepts and analysis which I present in this chapter and the following chapters have obviously been indebted to Fisher's pioneer work, although they differ considerably from his. My indebtedness to Wicksteed and Mises is equally great.

My main thesis is that, in order to understand the connected notions of consumption and saving, we have to recognize that every individual has four conceptually distinct economic roles, *which are normally exercised concurrently.* "The producer," "the consumer," "the saver," and "the entrepreneur" are normally to be regarded as the same person in what usually appears as one simple act! While it is essential to keep these *functions* distinct in our minds, it is equally desirable not to think about people, in the performance of the four roles, as belonging to four separate categories. Every person (apart from young children and the insane, who make no economic decisions of their own) ought to be seen as *continuously and simultaneously exercising* all the functions which these terms describe. Thus, when I refer to, say, "entrepreneurs," it must be remembered that I am referring to people who are exercising entrepreneurial functions, but recognizing that they are at the same time savers, consumers, and producers. We must, in particular, distinguish between the "entrepreneur" and the "producer," and between the "entrepreneur" and the "consumer-saver."

The producer as such is simply the provider of valuable services, creating value (that is, income) in the form of his personal services, or those of his assets. The *entrepreneur* expresses judgment in respect of choice of means to ends. To the extent to which any producer makes such a choice he is acting in an entrepreneurial role, supplying entrepreneurial services—the most important value-creating services in the whole system. Hence *the entrepreneur* is a particular kind of producer. He not only chooses means but bears responsibility for the interpretation of consumer preferences, and bets on the results of his choice. That is, he creates production functions through combining the services of men and assets in the manner which he predicts will prove most productive (in the sense that the ultimate final product will be most wanted—and hence demanded—by consumers). A successful (wise or lucky) bet brings him (the entrepreneur) a realized yield in excess of interest ("profit") and an unsuccessful (unwise or unlucky) bet a realized yield which falls short of interest ("loss"). The entrepreneur, *who is normally the residual claimant* on the value of the product,[3] may pay someone else (a manager) to make the choice of means on his behalf.

The *entrepreneur* as such is never responsible for the replacement and accumulation (or decumulation) of assets, but merely for *the form* in which this is done, that is, for the particular assets chosen for particular purposes and the particular workers employed. The demand to replace or accumulate net is the demand of savers, those who choose between consumption (of services or assets) in the

---

[3] I say "normally" because when contractual remuneration exceeds interest on the value of the resources or services invested in a venture, the excess is entrepreneurial remuneration. (See pp. 311–12.)

immediate future and consumption in the distant future,[4] that is, of savers. (See pp. 312–13.)

The *consumer* exercises preferences in respect of ends: (a) in respect of the particular services and assets of which he exterminates the value (through consumption), and (b) *in respect of the time pattern of that extermination.* Hence the *saver* can be envisaged as an important subclass of the *consumer,* just as the *entrepreneur* can be envisaged as an important subclass of the *producer.*

A morphology of the capital structure in the form of assets arranged in order of their prospective economic life spans can, I think, be of the greatest assistance in clarifying some of the problems to be discussed in this chapter. The classification envisages, at the one end, services consumed as they are rendered (that is, services regarded as goods of zero life expectancy) and, at the other end, assets of virtually infinite prospective *physical* life span, such as a tunnel (which may, however, be consumed *economically* if it becomes unprofitable to make any use of it). This conception of the classification of assets according to their economic life expectancy corresponds to the Austrian (specifically Böhm-Bawerk's) "stages of production" which are arranged according to their "distance from consumption." As I use this classification, it is irrelevant whether the assets are in "firms" or "households."

J. B. Say was the first, I think, to *define* "consumption" as "the extermination of value" and "production" as "the creation of value." The explicit acceptance of these realistic definitions enormously simplifies understanding of the issues. It must be remembered, however, that both the extermination and the creation of value may be not only purposeful, but unintended or accidental.

"Consumption," being the extermination of value, as well as the choice of the particular values to be exterminated, *is equally the extermination of the power to demand.* "Production," on the other hand, being the creation of value, is the creation of power to demand. *It follows that, in Keynes' equation, $y = c + i$* ("income" equals "consumption" *plus* "investment"), the word "consumption" ought to be recognized as a particular part of "production"! If "consumption" in the equation is to form part of "income," it must be the value of that portion of the flow of productive services (income) which makes up for value concurrently exterminated. There is, however, no way of physically identifying that part of aggregate produc-

---

[4] Consumption of assets or services.

tion which is called "consumption" and that part which is called "investment." The *value* of aggregate production over a period is the *value* of income. Consumption over a period is the *value* of services exterminated *plus* that of assets exterminated (depreciation being one example). Hence value produced *minus* value consumed *equals* something which is often called "investment."

So conceived, "investment" is a value residue. Yet (as we have seen) in *The General Theory* "investment" means the acquisition of nonliquid assets. But nonliquid assets also are subject to some value loss, in other words, "consumption." Indeed, even assets of the longest economic life expectancies are consumed through wear and tear, obsolescence, etc., and the devotion of productive services to their maintenance, renovation, and eventual replacement must therefore also fall into Keynes' category "consumption"; even the replacement of a huge machine must, for consistency, be classified under the "consumption" heading.[5]

Of course both terms are preposterously inappropriate. "Replacement" would have been a less confusing term than "consumption." But *all* productive services that are not consumed as they are rendered are *invested in,* that is, embodied into, a stock of assets covering the whole range of economic life expectancies for the nonmoney part of the stock[6] (whether in factories, shops, or households). The money valuation of the flow of productive services equals the money valuation of production, for not only are marketing services included but the contributions of entrepreneurs also—positive contributions when profits (realized yields in excess of interest) are being achieved and negative contributions (unintended consumption) when losses are being incurred.

Properly seen, what are called by such terms as "capital formation," the "development *tempo,*" "net investment," etc., are wholly and solely the result of the aggregate expression of individual saving preferences and prospective yields to investment (in the sense of the embodiment of productive services in assets of all kinds, whether for replacement or growth).

"Saving preference" (or "time preference") refers to a particular choice of ends: the people's valuation of satisfactions to be enjoyed in the relatively distant future in relation to satisfactions to be en-

---

[5] But such assets may appreciate in value—a special case of the creation of value or "production."

[6] Inclusion of credit money as part of the assets stock would mean double counting.

joyed in the immediate future—"the future" referring to various definite or indefinite times. "Prospective yields" reflect entrepreneurial predictions about the wantedness or productiveness of assets in general. Such forecasts are sometimes called (loosely) the demand for "savings." The actual rate of net accumulation (positive or negative) results from these preferences and predictions, that is, the rate of growth as distinct from the resulting composition of replacement and net accumulation.

As I see things, through a faulty perception of these distinctions, the Swedish economists since Wicksell, and the great majority of British and American economists since Robertson's *Banking Policy and the Price Level,* have been led into several different attempts to show that certain conceptually identical *magnitudes,* namely "savings" and what they most often seem to mean by "investment," may be unequal,[7] and that the distinction is of the very greatest significance. These attempts have received their most seriously fallacious development in Keynesian thought, in spite of Keynes' having tried to show the *necessary equality* (as distinct from the *identity*) of these magnitudes.

The use of the terms "consumption" and "savings" (as magnitudes) in *The General Theory* created, indeed, more confusion in the minds of critical readers than any other notions ever treated in economics. For Keynes seemed to be arguing, *first,* that savings and investment are necessarily equal; *second,* that savings tend constantly to exceed investment with grave consequences; and, *third,* that in some sense savings are a bad thing, causing income to contract, while investment is a good thing (like consumption), causing income to increase. In Keynes' words, "the decisions to consume and invest between them determine incomes."[8]

He defined "savings" as income *minus* consumption, which makes the residues, "savings" and "investment," alternative terms in his equation; hence we are not allowed to regard savings simply as *unspent* income. Accordingly, in my own attempt to reduce Keynes' use of the term to the least absurdity, I have assumed him to mean by it "that part of income which, given that expenditure on assets needed to replace the value of consumption, will be retained as money, bidding up M_r, unless it is spent on investment." But this does not

[7] Gunnar Myrdal says that the "distinction between saving and investment is the essence of the modern monetary theory which starts with Wicksell." *Monetary Equilibrium* (London: William Hodge and Company, 1939), p. 90.

[8] Keynes, *The General Theory,* p. 64.

get rid of the absurdity completely; for what are we then to call the parallel concept, that is, "that part of income which, given expenditure on investment, will be unspent unless it is spent on consumption"?

The extent of Keynes' confusion between spending and consuming (or between not spending and saving) is revealed in his reference to the objects "which lead individuals to *refrain from spending* out of their incomes."[9] (My italics.) *Yet in a money economy one spends to save* (for instance, to acquire long-life assets) just as one spends to acquire the kind of assets that are popularly called "consumer goods." To provide liberally for the future one cannot acquire (spend to obtain) services or perishable goods which cannot form part of one's inventories. One must spend to obtain durable goods or self-replenishing inventories of short-life goods. Nor, as we have seen (p. 238), does one buy out of money stocks, unless one is disinvesting from money stocks, but through the realization of *money's worth,* the liquidation of nonmoney. The truth is, as I once put it, saving preference and liquidity preference are as unrelated as demands for monocles and bubble gum.

But what makes it all the more difficult to guess what Keynes really meant, and what his disciples have not, as far as I know, ever come near to explaining is that in the present context, in spite of his reference to *refraining from spending,* he did not mention liquidity as an objective of such conduct, and referred simply to provision for "old age, family education, or the maintenance of dependents," the desire to enjoy "a gradually improving standard of life," etc. Under the eight headings he listed, only "miserliness" has any relevance to the choice of money, and yet he used the words "refrain from spending." He tried to find, instead, the supposedly depressing effects of saving in the fact that the saver may merely acquire existing and not new or additional assets, which "forces some other individual to transfer to him some article of wealth old or new," while such transfers "may be actively inimical to . . . the creation of new wealth."[10]

The failure of the attempts which have been made to *explain away* (as distinct from explaining) these confusions (for example, the suggestion that a lag is implied, the suggestion that it is *attempted* saving which reduces income and attempted investment which in-

---

[9] Ibid., p. 107.
[10] Ibid., p. 212.

creases it, etc.) has been demonstrated in Hazlitt's study,[11] and I propose in this chapter simply to confine myself to an independent examination of basic concepts.

The simple diagram which follows represents an analysis of the composition of income. The magnitudes indicated are those which are influenced by people in the four roles which I have specified.

The horizontal length of each rectangle represents income—or a part of income—the value of the flow of productive services during a given period. But the same diagram could be used to represent the rate of flow of services, measured in money terms.

Diagram I

(All magnitudes are in terms of actual money units)

Flow of Services (Output, Production or Income)		
Consumed Services	Embodied Services	
Consumed Services	Consumed Assets	Accumulated Assets
Consumption = Replacement		Savings

In the analysis of the flow of services or income, I have purposely given two names to one magnitude, namely "consumption" and "replacement," when value exterminated is at least fully replenished by value created. That they are *appropriately* and *usefully* defined, so as to describe the same things in different aspects, may have to be demonstrated. But if "consumption" exceeds "income," "replacement" falls short of "consumption," and the magnitude "savings" is negative: it is "dissavings."

I have defined "income" earlier as *the flow of valuable services,* which may be measured in actual money units, or in abstract money units of constant purchasing power ("real terms"). The former is "money income," the latter "real income." Income so defined is essentially a value concept. The notion of real income as a "quantity" appears to me to be absurd. Yet *all the difficulties but one* which have been raised by Keynes[12] and Lindahl[13] are avoided if we regard it as *the value* of the flow of services. The difficulty which is *not* avoided is that arising out of the satisfactoriness or otherwise of the measure

[11] Hazlitt, *The Failure of the "New Economics,"* esp. chaps. 8–10.

[12] Keynes, *The Treatise on Money,* vol. 1, bk. 2.

[13] Erik Lindahl, "The Concept of Income," in *Essays in Honour of Gustav Cassel,* pp. 399–407.

of value (including real value, or purchasing power) envisaged. (See above, pp. 191, 238–39.)

We are all too apt to forget, under the simplifying influence of price index numbers (as Heilperin has insisted),[14] "the heterogeneous reality that they are supposed to represent. . . . It is the changing *structure* of economic quantities that really matters most rather than changes in *averages*." It is not enough merely to perceive the difficulties of index-number interpretation. Even Keynes did that, but the "macroeconomic" method that he initiated in fact seemed to ignore these difficulties at the very point at which they were crucial.

Teaching in the Marshallian tradition has relied on the notion of "the national dividend," meaning by this a flow to be *divided* in a certain way. In this approach, *commodities* (not necessarily material) as well as services are included in the magnitude. That procedure has merits but creates difficulties. In statistical studies, however, it is easiest to include the value of final commodities, which equals the value of services embodied into those commodities. Included in that magnitude is the value of entrepreneurial services (a point to which I shall shortly return) *plus* the value of final services consumed as they are rendered. But to get to a rigorously definable idea of what pre-Keynesian economists really understood by *real income* or *net produce,* we need simply value the full flow of services.

Of this flow, a very small proportion of the value ("consumed services") is exterminated immediately, but the larger proportion is embodied into a stock of assets which is in process of concurrent consumption, replacement of consumption (partial or full), or accumulation of assets.

I could have adopted a terminology closer to that of some other writers and defined "output" as what is put into the stock of resources and "income" as what is taken out of the stock ("final services" consumed directly being regarded as part of both output and income). But it seems to be much more in keeping with everyday usage to regard the flow of services as identical with income, for it all "comes in" as remuneration—wages, interest, and profits. Moreover, my definition helps us to avoid such difficulties as arise inevitably out of attempts (not specifically Keynesian) to conceive of the saving process as an exchange between present and future *income.* As I use terms, the notion of any exchange between income

---

[14] Michael Angelo Heilperin, *International Monetary Economics* (London: Longmans, Green, and Company, 1939), p. viii.

now and income later has no meaning, whereas we *can* think usefully of the sacrifice of present for future *consumption*.

The services which form income include all services which have scarcity and hence value, *whether or not those services actually enter into the circle of exchange.* (See pp. 237–40.) It embraces those provided by natural resources (for example, the services of land, valued at rent), by man-made resources (for example, plant, equipment, houses, furniture, all stock and inventories, patents, and copyrights, etc.), by money, and by people.

The owners of all these four kinds of resources (including money!) are to be described as producers, for the production process—the creation of value—occurs as the supply of valuable services.

All valuable resources other than people are assets. And even people may be usefully regarded as assets for some purposes, for investment in human capital is of great importance.

Because entrepreneurial services are included in the total flow of services, the definition makes no distinction between "inputs" of services and "outputs" of products. The flow of services *is* the flow of "outputs" (or products). "Inputs" cannot then be reckoned simply as the value of the flow of services *minus* the aggregate value of entrepreneurial services.

Similarly (*apropos* of input-output analysis) it is common to distinguish prices (meaning the prices of physically completed products or other assets) from wage rates or from "costs." I propose, however, to regard the prices of final products and other assets as reflecting the prices of all services embodied into them. This is possible because I have included the supply of entrepreneurial services, the value of which (in the form of the entrepreneurs' residual claim on the value of output after contractual claims have been settled) is determined by demand for their services. And, in accordance with my definition of production and consumption, I must not only include as services those provided in the course of the marketing function, but treat as embodied services any increase in the capital value of assets, however caused (interest being constant). Similarly, I must include as consumption (disembodiment and extermination of services) any loss of capital value (interest being constant).

Services flow from assets automatically or through effort (effort being the complementary services of *people*). As we have seen, effort may be either simple effort, as when a person supplies his own services without the use of assets (a virtually nonexistent case), or effort combined with the services of assets.

Only those services which have scarcity (and hence value) are included in income. The services of valueless resources are themselves valueless and hence, however important to man's existence and well-being, are excluded. Thus, the sun's light and warmth, the air that we breathe, productive forces like gravity, and the accumulation of human knowledge, although essential for the material welfare and indeed for the survival of mankind, are, by reason of the fact that their use by any person does not deprive any other person of any part of their use, not economic goods. Similarly, when the services of valuable resources are temporarily valueless, then, whether they are used or not, their services may be regarded as entering into the flow of services, but not as entering into their aggregate real value or "quantity."

The waste of services which have been earlier embodied into assets, through the useless or accidental extermination of their value, is consumption. Unless such waste is covered by replacement, its value is a negative contribution to real income.

The income from money which is held in households[15] is nonpecuniary but can, nevertheless, be measured in money terms and hence in real terms. That is, the income can be valued at interest on the capital value of the resources providing monetary services. Such services form part of society's *real* income just as the services of one's house, one's lawn mower, and one's pipe form part of real income, consumed directly.[16] Hence they enter into money income as I have defined it and influence its magnitude.[17]

A distinction is made between those services which are *consumed directly*,[18] and the rest, *embodied services* (embodied into assets).[19]

---

[15] The phrase "held in households" excludes those who hold money (in a cash register, in a checking account, or in some other form) for business purposes.

[16] I value income from consumers' assets at interest on their capital value, regarding this as the market price of the services they render. That is, consumers' surplus is not regarded as entering into income. (See pp. 312–13.)

[17] Thus, the services we obtain from television certainly compete with and influence the real and money value of the services provided by theaters. The significance of households is discussed generally on p. 313.

[18] What I have called "consumed services" corresponds to what J. B. Say called "immaterial products, or values consumed at the moment of production" *(Political Economy,* 4th ed., vol. 1, p. 136), giving as examples the physician, the musician, the actor, the priest, the lawyer, the servant, and the immaterial returns of a public edifice, a bridge, a highway, or public gardens.

[19] The services of money are *embodied into assets* when they are used in business just as are, say, the services of the site of the undertaking. Monetary services may be regarded as *consumed directly* when used in households.

300 · *The Keynesian Episode*

Of those services which are embodied into assets, the value of some goes to make up *replacement* of all the value exterminated (of services or assets) and possibly replaced with assets some of which are physically quite different, while the value of the rest (if any) makes up *accumulated assets* or "savings."[20] And as I have shown, if replacement falls short of the value of what is being consumed, dissaving is occurring, and the deficiency may be called *decumulated (or consumed) assets.* It may be regarded as the disembodiment of services formerly embodied into assets.

Different parts of *embodied services* have different life expectancies—different rates of *turnover* (extermination matched by replacement), and it is this, rather than the vague conventional distinction between "consumer goods" and "producer goods," which is important in economic analysis (although it is not very important in the argument which I am developing here).

Broadly defined, the term "consumption" has reference to *the achievement of economic ends,* which culminates in the extermination of value. Consumption in this sense may be contrasted to production, which is *the response to the forecast expression of economic ends.* The *form* of production so envisaged is, in other words, the response to "consumers' sovereignty"; and consumers' sovereignty is effective to the extent to which it does determine the composition of subsequent production—that is, first, the form of the stock of assets, and second, the form of the subsequent flow of services.

Among the consumers' preferences so expressed are those of leisure preference, time preference, risk preference, and to some extent liquidity preference.[21] As we have seen, the form of the stock of assets, and the form of the flow of services (production), are influenced by the expression of these preferences in exactly the same way that they are influenced by the expression of all other preferences.

In the remainder of this discussion, however, I shall use the term

---

[20] For a rigorous discussion of the process of "saving" and the magnitude "savings," see pp. 400 et seq.

[21] When liquidity preference is expressed in the course of business, it may be regarded as a choice of means and not as preference concerning ends. When a private individual, or a firm on his behalf, holds money, it may be the result of a choice of ends *or* a choice of means. It is a *choice of ends* if the purpose is private convenience, the desire for security or miserliness. It is a *choice of means* if the money assets are accumulated speculatively. We can, if we wish, distinguish the two purposes for demanding liquidity by the terms "consumption liquidity" and "production liquidity."

"consumption" to mean either a *process or a magnitude.* The context will make clear what is meant.[22]

The *process* consists of the actual current extermination of the value of services as they are rendered and extermination of the value of some part of the stock of assets (including services previously embodied into assets, that is, the decumulation of the stock), a stock which (as we have seen) is in process of full or partial replenishment or growth.

The *magnitude* consists of the aggregate value of what is so exterminated over a period, or the rate of that extermination.[23] If "production" equals or exceeds "consumption," "replacement" will be another term for consumption.

When "final services" are consumed, nothing *physical* is exterminated; but the *value* of the services is exterminated. However, the valuable services of the assets used in a business, or assets used in some forms of home production (for example, a sewing machine), are embodied in products, which means that they are not consumed; whereas the valuable services of "consumption assets," like a stereo set or a picture, *are* exterminated, that is, consumed even though the assets themselves may not be subject to consumption (for example, as with a picture).

One *consumes assets* through their extermination, which can be seen as the decumulation of a stock.[24] But the physical extermination is incidental. As J. B. Say pointed out, consumption is "the destruction of utility, and not of substance or matter . . . an extinction of that which made [a good] an object of desire and/or demand," and, "being the destruction of value, is commensurate, not with the bulk, the weight, or the number of the products consumed, but with their value. Large consumption is the destruction of large value, whatever form that value may happen to have assumed."[25]

All services which *are not incorporated into assets* are consumed

---

[22] In the parallel concepts, the process and the magnitude of "saving," I have thought it desirable (for reasons to be explained) to use a separate term, "savings" (with an "s"), for the *magnitude* involved.

[23] Strictly speaking, the statement that such loss of value is consumption needs the assumption, "the rate of interest not having risen."

[24] We are accustomed to talk, loosely, of the "consumption" of fuel, materials, etc., in the course of production. Such resources are, however, to be regarded not as consumed but as embodied into other resources, just as, say, the services of the site, building, machinery, and liquid assets of a firm are embodied into its products.

[25] Say, op. cit., 2:221–22.

directly, even if sometimes wastefully. I have referred to them as "consumed services." The term covers all services which need not be embodied into assets before being consumed. The proportion to aggregate income of the flow of services which is so consumed is probably very small.[26] Most services are embodied into assets, that is, invested in, at least for a small period of time, before they are disembodied into consumption.

All assets which *are wasted,* in the sense that they lose value (at constant interest) without rendering unwasted services, are to be regarded as consumed. Assets which are *"used up"* in business and industry are to be regarded not as consumed but as transformed, if at least an equivalent value is embodied into other assets—products.

Consumption may be, as I insisted above (p. 292), deliberate or inadvertent, purposeful or accidental. Thus, a car may be consumed through wear and tear in use or through an accident which destroys it. Or any other particular item in a person's assets stock may lose value through a transfer of demand to something else. *Any such loss of value will represent consumption,* although there will be an increase of value experienced in other assets to which demand is transferred. *The increase of value in that case will be "production"* as I have defined it. Under constant income, the aggregate value of the assets stock will remain unchanged through *a demand transfer* of that type (ultimately, *a preference transfer*).

A special case of consumption is obsolescence. But similarly, the value of assets may increase while they are passively owned; and that also, being the creation of value, must be treated as production. It may occur through pure luck. The enormous fortune built up by Cecil Rhodes in the Kimberley diamond fields last century is said to have begun when his chance possession of pumps in an emergency enabled him to rent them to the highest bidders. Whether his possession of the pumps when the diamond mines were unexpectedly flooded had been due to his prescience, or to his differential good luck, the principle would have been no different. The increase in value was "production" in both cases.

But what *seems* to be passive ownership may be purposeful. For instance, red wine may be retained in storage because its owners

---

[26] The biggest contribution toward "consumed services" may well be that of the services flowing from "consumer assets," for example, from one's house, furniture, and car.

predict that a big improvement in its quality and sale value will sufficiently exceed the cost of carrying it through time to justify the venture. It is, however, often much more profitable to carry goods through time when no change in their physical condition is expected. For instance, to supply "time utilities," it is productive to incur the costs of carrying crops from one harvest to the next. Similarly, inventories held as reserves are productive.

When we express the results of "consumption" as a magnitude, it means the aggregate value of "consumed services" *plus* the value of services disembodied from assets (the value of resources exterminated). In other words, "consumption" as a magnitude is the aggregate value of output *minus* "savings" (the value of "accumulated assets").

He who consumes services or whose assets are consumed—exterminated—is a "consumer." Thus, the stockholder in a corporation of which the assets are used unwisely or unluckily, so that they lose value (through physical extermination or otherwise—but interest being assumed constant), must, in that role, be regarded as a "consumer."

What constitutes the magnitudes *consumed assets* and *replacement* may be conceived of in real or money terms. That is, by "replacement" we may mean either (a) the value of that flow of services which, when embodied into assets, maintains the real value of assets intact (that is, when their value is measured in abstractly conceived *money units of constant purchasing power*), which we can call *realized replacement,* or (b) the value of that flow of services which, when embodied into assets, maintains their money value intact (that is, their value in terms of *actual money units*), which we can call *supposed replacement.* Corresponding to these concepts, we have *realized consumption* and *supposed consumption.*[27]

Both realized and supposed replacement (or consumed assets) may be measured either in real or in money terms.

The value of consumed services *plus* the value of consumed assets make up the magnitude *consumption,* which can be described as "realized" or "supposed," according to whether it is reckoned in real or money terms. The value of the rest of the flow of services represents accumulated assets which, once again, may be realized or supposed.

---

[27] This distinction between "supposed" and "realized" does *not* correspond to the usual distinction made between "planned" and "realized" aggregates.

"Consumption" does not express demand but exterminates it; yet it is accompanied by demand for assets which normally replace consumption. Replacement demand takes the form of services being offered for incorporation into a stock of assets of varying life expectancies. Moreover, except in the case of consumed services, any "consumption *demand"* expressed is for replacement (which in the aggregate may be full or partial), and that contributes to or makes up saving preference.[28] In the case of *consumed services,* the demand is normally coterminous with consumption. When I buy theater tickets, however, I am demanding assets; and when I use them, I exterminate their value.

When the value exterminated is that of the services of relatively permanent, unconsumable assets, say, the services enjoyed during a visit to an art gallery, no value of assets is exterminated (except for wear and tear of the building, upkeep costs, and supervision). There is merely a transfer of power to demand from the visitor to the gallery to the owners of the gallery. But the owners' investment in the gallery meant that some other assets of which the community could have enjoyed the product were not provided. And he who has paid a dollar for admission can subsequently demand a value of noncompeting things which is one dollar less. That is, if he is to maintain his capital intact, he must reduce the value of his total subsequent *consumption* by one dollar, or increase the value of his *production* by one dollar.

Consumption as such can in no sense be a source of demand for anything.[29] But it *is* of the nature of a vote for the continued production of that thing. *Strictly speaking,* therefore, it is incorrect to speak of "consumption *demand"* at all (except, perhaps, when we imagine the consumer buying consumed services). For in the act of consumption, the consumer is always depleting his own stocks, and making no offer of any kind; and when he is replacing or accumulating, he is saving *and* exercising entrepreneurship. (See p. 312.) In demand-

---

[28] We shall see that the *offer* of *existing* assets for services to be embodied into new assets (for replacement or net accumulation) is society's demand for saving (the converse of the saver's *demand for assets*). Demand for saving is for services to make (ultimately) assets for replacement or additional assets. This demand, which is an expression of prospective yields, is conveyed through entrepreneurs, and is competing against consumers for the flow of services. This competition, in turn, contributes to the inducement for additional savings or diminished dissavings, namely, interest.

[29] I shall be forced to reiterate this truth in several later contexts.

ing consumer goods (assets of short life expectancies) he is *investing* in replacements with the intention of consuming these replacements. This part of demand to replace forms the greater part of "consumption demand."[30] But the consumers' inventories being replaced must normally be consumed (wastefully or otherwise) relatively soon[31] (at various times, depending upon perishability, storage costs, etc.). Such inventories are "unproductive" except for short periods of time because it is unprofitable to try to carry stocks greater than current stocks through time. Hence, continued reinvestment in replacement of consumer goods may, if we wish, be loosely termed "consumption demand," provided that it is always remembered that the origin of the ability to replace is not consumption but production—the flow of real income out of which the replacements are demanded.

The fact that consumption cannot be regarded as in any sense the source of any demand is vital to my thesis, and I return to it in the following chapter.

I shall use the term "saving" (without an "s") to mean *the act* of an individual or *a process* of society, namely, the acquisition of assets (capital) in return for services (income). When the individual saves, he expresses a particular preference concerning the use of the flow of services, which is the same thing as the use of the stock of assets. This choice or preference is being constantly made. Hence the term "saving" describes the action taken to sacrifice consumption in the immediate future for consumption later (of the assets acquired *or of their services*). It may be equally usefully envisaged as the result of an intention *not to exterminate* at more than a certain rate, the stock of assets which the services (of men or assets) are replacing or building up.

I shall, then, call the aggregate expression of all individual acts of saving, *the process of saving* or, for short, simply *saving* (without an "s"). It should be noticed that this term covers the general expression of time preference, *whatever its intensity,* that is, whatever the relative values placed by society upon consumption, at different future times, and *irrespective of whether the process results in full or incomplete replacement of assets, or accumulation.* In conformity with the above definition, I shall describe people as "savers" when they are exercising time (that is, saving) preference. They are dis-

---

[30] It must be remembered that "consumed services" form a very small proportion of income and consumption.

[31] Relatively soon, that is, in comparison with assets of long life expectancies—producer goods.

saving when their extermination of assets is not being fully replaced by their saving.

In order to stress the nature of the choice which has to be expressed, I have introduced the term "consumer-saver." All "consumption-saving demand" is an expression of preference. The distinction between saving preference and consumption preference, as I shall use these terms, is solely one of time. The process of consumption consists of the *current* extermination of services and assets, whereas saving preference is for *future* consumption in this sense (and hence expressed as a demand for assets which can be carried through time). That is why all investment in assets—the greater part of all output—has to be regarded as a response to saving preference although the inventories accumulated are partly or wholly in process of current consumption.

When I use the term "consumer-saver," I am thinking not only of individuals but of corporations, and even of governments themselves. For shareholders delegate to directorates, in addition to the right to invest or disinvest[32] (that is, to make entrepreneurial decisions on their behalf), the right to save on their behalf. And it is certainly possible for a government or its agencies to save net as well as to consume. For example, the government is contributing to savings when it pays off part of the national debt, or when it taxes for capital purposes.

I have used the terms "time preference" and "saving preference" as synonyms in contexts in which their meaning has seemed to me to be self-evident. But in rigorous language, I mean by these terms the *offer* of services for assets, including money assets (whether the current rate of consumption is leaving additions to, or only replacement of, or only *partial* replacement of the stock of assets). It should be noticed that an increased *offer* of services for assets does *not* mean that the flow of services *into* assets necessarily increases, but that the ratio of exchange between services and assets is altered. In the next chapter, I shall explain how if (as a society) we, say, double our offer of services for assets (income for capital), *ceteris paribus* we halve the rate of interest; that is, how we must then sacrifice twice as much income to get a given "amount" of capital (that is, an "amount" which will offer a given prospective annual yield). To be "saving preference" the demand expressed must originate in income, that is,

---

[32] The right to dissave purposely is seldom delegated by the shareholder, but merely the right to retain capital as dividends.

in the flow of services. I must repeat that the offer of assets for
assets *cannot be* an expression of saving preference if the assets are
of equivalent life expectancies. The offer of services for assets *is*. It
is because services cannot be carried through time, whereas assets
can be, that the process of saving *necessarily* involves a demand for
assets through the offer of services (a demand for capital through
the offer of income).

The term "assets" is intended to include such things as share
certificates, securities of all kinds and even unsecured rights for
the return of a loan. No double counting is thereby caused. Thus, the
value of any individual's assets consists of the gross value of the
assets of which he has custody, less the value of his "debts" (that is,
the assets which he may be called upon to return on demand, or on
a particular date, or following some contingency). And the value of
all assets is the present discounted value of the prospective income
stream they offer.

When the demand for assets expressed as saving preference causes
an embodiment of services great enough (or, the same thing, a rate
of consumption small enough) to result in accumulated assets (supposed or realized), I shall call the value of the additional resources
acquired, *savings* (with an "s"). When that demand is insufficient to bring about full replacement (supposed or realized), I shall
call the net shortfall, *dissavings*. The terms express, therefore, the
measurable results of *response to* time preference.

It has seemed convenient to call the expression of time preference
by one name—saving—whether it happens to induce partial replacement, full replacement, or an accumulation of assets (supposed or
realized); for in practice every individual has *some* preference for
the future.[33] Moreover, the word "savings," unqualified, and in its
usual connotation, has reference to *an excess* of income over consumption. I accordingly use it in that sense when I spell it with an
"s."

The notion of the aggregate *magnitude* of savings gives rise to
difficulties simply because the value of the assets acquired by a saver
is *inserted in* the aggregate value of a stock which is in process of
partial or complete replenishment or of net accumulation. To simplify exposition, I propose to use the phrase *"an increase in savings"*

---

[33] If he had not, he would always *immediately* consume the whole of his resources, exchanging any durable resources which he possessed for decumulable
resources.

(or similar expression) to cover also the notion of *"a decrease in dissavings,"* and the phrase "a decrease in savings" to cover also the notion of "an increase in dissavings."

It was Knut Wicksell, I think, who originated the practice of considering the significance of the *aggregate magnitudes* "saving" and "consumption"; but clarity was vitiated through his attempt to conceive of the supply of goods which constitutes real income as falling into two categories—"consumer goods" and "capital goods." For inventories of consumer goods are themselves capital goods (productive capital), until they are consumed—their value exterminated. And as we have seen, goods of relatively long life expectancy are nearly all subject to *some* physical consumption; for they are liable to depreciation (through use, physical deterioration over time, as well as obsolescence). The clarity of complete generality is, I think, obtained in the categories that I call "consumption" (which includes "replacement") and "accumulated assets." And when I wish to refer to the form in which income is being received, I distinguish simply (a) consumed services, (b) services embodied in assets of which it is judged that greater quantities than existing inventories cannot be profitably carried through time, and (c) services embodied in assets intended to be added to the existing aggregate of assets. The products of category (b) *could* be called "consumer goods" and those of (c) "capital goods." But that is *not* what is normally meant by these terms; nor would a distinction based on life expectancies (rates of turnover) conform to the vague conventional distinction between these categories.

The magnitudes *savings* or *dissavings* may, as I have said, be *measured* from two different points: (a) the point at which *supposed replacement* is complete or (b) the point at which *realized replacement* is complete (see above, pp. 303–4). The terms describe therefore either the amount by which (interest being assumed constant) the money value of the community's assets increases over a period, to be called *supposed savings,* or the amount by which the real value of those assets increases over a period, to be called *realized savings.*[34]

Before supposed or realized savings can begin to accumulate, a preference must have been expressed for *the continuance in the future* of at least the current rate of consumption. The response to that

---

[34] The same terms may, as I have said, be used to describe *the rate at which* the money or real value of assets increases or decreases.

preference covers replacement. Savings result, then, when people refrain from such consumption as *they believe* entails a reduction or fails to provide for an increase of the real value of their assets. But if such savings merely maintain the money value, and not the real value of assets, they are supposed savings only. In other words, when the magnitude of savings in either sense is negative (they can then be called *supposed* or *realized dissavings*), the cause—the act or process—is insufficient saving (which is another way of saying, too much consumption). I shall be dealing with objections to this assertion. If realized savings fall short of supposed savings,[35] all that the latter will show is the extent to which savers will have the right to *spend more* (in money units) in the future, while the former will show the extent to which they will have the right to *acquire more* (in real terms), whether for consumption or net accumulation.

The term "savings" (of a period) is, as I have shown, merely an alternative term for "accumulated assets" of that period. As I define these terms, they are synonyms for *different aspects* of the same magnitude. The "supposed savings" of a period always equal the "supposed accumulated assets" of that period (the amount by which the aggregate value of assets has increased when measured in terms of actual money units). Similarly, "realized savings" always equal "realized accumulated assets" (the increase in the value of the sum total of assets when replacement is measured in terms of money units of constant purchasing power—interest being constant). This definition of "savings" certainly does not correspond to Myrdal's definition of "savings," as that part of income "which is not used in the demand for consumption goods."[36] For incorporation of services into assets includes the replenishment of inventories of consumer goods; and it is theoretically possible for the aggregate value of consumer goods (conventionally defined) accumulated to increase

---

[35] The use of the word "supposed" depends on a simplifying assumption (a rather unrealistic assumption), namely, that people suffer from "the money illusion." It is assumed that they always regard the achievement of *supposed* savings, which has occurred when the money value of their assets has increased (interest being constant), as meaning that they have accumulated real assets. That is, they are assumed to "suppose," wrongly, that their real power to consume in the future has increased. I have felt it essential to make use of some such terms because the terms *money savings* and *real savings* (instead of supposed and realized savings) would be ambiguous. Both supposed and realized savings may be measured either in money or in "real" terms (as, indeed, may all the other magnitudes which the adjectives "supposed" and "realized" describe).

[36] Myrdal, op. cit., p. 90.

while, through depreciation, the value of the aggregate stock of producer goods (conventionally defined)[37] is declining.

The distinction (on which the Keynesians have attempted to build) between *expenditure* on "consumption," or what is devoted to making "consumer goods," and *expenditure* on "investment," or what is denoted to making "producer goods," is ambiguous; for earnings from the maintenance, repair, and replacement of equipment are equally "consumption" *in the sense intended.*[38] Thus, although I am using the term "savings" to mean the flow of services "devoted to *increasing* the future flow of income" (George Stigler's words,[39] my italics), it has to be remembered that the decision to replace (that is, to *maintain* the future flow of income, in whole or in part) is equally a decision as between consumption now and consumption later (of assets or the product of assets).[40]

"Consumption" is mainly out of inventories—out of capital (apart from the relatively small magnitude "consumed services"). "Saving" is refraining from the consumption of inventories (of *all* life expectancies) in process of production, and demand from income for the assets which form those inventories. Income (output, the flow of services) is *mainly* a contribution to inventories, in spite of concurrent consumption. Hence, to restate the point I made above (p. 292), *income = consumption + savings* could well be phrased, *income = replacement + savings,* in which form it is much less conducive to misunderstanding.[41]

---

[37] I am not dealing in this chapter with the notion that savings are "income" which is simply not "spent" on things intended to be consumed, implying that it may not be "spent" on assets. If income is accompanied by consumption of lesser value, it *must* be accompanied by savings. What Myrdal (and Keynes, who uses the same notion) seems to mean is that *nonmoney assets* (as distinct from income) may be used to demand liquidity, that is, offered in exchange for money, bidding up the value M_r.

[38] In any case, neither replacement nor accumulation of assets need involve *expenditure.* If a farmer working on his own account allows his flocks and herds to breed and does not sell the increase, he is saving and accumulating net. If he *employs* a shepherd or other labor in the process, however, and does not remunerate in kind, the remuneration of this labor (subsequent to the accumulation) *will* be effected through the medium of expenditure.

[39] George J. Stigler, *The Theory of Price* (New York: Macmillan, 1946), p. 325.

[40] Stigler talks in other places of "net savings," which are obviously what he means by the definition in the text.

[41] It would be possible, I repeat, to regard "consumed services" as forming part of inventories for an *instant,* in which case the identity *income ≡ replacement + net accumulation* could be stated without qualification.

The concept of saving has to do, then, with the exercise of time preference through the exchange of valuable services now (which confer the power to consume now) for assets (which confer the power to consume later). *Because saving is the acquisition of assets in exchange for services* (or the acquisition of assets of long life expectancy with assets of short life expectancy), there can be no such *thing as society saving more than can be invested. The separation of saving and investment decisions* (on which so much emphasis has been placed by the Keynesians) *is defensible only when the notion of "investment" is confined to the taking of responsibility for the form, that is, the composition of the assets stock.*

The consumer-saver's function is the expression of preferences concerning products and *concerning time*. We call him a saver when we are thinking of the latter preference. As a saver he accumulates resources—*any* resources—by refraining from using all his rights to consume (represented by his stock of capital into which his contribution to income is constantly flowing). His role is as *passive* as that of the producer in that, *as* a saver, he does not choose *particular* resources to hold. As a *pure* saver, he receives no entrepreneurial remuneration from his savings: he receives interest only. But as he must always choose (unless he acquires assets at random), he must always be an entrepreneur in some degree.[42] As a saver, his preferences influence the composition of income in one sense only, namely, the form appropriate for the distribution of the life expectancies of the specific assets that he, directly or indirectly, is demanding. Thus, a response to a rise in saving preference will be in the form of a greater proportion of assets of long life expectancies. But in all respects, the form of income is ultimately determined via entrepreneurial prediction of ultimate consumer preference.

The entrepreneur, as we have seen, *assumes responsibility for* choosing the means needed for the response to consumer-saver preferences. He thereby *determines the form* to be taken by income and hence *the form* of replacement and accumulation of assets. In doing so, he contracts with and directs *producers*. Given the definitions we are using, this is another way of saying, "by causing existing resources to be used in a particular way." He relies on his forecasts of

---

[42] We are forced to make an entrepreneurial choice at the stage in which our product or our claims are exchanged for money; for it is continuously in our power to change the form in which our assets are held. The decision to make no change is itself a decision. Hence, it can be maintained that there can hardly be such a thing *in practice* as a "pure saver."

future preferences as a whole, and among other things upon interpretations of two sets of factors: saving preference and all the factors which determine what Keynes called "the marginal efficiency of capital."[43] His direction of services into different channels is itself a valuable service.[44] Hence the entrepreneur may be regarded as belonging to a special class of producer. Indeed, in backing expert judgment—his own or that of others—the entrepreneur is vitally productive. The definitions I am using merely isolate this important kind of productive action.

But we are nearly all making entrepreneurial decisions all the time; and I must repeat that when a person who is saving deliberately *selects* certain assets (for example, money, gilt-edged securities, or equities, in a certain industry or firm, or fixed property) which he expects to bring him the highest return (pecuniary or other) compatible with the satisfaction of his risk preference, he is acting as an entrepreneur. In other words, because every person who is a saver *must* decide to keep his nonconsumed income in some form or other, every saver must have at least *some* entrepreneurial influence. *As a saver,* however, he is a *passive* purchaser of assets, concerned only with acquiring or retaining assets "in some form or other." *As an entrepreneur,* he chooses particular assets to use. This distinction can be clearly envisaged if it is remembered—as has just been stated—that the pure saver can expect a yield of interest only.

A further clarification of the distinction between entrepreneurs and *producers* may be helpful. The producer usually receives a defined contractual remuneration; but as the contract to which he is tied and to which he has tied others may turn out to be favorable or unfavorable (so that if he recontracted now he would get less favorable or more favorable terms), some element of his remuneration will be, strictly speaking, profit or loss. It again follows therefore that in entering into any contract, every producer is inevitably an entrepreneur.

---

[43] The schedule of the marginal efficiency of capital represents the complex of predicted productive potentialities, from the wise or lucky perception of which, wedded to the necessary initiative, the entrepreneur is able to win a profit or avoid losses (in the sense of a realized return above or below interest) by directing the embodiment of services in accordance with predicted demands.

[44] Some readers may wonder why the entrepreneur is here regarded merely as dealing with services and not with assets. But as we have seen, when assets are devoted to certain uses, it is really their services which are being utilized in a certain way, even when the resources are acquired in the expectation of capital gain.

Moreover, strictly speaking, even the person whom we usually think of as a *consumer* is performing the entrepreneurial function. Thus, we *acquire* durable consumer goods (replaced or accumulated net) up to the point at which we prefer their prospective services to what we can get from interest on the sum we invest in them. Similarly, we *retain* consumer assets when we prefer their services to what we can get from interest on the sum we can realize from their sale. For the interest we sacrifice equals the value of what we can obtain in the form of other directly rendered services or the services of other assets.

Durable goods in the household stand in this respect in exactly the same position as all other productive assets except that, in this case, we do not regard the prospective return exceeding interest (in "gratifications") as "profit," although Murray Rothbard has recently called it "psychic profit." But basically, all assets we retain, whether "privately" or in business, are held for the same economic reasons.

I have mentioned that the term *investment* is commonly used to mean what I call "accumulated assets." But when a firm *replaces* a machine, it "invests" in a new machine, just as it has been disinvesting (instead of merely consuming) the old one (if it has been making the needed arrangements to cover depreciation). I wish to avoid the potential confusions which lurk in such a terminology.

The position is complicated because, as we have seen (p. 306), the ordinary stockholder always delegates to the corporation in which he has invested, not only authority to make decisions for which he assumes entrepreneurial responsibility, but also at least a limited authority to make saving decisions on his behalf, namely, the right to maintain the firm's resources intact, that is, to replace. And to the extent to which the stockholder acquiesces in undistributed profits (that is, in corporate decisions to add to the firm's resources), the amount that he saves is not of his own direct choosing. But he is still the entrepreneur and still the saver. Hence directors or managers have a dual role, both sides of which are covered by the managerial function. They are salaried employees of entrepreneurs and of savers. They express simultaneously entrepreneurial judgment and saving preference: an entrepreneurial judgment because there is a calculation of the *most profitable* form in which to hold and use resources, and a saving preference because there is a choice concerning *the amount* of resources to be maintained or acquired (out of disinvested funds *plus* profits). Both roles are merged on behalf of entrepreneurs and savers among the stockholders. Obviously, the managerial function is of the utmost importance. But directors and managers are interpreters or agents, in spite of the fact that, in choosing means, they have the vital role of creating new production functions or assets mixes.

I have explained that, insofar as any person's decisions affect the real or money value of accumulated or consumed assets, he is acting in a consumer-saver role. To avoid confusion, therefore, I have defined the concepts of "investment" and "disinvestment" so that they have reference solely to *the form or composition* of accumulation. For entrepreneurs may be said to *invest* or *disinvest* when they allocate or withdraw resources or services, in varying combinations, to or from the manufacture of *different kinds of products or different methods of production,* and to or from *particular undertakings.* When an entrepreneur invests, he must use either his own resources or resources entrusted to him by (sometimes borrowed from) others. As an entrepreneur (for example, as a stockholder), he may disinvest from particular firms, which is what happens when he gets back capital as dividends. But whether he then decides to reinvest such dividend receipts in other assets or ventures, so as to maintain his capital intact, or to treat the receipts as though they were income and eat up the capital, the decision always is that of a consumer-saver and not of an entrepreneur. A preference is involved, not a responsibility concerning the use of services.

In each individual case, it is true, the entrepreneur invests a chosen value in chosen resources and operations. *But each amount of services so invested prevents some other entrepreneur from investing a similar amount. That is, it represents a particular way of using the services of scarce resources and is in no sense a determinant of the rate of growth in his assets stock.*

Appendix A

The Concept of Aggregate Demand

In Chapter 5 I referred to the defectiveness of the concept of aggregate effective demand.[45] But even without the tendentious adjective "effective," the notion of "aggregate demand" or "demand in general" is objectionable. We can, as I have explained (pp. 106–9), envisage *"demands* in general"; but *strictly speaking* we cannot, I hold, describe such demands as *"demand* in general" or "aggregate demand" without the danger of misleading ourselves and others. The source of all demands is the flow of services (income) and/or the stock of assets (capital).

Demands in general ("aggregate demand") *for assets* from *the offer of assets* are in no conceivable sense something which can be measured, because it is impossible to measure *preferences* in general! It is wholly a matter of changes in *relative values*. The number of exchanges of assets is no measure of anything. The relative value of particular assets or of different kinds of assets may change considerably (through changes in preference) without any exchanges actually occurring; and there is no way of *aggregating* the preferences or value changes so expressed.

But is it possible to measure that part of the demands for services which arise from the offer of services? The flow itself—the income —can be measured in value units; and in measuring in *value* units, *demands are assumed;* for without demands (that is, without the ability to exchange one thing for another thing or things) there will be no value. But I do not think that demands in general for services

---

[45] At the same time I have at times conformed to current usage to the extent of using the term "demand" (in general) in contexts in which it is synonymous with "income."

from the offer of services can be *measured* in any sense, any more than the aggregate demand from the offer of assets for assets can be measured. Again, it is purely a question of relative preferences. Of course, *income* can be meaningfully measured.

Services which make up the flow of income are either retained (consumed, or embodied into assets for the owner) or exchanged. In each case they are demanded. If retained, their owners *outbid* others, so to speak.[46] If exchanged, their owners *are outbid by* others. Now although the whole of the flow of valuable services *is demanded,* and although it is part of *the source of demands in general,* we surely cannot say that it *is* demand. But when economists have talked of "demand in general" or "aggregate demand," and they have been thinking of demand from the flow of services, then they have merely been using another term for "income." Income *is,* indeed, what they have meant by "aggregate demand." But they write as though they thought aggregate demand *causes* aggregate income. Actually, production as a whole *is* the creation of value; hence it is the creation of income and the source of all demands *from income.*

In the category "demands in general," however, are demands for services from the offer of assets, and demands for assets from the offer of services. Let us assume that we are measuring the flow of services in money units of constant purchasing power. Demands of this nature will clearly not affect the aggregate value of the flow of services. (See above, pp. 304–5.) They will influence only the rate of interest—*the ratio* between the values of services and the values of the assets from which services flow.

It is therefore imperative that we should separate quite clearly in our minds demands for services from the offer of services, and demands for services from the offer of assets (and for assets from the offer of services). Lumping together "demands" in such different senses, in a blanket concept of "demands in general," can only lead to the most serious confusions, still more so if it is thought of as forming part of a measurable complex called "aggregate demand."

Clarity on this issue will assist the reader in the chapters which follow.

---

[46] Thus, when I grow cabbages in my garden, I may myself demand them (preferring them to the products of the farms); and when I shave myself I am demanding (preferring) my own services instead of those of the barber.

14

The Consumption Fallacy

In previous chapters, I have used the term "savings" in its ordinary, everyday connotation. In such a sense its value magnitude as a constituent of the income of a period is identical with what I have called "accumulated assets." And I have suggested that, given the factors which determine interest, consumer-savers determine the *"amount" and value* of consumed services and assets, while entrepreneurs determine *the form* of the assets stock. But I am not optimistic enough to suppose that I shall have convinced all readers of the futility of those approaches which make use of the notions of the availability or nonavailability of "outlets for investment," or of the "absorption (or nonabsorption) of savings in investment." I propose therefore to examine further the nature of the response to consumption-saving preference.

An increase or decrease in the demand for assets by the offer of services, that is, an increase or decrease in saving preference, may be *induced* or *autonomous*.[1] It is *induced* if called forth by a rise in the rate of interest (brought about by a rise in prospective yields) or vice versa. It is *autonomous* if it is brought about by all the other factors, apart from the rate of interest, which influence saving preference. By a "change in the rate of interest" I mean a change in the relative values of services and assets (income and capital), as will shortly become clear.[2]

---

[1] The term "autonomous" is not *ideal,* for included under it is the reaction to all value changes other than those expressed in the rate of interest.

[2] In Diagram II, p. 334, "autonomous" changes in time preference are represented by shifts in the curve representing saving preference and "induced" changes by movements along this curve caused by shifts in the curve representing the demand for saving. (See p. 304 n.)

I shall argue that, given the entrepreneur's offer of interest, the magnitude of *services and assets consumed* (or consumption) is determined *solely* by the factors which are expressed in saving preference. Similarly, given saving preference, this magnitude is determined by prospective yields, which are reflected in the entrepreneur's interest offer. Changes in the rate of savings (or dissavings) being the same thing as changes in the rate at which assets are accumulated or consumed, shifts in the demand schedule of entrepreneurs competing for services to be embodied into the assets they use, can influence the magnitudes in question only insofar as the rate of interest they offer can influence the preferences which determine the rate of savings (or dissavings). Entrepreneurial optimism or pessimism can otherwise determine merely *the form* in which resources are replaced or accumulated.

A change in the form of the assets stock (indeed, the form of income generally) is then, in every case, due to an entrepreneurial decision. The entrepreneur's inducement is the *relative* prospective profitableness of investment in different kinds of assets. To the typical entrepreneur, a fall in the rate of interest appears as a fall in costs; and as the subsequent analysis will make clear, if realized savings increase, this will be due entirely to an additional flow of services having been made available for entrepreneurs to embody into the additional assets which savers are demanding.

I can at this stage anticipate an objection. It will be said that this reasoning can hardly hold if the market rate of interest is fixed below the noninflationary level (with a consequent increasing MV in relation to T). But unless people *wish* then to save a larger proportion of their increasing money incomes, it will cause no increase in the rate of realized accumulation of assets in real terms but merely a higher money valuation of the flow of income generally. (I refer to a slightly different form of the fallacy on pp. 322–24.)

We must keep constantly in mind two fundamental truths: (a) that replacement is a response to the same kind of saving preference and carried out to the same limits as net accumulation (the limits being set by the points at which the marginal prospective yield from the assets to be acquired[3] has fallen to the rate of interest); and (b) that the greater part of all output is a response to this preference, that is, a response to the demand for the *capital* represented *by*

---

[3] The embodiment of services into maintenance and renovation is, of course, regarded as the acquisition of assets in the form of replacement.

inventories and *stocks of all life expectancies.* The only services which are in no sense a response (through the entrepreneur, and indirectly) to saving preference are those I have called "consumed services," which are consumed as they are rendered, and those which are embodied into immediately perishable goods.[4] Thus, the replacement part of output is, *by definition,* accompanied by consumption at an equivalent rate (unless the magnitude of the assets stock is contracting). But it remains one part of the response to saving preference. That is, some part of production is *overlapped* by consumption. Hence, the inducement to the entrepreneur is the same whether or not growth occurs. Prospective profits (in the sense of a yield in excess of interest) are as essential to induce any measure of replacement as they are to induce growth.[5]

It is because the same kind of preference calls forth that value of production which overlaps consumption as well as the part which does not, that I call *the whole process* by one name, "saving." If we concentrate attention on the excess of production over consumption (in other words, "savings"), or on the excess of consumption over production (in other words, "dissavings"), we are apt to forget that production and consumption are independently determined magnitudes.[6] The former can be realized only out of income whereas the latter must be mainly out of capital. My approach endeavors to concentrate attention upon these magnitudes themselves and not merely upon the overlap.

Nevertheless, I expect to be told that it is straining the meaning of words to describe the process of demanding assets to replace inventories consumed as "saving preference," instead of confining

---

[4] Perishability means that inventories can never be more than negligible in magnitude.

[5] Of course, one cannot consider in isolation the prospective profitableness or replacement of or additions to particular assets. It becomes profitable to replace or add to the stock of one kind of assets because it is at the same time profitable to replace or add to the stock of various complementary assets needed. But this in no way weakens the principle stated.

Nor is the proposition disturbed in the case in which a firm decides to "run at a loss" for a temporary period in order to preserve the goodwill of staff or customers. It remains true that, from the long-term point of view, profits in the sense of an eventual yield above interest must be expected from the value of services embodied into assets. The fact that profits are expected from all replacements does not mean that *realized* profits (realized yields in excess of interest at the time of the investment) will *eventuate.* Still less does it mean that profits in the accounting sense will be made.

[6] When we consume anything, we need not replace with the same thing, or we need not replace at all—we may live on capital.

this term to demand for the excess above replacement (resulting in what I have called "savings"—plural). But saving preference in my sense is perfectly homogeneous.

Saving—*the process*—is always occurring even though dissavings are being realized and capital consumption is in progress! That is, *saving preference* may be effectively exercised, even if it is not currently leading to any replacement. This can be seen whenever the consumption of a decumulable stock is spread over time. For instance, if Robinson Crusoe carefully conserves his pile of grain from one harvest throughout the year in order to make it last until the next harvest, he is all the time exercising consumption-saving choice. And if he decides to consume more slowly (and his grain reserves are his only consumable stocks), the decline in the rate of consumption means, in effect, a rise in saving preference and decreased dissavings.

A decline in consumption always means an increase in real savings (or a decrease in dissavings) *and vice versa,* unless there is some other *conceptually quite independent* reaction. For instance, if Crusoe's decision to consume more slowly means that some of his stocks perish, or if similar action in an exchange economy means some discoordination and a shrinkage in the flow of income, this is what I have in mind in the reference to a *"conceptually quite independent reaction."* But we must always take into account the possibility of all sorts of predictable or unpredictable reactions upon the flow of services or the stock of assets, owing to such changes in preference.

Let us now notice in greater detail the process by which the individual, in achieving savings, contributes to savings by the community.

A person acquires savings by refraining from the consumption of a value of services and assets greater than the value of his contribution to the stock of assets into which his services (or those of his assets) are flowing. In practice, he either accumulates the product of his own efforts or property (for example, Crusoe building a hut), or accumulates assets in the form of *contractual claims* for remuneration, interest, or dividends in return for the product of his efforts or the services of his property. This stage in saving is almost always ended through the temporary conversion of the assets accumulated (products or claims) into money.[7] Thus, if the saver is an employee who is paid his wages weekly, he is saving from the beginning of the

---

[7] In the case of both the earner and the receiver of interest and dividends, this stage is the fulfillment of the contract which led to the personal services being rendered or the investment being made.

week until the end of the week; for he is accumulating assets in the form of his legal claim for wages on his employer. If during that week he has consumed a smaller value of assets (food, clothing, etc.) than the value of those he has accumulated as claims, he will have achieved savings. He neither saves further nor accumulates further in turning one form of assets into another (for example, in exchanging rights to wages for actual wages—money), or subsequently by investing in a savings account, subscribing to equities in an existing corporation or one in process of formation, or buying a television set. If he is working on his own account as a manufacturer of something durable, he will be achieving savings when he accumulates inventories at a rate of which the value sufficiently exceeds the value of his current consumption and accumulation of liabilities. If he is working on his own account selling services, like a doctor, he will be saving as he renders his services and is either paid or acquires the right to be paid. In each case, whether or not a contribution to society's savings is being made depends upon whether or not a person's acquisition of assets (*including money*) is exceeding his consumption of services and assets. Hence unless such contributions to *savings* have, in the aggregate, been offset by dissavings on the parts of others, there will have been an *equivalent* addition to *savings* (that is, accumulated assets) on the part of society. It follows that *the amount of realized savings by society must equal the sum of realized individual savings*—individual additions to the value of assets owned *less* individual dissavings, whatever initial form such assets may have happened to take.

We have seen that saving preference means the offer of services for assets and not the offer of assets for assets (see pp. 306–7, 317–18). Similarly the response to this preference—replacement and net accumulation *in general*—can occur only through the incorporation of *services* into assets—in other words, out of income. When economists talk of the investment of *capital,* they must mean (unless there is some subtle confusion in their thinking) the combination or recombination of capital assets. But mere combination of assets by entrepreneurs does not lead to any contribution to growth unless creating the new "assets mix" is productive. If, when combined, the capital value of two assets is greater than when they are uncombined, and no other services have been involved in the combination, it means that the innovators' (the entrepreneurs') services have been embodied into the assets, which is an act of production.

It should be noticed that, while from the standpoint of the individual saver assets may be accumulated in the form of *products, or claims, or credit money,* from the standpoint of society, assets are accumulated solely in the form of *products.*[8] For claims and credit money are offset by liabilities.

The fact that all persons may prefer to hold more or less of their assets in the form of money (and this may happen to accompany saving or dissaving), *does not cause any divergence between savings and accumulated assets.* Consider, for instance, the case in which a person acquires increased stocks of money equal to the value of his savings during a period. If those to whom he has sold assets (his original savings) have not consumed them, *the aggregate stock of assets will have increased. This is in spite of the fact that the stock of money cannot be increased by saving preference or a response to it* (neither M_r nor M). (I shall return to this point.)

To talk of "saving money," unless it is merely a loose or popular way of talking, is a serious solecism. One may save, and then invest in money; but the *saving* has occurred before the product into which services have been embodied has been exchanged for the money. If I grow potatoes, sell them, and retain the money receipts, *my saving occurs as I am accumulating the potatoes, not when I sell them.*

The point at issue is no mere verbal quibble. Demand for money must be recognized as an expression of entrepreneurship; and it is, I repeat, an act which is wholly independent of saving preference. The entrepreneur will, as we have seen, choose to hold his assets in the form of money to the extent to which monetary services appear to be more profitable than the services of other assets—that is, up to the point at which the marginal prospective yield in terms of monetary services has fallen to the rate of interest. Now what has to be explained is why this reaction to saving—why this particular entrepreneurial choice of productive factors—should cause the cessation of, or a falling off in, the rate at which services are supplied for immediate consumption or embodiment into assets. Any falling off or cessation in production must be due, in the circumstances being considered, to the services which are capable of use for that purpose not being offered at prices which are correctly coordinated with prospective demand for them.

It is never argued that the scope for growth contracts because potentially available services are wrongly thought to be more

---

[8] I should remind the reader that if certain assets increase in real value passively (interest being constant), I regard the increase as a product.

profitably employed in producing things of short life expectancies, instead of things of long life expectancies. Hence the implication must be that such services are withheld through being priced above market-clearing values, that is, higher than people *can afford* to pay, or higher than they *are willing* to pay (that is, too high in relation to the future prices which buyers anticipate).

It follows that those economists who talk of savings not being fully absorbed in investment, or of a lack of investment outlets for savings, or of "the thrift of the community" (being) "too great for the demands put upon it" (as the Radcliffe Committee expressed the fallacy)[9] cannot justify their position on the grounds that they have had in mind "past savings"—"hoarded savings." For as we have seen, the exchange of money for nonmoney does not, in itself, bring about additions to the aggregate assets stock.

The same misconception in a different makeup is found in the notion that growth may be "financed," not out of current savings but out of inflation. Savings, it is thought, will then be unnecessary. The answer is that inflationary credit issued, or notes forged, may be spent to buy either "consumed services" or "embodied services" while the proportion of assets of long life expectancies in the total stock may rise if that is the entrepreneur's choice. To use the common terminology, if "new money" happens to be "injected" so as to provide additional producer goods, the decision to depreciate the money unit is linked with a command to save,[10] provided, of course, (a) that the supposed production financed does not partake of the nature of boondoggling, which is disguised consumption,[11] and hence a depressant, and (b) that it does not induce additional unintended consumption elsewhere in the economy.

A similar error sometimes arises in the opposite form. Growth is assumed to occur "autonomously," the failure to achieve correspond-

---

[9] Report of the Radcliffe Committee, para. 42.

[10] It need hardly be stressed that, if the accumulated assets are sufficiently productive, they are financed by noninflationary credit, and not by inflation.

[11] In attempting to answer Bertil Ohlin's criticisms in 1937, Keynes argued that "finance" (meaning credit expansion which may or may not be inflationary) "has nothing to do with saving," which is certainly true. But he continued, "At the 'financial' stage of the proceedings no net savings has taken place on anyone's part, just as there has been no net investment." Keynes, "Alternative Theories of the Rate of Interest," *Economic Journal,* June 1937, p. 247. This misses the real issue, with which I have dealt above. "The financial stage of the proceedings" can only be said to begin when the money valuation of a given flow of services has changed, and *someone* must have decided how the newly valued flow is being utilized.

ing savings being supposed to force inflation, through which the necessary savings are induced. For instance, the Radcliffe Committee wrote of "heavy investment in *new* capital assets" having occurred "without the corresponding rise in current savings necessary to finance their production without inflation."[12] (My italics.) But if the word *new* is intended to mean *additional,* savings *must* have been forthcoming through decisions somewhere.

It is far from certain, however, whether the Committee regards the inflation as having been *beneficent* in permitting investment in heavy industry; for it referred also to "excessive demand," resulting from too little thrift. Yet any inflation in the circumstances mentioned can arise only from monetary policy, which an official desire for investment in a particular form—heavy industry—*may cause to be expedient.* And the expediency can in turn arise only because, given existing prospective yields in that field, freely expressed saving preference does not itself make the objective sufficiently cheap. Abnormally low (or declining) thrift is not *inflationary,* as the words "excessive demand" imply, unless it is assumed that the noninflationary level of interest being raised by rising consumption, any formerly existing market rate will be inflationary, or that a rise in consumption happens to be accompanied by an uncompensated rise in V.[13] The only sense in which there can be said to be "too little" or "too much" thrift implies a moral judgment, or the assumption that people do not know their own interests in exercising consumption-saving preference. In this sense alone can a "deficiency" or "excess" of thrift be alleged.

The most important conclusion of this and the previous page is, however, that *the notion of an insufficiency of openings for investment in relation to the flow of savings is absurd.* It is impossible to save without replacing or adding to one's assets, that is, without exercising the entrepreneurial decision of choosing the form of assets judged to be most *productive,* that is, of greatest prospective usefulness to oneself or others (including, of course, money assets).

A rather different form of the same fallacy is that "saving as such is merely not spending," so that a person may save "without demanding anything at all." When we accumulate money, it is said, we

---

[12] Radcliffe Report, para. 31.

[13] For a change in saving preference implies (a) changed demands for assets in terms of services and (b) increased demands for certain services which offset reduced demands for other services. (See pp. 329–31.)

postpone consumption, but there is no "current demand for additional assets." As one objector put it to me verbally, "In the case in which some *individuals* postpone consumption and accumulate money, *society* accumulates nothing more of anything." There are two cases to consider here.

First, we have the case in which money is *deliberately* accumulated. This may be either (a) for motives of convenience, etc. (the normal business and private demands for monetary services), or (b) for speculative reasons (for example, when the value of the *money unit* or the rate of interest is expected to rise). But why, in either of these circumstances, should we not regard the assets so held as having been "invested in"? One invests in money up to the point at which we judge it to produce more income than nonmoney. We enjoy a valuable yield in liquidity.

Second, we have the case in which money assets are accumulated solely through inertia, as when we "just allow bank balances to pile up." Let us consider a parallel example. On occasion, I have signed a banker's order for a certain periodical in which I have later ceased to be interested, eventually throwing the unopened copies into the wastepaper basket, but in the meantime forgetting to cancel my subscription. Can it then be said that I am not demanding the periodical? My "inertia" has meant a claim on the scarce resources, paper, etc., which have gone into the journal. Similarly, when I "allow cash to pile up," my action is still tending to bid up the aggregate real value of money, just as it does when my demand to hold cash is deliberate and purposive. *Hence my contribution to savings is a contribution to society's savings, unless those from whom I obtain the money happen to dissave in consequence.*

The possibility that the individual saver *may,* through sheer inertia (and in another—that is, an entrepreneurial—capacity), retain an abnormal value of assets in the form of currency or in his checking account, and for an inordinately long period, has received much stress in Keynesian literature.[14] Now if people *are* inclined at times to bid up M_r, the aggregate real value of money more than in propor-

---

14 It is seldom considered whether a person may not be equally passive in respect of his whole portfolio of assets. The truth is, I think, that in general people are *less* passive and uncritical about money holdings than they are about any of their other resources. They realize usually that it is wasteful to hold "idle money"—money without a purpose—while they perceive less often that some of their *nonmoney* assets offer prospective yields below interest on their current sale value.

tion to the increase in real income,[15] and monetary policy is inflexible, that will not prevent growth, unless this "hoarding" of money somehow causes (a) the growth of real income to cease (through the withholding of capacity) and partly for this reason, (b) the achievement of real savings to cease or fall.

In each case, however, when a rise in saving preference happens to be accompanied by a rise in liquidity preference, the aggregate value of assets held for the monetary services they can perform rises; and the individual who, having saved, holds more money assets than previously, will have more assets of all kinds than previously. And as we have seen (pp. 321–22), if those who acquire from him nonmoney goods or services (in return for the money which he accumulates) refrain from decumulating the goods, or use the services in the production of assets, they will still not have fewer real assets than before. *In that case, society must have accumulated.* In other words, unless the rest of society *wastes or consume*s what he (the hoarder) would otherwise have withdrawn from the flow of nonmoney products, an increase in the assets stock must have been achieved. *The future flow of all wanted things will be greater by reason of his savings having occurred.* If waste *does* occur, however (and in our contemporary world we all know that it can occur— because capacity may be withheld), it may be at the expense of growth. But in that case a rise in saving preference, even when it is accompanied by a rise in liquidity preference, cannot be held responsible for the waste. Blame must fall wholly on whoever may have been responsible for pricing inputs or outputs at above market-clearing values.[16]

We must beware of misinterpreting the fact that the entrepreneur's demand for services seems in practice to be *financed* by the saver's demand for assets. Certainly, in a common case, the saver buys securities, thus passing the power to demand services to entrepreneurs; but that is just how the original saver may escape the making of *the more difficult* entrepreneurial decisions[17] and remain more of

---

[15] The aggregate value of money (in real terms) tends to vary in proportion to real income, in the same sort of way that the aggregate real value of land *tends* to change in this way. (See pp. 192–93.)

[16] James Tobin's interpretation of Keynesian teaching to the effect that expenditure on the flow of services from a given income may decline without hoarding is dealt with in Appendix B.

[17] He still makes an entrepreneurial decision in choosing a particular security to purchase, or a particular borrower.

a "pure saver" (that is, simply a demander of assets). The aggregate entrepreneurial demand for services for embodiment into assets is not increased by the passing of that power. The partial and very useful specialization in practice of saving preference on the one hand, and entrepreneurial judgment and action on the other, in no way upsets the argument. For instance, when a "pure saver" lends to the entrepreneur (short term, long term, or permanently), he acquires *assets,* in the form of *securities,* from the entrepreneur; while to the entrepreneur is transferred the power to decide what services to purchase for replacement or growth. This is one aspect of *the constant offer, through the medium of entrepreneurs, of assets for services;* and it occurs in the same sort of way when the same person is the saver and the entrepreneur, as it does when the saver *lends* to the entrepreneur.[18]

Entrepreneurial decisions can, therefore, have no direct effect upon the rate of growth of the assets stock from a given income. Entrepreneurs can merely (a) change the composition of replacements to and additions to the stock of assets and (b) offer interest to savers in the process of, so to speak, bidding for a given flow of services. They can only *utilize* the flow of services by arranging those combinations of assets which they forecast will be most profitable. Certainly, through their determination of new "assets mixes," which result in new compositions of embodied services, and especially through the economizing displacements they bring about,[19] their activities are constantly tending to magnify the flow of services providable from a stock of assets of given value, and a given stock of knowledge, skills, effort, and muscular power. But *as entrepreneurs* they cannot control the rate at which concurrent consumption—the accompanying extermination of the value of the assets stock—is occurring. They cannot, for instance, prevent consumption from increasing more rapidly than income is increasing or vice versa. That is, they cannot add to the excess of income above consumption (except insofar as they are, in another role, savers). Subsequent exchanges of one kind of assets for another involve no further accumulation of assets. We

---

[18] If a person uses services for embodiment into assets, through the offer of his personal services or the services of his own property (that is, out of his own income), he is at one and the same time a saver and an entrepreneur. He is a saver in that he demands assets. He is an entrepreneur in that he demands services for embodiment in *particular* assets.

[19] Producing given outputs at reduced labor or capital costs. See my *The Strike-Threat System,* pp. 19–20.

must remember, however, that the common assumption that "saving" is done by one set of persons and investment in assets by another set of persons is wrong, even though investment decisions may be said to be made *in some degree* by a specialized class of persons. Savings or dissavings are always due to the decisions of those who refrain from consuming or who consume. In short, changes in the sum total of assets are determined solely by saving preference; and they can be studied only through the factors which determine that preference.

If the above argument is valid, then entrepreneurial optimism and pessimism are irrelevant to the rate of savings except through their influence on *prospective* supplies in general (the source of prospective demands in general and hence prospective yields), which may influence (a) (through the interest offer) the expression of saving preference,[20] and (b) the release or withholding of productive capacity.

Hence these psychological attitudes *are* relevant to the development *tempo*. But the important consequence of optimism in this respect is not that it causes the accumulation of assets but that it causes the growth of real income; for normally it results equally in an increase in consumption (and replacement). The reaction upon income must be kept distinct in our minds, therefore, from both (a) the rise in the entrepreneurial demand for services, that is, the increased bidding which raises the rate of interest, and (b) the effects upon the prospective productivity of money, that is, upon any change in M_r. In many treatments all three influences[21] seem to me to be confused.

I am not denying—indeed I wish to stress—the enormous importance of the decisions which determine investment (as I have defined it). In proportion to the extent to which entrepreneurs correctly discern the most profitable and productive forms of gross accumulation, they will not only influence their own contribution to the flow of services but *stimulate* it and hence cause an increase in *the ability to save.* At the same time, the boost to supplies is likely

---

[20] That is, to the extent to which the offer of interest induces a reduction of the relative rate of consumption, it *can* cause an increase in the accumulation of assets.

The confidence which induces people (1) as producers, to release capacity and (2) as entrepreneurs, (a) to raise their interest offer, and (b) perhaps dishoard, is justified when it is based on the correctly discerned bringing of relative prices into a coordinated relationship.

[21] That is, upon income, the offer of interest and the productivity of money.

to raise prospects, and hence the interest inducement, and so (perhaps) an induced *willingness to save*.

Hence entrepreneurs, in predicting and devising what they judge will be the least-cost production functions, can affect the rate of growth only because they can influence the composition of production in response to thrift; because their interest offer may influence the expression of thrift; and because their successful activity causes real income to expand and so *facilitates* the achievement of savings.

If at any time the aggregate real value of productive capacity is not increasing, that means *the representative consumer-saver* cannot be achieving savings. At best, he can merely be replacing. Now obviously, saving preference *may* sometimes be like that. Indeed, it is the only explanation of nonexpanding societies. But I find it difficult to conceive why, in the conditions which we can observe to be ruling in all countries of the contemporary world, it should ever be assumed to be *impossible* for all would-be savers to accumulate assets. Only if it can be assumed that for some reason the reaction to a rise in saving preference must be a fall in real income, while consumption *cannot* fall to compensate, can it be said that *savings* are impossible of achievement. And if it is so assumed— that the representative consumer-saver *cannot* curtail current consumption, as his income falls—that is an assumption about the nature of preferences. But of course in a free society, the *process* of production is a cooperative activity coordinated by pricing under the discipline of competition; and, if governments favor private interests, as against the collective interest, (a) by allowing certain prices to be forced above market-clearing values (through the private use of coercive power), or (b) by themselves acting on behalf of politically powerful private interests and fixing prices above market-clearing values, the flow of productive services *must* shrink. In such circumstances, it is very easy to fall into the error of blaming certain autonomous or induced changes in preferences, like saving preference or liquidity preference, for contributing to depression.

We are unable to assume, however, that in practice there is always a flow of services available not only for replacement uses, or to maintain any existing rate of net accumulation, but also for an *increased* rate of net accumulation. The *additional* services needed for that purpose *can* become available (a) through market-selected downward price adjustments to release withheld capacity of the required type; or (b) through the release of some of the services of *versatile* resources at present devoted to the replacement of inventories of short life expectancies (a release made possible through a decline in the rate of consumption) for use in the manufacture of assets of longer life expectancies; or (c) through the form of current replacement and net accumulation of assets happening to favor further accumulation. But such reactions will not necessarily follow (for example, if there is "full employment," or if the resources making goods of short prospective life span are, in the short run, absolutely specific,[22] or if the form of current growth is not such as facilitates more rapid growth). In that case, what will be the effects of changes in consumption-saving preference?

There are two aspects of such changes: (a) a change in values and (b) a consequent *gradual* change in the composition of the future flow of services, in spite of short-run specificities. Theoretically, the former can occur without the latter. For instance, the desire to save more may simply cause the values of those services which replace inventories of goods of short life expectancies to fall while causing the values of those services which replace or add to relatively long life expectancies to rise. Moreover, when this occurs, the values of assets in general will increase in relation to the values of the services they provide. In other words (as we shall see), the rate of interest will fall. But if there is any versatility as between these broad uses of the resources employed—if it is possible to replace any kind of worn-out specific assets by another kind—the discrepancies in the relative values will induce *action* (response to demand). It is solely because such action may occur that, as we have seen, any desire to increase the rate of provision for the future can ever be realized *by society.* Unless the composition of current income is appropriate for growth, or unless resources can be and are released from replacing inventories of goods of which net additions to current stocks *cannot be profitably carried through time* in order to produce additions to the stocks of those assets of which additional stocks *can be profitably carried through time,* it is possible for one set of persons to acquire savings only as fast as others are simultaneously consuming their assets (by exchanging long-life assets for short-life assets or consumed services).

It is important, therefore, to distinguish changes in "consumption-saving *preference*"—changes in the relative value placed on current

---

[22] I say, "in the short run," because according to the rate at which depreciation occurs there must always be possibilities of making large changes in the form of the assets stock at the time of replacement.

consumption—from changes in *actual* consumption. In pure theory, at least, the *value* of consumption may decline, owing to a rise in saving preference, without any change in its physical composition (the "amounts" of different things consumed); and this is simply another way of saying that the value of accumulated assets may increase without any change in the composition of the stock. Such changes in relative values will be experienced when changes in demand (expressing saving-consumption preference) induce no response or an incomplete supply response.

For simplicity, let us imagine that there is no withheld capacity and that the resources used for replacing inventories of short-life goods are sufficiently unversatile to prevent their being transferred to the production of long-life, "economically durable" assets, and that no net accumulation has been occurring. In these circumstances what will limit the acquisition of savings *by individuals?* The answer is, exactly the same factors as limit the achievement of all other economic ends, the cost of so doing.

In the sort of world of which we have had experience, the acquisition of savings has nearly always been subject to the additional inducement that savings bear fruits through positive interest. But in an imaginary society in which aggregate accumulation of assets is impossible (that is, in which it is impossible for people in general to refrain—except by obvious waste—from consuming an aggregate value which falls short of the value of their product), and in which the desire by some to provide for the future (at the current cost of so doing) is not wholly offset by the desire on the part of others to enjoy the fruits of past provision for the future (through consumption), *the rate of interest can be negative.* Instead of thrift being, so to speak, subsidized by positive interest, it may be penalized by negative interest.

Let us consider the implications of such a society, assuming that all products are *perishable.*[23] In this case *society* would no more attempt to achieve savings than a country in the twentieth century would attempt to improve its climate by changing the angle of inclination of the earth's axis! People *in general* would not want to provide more for the future because the cost of so doing would be prohibitive. But individual savers might well wish to pay now, in

---

[23] We can think of Keynes' banana community example, used in his *Treatise.* The rate of interest could equate consumption by some with the accumulation of assets by others.

order to provide for consumption in the distant future, instead of being remunerated for doing so by positive interest. They might, for instance, offer to pay $10,000 now in return for, say, $5,000 in ten years' time. That situation could arise, however, only if there were no durable assets to acquire. But consideration of these rather fantastic possibilities does not make necessary any modification of the principle that the achievement of savings by individuals, not countervailed through consumption by others, will always and necessarily mean accumulation of assets by society.

To sum up, changes in consumption-saving preference may, theoretically, influence interest only and cause no change, or a nonproportional change, in the rate of embodiment of services into assets or their consumption. And when I talk of such changes, I envisage them as being expressed partly or solely in value changes (including interest), as distinct from changes in the form of output.

It follows that thrift—positive saving preference—is the source of all growth of productive capacity which does occur, although it may not always be strong enough actually to bring forth growth. But an increase in savings *bids down* the value of services in terms of assets, with owners *offering* services (income) for assets (capital); and in so doing, causing the rate of interest to fall. But the demand for those services is initially expressed by consumer-savers via entrepreneurs, and the latter accept *responsibility* to society for their prediction of consumer-saver preferences.[24]

Interest (the noninflationary, nondeflationary level) is *determined* when entrepreneurs offer assets for services and savers offer services for assets; but interest is not affected when services are offered for services, or assets are offered for assets, unless the distribution of life expectancies within the stock is changed.[25] *Even the exchange of money for nonmoney assets, in itself, leaves the noninflationary, nondeflationary level of interest unchanged.*[26] The services offered by savers are those contributed as income (for only income can be devoted to replacement or accumulation of the aggregate assets stock). The assets offered are the existing stock, of which different components have different life expectancies.

---

[24] Entrepreneurs interpret saving preference in that they predict the extent to which savings are adding to unwithheld productive power; and the rate of interest they offer will vary with their prediction on this point.

[25] For assets of short life expectancies resemble "pure services" in some respects.

[26] But obviously, if M *is changing* in relation to M_r, there will be a divergence of market interest from the noninflationary, nondeflationary level.

Diagram II, p. 334, illustrates (a) the determinants of interest as I see them, and (b) the difference between *induced* and *autonomous* changes in saving preference. "Interest" is represented on the vertical axis, while on the horizontal axis "income" is represented (to the right and left of the origin), and "income" (in this case) is the aggregate value of the flow of services measured in abstractly conceived money units of constant purchasing power.[27] Of this flow, almost the whole represents services embodied into the stock of assets, "consumed services" being realistically assumed to form a very small proportion of the whole. But for simplicity, I go further and ask the reader *to assume that the whole of income consists of services embodied into assets which cover the whole range of life expectancies, so that no allowance need be made for services consumed directly.* It is assumed also that income (in this case "embodied services") is constant (that is, that no withheld capacity is being released) and no growth or contraction in the assets stock is in progress *initially.*[28] Income or "embodied services" is EA, or OB, or OC + OF.

The model is dangerously unrealistic. For in practice savings increase normally and most easily, not through a sacrifice of the former rate of consumption but through income increasing (owing to past savings or the release of capacity) with some part of the additional income being added to previous savings. Moreover, the representation of "embodied services" in this way makes abstraction of the *composition* of the assets stock in terms of life expectancies and the potentialities of growth in different forms. The form of any unutilized capacity will influence the form in which income is likely to increase and the manner in which it will be devoted to the different purposes indicated in Diagram I (p. 296). Finally, movements in the demand schedule represent changes in circumstances which may (as we have seen) influence pricing and hence the withholding or release of capacity—that is, the magnitude of real income. The model represented in Diagram II makes abstraction of these very important

[27] The fact that this measurement is based on an index-number conception and hence a particular measure of *the value,* and not of *some supposed physical quantity,* of the flow of services (and parts thereof), is very important at certain stages of the argument.

[28] In other words, the *assumption* in Diagram II (which is about to be explained) is that the "saving preference schedule" is at S_1. When the "saving preference schedule" moves from S_1 to the position S_2, accumulation of assets (savings) will occur, and real income must then be increasing (unless additional capacity is withheld—a possibility which is excluded in the assumptions).

Diagram II

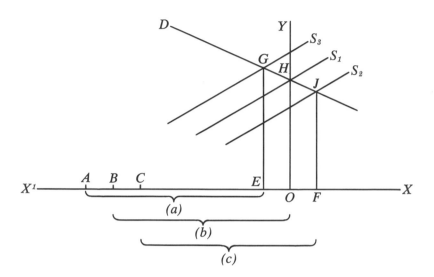

aspects of the topics we shall be discussing. But I use this very simplified model solely to *illustrate* my argument. *In itself it proves nothing.*

Curve *D* is a demand schedule representing the rates of interest at which entrepreneurs (in competition with one another) estimate that it will be profitable to bid for services which are embodied into the stock of assets at different rates of concurrent consumption. Alternatively, it may be said to represent the rates of interest at which entrepreneurs find it profitable to offer for the hire of the capital with which they can acquire (by barter or purchase) the services made available for different kinds of uses. The height of the schedule is determined by prospective yields to the embodiment of services in assets. From the angle of the community, the curve represents the prospective profitableness (as interpreted by entrepreneurs) of resources to replace, or add to, power to consume at different times in the future.

I have explained that entrepreneurs take responsibility merely for *the form* in which the flow of services priced for market clearance is embodied into assets and not for the rate at which this occurs (which is solely the consumer-savers' decision). In accepting such a responsibility, entrepreneurs are "demanding" the full flow of services; and the shape of the demand curve merely represents the extent to which their demand influences the value of services in terms of assets (that is, the rate of interest). Entrepreneurs always demand the full flow of services offered, for by definition all *services* have value, and if they have value, someone must be choosing the assets into which they are being incorporated.

Curves S_1, S_2, and S_3 are three different positions of the supply schedule representing three different consumer-saver reactions to scales of interest rates. For brevity the supply schedule is called the "saving preference schedule." *EA, OB,* and *OC + OF* represent the same amounts of "embodied services" under the three different positions of the saving preference schedule. Each curve shows how, at different rates of interest, consumption-saving preference will cause the form of "embodied services" to change in respect of the relative real values of replacement (consumption) and accumulated assets (savings). From the angle of the community, these curves may be interpreted as representing the cost of making provision for future consumption (that is, replacement and growth), namely, the sacrifice of consumption in the immediate future for consumption in the more distant future.

It is possible now to restate the above propositions. The shape of the demand schedule is determined by prospective yields. With the supply schedules, the diagram shows the way in which changes in consumer-saver preference are assumed to influence the interest entrepreneurs will have to offer, and hence the relative value of assets and services.

An increase in consumption (whether a reaction to a shift in the demand schedule *or* expressed directly by a movement in the supply schedule) is represented by a shift to the left of the flow of "embodied services," for example, from *OC + OF* to *OB* (or to *EA*) —or from (*c*) to (*b*), or to (*a*)—while a decrease of consumption is represented by a shift to the right.

The magnitude of dissavings is shown to the left of the origin and the magnitude of savings to the right of the origin. Thus, when *EA* [that is, (*a*)] represents the flow of embodied services, *OE* is dissavings. And when *OC + OF* [that is, (*c*)] is the flow of embodied services, *OF* is savings.

To state some of the implications assumed in the diagram in another way, we can say that, with the saving preference schedule in the position S_1, "embodied services" being *OB* [that is, (*b*)], "consumed assets" will be the same. The diagram assumes, that is, that (the demand schedule D being given) when no savings or dissavings are occurring, the rate of interest will be OH unless inflation or deflation is occurring.

In the position S_2, "embodied services" being $OC + OF$ [that is, (c)], "consumed assets" (replaced) will be OC and savings ("unconsumed assets") OF. The diagram assumes, that is, that when realized savings equal to OF are occurring, the rate of interest will be FJ.

In the position S_3, "embodied services" being EA [that is, (a)], "consumed assets" will be OA and unreplaced consumption, that is, "dissavings," OE. Thus, if the desire to postpone consumption is negative, not only will there be incomplete replacement, but stocks of assets will be depleted. The diagram assumes, that is, that when "dissavings" equal to OE are occurring, the rate of interest will be EG.

Starting with the saving preference schedule in the position S_1, a shift to the position S_2 will mean that *the composition* of the contribution to accumulated assets will change, because it will be profitable, in view of the reduced interest, *to divert services* equal to the real value OF, from incorporation into assets of relatively short life expectancies ("consumption uses") into assets of relatively long life expectancies ("growth uses"). (The extent to which this can actually happen will depend, as we have seen, upon the versatility of resources as between the two broad kinds of assets.)

It has so far been *assumed* that, as the prospective profitableness to entrepreneurs of embodying services into assets rises (a rise in schedule D),[29] causing the rate of interest to rise, a response occurs in the form of the release of services from providing for replacement of consumption in the one form in order to provide for replacement in the other form. The release is effected through a decline in consumption. It *can* take the form simply of a decline in consumption of durable, physically completed assets in households, warehouses, or shops of which (through the saving induced) it becomes profitable to carry larger inventories through time. In other words, the form of income may change either because the physical nature of output changes or because (for short periods) more of the same physical output is accumulated net in order to produce time utilities.

---

[29] The rise in the demand schedule may be due to entrepreneurial forecasts of general prosperity (large future outputs) or (a special case) to an increasing relative profitableness of capital-intensive methods of production.

The diagram has assumed (for simplicity but unrealistically) a *perfect* response in the composition of output to changes in saving preference. But if we now again make the opposite assumption, namely, that there is no response at all of this kind, we can still represent it on a similar sort of diagram, using it to show changes in the *relative* values of different parts of the flow of services. (See Diagram III in footnote 30, p. 338.)

Let us assume that services embodied in assets of short life expectancy and those embodied in assets of long life expectancy are absolutely specific to their respective fields, although the former are produced by the latter. In such a situation it will be quite impossible for society to add more rapidly to the stock of assets by sacrificing current consumption. Changes in saving preference will then merely affect values—the rate of interest and the relative values of the two categories of assets. When the saving preference schedule moves to the right, entrepreneurs will find it possible to borrow at lower interest, but they will be forced to offer more for a rigid flow of services specialized for embodiment in long-life assets (producer goods). At the same time, consumers, that is, replacers, will be able to bid down the value of an undiminished flow of services into short-life assets (consumer goods). In such circumstances, the value of the services embodied into short-life goods must fall, while that of those embodied into long-life assets must rise.[30]

The savings preference schedules which I am using correspond in some respects with Ohlin's notion of *ex ante* saving, just as the demand schedules I use correspond roughly to his conception of *ex ante* investment. But the interest determined (vertical axis) and the values, including real values (of the flow of services and its components), determined (horizontal axis) are *current valuations*.

---

[30] The reader is reminded that the magnitude "embodied services" is measured on the diagram in abstractly conceived money units of constant "real value." It is a *value* aggregate, not a supposed *physical quantity* aggregate.

Let us begin with the assumption that "savings" are being realized, of the value OC. (There is, of course, no *physically identifiable* part of "embodied services" which represents "savings" but that value of the flow of services which is still represented to the right of the origin.) Saving preference is shown to shift from S_1 to S_2, "embodied services" from OA plus OC to OB plus OE. Interest falls. The assumption is that the *physical compositions* of OA and OB are identical, as are those of OC and OE. The changes are in relative values. The fact that physical adjustments are ruled out does not mean that value changes are prevented!

It might be thought that the assumed absolute specificity between the two categories of assets implies vertical supply curves. But induced as well as autonomous changes in saving preferences are *theoretically* conceivable (how-

It is theoretically possible that the offer of higher interest, represented by a rise in the demand schedule, may be responded to by an
increase in the desire to consume in the immediate future. In that
case, fewer resources will be available for expansion. There seems to
be some inconsistency in such a situation, however; for the demand
schedule is most likely to rise because prospective yields are high,
and prospective yields are most likely to be high only because demands for outputs in general are expected to be high in the future;
while the situation which we are considering assumes that people are
induced to sacrifice consumption in the distant future for consumption in the immediate future. It does not seem to be worthwhile
discussing further such highly unlikely preference reactions. But I
claim that *all my arguments stand whatever preferences happen to be.*
As I have insisted more than once, under competition, *there is never
any obstacle to the self-consistent use of scarce resources in the
satisfaction of any set of noncontradictory preferences.*[31] If people
cannot be induced to increase their provision for the future by the
offer of higher interest, that is all there is to it.

The argument the Keynesians have to answer is not that if the
desire to save increases, the rate of additions to physical productive
capacity must necessarily increase. In order to substantiate their

---

ever purposeless under present assumptions) and they would have similar effects
upon the relative values of "embodied services" replacing consumption or
entering into savings.

Diagram III

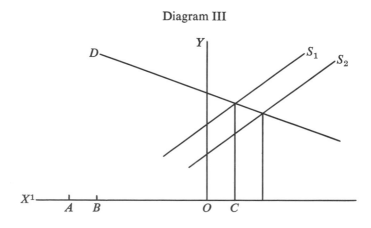

contention, they must show that the sacrifice of consumption out of a given income *without waste* does not necessarily result in savings. In other words, what they have to deny is that an autonomous increase in that part of the flow of services which is not matched by extermination of value always means increased realized savings. Under my definitions, however, this would be denying a truism—a tautology. But this does not imply that a reduced rate of interest due to a shift in the supply schedule *causes* an increased rate of savings *unless it can be assumed that at the lower interest entrepreneurs, interpreting prospective yields, do in fact compete more successfully for services to be embodied in assets of long life expectancy which would otherwise be incorporated into short-life assets.*

Such a situation is one which, it is commonly held, cannot exist in the real world. For instance, at times the Keynesian view is that realized savings cannot be achieved simply through the reduction of current consumption. But I maintain that it is *only* through the sacrifice of *possible* present consumption that productive capacity can ever grow, and that there are no important exceptions to this truth.

Let us now drop the assumption that there is no initial growth in utilized productive power and suppose that real income grows solely through the achievement of savings assisted or induced by the economizing process. The same analysis applies, but the extent to which realized savings can occur—through the changes represented—will now depend not only upon the versatility of the services which can be diverted from embodiment into short-life assets into long-life assets, but also upon the extent to which the increasing real income (from the release of withheld capacity or from realized net accumulation in progress) happens to be in the form of services appropriate for the two vaguely differentiated categories of assets. *Saving-consumption preference, however, plays its role in exactly the same kind of way.* The greater consumption preference, the smaller will be the rate of realized savings and vice versa.

That saving means bidding for assets is least obvious, and may at first seem to be wrong in the case of short-life assets (for example, inventories of consumers' goods); but it is equally saving preference which bids for such goods *as capital,* that is, as inventories in process of sale and replacement, or, in households, consumption and replacement.[32]

---

[32] Investment in such inventories may, as with all other investments, prove "unproductive" except for short periods of time, during which they contribute,

I expect the objection that demand of that nature is "consumption demand." (See pp. 300–303.) The consumer, it may be said, expresses his demand by purchasing commodities—services or assets—in the market. But unless the consumer exterminates services as they are rendered, *he invests* for short periods in whatever he consumes. This may well sound like an outrageous and paradoxical verbal quibble. In reality, the distinction (which I stressed in the previous chapter, pp. 300–303) is vital for clear thinking. The demand for "consumer goods" *from those whom we usually call "consumers"* is a demand for assets of short life expectancies. *"Consumers"* certainly do hold stocks (in pantries, wardrobes, etc.) for consumption convenience; and such "consumers" are constantly replacing these stocks as consumption exterminates them. But to the extent to which so-called consumers do this they are, strictly speaking, (a) performing the entrepreneurial function—choosing assets—(b) performing the productive function of trading on their own account, and (c) *saving* (chiefly in its replacement form), using their own income for the purpose. When it is perishable goods which are demanded, then demand for short-life goods is solely for the necessarily small and rapidly turning over stock which is being maintained by replacement. The fact that this demand is *necessarily accompanied by consumption* must not cause us to confuse the two. (See pp. 279–82.)

I repeat, consumers, as I have defined them, either consume services as they are supplied or exterminate assets, just as producers embody services into assets. Thus, consumption proper is the opposite of saving demand, the opposite of the demand for assets. It is the opposite even of that part of saving demand which only covers replacement. "Consumption demand" (if we use that term at all) must be regarded as consisting of (a) demand for "consumed services" *plus* (b) demand for that part of "embodied services" *which makes* up the value of replacement. But (b) has its origin in a consumer-saver's decision, while *the form* taken by replacement is an entrepreneurial interpretation of consumers' preference.

Because on the whole people try at least to maintain their capital intact (annuitants and the old generally are the important exceptions), consumption is usually accompanied by sufficient investment in assets to replace the real value of assets in general. But this must

---

as inventories, to the sum total of marketing costs. The periods must often be short, mainly by reason of perishability, storage costs, or interest costs. The services which have been embodied into assets in this form must be consumed early or they will be wasted—consumed for no one's benefit.

not lead us to the quite wrong conclusion that consumption itself *is* demand for (or even *the origin* of demand for) goods which replace what is being decumulated. The exact manner in which changes in the magnitude of consumption of particular things at any time affect the *composition* of the future flow of services, I shall discuss shortly, but I must insist, possibly *ad nauseam,* that consumption is always the *extermination* of power to demand. The failure of the Keynesians to understand this simple truth lies at the root of what I believe to be the most outrageous intellectual error of this age.[33] The creation of power to demand, whether for replacement or growth, is production. Certainly production also creates the power ultimately to consume or accumulate. But with consumption the power to demand (the offer of one thing for something else) is wiped out.

Replacement demand may be seen simply as that part of saving demand which is insufficient to bring about growth. It is wrong to think of it as *a response* to consumption. Replacement is a response to saving preference, even if this response takes the form of maintaining stocks of short-life goods constant. *All* demand for assets which is expressed out of income (that is, out of the flow of services) is a contribution to the process of saving.

When goods with short life expectancies are accumulated by those who propose to consume them, this act of investment *enables a forecast* (of almost perfect reliability) of their early consumption. Thus, when we restock our wardrobes and pantries, we are investing in things which we predict *we* are going to want to consume in the near or relatively early future. Although in doing so we are not consuming; *we are indicating our preferences as consumers.* Our acts (which are influenced mainly by the fact that the sort of things which we have been consuming we are likely to want to consume again) form the data on which other entrepreneurs—merchants or traders—base their predictions. Similarly, the reduction, full replacement, or accumulation of traders' inventories create the data (the market signals) to which entrepreneurs (producers) or marketers of physical products react. In that way consumers' sovereignty is exercised, and this ultimately controls the form of investment of services in replacement *plus* growth and, indeed, the total assets mix and the composition of

---

[33] It is only just to remind the reader that not all pre-Keynesian economists had J. B. Say's clear perception that consumption represents extermination of demand. Thus, even Ricardo and J. S. Mill wrote at times as though they were assuming that consumption, and not production, is the source of demands in general.

subsequent income as a whole. But while the current rate of depletion of different kinds of assets is *evidence* on which the entrepreneur can attempt to forecast *the composition* of preferences in the future, and so the *relative profitabilities of different kinds of accumulation, it is irrelevant to the amount or rate of growth.*

Certain services are enjoyed, certain inventories are consumed, and certain equipment is used up or otherwise depreciated. From this, entrepreneurs can predict that, *on the whole,* the same sorts of things are going to be consumed in the future, so that there will normally be a demand for the replacement of inventories and the making good of depreciation *in the same form.* Profitable investment in inventories of particular short-life goods depends upon the current rate at which they are being consumed *and* their present and prospective prices. And each such entrepreneurial decision influences, of course, other entrepreneurial decisions at different stages of the consumption, marketing, and physical production processes.

Yet the notion has become deeply ingrained in modern teaching that "investment opportunities" are created by consumption. Students in most universities are today taught that an increase in demand for consumers' goods and services will lead in turn to an increase (an accelerated increase) in demand for the producers' goods which make them. If we ignore the acceleration notion (which I propose to criticize in a later chapter), this is undoubtedly true of the predicted demand for any *individual* consumers' good. But this has led some economists to jump to the false conclusion that consumption in general is the source of demand in general, while thinking of "demand" as an aggregate magnitude. (See pp. 315–16.)

I have shown that, in expressing a demand for *particular* assets, entrepreneurs must choose *inter alia* between two broad, vaguely differentiated categories of investment: (a) into inventories of goods of short economic life expectancies, which are destined to be relatively rapidly consumed, and (b) into stocks of all other assets of long economic life expectancies, which are normally consumed slowly (through depreciation).[34] Thus, while as entrepreneurs people neither save nor dissave (being classed as savers or consumers when they do that), in assuming responsibility for *the form* of the assets

---

[34] This is another way of stating what has already been shown, namely, that the greater the magnitude of savings the greater will be the proportion of the flow of services embodied into assets of which it is profitable to carry greater stocks through time, and the smaller the proportion embodied into products of which greater stocks cannot profitably be carried through time.

stock as it shrinks or grows, they interpret among other things the relative weights of the two competing sets of demands which make up the expression of consumption-saving preferences.

It should now be clear that *the extent to which* processes of replacement and/or growth as a whole occur is always determined through the basic choice between current and postponed consumption; and that only if services are released from withholding, or diverted from investment in short-life assets to investment in long-life assets, or supplied through the form of current replacement and growth, *and directed through consumer-saver preference,* can society *increase* any rate at which the total stock of assets is accumulating. In other words, we again reach the conclusion that *there is but one way in which productive capacity can increase, namely, through thrift being strong enough to bring it about, given any specificity or versatility of men or assets.*

And as I demonstrated above (p. 317), the case of savings achieved out of income which is in process of inflation constitutes no exception. Growth still requires the exercise of preference against current consumption.[35] I must repeat, however, that for the rate of growth to increase without the concurrent release of capacity, versatility is essential. In its absence, entrepreneurs are powerless to accumulate more rapidly.

Indeed, there are no real exceptions[36] to the rule that increased preference for *current consumption in general* tends, in itself, to reduce the rate at which those long-life assets which maintain or increase the flow of output (and ultimately the flow of *short-life goods*) are replaced or accumulated.

This does not mean that consumption and growth cannot increase together. But such can only happen if real income increases concurrently. Such is, of course, the usual case. Economic growth normally takes this form. Productive power expands although consumption does not decline or even continues to increase; for the growth of real income can permit the accumulation of assets without any fall in the *absolute rate* of realized consumption.

---

[35] At one stage Keynes *appears* to have recognized this point; for his argument that "the savings which result from this decision" (the decision to "invest") "are just as genuine as other savings" (*The General Theory,* p. 83) is really suggesting that, if any entrepreneur uses inflationary credit to provide new assets, *society* will have achieved net accumulation through a thrift decision having accompanied the entrepreneurial decision.

[36] The imaginary case in which all output is perishable is not a "real exception."

I anticipate the objection that I have given insufficient weight to the possibility of savings increasing *only apparently* through an unanticipated depreciation of the money unit, which will provide entrepreneurs with more funds (savings) with which to bid for rigidly priced services in the capital goods field. The consequent increase in the money valuation of income may lead to the release of services formerly priced above market-clearing values, with a rise in the marginal efficiency of capital, and multiplied repercussions. Such a possibility is clearly not incompatible with our present analysis.

Alternatively, it may be objected that the mere occurrence of a rise in saving preference may cause real income to decline because, owing to price rigidity, resources will be withheld in the short-life goods industries. But the thesis which I have stated does not deny (as I insisted above, Chapters 4 and 7) that price rigidity, confronted with a change in saving preference (or any other change in preference), may throw the economic system out of coordination. As I must continue to stress, when the price mechanism is prevented from carrying out its coordinative functions, wasteful idleness must certainly follow, no matter what the original change in economic ends may have been. In such circumstances, it is almost fatuous to say that an increase in savings is responsible for unemployment. If the demand for the services of a specific piece of equipment falls off, so that it is essential for its hire value to fall from $10 to $9 in order that it shall continue to be used, while the charge for hire is maintained at $10, we can hardly usefully say that the decline in demand is the cause of the idleness. *For its employment is compatible with the decline in demand while it is inconsistent with the maintenance of the charge for hire.*

Is there, then, any possible justification for the view that an increased demand for short-life (consumer) goods can be an inducement to the accumulation of assets in general? *We can use such a phrase of predicted (not current) demand for short-life assets as the inducement to a favorable entrepreneurial offer of interest (which may evoke a response in savings) if we make it clear that it is growth of output in one industry which is providing the source of future demand for the product of the increasing capacity of noncompeting industries.* We carry assets through time either because we wish to consume them or use their services ourselves, or because we count on others demanding them in the future for these purposes. What may be called "the demand for savings"—the demand schedule of

Diagram II—is derived from prospective yields, which are calculated from (a) the *anticipated flow of products* in the future, and (b) the belief that these products will be priced for exchange, so that each will give rise to demand for noncompeting things. This view of "demand in general" depends, of course, upon a recognition of Say's law and the essential complementarity of capital resources as a whole. *If a predicted rise in demands to replace consumption induces a rise in saving preference (through a response to a rise in the rate of interest), while the required versatilities exist,*[37] *it will cause an increase in the rate of accumulation of assets, but not otherwise.* Realized demands for short-life goods (which may be the confirmation of the predicted demands which led to the rise in the marginal efficiency of capital) are derived from the complementarity of the accumulated assets and not from *current* consumption. And (unless the release of capacity can be forecast) predicted future demands for short-life goods are, as we have seen, the outcome of past thrift decisions against consumption.

Hence, when the entrepreneur is trying to predict, not the relative preference of society for the different kinds of goods of which he is contemplating production but, given his predictions on this point, *the general ability* of the community to purchase these goods, he is trying to forecast utilized productive power in the future. He will normally conceive of the degree of prospective utilization of productive power as "the degree of prosperity," or "the amount of purchasing power" to be anticipated, without realizing very clearly the reality that the source of all power to demand is production, current or past, not offset through extermination by consumption.

This brings us to a widely held fallacy which is relevant to the inducement to accumulation. It is assumed that increasing savings *must* force down the long-term rate of interest in the absence of autonomous progress.[38] The fallacy stresses not the lack of versatility in productive capacity, which was discussed above (see pp. 329–31), but the decline in prospective yields which is supposed to accompany the growth of productive power. Now an increased flow of savings need not cause a decline in interest if (a) there is autonomous growth in progress, or (b) withheld capacity is being released, or (c)

---

[37] The shape of the supply schedule in Diagram II reflects preferences in the light of versatilities.

[38] The works of some of the most careful economists are *misleading* on this point when they use static analysis but fail to point out to the student the possible dynamic repercussions of complementarity.

accumulation of one kind of assets is creating additional demand for net accumulation of another kind: (a) is universally admitted; (b) is seldom understood; while (c) is usually denied, implicitly or explicitly. Insofar as the *complementarity* referred to under (c) exists, increased savings are partly or wholly offset by a rise in the demand schedule for savings! In other words, the long-term demand for and supply of *aggregate* savings are not independent, and static analysis can assist very little in explaining the long-term rate of interest.[39]

This is not to deny that, for reasons noticed above, there will be, in each particular case, in the short run, and beyond a certain point, diminishing predicted and realized returns to an increasing rate of accumulation. And it may be legitimate to assume that the schedule of the marginal efficiency of capital will not rise sufficiently, following an increased rate of savings, to prevent some temporary fall in the rate of interest. In explaining the particular case and the short run, it is permissible to make abstraction of the repercussions of complementarity. But to imagine that growing savings could cause the value of services in relation to the value of assets to fall toward zero is to imagine an approach toward a utopian state of satiety, in which productive services (those which are consumed directly, or those which flow into replacement) are tending to become as plentiful and cheap as the atmosphere. The truth is, of course, that provision for the future has no such tendency. The law of the insatiability of human wants remains without substantial challenge. Indeed, the building up of physical productive power has no greater tendency to force interest toward zero than has the growth of population a tendency to reduce the value of labor to zero.

I can now state categorically the thesis that consumption does not call forth replacement or accumulation of assets, and that the growth in the preference, tendency, or propensity to consume releases no inducement to economic expansion. Indeed, if real income remained constant in the absence of the accumulation of assets, the reverse would be true. Only a decline in the preference for current consumption could then make net accumulation possible. And if real income is then increasing in the only way possible, namely, through

---

[39] As the accumulation of capital resources proceeds, it may be possible to use more economic (for example, more roundabout) methods, so that the demand for savings is actually *enhanced* by savings. But that brings in factors which may be regarded as autonomous. The present argument rests only on the contention that each act of accumulation of assets creates a demand for non-competing accumulation.

the release of withheld capacity or continuous realized accumulation of assets (as influenced by autonomous economization), an increased preference for current consumption will slow down, bring to an end, or reverse the rate of accumulation of assets and any rate of growth of real income.

To sum up, an increase in society's rate of growth *normally* arises not through a decline in consumption leaving an accumulation of unconsumed assets, but (a) through the diversion of the services of some versatile resources from producing short-life goods to producing long-life goods, or (b) through additional services, due to an increasing real income, being directed to long-life goods rather than short-life goods, a process which is influenced by the form in which the flow of services (real income) increases. Such "additional services" can arise from two sources: (1) the accumulation of assets in progress (the growth of productive power itself); or (2) the release from wasteful idleness of services provided by existing resources. A special case of (1) is that in which the "additional services" arise from the growing productive power due to "autonomous developments," that is, economizing displacements—innovations, inventions, and discoveries which are not offset by growing consumption.

We reach the five following conclusions: (1) Economic growth, when technically possible (within limits set by the versatility of resources), is caused by saving preference alone; although savings may be *induced or facilitated* by the current form of income, by the release of withheld capacity, by economizing displacement (autonomous growth), or by increased interest. (2) The mere wish, or will, or propensity to consume at the current rate, or at a greater rate, must not be viewed as the source of demand for the future services of capital resources and so for their replacement or accumulation respectively, unless that wish, will, or propensity is explicitly regarded as creating the incentive to produce. (3) Production to *replace or add* to the assets stock must be seen as the *source* of maintained and increased demands respectively for all inputs and outputs. (4) The predicted preferences of consumer-savers determine the *form of utilization of productive resources* in the short run, and the *form of these resources themselves* in the long run. (5) Nothing can be more *misleading* than the contemporary tendency to talk about "the absorption of savings into investment," or similar phrases, although some of the most rigorous economists have conformed to this usage. For if savings have been achieved, the savers *must* already have chosen to invest in *some* assets. This contention is not upset by the important facts that, in selecting *particular* assets the savers *must* have acted also as entrepreneurs, and that they can subsequently (as entrepreneurs) disinvest (a) from assets of short life expectancy and invest in assets of long life expectancy, or (b) from assets of high liquidity and invest in assets of low liquidity.

This last conclusion demands special emphasis. There is *always* a "demand for savings"; and in the absence of pricing barriers, there are *always* "investment outlets" or "investment opportunities." *Such opportunities can be "created," as well as filled, only by thrift* in the presence of versatility of resources, or the release of withheld capacity, or the current growth of productive power due to past thrift, or economizing displacement.

And this last process includes discoveries, inventions, innovations, and managerial ingenuities which economize resources and so cause prospective yields to rise; while the resulting high interest (or sometimes rising prospective yields directly)[40] *may call forth* a larger flow of savings, in other words, cause the flow of "embodied services" to rise in relation to replaced consumption and in that sense lead to real expansion. Nor is there any implication that autonomous progress or the release of withheld capacity may not *facilitate* thrift (and hence real expansion) through permitting savings to occur with little or no sacrifice of the former rate of consumption or even of its former rate of growth. But we cannot escape the basic truth (paradoxical to Keynesians) that *only decisions against current consumption can permit the emergence of "investment opportunities."*

It is in the light of the above conclusions that all variants of the underconsumption theory of depression or stagnation, as well as all notions which involve the Keynesian consumption concept (such as the "propensity to consume," the "acceleration theory," and the "multiplier theory"), must be pondered.

I anticipate the objection that my analysis has overlooked most important issues, particularly those connected with the effects of saving upon the velocity of circulation or the aggregate rate of spending. But these issues have been treated in Chapter 8; and the

---

[40] While Diagram II (p. 334), with which I have illustrated the above analysis, represents the assumed aggregate influence of prospective yields in general upon the incentive of people (as entrepreneurs) *to borrow* for investment (including from themselves, as savers), it cannot represent the aggregate influence of prospective yields in particular undertakings upon the incentive *to save* (in order to invest in such undertakings) on the part of those who perceive (as entrepreneurs) such yields. But, of course, prospective profits as well as current interest must be assumed to have some influence on the expression of all consumer-saver preferences.

argument presented here cannot, I think, be upset merely by bringing such monetary factors into the reckoning.

A different objection which may be expected is to the effect that while savers may be prepared to offer a flow of loans (for example, in the form of the purchase of fixed interest securities), entrepreneurs may not think it profitable to use the funds under such conditions, however low the savers bid down the rate of interest. At the same time (to translate the argument into my own terminology) *the managers* would be prepared to advise the flotation of plenty of new ventures, and could do so, if the savers would only supply "risk capital," that is, if the savers would also be prepared to serve as active additional entrepreneurs and become residual claimants by investing in equities. The argument amounts to the contention either that people as entrepreneurs are insufficiently enterprising,[41] or that prospects are not favorable enough to evoke the required enterprise.

Now if the value of *assets* in the form of securities is being bid up and entrepreneurial demand for the *services* of nonmoney resources does not increase, the implication is that entrepreneurs are adding to their money stocks. But why should they do so unless they believe that investment in money offers a higher yield than investment in other assets? Such a situation can emerge only if they expect more favorable opportunities to present themselves later than are available at the moment (for example, a more favorable price-cost ratio or other forecast value relationships). It is quite wrong to assume that unfavorable prospects can deter net accumulation, otherwise than through the discouragement of saving preference, or—indirectly— through the encouragement of the withholding of capacity (although such prospects certainly do influence *the form* taken by accumulation). We must regard entrepreneurs as interested in *relative,* not *absolute* prospective yields.[42] We can equally appropriately say that their function is to choose the "least unfavorable" as the "most favorable" openings for investment.

I am not suggesting that risk preference is irrelevant, that the

---

[41] Ironically enough, the Keynesian system, in its ultimate effects, works to dampen and discourage enterprise, especially through the inevitable eventual repression of latent inflation. And Keynes himself disparaged the entrepreneurial function as it is performed in practice, implying that supposed enterprise depends upon "animal spirits" more than upon careful prediction and calculation. He was, I think, envisaging then rather the stock exchange speculator, whom he understood, than the typical business administrator planning his budgets, whom he certainly did *not* understand.

[42] I am here ignoring the argument, which I regard as unimportant, that the cost of investing may exceed interest.

widespread existence of an enterprising temperament may not cause
a more productive *form* of accumulation and hence *ultimately* a
more rapid rate of net accumulation.[43] And I have already explained
why, in the circumstances in which withheld capacity exists, optimism
may have considerable expansive effects through inducing the release
of that capacity.

The failure to recognize thrift as the sole ultimate source of
expansion has been due, I believe, to two main sources of confusion.
(a) The implications of the facilitation of savings by pricing nearer
to market-clearing values (that is, released capacity), the economization process, or current growth itself have not been understood.
(b) There has been an age-old misinterpretation of that general
discoordination which so often attenuates prospective yields (and
causes therefore entrepreneurs to wait for market-enforced readjust-
ments before embarking on the more productive, capital intensive
and hazardous undertakings). For in the presence of price rigidities
which are regarded as unstable, a tendency for the purchasing power
of the money unit to rise leads to what is regarded as a decline in
the *willingness to spend* (on services of all kinds), accompanied possibly by increased thrift.[44] Some productive services which were
formerly embodied into assets of relatively short life expectancies
(that is, into inventories of goods for early consumption) will then
be embodied into assets of relatively long life expectancies. It is
possible also that, in waiting for "investment opportunities" to appear,
entrepreneurs may bid up the real value of aggregate money stocks.
Then, unless the aggregate "nominal money supply" is increased to
maintain a constant relationship between M and M_r, a deflationary
pressure on prices will be exerted. But if a proclamation of a nondeflationary policy is generally believed, it will bring to an end the
speculative element in the demand for money. The avoidance of
deflation will of course create a *latent* inflation, although of a kind
which is easily rectifiable as soon as V begins to rise.

But if a policy of this kind is not effectively carried out, the result-

---

[43] Enterprise and conditions conducive to the exercise of wise risk taking are,
indirectly, important factors favoring economic expansion—through the reactions of interest upon savings, and the tendency of wise risk taking to bring
about the most productive forms of replacement and net accumulation.

[44] Until successive breaches in the rigidities have brought the average of prices
down to the height to which it is generally expected to fall, or until the belief
in the instability of the rigidities has passed, either of which circumstances will
cause the market rate of interest to assume the noninflationary, nondeflationary
level.

ing situation can easily *appear* as a low "propensity to consume" with a concomitant "absence of investment opportunities." For if there is idle capacity in the consumers' goods industries, it hardly seems rational to add to that capacity.[45] The whole deplorable situation then *appears* superficially to be due to one simple and obvious cause. People are not consuming enough. If they can only be set consuming again, it is thought, there will again be prospects for investment, and expenditure on investment will in turn create purchasing power for still further consumption. But the trouble does not lie in any insufficiency in the desire or propensity to consume, nor in any insufficiency in the incentive to replace or add to the assets stock in the form that entrepreneurs judge to be prospectively most profitable. It is to be found simply in the failure to coordinate—to adjust prices when the underlying values change. And if the changes in these underlying values are due to a deflationary policy, adopted in the interests of distributive justice, or as a matter of honor, then it is obviously a grossly inefficient way of serving the causes of justice and honor to do nothing effective to permit or enforce directly the price coordinations which such a policy demands.

It is easy to reach the defeatist conclusion that political factors appear to render coordination through the price mechanism out of the question in the modern world.[46] But if that conclusion is reached, the student ought never to be left with the impression that unemployment, depression, and stagnation are due, *in any sense,* to too much thrift or insufficient consumption or insufficient investment.

It is true in a sense that the Great Depression of the thirties, in the United States and Western Europe, was attributable to the failure of society to permit mass consumption. But potential consumption was not frustrated through too little income being left in the hands of those with a high propensity to consume; nor was it due to an excess of thrift of any type; nor was it the consequence of a monetary policy which somehow created *a barrier* to the required consumption. I repeat, it was wholly attributable to the defective pricing of inputs and outputs generally, and not specially of con-

---

[45] If price rigidity did not exist in the producers' goods industries also, it would pay to add to productive capacity with a view to breaking down the price rigidities in the consumers' goods field, and selling at prices (in relation to anticipated prices) at which consumers would be willing to buy.

[46] It would then seem to be the duty of statesmen to point this out, and face the consequences, during the inflations which deliberate deflations are intended, tardily, to rectify.

sumers' goods and services, above market-clearing values, that is, beyond the reach of uninflated income and out of consistency with price expectations.

The approach of this and the previous chapter illustrates, incidentally, the folly of the Keynesian notion that there is some "amount" or "level" of *real income* or *employment* corresponding to each level of the rate of interest, or to each "amount" or "level" of accumulation of assets ("investment"), and so the folly of the remedy implied (and advocated) for unemployment, namely, that government should determine, by monetary or fiscal policy, a rate of interest which is regarded as consistent with full employment, or alternatively undertake such expenditure (on "investment" or other) as is necessary to achieve the same end. Admittedly, in depression, the values of both consumption and investment are unduly low. But that is the *manifestation,* not the cause, of depression.

Appendix A

The Relevance of "Expenditure" by Government and Foreigners

A possible source of confusion needs to be mentioned. It has become usual since Keynes for aggregate income to be regarded as divided into money *expenditures* by consumers, investors, governments, and foreigners. But that part of "income" (the flow of services) which is earned or seized by the government has, *in this context,* the same significance as that part of which the ownership is retained by the private producers who earn it or receive it as a handout. That is, unless the services which make up income are immediately consumed, they are in both cases embodied into assets ranging over the whole gamut of life expectancies. Nor does the fact that consumption-saving preference may be expressed collectively as well as individually in any way affect the analysis of this chapter. In the economic field, the government is inevitably a consumer-saver.

Nor is the argument affected because there are cases in which assets in a national area are owned by foreigners (whether they are domiciled in that area or not) and contribute therefore to the flow of services; or where the gains from exchanging goods from within the national area for goods from outside the area contribute to the value of the flow of services (aggregate national income); or when goods and services owned at home are exchanged for goods and services owned abroad; or when services are exchanged for assets across national boundaries. Moreover, the extent to which people (as income producers or as income receivers) decide to exterminate ("consume") the value of the services they provide, or "consume" any proportion of the assets they own, is determined by the same factors *whatever the origin of the income may have been.* Hence in the study of any community, its gain from external trade is—in the context of the present argument—best regarded as one form of profitable production.

The export or import of capital can be similarly considered. Capital is exported when the prospective yield from that use (the expected future flow of services from it) is greater than that predicted from any available internal use; and capital is imported when the prospective yield from its employment exceeds the payment for its employment.

It might be thought that so simple an approach hides a fallacy because the balance of expenditures and receipts in foreign trade must influence the real value of money assets, M_r, and hence, if M is constant, the value of the money unit. But insofar as international transactions in goods and money do influence M_r or MV, they have the same effect as all other factors which have this influence. There appear to be, therefore, no valid reasons for supposing that international economic relations in any way upset our conclusions that economic growth is a response to thrift and therefore that investment outlets are created by thrift.

Appendix B

The Notion of "Failure to Spend" Without "Hoarding"

An attempted rationalization of Keynesian teaching which I do not understand is one which is well illustrated in an article by James Tobin, who holds that "an individual may fail to spend all his income on goods and services currently produced without hoarding—adding to his cash balance—any of the remainder. He may, instead, purchase obligations of indebtedness, real estate, or other existing assets."[47] Let us assume that Tobin is not here thinking of bidding for "hybrid assets"; for that *is,* of course, a particular form of bidding up of M_r (see p. 72). When we exercise saving preference we use our income (*a flow* of services) to bid up the value of assets (*a stock*), and (for reasons which we have noticed) this effect may not be wholly offset by concurrent additions to the stock of assets. In consequence, we may simply bid down the rate of interest. But our demand for the stock remains the source of a demand for additions to it, and so indirectly for demands for that part of *the flow of services* which can add to the stock. The greater the response in any case, the smaller will be the tendency for the rate of interest to fall. All demands for replacements and additions to the stock of assets (through "goods and services currently produced," as Tobin puts it) proceed via demands for assets as a whole. But changes in such demands affect the *relative money values* of different parts of the flow of services, and not their *aggregate money value* unless general changes in demand for money, or other monetary phenomena, are affecting the value of the money unit; while *the whole flow of "goods*

---

[47] "Comment on Jacques Rueff's "The Fallacies of Lord Keynes' 'General Theory,'" *Quarterly Journal of Economics,* May 1947, pp. 353–67; ibid., November 1948, p. 764.

*and services currently produced" will always be demanded if priced
at levels consistent with coordination of the economy.*[48]

If savings are defined as "money income *minus* expenditure on
consumption goods," and "savings" are supposed to differ from
"investment" (defined as "expenditure on additional capital goods"),
then the only conceivable discrepancy *must* be due to hoarding or dishoarding of money. In other words, if "savings" in that sense exceed
"investment," M_r is being bid up and, M being constant, the *money*
value of nonmoney services will be bid down. But that *is* hoarding
(an increased demand for money which is not due to an increase in
T), and a condition which monetary policy can easily rectify by a
temporary increase in M, the nominal money supply.

---

[48] In the hypothetical case noticed above, in which growth is physically impossible, this remains true; for the whole flow of services will be consumed
directly or embodied into assets which—because increased stocks cannot be
profitably carried through time—are being consumed at an equivalent rate.

15

The Marginal Propensity to Consume

The concept of the marginal propensity to consume describes the division between "consumption" (*presumably* the value of production needed to replace the value of services and assets exterminated) and "investment" (*presumably* the value of production which is in excess of value exterminated) which it is assumed will take place in the expenditure of an additional increment of income. This concept plays a vital role in Keynes' theory of the multiplier, a theory which attempts to explain how the use of income so described may cause a deficiency in aggregate demand, which may be rectified by an addition to aggregate expenditure upon "investment," the effects of which (upon aggregate demand) are supposed to be automatically multiplied.

Before examining this thesis it will be useful to notice, by way of contrast, certain aspects of what pre-Keynesian economists were teaching about the dynamic relations of monetary policy and employment. The following impressions of that teaching are expressed in a manner which may well have been influenced by Keynes' terminology and post-Keynesian discussions, but they are phrased to some extent in my own terminology which I have already been employing. They state what I believe would have been almost universally accepted before *The General Theory* appeared.

It has always been recognized, I think, that any event which leads to an increase in MV relative to T can induce a further increase in V through the effect upon expectations. Whether, in such a case the increase in MV initially leads to an increase in demands for goods of zero or short life expectancies (services immediately consumed and "consumer goods"), or increased demands for goods of long life expectancies ("producer goods"), or through private or governmental demands for these things, or whether the rising money income offered for things is due to M or V or both increasing, the effect is the same. It has been recognized also that under a monetary system with any degree of flexibility (for example, as normally under the gold standard) one expansion of real income, financed by noninflationary credit expansion—that is, an appropriate increase in M —would evoke a further increase in M if T tended to rise in relation to MV. In other words, it has been understood all along that a greater *money income* than that due to any original increase in MV may emerge, either owing to the commitments of a monetary policy or owing to speculative reactions upon V, and that the emerging additional money income may cause the release of any capacity the services of which may have been previously priced above market-clearing levels, and so through policy obligations, require a further noninflationary increase in M. I explain further in Chapter 16.

The theory of the multiplier, based on the concept of the marginal propensity to consume, is an attempt to show that there is something seriously wrong about this view. It alleges that a crucial source of instability is lurking in the fact (alleged) that a rise in savings per se (not savings accompanied by a rise in liquidity preference) causes "a gap" in aggregate demand, which only additional expenditure on "investment" can fill. It is held further that the withheld capacity (or other idle capacity) causing "the gap" in aggregate demand, which it is supposed only additional expenditure on "investment" can fill, can be coaxed back into use only through additional initial expenditure on "investment." In contrast, the pre-Keynesian view was that additional "demand," whether arising from an increase in M or in V, could rectify price-caused unemployment (provided that prices were not raised further in anticipation, or in consequence, of this reaction).

While pre-Keynesian thinking recognized the possibility of repercussions from the initial demands so caused upon expectations, and hence upon V, or through the reactions upon M (if capacity is released), the multiplier theory confines attention to the repercussions upon those incomes which are affected, in turn, by the money spent initially passing from hand to hand. Pre-Keynesian thinking laid stress on (a) the flow of products (or of productive services) as the source of aggregate demand (in the sense of real income), a magnitude which increases with every release of withheld capacity or with every growth of capacity (not neutralized by withholding or additional consumption elsewhere); and (b) the determinants of the value of the money unit (which value determines the money valuation of income). The multiplier theory, on the other hand, lays stress on the *expenditure* which is set going, an expenditure which is supposed to precede the release or growth of capacity and so to rectify the community's disinclination or inability to *consume* enough. Now if the word "consume" here refers to the extermination of value, which means extermination of part of the source of demands, it does not make sense. Suppose therefore that what is meant is that too small a proportion of the flow of productive services is devoted to *replacement* of the value consumed, would it then make sense? Hardly, for by definition the value of replacement is identical with the value of consumption when there is no capital consumption.

In the pre-Keynesian era, economists remembered the operation of the gold standard. They tended to think of that standard, or some improvement of it, but always assuming the use of some money unit of defined value, as the *normal* money and as the best conceivable system provided it was expertly administered. For the credit system and the demand for monetary services operated under the discipline of the convertibility obligation. It was *believed* that the system would cause money income and real income to vary more or less in proportion. But monetary policy was certainly not regarded generally as a legitimate means of "creating employment." Where increased idleness of certain men and certain assets had emerged, reduction of those prices which exceeded market-clearing levels (which would mean, *ceteris paribus,* a rise in such prices as had *not* previously been above such levels) was thought to be the required remedy for increasing the source of demands. Certainly any economization achieved in what they thought was a good monetary system could be held to "stimulate" the economy, but only in the same way that an improvement in the transport industries which reduced freights and fares could be expected to add to the source of demands, generally. Yet, the multiplier theory ignores the possibility of continuous coordination through those price adjustments which affect the value of the money unit.[1]

This possibility of adjusting prices to correspond with changes in market-clearing levels is so fundamental in the non-Keynesian ap-

---

[1] But as we shall see in the following chapter, what I call the "employment" and the "real income" multipliers tacitly assume the release of capacity through inflation-induced price adjustment.

proach that it cannot be fruitfully omitted, as a determining condition, from any situation studied. Yet its exclusion by Keynes was not merely an assumption made for the convenience of theoretical simplicity—that is, as an expositional device. As we have seen, the assumption of price rigidity[2] is looked upon as a realistic and practically useful premise for the study of the short run in the world that we know, and consideration of coordinative price adjustments is excluded through the very choice of concepts employed.

The concept of the marginal propensity to consume is used in the discussion of an assumption—a supposed "psychological law"—that, *as real income increases, consumption increases but by not so much as income.* That is, the increment of consumption is assumed to be less than the increment of income. (Even if *the proportion* of the increment of income consumed *exceeds* the proportion which consumption bears to income, the multiplier is supposed to hold.)

It should be noticed that the same proposition can be stated the other way around, as follows: *As real income increases, savings and investment increase, but by not so much as income.* Keynes himself stated the law as follows: "If C_w is the amount of consumption and Y_w is income . . . ΔC_w has the same sign as ΔY_w but is smaller in amount, i.e., $\dfrac{dC_w}{dY_w}$ is positive and less than unity."[3] But this "law" can be equally well stated as follows: "If S is the amount of savings and Y is income . . . ΔS has the same sign as ΔY but is smaller in amount, i.e., $\dfrac{dS}{dY}$ is positive and less than unity." It is, I think, significant that the "law" is never stated in this form.[4] Yet it is an equally valid statement. In short, the "fundamental psychological rule" on which, Keynes argued, the stability of the economic system depends in practice,[5] merely states that the marginal propensity to consume is neither unity nor zero, that is, that people will neither consume the whole of any increase in income (but save the rest

---

[2] It is wage-rate rigidity which Keynes particularly stressed. The thesis that price adjustments are self-frustrating has been dealt with in Chapter 12.

[3] Keynes, *The General Theory,* p. 96. Keynes regarded these quantities as measured in wage units, and he therefore gave each of the terms the subscript *w*. But the argument is not affected by the units in which these amounts are measured.

[4] It *is* sometimes said that the propensity to consume is merely another term for the propensity to save.

[5] Keynes, op. cit., p. 97.

of it) nor save the whole of any increase (but consume the rest of it).

So stated, one would think that the law could hardly be of any importance, even if one could accept the further assumption that the ratio $\frac{dC}{dY}$ is rigid in the short run.[6] But Keynes deduced from it that, "if employment and hence aggregate income increase, *not all* the additional employment will be required to satisfy the needs of additional consumption."[7] Well, this is self-evident if we assume, as he did, that capacity has been released. Some of the "additional employment" will be required to satisfy the needs of additional savings. It did not occur to Keynes that we can equally usefully say: "Not all the additional employment will be required to satisfy the needs of additional savings, but some will be needed for additional *current* consumption." Nevertheless, he maintained that "this simple principle" leads to the conclusion that "employment *can only* [my italics] increase *pari passu* with an increase in investment; unless, indeed, there is a change in the propensity to consume."[8] He reached this conclusion because, he said, consumers "will *spend less* [my italics] than the increase in aggregate supply price," which will lead (in my terminology)[9] to the withholding of capacity unless there is additional investment "to fill the gap."[10] I propose to argue that it is solely the assumption (through the phrase "will spend less") that the short-term demand for money somehow increases more than proportionally as income increases (a notion which is due to defective concepts of consumption and savings) which can justify further consideration of the argument.

But Keynes failed completely to perceive the significance of these words "will spend less." Indeed, throughout the whole of his discussion of the propensity to consume, a fundamental confusion is lurking. At times he appeared to be assuming that when people do not devote the entire increment of income to acquiring consumer goods, they bid up the value of money with the rest. But at other times the context appears to make it obvious that "the gap" which

---

[6] That is, in Keynes' words, "unlikely to undergo a material change over a short period of time except in abnormal or revolutionary circumstances." Ibid., p. 91.

[7] Ibid., p. 97.

[8] Ibid., p. 98.

[9] Keynes said that the increased employment "will prove unprofitable." He assumed, of course, a rigid price of labor or other rigid factor prices and hence withheld capacity.

[10] Keynes, op. cit., p. 98.

"needs filling" is that caused by *saving* as such. The acquisition of savings is not the same thing as postponing spending, whereas Keynes wrote as though it were, and used concepts which prevent us from continuously making the distinction. It requires as much "spending" to acquire $1,000 of goods of long life expectancy as it does to acquire $1,000 of goods of short life expectancy.

I have a big expositional difficulty in this chapter and the subsequent chapter. Most Keynesians vehemently deny that the theory of the multiplier and the concept of the marginal propensity to consume rely tacitly upon the assumption of liquidity preference, or what most pre-Keynesian economists used to call "hoarding." Moreover, Keynes expressed himself several times in a manner which excludes such a suggestion. Yet the assumption that a rise in real income leads to a more than proportional rise in the demand for money *is* implied, and often seems to make the multiplier argument intelligible (although not acceptable). Some economists, in an attempt to rehabilitate the multiplier theory, have in fact turned to an explanation along these lines.[11] (See my references to Goodwin, pp. 392–94.) I have always had the feeling that, in thinking of the "gap," that is, the amount by which the value of consumption is supposed to be deficient (when income is increasing), Keynes and his disciples have been, in a muddled sort of way, thinking of this sum as not having been spent at all. Hence, in handling these issues, I have found it to be desirable not only to treat the argument of *The General Theory* in its own terms, but to deal also with the same arguments as rationalized by the assumption that the value of any additional increment of income which is not consumed *is* partly or wholly invested in money inventories. Unless I do this, I have the feeling that I shall not be answering the real objections which will be in the minds of those modern economists who still seem to find meaning in Keynes' "multiplier" notion.

Consider, for instance, Keynes' discussion of the depreciation of a house. He said that if the landlord "neither spends on upkeep nor regards as net income available *for consumption*" (my italics), the

---

[11] It could then be expressed as a high *propensity to* invest in money when real income is increasing (due to our not immediately having anything on which to spend the increases). But it is, I am afraid, a pure rationalization of Keynes' case to suppose that he was concerned with demand for money. It is saving, not hoarding, which he regarded as to blame for "the gap" (discussed on pp. 323–25)—"increased investment" (at the expense of consumption). Ibid., p. 105. Yet his remedy is additional expenditure on "investment."

provision he makes for depreciation "constitutes a drag on employment all through the life of the house" until the fund so accumulated is used for rebuilding the house. Again, one would think that the tacit assumption is that, in the meantime, the landlord invests the whole of the depreciation provision in money, thus tending to bid up the aggregate real value of money assets. For to the extent to which the landlord does not regard it as more profitable to retain rents received in the form of money, he *must* acquire *some* assets (whatever their life expectancies may be). His only alternative would be to cash the rent checks and then destroy the cash! Hence, Keynes concluded that "sinking funds, etc., are apt to withdraw spending power from the consumer. . . ."[12] But why only from the consumer? If it is "spending power" which is withdrawn, why is it not equally at the expense of those who would otherwise purchase services for embodiment into assets of *all* life expectancies?[13] And if further increments of investment in money *are* judged to offer higher yields than further increments of investment in nonmoney, why should this cause consumption to contract, that is, cause a smaller value of services and assets to be exterminated and therefore cause, perhaps, a smaller subsequent investment in assets of short life expectancies to be prospectively profitable?

Of course in the absence of the coordination which price flexibility permits, *deflation* certainly can reduce the flow of services (which, I repeat, is often what is meant by "aggregate demand").

---

[12] Ibid., pp. 99–100.

[13] Actually, it seems to me absurd to suppose that "financial prudence" and "sound finance" (about which Keynes waxed so ironic in the passages in which this argument occurs) lead to sinking funds being invested in money to any extent in normal times, although hybrid assets might well be chosen in some circumstances. Sinking funds are in practice invested in securities (unless they can find temporarily profitable employment in the business itself); it is only to the extent to which these securities offer prospective *pecuniary* yields of below the rate of interest that they form (as hybrid money) part of the aggregate stock of money; and only in that case will demand for them tend to raise the aggregate real value of money. But the demand for hybrid money which arises from the investment of sinking funds (for example, for securities of appropriate maturities) is wholly normal demand for monetary services; and there seems to be no reason why demand for money from this source should not be stable in normal times, and no reason why abnormal changes in it should not be met by noninflationary credit adjustments. There can be no tendency for a decline in V, with a consequent inducement to withhold capacity, unless the aggregate real value of money is in process of being bid up and M remains fixed. Keynes' objection to "financial prudence" was a plea for inflation rather than an objection to deflation.

But as we noticed above (pp. 184–85, 189–90, 197–98), an increased investment in money need not be accompanied by deflation if the monetary authority is under instructions to maintain a money unit of constant purchasing power (by preserving a constant long-term relationship between MV and T). Under such a policy, the inevitably created condition of *latent* inflation would, as we have seen, cause no difficulty when V returned to normal; for bank credit could be withdrawn as money inventories were replenished through increased sales.

But most important of all, even if we do try to assume (in wishing to interpret the crucial passages under discussion in the most friendly and lenient way) that Keynes' words "withdraw spending power from the consumer" were intended to mean "invest in money," Chapter 8 of *The General Theory* rules it out. Thus the term "liquidity preference" does not appear in Chapter 8, in which he introduced the idea of the marginal propensity to consume. Certainly he talked there of the imperfection with which man adjusts "his *expenditure* to changes in his income" (my italics), yet he went on to say: "Thus a rising income will often be accompanied by increased saving, and a falling income by decreased saving. . . ." But he had defined "saving" as the excess of the value of current output (income) over consumption. Saving so conceived *is* what I call "savings," that is, the value of output produced over a period *minus* the value of output exterminated over that period. Moreover, he followed the passage just quoted by a discussion of the motives for adjustments to income changes "which only acquire effective sway when a margin of comfort has been attained"[14]—again an indication that he was thinking of the devotion of saved income to the acquisition of *non-money assets*. This interpretation is strengthened by his argument in Chapter 9, in which he developed further his explanation of the propensity to consume. He discussed the motives which lead to provision for the future, but brought in "the motive of liquidity" merely *as one of many reasons* for the desire to accumulate capital assets.[15] He did *not* state that, when this reason accounts in part for the saving, there is a special case to be considered. Finally, his attitude on this point is brought out in his discussion of the implications

---

14 Keynes, op. cit., p. 97.

15 This is one of the contexts in which Keynes' failure to distinguish between the saver and the entrepreneur roles, and his consequent failure to perceive that demand for money is the expression of an entrepreneurial judgment, appear to me to have caused great confusion.

of the fact that "Consumption is satisfied partly by objects produced currently and partly by objects produced previously, i.e., by disinvestment." He contended that "To the extent that consumption is satisfied (out of existing stocks), there is a contraction of current demand, since to that extent a part of current expenditure fails to find its way back as a part of net income."[16] In reality, *all* consumption (except for consumption of "final services," which forms a small proportion of income) is satisfied out of stocks which have been finally produced in a physical sense *over a wide range of points of time,* and which have a wide range of life expectancies. The fact that a larger proportion of goods being currently consumed got their physical form a long time ago (as with the using up of an old locomotive or the drinking of a bottle of old wine) does not cause a contraction of "current demand" in any sense of that term of which I can conceive.[17] Only if there is a failure to embody services of a real value equivalent to any current extermination of value, will "aggregate demand" decline; and *the demand will decline owing to a failure of production, not of consumption.*

If we were able, then, to interpret Keynes' phrase about "current expenditure" failing "to find its way back as part of net income" as referring to a rise in liquidity preference, controversy would be shifted to a different plane. But even so the implications of his argument would be unacceptable. Consumption of previously accumulated stocks creates no "gap" due to savers being somehow prevented from "investing" in nonmoney and so forced to accumulate money. As I have consistently insisted, virtually all consumption (extermination of value) is out of an existing stock of assets.[18] Hence, if Keynes *was* subconsciously thinking of abnormal demand for money when he concluded that the "problem of providing that new capital-investment shall always outrun capital-disinvestment sufficiently to fill the gap between net income and consumption, presents a problem which is increasingly difficult as capital increases,"[19] he seems to have been confused by a reversal of cause and effect. No "gap" is caused by investment in additional money when people regard that as more productive than investment in nonmoney.

---

16 Keynes, op. cit., p. 105.

17 The most reasonable meaning of "current income" is surely "the aggregate value of the flow of services of an understood period."

18 In this context Keynes obviously intends "disinvestment" to mean "consumption," not the mere sale of assets or the failure to replace used up assets.

19 Keynes, op. cit., p. 105.

There is yet another passage in which Keynes appeared about to recognize that the real problem concerns demand for money, namely, when he referred to the possibility that financial provision for the future might be separated from physical provision for the future.[20] But financial provision to make good consumption of assets of short life expectancy is equally likely to be separated from physical provision of such assets! That is, payment may be postponed for services which are normally devoted to replacing current consumption just as easily as for those which are normally devoted to current accumulation. But Keynes did not show why an increase of income should aggravate the separation (cause hoarding and so "a gap") in either case.

If monetary policy aims at maintaining convertibility, parity, or a tolerable scale of prices, the effect of growing utilized capacity must, *if it is recognized as such,* bring about an expansion of credit (that it, an increase in M). Hence, unless the convertibility obligations, or the parity sought, or the price index objectives are *in themselves* deflationary, or unless (through a misunderstanding of the situation) the attempt to administer an intendedly neutral policy works in a deflationary manner, we have no grounds for supposing that a stimulus to the cumulative withholding of capacity will be induced.

Let us consider further what Keynes meant when he argued that the "gap" must be filled in order to provide *future* consumption demand.[21] Extra *expenditure* on investment, he appeared to suggest, can alone create the purchasing power necessary. Thus he wrote: "New capital-investment can only take place in excess of current capital-disinvestment if *future* expenditure on consumption is expected to increase." Of course, whenever capital is maintained intact or accumulated, because a prospective yield in excess of interest is expected from the embodiment of services in assets, it can occur only because (excluding the case in which the purpose of the investment is ultimate consumption of the product by the investor himself) marginal prospective sales of the outputs are predicted to exceed the cost of the assets acquired and the prospective cost of operating them. Keynes continues, "Each time we secure today's equilibrium by increased investment" (at the expense of consumption) "we are aggravating the difficulty of securing equilibrium tomorrow."

---

[20] Ibid., p. 104.

[21] "Consumption demand" meaning, presumably, demand for final services or goods of short life expectancies.

Well, every time income receivers decide to reduce their demand for *A* in order to acquire more *B,* then *ceteris paribus* the price of *A* will fall and that of *B* rise; while to the extent to which entrepreneurs are permitted to coordinate, fewer resources will be devoted to producing *A* and additional resources to producing *B.* Any rise in saving preference is simply a special case of this effect. It tends to reduce the rate of interest and, in so doing, it tends to release resources for cheapening *immediately* the production of assets of long life expectancies (producer goods) and *eventually* assets of short life expectancies (consumer goods). In other words, such a change in preference is itself automatically reducing the burden of the co-ordinative adjustments which will be needed tomorrow.

Is not this exactly the opposite of Keynes' contention? I have already exposed what I believe to be the error. If the rate of interest is declining, it is simply a manifestation of the value of services being reduced in relation to the value of assets. But, Keynes continues, "A diminished propensity to consume today can only be accommodated to the public advantage if an increased propensity to consume is expected to exist some day."[22] That is, an increased propensity to consume will be expected in the future and therefore will encourage investment in long-life assets in anticipation of later demands for the product of these assets. Yet somehow Keynes fails to see the issue in this way.

His reference to "future *expenditure* on consumption" instead of "future *production* to enable future consumption and growth," brings out the nature of his thinking. *He tended always to think either of consumption or of spending as the source of demand.* Yet consumption is extermination of the power to demand. The truth is, as I suggested in the paragraph above, that the mere fact that there is a diminished *propensity* to consume now ought, in the minds of economic advisers, to cause an expected higher *ability* to consume in the future. I have shown that if we exclude population growth, then *all* expansion of the ultimate source of demands, that is, all real accumulation of productive power, *with no exceptions*, is the result of a consumer-saver decision against current consumption. And far from "every weakening of the propensity to consume regarded as a permanent habit" reducing "the demand for capital as well as the demand for consumption,"[23] it must always represent a demand for

---

22 Keynes, op. cit., pp. 105–6.
23 Ibid., p. 106.

a more rapid piling up of capital resources, as well as grounds for the prediction of an accelerated growth of "aggregate demand" in the future. (See pp. 345–47.) Of course, if it happens to be accompanied by the pricing of inputs and outputs above market-clearing levels and hence the withholding of capacity, a stronger saving preference will be necessary to achieve this result. And, in the absence of price coordination (that is, if price rigidities regarded as unstable cannot be rectified) such a withholding may be induced through deflationary investment in money, which can in turn—it might be argued—be caused through pessimistic expectations about the *immediate* future. It is admittedly *conceivable* that the very phenomenon which ought to cause optimistic expectations concerning prospective future "aggregate demand," in practice causes pessimism. That is a quite separate point.

We can, I think, get a further insight into Keynes' ideas in his apparent paradox that "a rise in the rate of interest will have the effect of reducing the amount actually saved."[24] He contended that the higher interest will diminish "investment" and hence reduce income, the rate of saving falling by the same amount as the decline in income. But the cause of increased interest is always either a rise in the schedule of the marginal efficiency of capital (which, he says, will "offset" the rise in interest!) or a fall in saving preference, *unless monetary policy is deflationary.* In other words, if the marginal efficiency of capital remains unchanged, interest can rise only through an *increased* propensity to consume, or through those influences which Keynes appears anxious to exclude (until they are brought in, *as an independent factor,* in the last paragraph of his Chapter 9), namely, the determinants of M and V.[25] The vital truth is that decisions which cause *value produced* to exceed *value exterminated* are responses to saving preference, not to liquidity preference.

A rise in saving preference as such can exert no deflationary influence.[26] If the resources devoted to production of goods with short life expectancies are highly specific and the prices of their services rigid, then admittedly an increase in saving preference may result in

---

[24] Ibid., p. 110.

[25] It is very difficult to know from the chapter under consideration (Chapter 9) whether Keynes intended "income" to mean money income or real income or whether he expected the reader to assume that income in the two senses varies more or less in proportion.

[26] Except in the sense that, if it causes the natural level of interest to fall, any formerly nondeflationary market rate will become a deflationary rate.

additional withheld capacity in those resources. But on the assumption that there is withheld capacity also in the industries specialized for production of goods with long life expectancies ("investment industries"), an equal *release of capacity* can be expected there.

Hence, Keynes' conclusion that "the more virtuous we are, the more determinedly thrifty . . . , the more our incomes will have to fall when interest rises relatively to the marginal efficiency of capital"[27] is based on a serious fallacy. For in the absence of deflationary policy, interest can rise "relatively to the marginal efficiency of capital" only through an increase, not a decrease, in the propensity to consume. And the rather cryptic qualification at the very end of Keynes' argument (at the end of Chapter 9) to the effect that if the rate of interest were always such as to maintain full employment, "Virtue would resume her sway" (in other words, a high rate of accumulation of assets *would* then be caused by a weak propensity to consume), seems merely to imply once again that all the time, in the course of the argument we have been examining, Keynes was really tacitly assuming what the Keynesians usually emphatically deny,[28] namely, that monetary factors are causing discoordination of prices through deflation.

The truth is that *deflation plus price rigidity would have that effect no matter what consumption-saving preference was expressed.* Obviously, if the market rate of interest is so fixed that, irrespective of the extent to which the services of productive capacity are being priced in excess of market-clearing values, the monetary unit (and so money income) is always depreciated to the extent necessary to induce the release of that capacity,[29] there can be no decline of real income due to unemployment of resources. But that does not enable us to assume that, when this condition is absent, the failure to spend enough and the withholding of capacity are due to saving.

There is no doubt, I think, that in Chapters 8 and 9 of *The General Theory,* Keynes was assuming that the source of ultimate demand lies in consumption instead of in production. Certainly he wrote as though he held that, because the whole of each increment

---

[27] Keynes, op. cit., p. 111.

[28] On this point see Fritz Machlup, "Period Analysis and Multiplier Theory," *Quarterly Journal of Economics,* November 1939, pp. 1–27.

[29] If an increase in M would induce the release of capacity without any depreciation of the money unit, that is, if the supply of services in general were perfectly elastic, then it could be said that the required depreciation was infinitesimal.

of a growing real income may not be *consumed,* demand may be insufficient to absorb the growing product. We shall see this sort of conviction reflected in the Keynesians' treatment of invested savings as "leakages" in the multiplier theory. Keynes wrote: "Consumption —to repeat the obvious—is the sole end and object of all economic activity." No one, I think, has devoted greater attention to the significance of this "obvious" truth than I have myself.[30] But it does *not* imply that consumption is the origin of aggregate *demand* in any sense. If I have an apple I can demand with it by, say, offering it for an orange; but if I eat it I have eradicated any power to demand with it. Because we all envisage the future, and because people generally wish to be able to maintain their power to produce (and hence to consume, or to consume better), the incentive to replace or more than replace consumption is enormously powerful. But because both "consumption" and "replacement" are identical in magnitude, that does not make them identical concepts! Keynes' words (in the context of a passage that is quoted on page 371), "our dependence on present consumption as a source of demand," seem to indicate something much more serious than careless or misleading exposition. Keynes continues: "Opportunities for employment are necessarily limited by the extent of aggregate demand. Aggregate demand can be derived only from present consumption or from present provision for future consumption."[31] The wording here is significant. His statement *would* have been more acceptable if he had said "aggregate demand can be derived only from *present provision for both present and future consumption,*" that is, the production of *valuable services.*[32] Whether the *value* of those services is derived from the expectation that the products into which they flow will be consumed or utilized in the early future or in the distant future is irrelevant. Was it not Keynes' failure to perceive that consumption is an essentially depressive force and production an essentially stimulating force which must be identified as the basic defect in his thinking and that of his disciples?

He contended, for instance, that "whenever an object is produced within the period with a view to satisfying consumption subsequently,

---

[30] See Hutt, *Economists and the Public,* Chapter 16, "Consumers' Sovereignty"; "The Concept of Consumers' Sovereignty," *Economic Journal,* 1937.

[31] Keynes, op. cit., p. 104.

[32] Actually, expenditure on replacement (which makes up the greater part of all expenditure in practice) must be covered in the term "future consumption." The true distinction is between the immediate and the distant future.

an expansion of current demand is set up."[33] This is quite wrong in what it apparently implies. It is the *form* of real income (the source of "demands in general") and not its *amount* which is affected. *Aggregate real demands* can expand only through a growth in *utilized* productive capacity, and whether this increase in the flow of services is embodied into goods for early or late consumption or utilization makes no difference.

Similarly, *aggregate money demands* can expand only when M and/or V increases; and the saving-consumption choice concerning the use of the increased money income is equally irrelevant, *unless it can be shown that the manner of spending influences one or both of these terms,* and that is just what Keynes fought shy of saying. Hence his thesis that saving as such—thrift—is a contractionist force is untenable. He has *not* shown that a high *propensity to consume* is favorable to employment. He has *not* shown that employment will be more difficult to achieve in a rapidly expanding economy (which will be the position when there is a high propensity to save) than it will be in a slowly expanding economy.

Possibly, at the back of Keynes' mind there was lurking the fallacy of the satiability of human preferences or wants. This impression is left by his view that "The greater . . . the consumption for which we have provided in advance, the more difficult it is to find something further to provide for in advance, and the greater our dependence on present consumption as a source of demand."[34] The only *real* point here is, I suggest, that there are limits to the expression of saving preference, that is, that there are diminishing returns to provision for the future. The postponement of current consumption is constantly increasing *the ultimate power to consume,* while the exercise of that power at any time is purely a matter of choice and freedom.[35] Was it not due to his failure to understand this that Keynes saw in thrift—in saving—and not in an uncompensated decline in MV in relation to T, the villain of the piece, while constantly writing as though he were identifying or confusing saving preference and liquidity preference?

It may be objected that all these criticisms I have presented ignore

---

[33] Keynes, op. cit., p. 105.

[34] Ibid.

[35] The withholding of capacity which is capable of providing currently valuable services is always a case of restraint on freedom, even if it is due merely to rigidity, for the rigidity prevents access to demanded services which are running to waste.

the vital contention that a fall in the marginal propensity to consume does not imply the achievement of, but only the attempt to achieve a greater flow of savings. But rationalization of the argument along these lines is equally indefensible; for it cannot be said that the *attempt to save* (through a reduced valuation of consumption) can (a) reduce *monetary* income, unless it can be assumed that it induces an uncompensated rise in the demand for money, or (b) reduce *real* income, unless it can be assumed for any reason to induce the withholding of capacity. In the absence of one or both of these effects, it cannot reduce the source of supposed or realized savings. Paul Samuelson suggests that one of the great contributions of Keynes is his demonstration that "the *attempt* to save may lower income and actually *realized* saving."[36] Once again, it is only if Keynes meant that saving may be accompanied by deflation and/or induce the withholding of capacity, that he can be said to have been right. And if Keynes did mean that, then he was merely stating in a tortuous way what I imagine every pre-Keynesian economist would have accepted. In short, arguments to the effect that "attempts" to increase savings may fail, that is, in the words of John Lintner, that they "do not necessarily or automatically increase new investment expenditures,"[37] can merely mean that a rise in saving preferences and an increased demand for money may occur together,[38] or that increased withheld capacity may emerge and cause *subsequent* savings to fall. It is quite true that a rise in saving preference does not necessarily mean that savings are achieved. As I have stressed several times, to the extent to which the services which make up income are nonversatile in respect of producing goods of differing life expectancies, attempts to provide for the future may merely bid down the rate of interest and cause the emergence of a new equilibrium under which a transfer of value from would-be savers to entrepreneurs is brought about.

The sound approach to all these problems may be found, I repeat, in a recognition that the rate of growth of real income is always conditioned by the extent to which *the forces which facilitate growth* (namely, thrift, economizing innovations, and the release of capacity) *in certain parts of the economy* are being offset by *the forces making*

---

[36] Paul A. Samuelson, *"The General Theory* (3)," in Harris, ed., *The New Economics,* p. 159.

[37] John Lintner, "The Theory of Money and Prices," in ibid., p. 527.

[38] It must be remembered that this does not mean that real accumulation is not caused, in the absence of the withholding of capacity.

for contraction (namely, consumption and the withholding of capacity) *in other parts of the economy.* If real income is growing, it must be because the forces making for growth are winning. It is, I maintain, impossible to find in the fact of that victory any reasons which might explain why contractionist influences should then tend to exert a relatively greater influence—unless offset by additional expenditure on investment.[39] Indeed, the contrary is true. The principle that growth and the release of capacity tend to call forth further growth and the release of further capacity, while the withholding of capacity tends to induce further withholding and reduce the profitableness of growth (in the absence of unanticipated inflation), has already been stated. Hence when utilized productive capacity is expanding, only monetary factors *plus* rigidity or such extraneous factors as a wave of labor union aggression, or monopolistically efficient acquisitiveness in some other form, will be able to account for the withholding. In short, if it is recognized that the source of all real demand is utilized productive capacity, the withholding of which is the withdrawal of real demand, many of the problems appear to solve themselves. And it then becomes clear, in particular, that the conclusion on which Keynes based his Chapter 16 (on the multiplier), namely, that "employment can only increase *pari passu* with investment,"[40] is false. It is *not* true that the pricing of services above market-clearing levels can be corrected only in the presence of growth.

As I argued in Chapter 7, permitting the pricing system to coordinate under the loss-avoidance, profit-seeking incentives is capable of exerting continuous pressures for the elimination of wasteful idleness in men and assets, quite irrespective of society's preferences in respect of satisfactions in the *immediate,* as distinct from the *distant* future.

---

[39] I need hardly repeat that if growth due to such factors is not accompanied by an increase in M, deflation must follow (unless V is increasing). But that is what Keynes seemed determined not to say in this context.

[40] Keynes, op. cit., p. 113.

16

The Multiplier

Some economists are today treating the "multiplier" as the process of "credit creation" through the banking system, that is, by way of the process which F. W. Crick explained with great clarity in a seldom-quoted contribution in 1927,[1] thereby clearing up much current confusion. Keynes had praised Crick's article, which was entitled "The Genesis of Bank Deposits," in his *Treatise*,[2] in which he treated the subject ably. Yet it seems to me that in writing *The General Theory,* Keynes had forgotten Crick's contribution. The phenomenon that Crick analyzed was exactly that which Keynes tried to explain through his multiplier theory. But the process of credit creation—the issue of credit by depositors who are not themselves indebted to the banking system—and the process of lending by all sellers who advance credit but do not borrow a corresponding amount from the banks or otherwise, are perfectly understandable without being linked to "the propensity to consume" and supposed "leakages."

In the actual world, with the fractional reserve system recognized as relevant to monetary policy, the value of the money unit (short-term and long-term) is, I suggest, what matters. But there is no definite limit, apart from the obvious concern of lenders for the safety of their loans, to the extent to which a central bank's "injection" of "new money" ("high-powered money," it is often called today) may make it profitable to expand credit. The expansion may "multiply" the nominal money supply (the number of "actual money units"), and cause an average of prices to rise unless the flow of productive services increases in proportion. Under any sys-

---

[1] *Economica*, June 1927, pp. 191–202.

[2] Keynes, *Treatise on Money,* p. 25 n.

tem in which the money unit has a defined value, for example, as under the gold standard, the monetary contract for convertibility of all money units into gold imposes the required discipline on the increase in M. When there is a central bank, its *main function* is to impose such an expedient or legally enacted limit to the "multiplication" of money, and it can successfully aim at any desired magnitude for the "nominal money supply."[3] But it must always act in the light of evidences of current and forecast demands for money. In other words, under central banking, the magnitude M is policy-determined. Irrespective of the particular mechanism through which a given injection of "newly created" (or "newly activated") money causes an expansion or contraction in M or in V, the *new* magnitude M, and its relation to M_r, is still wholly determinable by a central bank (or other monetary authority) whether it operates by discount rate, by open market, or by enacted reserve requirements. It is always capable of offsetting any inflationary or deflationary effects due to the changing profitability of issuing credit or to other causes, for example, budgetary deficits or surpluses.

Thus if, say, through open-market operations, the central bank "injects" another ten million dollars into the economy, it does not assume that MV will increase simply by that amount *unless that increase happens to be its target for* M. For instance, if its monetary policy is based on an obligation to maintain a money unit of constant value,[4] the central bank will have achieved its greatest success when the oscillation of the price index about a trend of zero is minimized. Or if the aim of government policy is not monetary stability, but to offset, say, the universal tendency of the strike-threat system to repress the flow of income and the source of demands, the central bank can, if so instructed, aim at a steady depreciation of the money unit (secretly, of course, for maximum effect). Or, if the aim is to raise the long-term value of a depreciated money unit on the old-fashioned moral principle that a civilized society depends on the keeping of promises, this also can be done, whatever the preferred or chosen mechanism by which credit can be withdrawn.

Stigler has described the "multiplier" as "the fuzziest part of his

---

[3] This magnitude, I repeat, not only includes the pure money equivalent of "hybrid money"—"near money," "money substitutes"—but allows also for the influence of "bank credit," *as well as all other lending and borrowing.*

[4] Because that is believed to be conducive to the most successful coordination of the economy through responsible entrepreneurial decision making (subject to the social forces of the market).

[Keynes'] theory."[5] I believe that the hold which the theory has obtained is chiefly due to this "fuzziness"; for when we have dispelled it by explaining what might have been meant (or should have been meant), we find that all possible explanations are fallacious. I propose to show that it has been built on (a) the fallacy (which I have already exposed in many different contexts) that only some change in the relationship between prospective yields and the rate of interest, which relationship Keynes assumed would influence expenditure on something called "investment," can cause MV and the money valuation of income to change,[6] (b) the fallacy (which was refuted in Chapter 11, above) that spending produces income, and (c) the wholly arbitrary tacit assumption that, subsequent to its initial "injection" as expenditure on "investment," "newly created money" is *spent* only if then devoted to consumption and not if devoted to further "investment."

Three points immediately arise.

(1) If it is being argued that the relation of the rate of interest to prospective yields somehow needs rectifying, how can this be reconciled with the obvious fact that prospective yields (envisaged by Keynes through his notion of the marginal efficiency of capital) are already a determinant of the rate of interest?

(2) In exactly what way is "expenditure" on services embodied into assets to replace consumption different from expenditure in excess of that value? Or alternatively, in what way is expenditure on services to be embodied into assets of relatively short life expectancy different from expenditure on assets of relatively long life expectancy? After many years of thinking about the issue, I still cannot suggest any answer.

(3) No economist would deny (a) that demands for particular services which are not consumed as they are rendered are derived from demands for noncompeting outputs of other services, and (b) that demands for goods of long life expectancies are derived from demands for goods of short life expectancies, which the services of long-life assets helped to produce.

---

[5] Stigler, *Five Lectures on Economic Problems*, p. 43.

[6] That this notion does lie at the root of the multiplier notion was also the interpretation of Hawtrey, who wrote: "Investment is relevant, because he [Keynes] maintains that only through investment can the flow of money be regulated." Hawtrey referred also to "income being tied down by the multiplier to the limit allowed by the volume of investment." R. G. Hawtrey, "Keynes and Supply Functions," *Economic Journal*, September 1956, pp. 483–84.

In its simplest and least unreasonable form, the multiplier thesis can be expressed by saying that the stimulation of industries producing for investment stimulates in turn the industries producing for consumption. At one point, the theory was so expressed by Keynes.

T. Wilson claims this much for the multiplier, that it has attracted attention to the consideration, "that, at a time when large numbers are out of work, the beneficial effect on employment of a rise in investment will not be confined to the industries making capital goods; that, if there are idle resources, consumption and investment are likely to move in the same direction instead of being alternatives as the earlier theories, which usually started with the initial assumption of full employment, were wont to suggest."[7] But if Keynes had said anything like this, no one would have objected, except to the quite untenable suggestion that earlier theories had implied anything different.

In Keynes' rigorous enunciation, the theory assumes that every additional increment of income is *caused by* an additional increment of expenditure which has been devoted to investment. An increase in "investment" of x will cause an ultimate increase in money income received of Kx.[8] If the marginal propensity to consume is 4/5ths, so that the multiplier (K) is 5, the increase in income will be $5x$. The multiplier will, then, be greater the greater the marginal propensity to consume, that is, *unity* when the propensity is *zero,* and *infinity* when the propensity is *unity* (an absurdity to which I must later give some attention).

In the usual statement of the theory, it is *tacitly assumed* that an increased rate of "investment" expenditure is *maintained,* in the sense that if for any reason the new level of "investment" due to the initial increase in M declines, M will be further increased to maintain "investment" at its new magnitude. This necessary assumption does not seem to be stated in most of the textbooks. I deal later (a) with the case in which an additional investment expenditure is assumed *not* to be maintained, as a decline in V is assumed gradually to absorb some of the initial addition to M; and (b) with the extreme case in which no part of the additional income which is unconsumed is "invested."

---

[7] T. Wilson, "Professor Robertson on Effective Demand," *Economic Journal,* 1953, p. 564. Surely every pre-Keynesian economist would have agreed that the *most probable* result of changes in income would be that the magnitudes consumption (replacement) and net accumulation would vary in the same direction, although improbably in the same proportion in each case.

[8] Keynes' own exposition does not, of course, justify this use of the word "ultimate."

The case chosen by Hague and Stonier to illustrate the principle makes it clear that they are assuming "not a mere once-for-all act of investment, but that the government undertakes to carry out the new, increased volume of investment in each succeeding year—or whatever period of time is most convenient. . . . Government expenditure . . . is constant at its new level."[9]

In stating the principle, I used the words "eventually" and "ultimate." But Keynes' multiplier was imagined by him to be *instantaneous*. The consumption goods industries were thought of as advancing *pari passu* with the capital goods industries.[10] Only imperfect foresight, he seemed to think, could account for any time lag; and, after consideration of this possibility, he restated his position as follows: ". . . *in every interval of time* the theory of the multiplier holds good in the sense that the increment of aggregate demand is equal to the product of the increment of aggregate investment and the multiplier as determined by the marginal propensity to consume."[11] (My italics.) (The words "the marginal propensity to consume" here are a slip for "the multiplier.")[12] But as a result of criticisms, subsequent Keynesians have rationalized the theory in what has been termed the "serial interpretation," which I shall in due course examine.

I have a general objection at the outset. Why should the "stimulation" due to the release of productive services formerly priced inconsistently with market-clearing values, and now devoted to the satisfaction of one set of economic ends (namely, planned provision for the future), "stimulate" the release of overpriced services of capacity devoted to the satisfaction of all other economic ends in any manner which is not just as possible the other way round? In other words, why should the field in which the initial expenditure is incurred be regarded as having some special significance? Under Say's law, any release of formerly overpriced services "stimulates" investment in inputs in noncompeting sectors of the economy; and if emphasis is placed upon "spending," why should expenditure in one sector of the economy have any special significance for the magni-

---

[9] Douglas C. Hague and Alfred W. Stonier, *The Essentials of Economics: An Introduction and Outlook for Students and the General Reader* (New York: Longman, Green, 1955), pp. 87–88.

[10] Keynes, *The General Theory,* p. 122.

[11] Ibid., p. 123.

[12] I pointed out this slip in my 1963 *Keynesianism,* but the slip was tacitly removed in later printings of *The General Theory.* This fact came to light only very recently. I worked from the earliest printing.

tude of aggregate money income unless, in that sector, the prices of services happen to diverge differentially from market-clearing levels? According to Keynes it is the "increment of aggregate investment" which must initiate the first impulse of the multiplier, and hence is the ultimate cause of an increase in money income and real income. But why should not any *initial* expenditure in a given situation have exactly the same kind of effect?[13] On this point, Haberler, shortly after *The General Theory* appeared, asked a simple but devastating question. Referring to Keynes' illustration of the increment of investment taking the form of public works, Haberler asked: "But how are we to classify money paid to unemployed workers to perform 'public works' of very doubtful value? Suppose these works consist of digging holes in the ground and filling them up again. Or suppose a road is built at a cost which far exceeds its value to the community."[14] In merely asking this question, I believe that Haberler exposed the total irrelevance of the broad field in which an initial expenditure is incurred. Only if we distinguish between the degrees of withheld capacity in the field of initial expenditure, is the field of spending relevant.[15]

Curiously enough, Haberler does not seem to perceive just how damaging his question is. He sees the arbitrariness of the distinction between investment and consumption (replacement) in this special case; he states that in practice the classification of additional expenditure "as consumption or investment is generally of minor importance" and he contends that "What matters are the factors stressed by traditional theory; the methods used by the government in raising the money, the rapidity with which the successive recipients spend it, the manner of spending, etc."[16] I agree completely, except that I believe that *the manner of the spending, or where it occurs,* has nothing to do with the position at all, either in respect of initial additions to expenditure or the subsequent additions which are induced.

---

[13] Later on, dealing with criticisms which had raised these issues, Keynes said that he chose new "investment" as the multiplicand because it is the "factor which is most prone to sudden and wide fluctuations." (Keynes, "The General Theory of Employment," *Quarterly Journal of Economics,* February 1937, pp. 209–23.) I fail to see why that should be a justification.

[14] Haberler, *Prosperity and Depression,* p. 250.

[15] On the assumption that "increased expenditure" can induce the release of capacity, the only reason why a release so effected in one large group of industries should not tend to stimulate a similar release in all the rest is that there happens to be no withheld capacity in the latter.

[16] Haberler, op. cit., p. 230.

The entrepreneur's incentive to spend on services which equal the value of consumption for embodiment into assets as a whole and hence for "replacement," is identical with his incentives to spend on whatever services are to be embodied into whatever assets Keynes meant when he used the word "investment." We can hardly hold that there is some special significance in society's expenditure in buying services for embodiment into assets as soon as this expenditure exceeds the value of replacement. This has never been shown and it cannot be shown. Moreover, in practice some undertakings are always disinvesting—failing to replace—while others are expanding. Thus it is impossible to say of any specific item of net accumulation of assets by one firm or person that it represents accumulated assets (that is, "investment") *on the part of society.* It seems to me that, in the light of this single criticism alone, the whole theory collapses unless it is revised to imply that all *additional* expenditures effect the same kind of stimulus. And the *typical* exposition explicitly denies this.[17]

But if the argument of my Chapter 11 is accepted, the theory collapses for another simple reason. I have shown that it is fallacious to suppose that *expenditure* either produces real income or the money valuation of income (determined by the value of the money unit), but that, on the contrary, it is the value of the money unit which determines how much expenditure is necessary in order to acquire a given *quantum* of services or assets. Real income *may* be produced through the release of overpriced capacity, and unanticipated inflation may bring this about, but it is still the reduced value of the money unit which makes increased expenditure necessary and not vice versa. Every time a money unit passes, the commodity or service which it buys is in turn demanding *it.* The offer of money for nonmoney no

---

[17] For example, Hague and Stonier write: "The multiplier . . . will not operate at all unless an initial change in *the volume of investment* takes place. In other words, the multiplier cannot operate unless there is something to be multiplied; and that something *must be* a change in investment." Op. cit., p. 90. (My italics.)

Paul Samuelson briefly admitted in 1941 ("Period Analysis and Income Distribution," *Quarterly Journal of Economics,* August 1942, pp. 577 et seq.) that relief expenditure (that is, on consumption) could be treated as entering into the multiplicand (the multiplier reaction then being expressed in "investment"); but he did not explicitly answer Dennis Robertson (whose ironic reference to "honorary investment" probably forced the admission); nor did he consider explicitly the implications which Robertson and Haberler had discussed. Subsequent teaching has scarcely been affected. (I refer below to Goodwin's treatment of the point, pp. 392–94.)

more tends to raise prices than the simultaneous offer of nonmoney for money tends to reduce prices. The one cannot occur *more frequently* than the other. In other words, changes in both M and V indicate changes in people's valuations of the money unit. But (a truistical proposition) if the number of money units increases in relation to the demand for money, the purchasing power of the money unit must contract.

I am not optimistic enough, however, to suppose that I can so simply convince those who have long become habituated to thinking in terms of the "generation" of income by expenditure, still less those economists who have taken their first steps in the study of economics by mastering the multiplier theory and painfully learning its mechanism from the textbooks. I must therefore examine it in some detail, *assuming for the time being that expenditure does generate income!*

We have first to distinguish between three sets of supposed effects of *additional* "investment" expenditure (that is, expenditure by society in excess of the previous value of the flow of services): (a) the effects upon money income, or what I shall call *the money income multiplier;* (b) the effects upon income measured in wage units, or what Keynes called—most inappropriately—"the investment multiplier," but which I shall call *the real income multiplier;* and (c) the effects upon employment, or what Keynes called *the employment multiplier.* All three multiplications start with expenditure on "investment," but the first is supposed to multiply the money income which results, the second the real income, and the third the employment.

Keynes seemed to think that there are difficulties involved in measuring income in real terms (he said, "in terms of product") which are escaped in the case of wage units. He said, however, that it is often convenient to regard income expressed in terms of wage units as "an adequate working index of changes in real income."[18] As his disciples have not followed his use of wage units as a measure, I propose to dispense with the wage-unit concept and discuss merely the real income multiplier, in the sense in which I have already used the term "real income."[19]

Because Keynes meant by "employment" the use of only one factor of production, labor, and not the use of all factors, the real

---

[18] Keynes, *The General Theory,* p. 114.

[19] That is, the value of the flow of services measured in imaginary money units of "constant purchasing power."

income multiplier (his "investment multiplier") will not be *identical* with the employment multiplier. He discussed the relations between them and explained that, while there is no reason in general to suppose that they will be equal, he found it convenient to deal with the simplified case in which they are assumed to be equal.

But the fundamentally important distinction which is essential for clear thinking is not that between the real income multiplier and the employment multiplier, but that between the money income multiplier and the real income multiplier. For while the effects of both the *employment multiplier* and the *real income multiplier* are envisaged as ceasing when a state of "full employment" has been reached (at which stage, additional expenditure on investment is regarded as causing no further increase in real income), the effects on money income (the *money income multiplier*) are supposed to continue and to be expressed in "true inflation,"[20] although the Keynesians do not *explicitly* use the concept of the money income multiplier.

One of the most serious difficulties about Keynes' exposition on this topic arises out of his use of concepts which cause the notions of the real income multiplier and the money income multiplier to be confused.[21] The clumsy wage-unit expression leads students to inhibit concern with the price consequences of the policies Keynes was envisaging. It obscures the fact that his nostrum was essentially inflationary. The wage-unit formulation facilitates the tacit assumption of perfect elasticity to increasing expenditure in *the release of capacity previously withheld through overpricing*. Only when the "full employment" condition has to be considered does the argument of *The General Theory* face the price consequences, that is, in the state in which rising prices no longer result in those improved price-cost ratios which raise prospective yields to investments in inputs, again presumably the condition which Keynes called "true inflation."

Now as we have seen, by "true inflation" Keynes meant neither a loss of parity on the part of the money unit in terms of a monetary standard nor a loss of parity in real terms. He argued in effect that, as long as any overpriced potential services are being released, any decline in the value of the money unit—that is, any rise in the scale of prices—is not truly inflationary. Until that point is reached, he

[20] Keynes, *The General Theory*, p. 119.
[21] Henry Hazlitt also has made this point. He writes, "Keynes' 'multiplier' jumps without notice from 'real' terms to monetary terms." *The Failure of the "New Economics,"* p. 145.

admitted that increases in "effective demand" will influence both the cost unit and output. But all this is explained in *The General Theory* very much later than the discussion of the multiplier itself, which leaves the impression with the student that, up to the point of "full employment," there will be perfect elasticity of supply in respect of the whole flow of services (those of the value needed for replacement as well as those in excess of that value).

If such a condition did exist, then the real income multiplier and the money income multiplier would be equal until no further capacity could be released. But unless they are equal, *the effect of seeking full employment (the release of withheld capacity) through the device of an increase in* M *(whether spent initially on "investment" or anything else) instead of through price adjustments, must be inflationary in the ordinary sense, as opposed to Keynes' sense.*

Nearly all subsequent discussions of the multiplier and especially those employing "the serial interpretation" (see below) appear to discuss the effects, not upon real income (or income measured in wage units), but upon money income. Nevertheless, they still typically treat the subject in such a way as to leave the impression with the student that the elasticity of supply is so perfect that an increase in M (and any consequent increase in V) will induce a rise in T as rapid or almost as rapid as the rise in MV.[22] The tacit assumption seems to be that deflation has previously caused idle capacity without causing prices to fall—in other words, that there has been a purposeless deflation (as distinct from a rectifying deflation).[23] But if that is the position, if *overpriced potential services* can be *coaxed back into use as easily as this, why should not very slight price adjustments be sufficient to secure the same objective?* (See pp. 229–32, 401.) I must remind the reader that this very reasonable possibility was excluded by Keynes in his assumptions and concepts.

Let us now consider the *money income multiplier*. The case usually chosen to illustrate it in the textbooks is that in which the initial

---

[22] For example, Hague and Stonier, whose treatment is quite typical of the textbooks, maintain that, until a condition of full employment is approached, increasing expenditure will mean an increase in employment but no (or little) increase in prices. Op. cit., p. 97.

[23] Yet there has never been any political or monetary *motive* for such a deflation; for credit contraction tends to follow rather than to cause the withholding of capacity. (See pp. 228–30, 246–48.) At the same time, *purposeless* deflation may occasionally have occurred inadvertently or by reason of the nature of a metallic standard.

expenditure arises through an increase in M ("newly created" money as distinct from "newly activated" money).[24] The present discussion will therefore be confined to this case. The additional expenditure on "investment" (public works, for example) is envisaged as being received in due course in the form of wages which go to buy goods in shops, then to buy goods which replace the stocks sold, which means in turn buying the services of producers, and so on. According to this "serial interpretation" of the theory, in each transfer of the money, *part of the sum passed,* being spent on consumption, enters into the income receipts of those who are paid for goods or services; and as each unit of money goes on circulating, it goes on entering into the income receipts of later recipients. If the marginal propensity to consume is $1/2$, so that the multiplier is 2, an initial expenditure of 100 is supposed to lead to successive increases of income in each subsequent *income period*[25] of the increments spent on consumption, namely, 50, 25, 12.5, 6.25, etc. That is, as the additional income receipts at each stage of the process are again spent, in part, *on consumers' goods,* each of these expenditures (as distinct from the part spent on goods which add to net "investment") is supposed to set up a further process of "generation" of money income. In this way, we are told (George Halm's words), "the money seeps down again through many productive processes and contributes to the income of an ever widening circle of people working in stores, offices and factories,"[26] and *the consumed part* carries on the "income generating" process. In short, each successive act of spending *on consumption* is thought to result in an addition to money income, while because some part of each increment of spending is assumed to be on investment, the successive *additions* to money income *from this cause* must, it is thought, dwindle. For insofar as the income of any subsequent recipient is saved, it is regarded as a "leakage" and believed to offset the multiplier effect. *These consequences are supposed to follow whether the "leakage" (the unconsumed part of the*

---

[24] George N. Halm, *Monetary Theory: A Modern Treatment of the Essentials of Money and Banking* (Philadelphia: Blakiston Company, 1942), pp. 399, 402. The term "newly *created* money" here means simply an increase in M, the number of units into which M_r, the aggregate real value of money assets, is divided.

[25] That is, the period in which each money unit is supposed to become income once.

[26] Halm, op. cit., p. 400.

increment of income) is spent in the acquisition of nonmoney assets or retained as money.[27] But in any case, people in general do not accumulate money, and must therefore "invest" the balance. Hence it is difficult to conceive of exactly what it is that *leaks away*. I shall, however, shortly show that the assumption *is* sometimes that what is not spent on consumption is not spent at all. Yet the Keynesians always try to maintain at the same time that the failure to spend on nonmoney is not investing in money. That is what is so confusing. What is equally confusing here is the fact that, in a literal sense, one only "spends on consumption" when one consumes services as they are rendered. Otherwise, what is really meant by the phrase is "spends on replacement."

Haberler has argued that the true multiplier will depend upon many other circumstances than the propensity to consume. He mentions, for instance, the marginal efficiency of capital and "the velocity, especially the income velocity of money."[28] It is to be my contention that no dynamic reactions have their origin in the propensity to consume, except insofar as this propensity *happens* to combine with other factors in influencing V (as I have defined it); and I do not think it has been shown that this propensity must have, or that it is likely to have, this effect. Haberler specifically mentions "leakages" in this connection. Only if he is thinking of "leakages" as accumulated money, an interpretation of the multiplier which true Keynesians reject, is it comprehensible, while the theory ignores the reality that investment in money has the same economic status as investment in nonmoney. (See below, pp. 389–91.)

As I have already insisted, Keynes certainly did *not* have liquidity preference in mind. His thinking on this point, as on others, seems to have been dominated simply by his tendency to think of consumption, and not production, as the source of demands in general. It was this belief which gave rise, I suggest, to his notion that money spent on consumption somehow goes on adding to the effective demand of subsequent recipients, while money spent by them on "investment" is treated as responding to, not adding to demand.

---

[27] I refer to income being *retained* as money, simply because that is the way the Keynesians always look at it. In reality, however, as we have seen, income always *accumulates* in the form of nonmoney assets. It is later exchanged for money.

[28] Gottfried Haberler, "Mr. Keynes' Theory of the 'Multiplier': A Methodological Criticism," in *Readings in Business Cycle Theory* (London: Allen and Unwin, 1950), p. 199.

And yet, as I have insisted, consumption as such is *the extermination of power to demand.* A similar way of reasoning appears to have caused his successors to think that expenditure on investment causes the "leakages" which we have been discussing. Thus, if the additional income resulting from the initial increase in expenditure (due to an increase in M) is in turn spent wholly on "investment," there will be (the Keynesians suppose) a complete "leakage," the multiplier will be unity, and money income will increase only in proportion to the increase in M. Expenditure on consumption (replacement) is alone thought of as giving any further *stimulus.*

But suppose the income resulting from the initial expenditure on investment is devoted wholly to consumption, that is, suppose the marginal propensity to consume is unity. Then the money income multiplier is assumed to be *infinite!* In Keynes' words, if people "seek to consume the whole of any increment of income . . . prices will rise without limit."[29] Haberler's explanation of this apparent absurdity is that, "In plain English, there *can be* no increase in I."[30] (My italics.) Why *"can be"?* The proposition itself *states* the assumption that there *will be* no voluntary attempt to acquire additional assets out of the resulting money income. But the initial increase in M is tacitly assumed to be spendable in any way which the original recipient of the money "invested" may choose.

I do not see that the absurdity can be explained away on these lines. I shall shortly suggest that the multiplier of infinity has a quite different meaning, and that consideration of this extreme case may serve as a *reductio ad absurdum* of the assumption that the marginal propensity to consume and any multiplier reaction are related, by some stimulus which originates in consumption. (See pp. 398–401.)

Surely the truth is that an increase of either M or V, spent initially on *either* "investment" *or* "consumption," will *ceteris paribus* enter into the income receipts of those paid for output and thus cause an increase in money income, while there are conditions under which it may be validly supposed that any such initial increase (however caused and wherever spent) will induce a further increase in V or a succession of increases in V, or (and this is an assumption about the nature of monetary policy) a further increase in M or a succession of increases in M. But the Keynesians refuse to admit this, even when their own attempts to explain what they think Keynes really meant,

---

29 Keynes, *The General Theory,* p. 117.
30 Haberler, *Prosperity and Depression,* p. 226.

or ought to have meant, seem to be leading them to the same conclusion. They are at pains to deny, for instance, that the multiplier and "income velocity" are one and the same thing. That is obvious. But is it not equally obvious that the multiplier effect must have time dimensions, and if so and unless we are tacitly assuming a succession of increases in M, that this will be expressible in terms of "income velocity"? (Machlup has made this point.)[31] Thus, if an additional expenditure (initiated by an increase of M_1 to M_2) in a particular field results in an ultimate increase of money income by more than $M_2V — M_1V$, it simply means that V must have increased![32]

Keynes himself recognized *other* factors which he thought *did* affect V; but he treated them as quite independent. He explained, for instance, that owing to what he called "the confused psychology which often prevails," expenditure on public works which ought to result in the multiplier effect being experienced is prevented through repercussions upon "confidence" which may "increase liquidity preference." He did not, however, regard this as affecting the multiplier. He classified it as a factor which may have adverse reactions on investment *"in other directions."*[33]

My contention is that these "other factors" are the only factors. The true *money income multiplier* is not explicable through any analysis of the way in which additional money units are passed on through the hands of the successive recipients and the kind of services purchased with them. It is explicable solely through an analysis of the determinants of V and M (in *my* sense of these terms).[34]

Some Keynesians perceive that we cannot concentrate our attention *solely* on spending by the first and subsequent recipients of the initial addition to money spent. Thus, Benjamin Higgins points out that, for the pump-priming effect of the multiplier to work, *"induced* private spending (*new investment* and consumption by those whose incomes are *not* directly affected by public investment, but whose anticipations are changed) would have to be positive and large."[35] I

---

[31] Fritz Machlup, "Period Analysis and the Multiplier Theory," in *Readings in Business Cycle Theory* (London: Allen and Unwin, 1950), p. 220 n.

[32] There seems to have been no textbook reaction to Vera Lutz's 1955 challenge on the broad issue discussed here. See her "Multiplier and Velocity Analysis: A Marriage," *Economica*, February 1955, pp. 29–44.

[33] Keynes, *The General Theory*, pp. 119–20.

[34] See pp. 188–90.

[35] Benjamin Higgins, "Keynesian Economics and Public Investment Policy," in Harris, ed., *The New Economics*.

have not seen this notion related explicitly to the multiplier theory as a whole (although, in italicizing the words *"new investment,"* the passage stresses the similarity to the effects of both kinds of expenditure).

Haberler, although an early, acute critic, seemed not to have the idea that it was only through *expenditure on consumption,* of the income resulting from an initial investment, that the income velocity of circulation would be multiplied. He retained the Keynesian view that receipts which are reinvested are "leakages," and cause a contraction in the multiplier. As I suggested above, I think this is because he is really regarding the saving of any part of the additional increment of income which is not spent on consumption goods as added to money stocks; and this can sometimes be seen to be the *tacit* assumption of many of the Keynesians.

Thus, in Alvin Hansen's rationalization of the multiplier, some "leakages" were obviously regarded as due to investment in money, although he did not recognize that this is what was *implied in each of the five "most important" cases he mentions.*[36] For instance, the purchase of consumers' goods which are not replaced by the seller can cause a "leakage," not because the goods are "excess," as Hansen believes (for the word "excess" has no meaning in his context), but because the money spent and received is tacitly assumed to be retained by the receiver.[37] Yet the Keynesians are emphatic in their denials that the leakages have anything to do with such a process. If, however, Haberler had argued that the marginal propensity of individuals to prefer money to nonmoney or (the same thing from a different aspect) their marginal propensity to spend to reduce their money stocks in order to buy nonmoney[38] will influence sub-

---

[36] Alvin H. Hansen, *A Guide to Keynes* (New York: McGraw-Hill Book Company, 1953), pp. 89–90.

[37] At one point Keynes came near to admitting that his whole aim was merely to prevent what I call the bidding up of M_r. He wrote: "The only radical cure for the crises of confidence which afflict the economic life of the modern world would be to allow the individual no choice between consuming his income and ordering the production of the specific capital-asset which, even though it be on precarious evidence, impresses him as the most promising investment available to him." (*The General Theory,* p. 161.) This certainly *implies* that he would wish to prevent the income receiver from preferring to hold money rather than other assets. But inconsistencies elsewhere prevent us from accepting so simple an explanation.

[38] That is, to buy nonmoney *services* (for immediate consumption, or for embodiment in replacement, or for embodiment in additional assets), or to buy nonmoney *assets* covering the whole range of economic life expectancies.

sequent changes in money income and the release of capacity, he would have refashioned the Keynesian multiplier into a more easily intelligible and more acceptable theory. But apparently because of some lingering conviction that the purchase of services flowing into additional assets of long life expectancy ("investment") has different effects from the purchase of services flowing into assets of short life expectancy, or into maintenance, repairs, replacement, and direct consumption, he appears to have been prevented from seeing and describing the whole problem simply as one of the effects of changes in "income velocity" or (given a certain monetary policy) upon the value of the money unit.

Investment in money (hoarding), which may accompany saving, or the settlement of debts without an equal amount of further borrowing on the part of others, *may* perhaps be usefully described as "leakages," in the sense that such a use of income will reduce the multiplicand (the initiating increase in aggregate expenditure).[39] But Halm argues—with seeming uneasiness—that the practice of treating *nonhoarded savings* as leakages "has its great advantages" (although he does not mention the "advantages"). He says, the effect of such expenditures is not "entirely ignored" because "they are treated under the so-called acceleration principle." It is merely "a terminological decision. . . . We are driven to the rather artificial construction that invested savings are first considered as leaking out of the monetary circulation and that they are, then, recreated to finance induced investment."[40] This looks like an attempt at justification of a wholly unjustified distinction between expenditure in two fields.[41]

---

[39] Halm has made the point that if "primary investment (financed by credit creation) is *supplanted by* investment which is financed out of savings, the multiplicand of the multiplier is reduced." Op. cit., p. 404. (My italics.) If all that is meant by the words "supplanted by" is that instead of a particular project (for example, public works) being financed by inflationary credit expansion it is financed by noninflationary borrowing, then, obviously, there will be no multiplier effect on money income from "investment which is financed out of savings," because the inflationary effect on aggregate expenditure is avoided. In other words, the multiplicand is *nil*. "Reduced" is hardly the correct word. I feel that Halm uses the word because he is still thinking of savings as a *leakage*—as something which permits the beneficent multiplier effects to escape. On the other hand, if "financed out of savings" is supposed to mean dishoarding, then it *is* logically an initiating expenditure in the multiplier sense.

[40] Halm, op. cit., p. 404, including footnote.

[41] Keynes himself did not recognize that recourse to the acceleration principle (to which he attached little importance) might be a way out of the difficulty.

Machlup, whose 1939 article has obviously influenced Halm's argument, discusses the unsatisfactory nature of the Keynesians' reply to those critics who have maintained that the "leakages" are nothing more than hoarding (the accumulation of idle cash balances and the cancellation of debts). "This identification of the leakages with hoarding," he says, "is liable to make full-blooded Keynesians furious. They usually react to it with an explanation of the meaninglessness of the concept of hoarding—in the Keynesian language —but they do not tell their misinterpreters 'what happens to the leaked-out funds.' They confine themselves to the contention that all that matters is the fact that these amounts are not spent on consumption. This answer, in turn, is apt to make their opponents furious."[42]

In forcing the discussion to this vital issue, Machlup appears to be maneuvering the Keynesians into a corner. But like Haberler, just as he seems to be ready to knock them out of the ring, he somehow pulls his punches and appears reluctant to carry on the fight. He continues, "As a matter of fact, it *is* irrelevant for the immediate effect what the nature of the leakage really is. It *is* true that it does not make any difference 'what happens to the leaked-out funds.' But the critics have nevertheless a perfect right to know what happens if the funds are not 'hoarded.' "[43] *Surely the whole question centers around this very issue.* If the leakages *are* merely hoarding, that is, savings which are "considered as leaking out of the monetary circulation" (Halm), then it can be argued that the *Keynesian* multipliers have to be abandoned on this ground alone. Machlup says that the critics of Keynes are unable to see that if, say, $100 which is "created" as bank deposits, for the purpose of purchasing securities to finance public works, is accompanied by the expenditure of $36 out of savings for the purchase of these securities from the banking system, it will *alleviate* the demands on the bank system, so that "only $64 will flow from new bank credit as a 'contribution to income.' "[44] The $36 is "invested," he says, but it is still a "leakage." But if there is a "leakage," surely it is due not to saving but to the policy of the monetary authority which, on parting with the securities it had originally

---

Yet it seems almost as though Keynes' successors, having made the multiplier a valued part of their apparatus, have been loath to recognize a weakness which renders it utterly worthless.

[42] Machlup, op. cit., p. 223.

[43] Ibid.

[44] Ibid., p. 225.

purchased, fails to reinvest the money proceeds, $36. Machlup is simply supposing that one *increase* in M is followed by a subsequent *decrease* in M.

If Keynes or any of his disciples had meant this, they would have said it and no economist could have misunderstood them. This sort of factor has nothing to do with the multiplier, but merely (as Halm perceives) with the multiplicand. And so, it seems to me, Machlup surprisingly abandons the fight when the multiplier is tottering.

Since Machlup wrote, I have noticed one other attempt worthy of consideration (this time by a would-be Keynesian), to rehabilitate "the multiplier." In his attempt to refine his theory, Richard M. Goodwin[45] seems to have been groping toward the same truth. He reaches the following conclusions (Robertsonian definitions are used in the passage): "Income increases, decreases, or remains stationary, depending on the difference between saving and investment."[46]

This makes the multiplication dependent not on the increases of investment but on the increase, constancy, or decrease of MV. The form in which it is expressed seems to imply that, *ceteris paribus,* the money valuation of income increases when uncompensated "dishoarding" is in progress and decreases when uncompensated "hoarding" is in progress. If that *is* what is meant, no one will dispute it. But if it implies that the money valuation of income cannot increase through an increase in M or V unless investment (in the Robertsonian sense) exceeds saving, it is wrong.

Goodwin explains that whether *subsequent* spending "generates" additional income (that is, whether the serial multiplier effect is realized) depends in each successive spending upon whether the expenditure is an "injection." It is an "injection," he says, if it is an expenditure otherwise than out of income (that is, *presumably* out of the "dishoarding" of money[47] or credit expansion). Does it not follow, therefore, that, in every case, the multiplier effect must simply be that of an increase in M or $V?$ All expenditures, says Goodwin, fall "into two classes, those springing from previously received income and all others."[48] But is it not just as easy to spend otherwise than out of "previously received income" on investment as on con-

---

45 Richard M. Goodwin, "The Multiplier," in Harris, op. cit., pp. 482–99.
46 Ibid., p. 493.
47 Of course, *all* expenditure is out of *holdings* of money!
48 Goodwin, op. cit., p. 486.

sumption? The explanation in the passage just quoted from Goodwin is, however, preceded by another passage of extraordinary obscurity. "To determine in practice what an injection is," says Goodwin, "requires much ingenuity, even though the principle is clear and fairly simple. When once understood, the distinction disposes of the spurious objection that what is done with savings has been ignored. If they lead to injections then it is obviously not so, and if they do not, then they ought to be left out of account so far as income is concerned."[49] The only meaning which I can attribute to these sentences amounts to an admission of, rather than the "disposal" of, what he calls "the spurious objection" that Keynes ignores "what is done with savings" (that is, whether they are "hoarded" or spent on the acquisition of additional nonmoney). Goodwin clings to the view that the extent to which successive expenditures are "injections" depends upon the marginal propensity to consume. He does so quite inconsistently, it seems to me. For once his criterion of an "injection" is accepted, the propensity to consume is admitted to be wholly irrelevant. No reasons remain for regarding successive expenditures on "consumption" as "injections" while successive expenditures on "investment" are regarded as "leakages." Yet he stands shoulder to shoulder with Keynes in regarding "consumption expenditure" as somehow different in kind from "investment expenditure." For instance, he describes as "a constant new injection . . . *that* consumption which people would make if they had no income."[50] (My italics.) Admittedly, if people who are receiving no money *buy* things to consume, their expenditure must be an "injection," that is, they must perforce buy on credit or dishoard. But this does not confer upon *consumption* in general some special attribute which causes expenditure to replace it necessarily to involve "dishoarding" or even to make "dishoarding" more likely. If people acquire nonmoney by "dishoarding" without increasing their consumption, the position is just the same. Moreover, there is no reason to suppose that, because there are always some people who will be living on the consumption of capital (for example, holders of annuities), the demand for money should be less. Thus, the sale of nonmoney assets by those receiving no income in order to spend the proceeds on consumption is *dissaving,* and as such will tend to raise the rate of interest and depress

---

[49] Ibid.
[50] Ibid., p. 485 n.

capital values. But dissaving is not dishoarding; it has no inherent tendency to cause dishoarding; and that means that it is irrelevant to the demand for money.

The initiating expenditure, and each subsequent expenditure which continues the multiplier effect, it is said, must be spending which does not originate out of "current income." But one does not *spend income.* One *consumes income and capital* (income being "consumed services" *plus* the capital which would have been accumulated [net] over a period if there had been no consumption of assets over that period), and one *saves income. But one spends by changing the form of one's capital,* that is, by decumulating holdings of money in exchange for nonmoney. One *spends,* not income but money. If one buys without reducing one's money stocks (that is, replenishing them), however, one buys with nonmoney, that is, with "money's worth."

All spending is *out of holdings* of money which are in process of depletion, replenishment,[51] or growth. The logical distinction is a twofold one. We have spending (a) out of *individual holdings of money* which people do not wish fully to replenish or people wish exactly to replenish, or people wish to hold more of (in short, all the factors which determine V),[52] and (b) out of *aggregate holdings of money units* which are in process of depletion or held constant or in process of growth (in short, spending which is possibly accompanied by changes in M). The factors under (a) influence only M_r, the aggregate real value of money, and the factors under (b) influence only M, the number of money units into which that real value is divided.

When I published my *Keynesianism* in 1963, Keynesian economists as a whole had not, I thought, progressed even as far as Goodwin. They still generally held (John Lintner's words) that, once the schedule relation between consumption and saving is assumed fixed, a "stable relationship between fluctuations in investment and changes in the level of income"[53] has been determined.

It has been suggested to me by an able critic (after reading my argument to this stage) that the notion of the "leakage" *can* be defended if it is treated merely as an analytical device for excluding from consideration all repercussions other than those which are

---

51 All replenishments are, of course, out of holdings of "money's worth."
52 T being given.
53 John Lintner, "The Theory of Money and Prices," in Harris, op. cit., p. 527.

implied in *the assumption* of a mechanical relationship between consumption and money income. His argument—put forward, I feel, more or less in the role of devil's advocate—is as follows:

> When money income increases (necessarily—or probably—under the multiplier assumption, through an increase in expenditure on "investment"), consumption will increase at a rate determined by the propensity to consume. Now while it is true that further investment spending *might* occur as a consequence, we do not want to consider that, because it must be regarded either as initiating a new multiplier series superimposed, so to speak, on the first, or as introducing an accelerator effect. Hence from the standpoint of an analysis of the direct consequences of the original increase in money income, we must treat not only any hoarding induced, but any expenditure on investment induced, as a "leakage."

In developing this thesis my critic asks us to imagine M to be 100 at the outset, the income of the "income period" being therefore assumed to be 100. (The Keynesian "income period" is that in which income reproduces itself, each money unit becoming income once.)[54] He assumes then one single increase of expenditure on investment (due to an increase in M) of 10. (We can imagine the central bank or Treasury failing to do anything to maintain this additional expenditure on investment after the single initial "injection".) Assuming a multiplier of 2, money income for successive periods will be, according to the theory:

| 100 | 110 | 105 | 102.5 | 101.25 | 100.625 |

and the saving increments will be

| 0 | 0 | 5 | 2.5 | 1.25 | 0.625 |

An ultimate addition of 20 will have been contributed over time to money income received, but the rate of receipt of this income (per income period) will gradually have fallen back to its original magnitude of 100.

Now my own interpretation of this example is that the increase in money income in the proportion 100 to 110 which, if V (expressed

---

[54] This is a method of making abstraction of V which has, I am inclined to think, been partly responsible for the Keynesian failure to see that unconsumed "income" which is not "invested" *must* be hoarded. An assumed decline in V is fallaciously treated as a decline in M. The fallacy is due to the Keynesian concept of "income" as receipts of money.

in terms of some fixed time interval) is constant, will remain at 110, is assumed to be continuously reduced because the so-called saving increments are *assumed* (for purely analytical reasons) to be absorbed into hoarding. (This could be expressed as a decline in V, in terms of a fixed time interval.) "Hoarding"—investment in increased money inventories—remains the only conceivable alternative to the "investment" of the "saved" increment; yet there is never the slightest reason for assuming it!

My critic seems to claim that describing what is *assumed* to be held as money by the adjective "saved" is a means of isolating the direct consequences of the initial "investment" increment. But that does not make any clearer to me what is meant. For as there is no reason why what is saved *should* be invested in money, all that is isolated is what would happen *if* all income saved *were* so treated. It does not tell us *why* income does not continue at 110, which, on my critic's argument, is what would happen if income receivers did not invest in money.

Then, to illustrate the effect of *maintaining* a certain increase in the rate of "investment" (M increasing by "injections" of 10 in each income period) my critic illustrates his position in the following table which shows, he thinks, "the direct consumption effects of each period's investment increment [of 10] superimposed one on the other in the subsequent periods."

MULTIPLIER OF 2

Immediate and subsequent effects of an increment of investment of 10 in period:	Income Period				
	1	2	3	4	5
1	10	5	2.5	1.25	0.625
2		10	5	2.5	1.25
3			10	5	2.5
4				10	5
5					10
Sum total of income increments:	10	15	17.5	18.75	19.375

The assumption is that the aggregate absorption of the successive additions to M (through the accumulation of money) increases continuously until eventually these additions become wholly absorbed.

It is a fantastic assumption. M is supposed to grow bigger and bigger while money income becomes stabilized at 120!

An ultimate doubling of the initial increase in M has resulted, and so an increase in the money income of 20 percent *per income period* (and hence—V being constant—*per annum*) has eventuated through the maintenance of the 10-percent increase in "investment." But that is not a *multiplication,* except in the sense that successive (decreasing) additions in M are *assumed* to have raised the original injection from 10 to 20! In this case, the explanation is not that an additional "injection" is needed to offset hoarded money, but that the maintenance of the initial rate of increase in "investment" requires what is *regarded* as the multiplicand to be raised by successively declining amounts or, in the extreme case in which the marginal propensity to consume is unity, by constant amounts in each period. But if the initial increase in M is regarded as a multiplicand, so should subsequent increases in it. The true multiplier is then always unity! In other words, *the monetary authority, in deciding to maintain a given increase in the rate of "investment," in the face of the hoarding of half of the successive injections of money, commits itself to a series of declining increases in* M. And the greater the marginal propensity to consume, the larger the successive additions to M which it is assumed are required, via monetary policy, to achieve this end. Thus if the marginal propensity to consume is thought to be 3/4, the *commitment* undertaken by the central bank will be ultimately to multiply the initial addition to M by 4. Only if the propensity to consume is zero (the multiplier being unity) so that the initial increase in "investment" maintains itself, will the central bank escape the obligation to increase M in the series I have explained. And when (owing to the marginal propensity to consume being judged to be unity) the same net addition to M is assumed to be made in each income period, the ultimate increase in M will be infinite. *This is, I suggest, the true explanation of what has been thought of as the infinite multiplier.* But there *is* no multiplication of anything.

The propensity-to-consume notion provides a wholly arbitrary formula for the assumption of a certain degree of inflation—a diminishing rate of increase of M in each income period, but a steady rate of increase when the marginal propensity to consume is judged to be unity, and no subsequent increase when the propensity is zero.

Exactly the same kind of effects will follow if a given level of additional expenditure is maintained on consumption, except that if the marginal propensity to consume is judged to be unity, the so-

called multiplier will then be unity, and if the marginal propensity
to consume is judged to be zero, the so-called multiplier will then
be infinity. Obviously such effects have nothing to do with leakages
or with hoarding. They represent *the purely formal consequences
upon the magnitude* M *of a certain monetary policy,* that is, with
Keynes' multiplier, of maintaining a given additional rate of expenditure on "investment" when the marginal propensity to consume is
positive. Exactly the same reasoning applies when the initiating increase in investment (or consumption) expenditure is supposed to
be due to an increase in V ("newly activated money"), except that
there are obvious limits to the extent to which dishoarding can occur
and no limits to the extent to which M may be increased except under
some form of convertibility.

At this stage it is convenient once again to drop the untenable assumption that *spending* generates income. The rate of *spending* is a
consequence not a cause of the factors which determine the relative
values of M_r and M. *Spending* does not influence money values. But
demand (which may be measured in money terms) does. Thus, an
initial increase in M may have its influence on prices *before* it is
spent, that is, through the negotiations to purchase something on the
part of those who have raised credit, or even the mere knowledge
of sellers that prospective purchasers have raised this credit. The
ability to spend influences values because it confers the power to
demand. The actual spending is a consequence. (See Chapter 11.)

But every act of demand (which, *when it has done its work,* may
lead to the passing of money) has the same relevance to the value
of the money unit, and hence to the money valuation of income, and
therefore in turn to the consequences of changes in that valuation
upon the withholding or release of capacity. It follows that, if expenditures on investment initially and consumption subsequently, do
have a different effect on the money valuation of income from expenditures on consumption initially and investment subsequently,
there must be some reason why they have a different effect upon the
demand for monetary services or upon the number of money units.
It is this simple thing which has never been shown.

Although Keynes' multiplier effect rests on an arbitrary formula
for a certain rate of inflation (or noninflationary credit expansion if
the release of withheld capacity is induced), neither Keynes nor his
disciples have perceived or explained this. They have been concerned
in a muddled way with all the factors which determine demand for
the services of money. The phenomena which they have been trying

to explain may be clearly envisaged, I think, through the following very simple and wholly truistical proposition (a proposition which remains true even in the extreme cases in which the marginal propensity to consume is unity or zero). An increase in M will not cause an increase in money income if it is accompanied by *an offsetting decrease in V*. Nor will any cumulative monetary effects be experienced (apart from the multiplication of an increase in M by V, or the multiplication of an increase in V by M!) unless an increase in V is induced or a further increase in M follows *in consequence of some obligation contained in monetary policy.*

Now it is conceivable that, *owing to mere inertia,* a tendency for money income to grow will be accompanied by a desire to hold *relatively* large cash balances. All sorts of conditions may be responsible for the changing usefulness (that is, productiveness) of money over short periods, and so its aggregate real value. But this possibility (the recognition of which has, I think, prompted the unacceptable multiplier thesis) seems to be of little practical importance. For such fluctuations in nonspeculative demand, if identified, can always be met by the issue or withdrawal of credit. It could be argued for instance that, if people do find it convenient to hold more cash while they are deciding what they can do with their increasing incomes, credit *can* expand without any tendency to weaken the ability of the monetary authority to honor its obligations. Hence, if it can be accepted that growing *real* income is a cause of a more than proportionate short-term expansion in the aggregate real value of money,[55] and that credit policy does not *automatically* cause the number of money units to increase in proportion to this expansion in real value (obviously through some misinterpretation of the situation), then it could be seriously argued that there is a problem to be tackled. The description of this problem in terms of the *marginal propensity to hoard* could then conceivably assist.

I suggest, therefore, that even if we accept the notion that expenditure influences the money valuation of income, it cannot be said that the reactions of "investment" expenditure upon "consumption" expenditure have any special consequences. But all factors which influence the money valuation of income initially may (a) *affect*

---

[55] Generally speaking, the aggregate real value of money (M_r) tends to increase, as real income increases, in the same way that the aggregate value of land tends to increase, that is, more or less *in proportion*. The theory under examination implies that M_r expands *initially* more than proportionally to the real value of an expanding income.

expectations and hence M_r, and (b) *cause a reaction in monetary policy and hence affect* M; while (c) *both reactions may affect the release or withholding of capacity,* in which case the notion of multipliers (the "real income" and "employment" multipliers) might not be inappropriate ways of envisaging Say's law reactions.

T. Wilson states that the multiplier (presumably both the "money income" and the "real income" multipliers) assumes "complete elasticity in the supply of funds" and "complete elasticity in the supply of consumers' goods."[56] Yet Keynes himself, and for a long time his disciples, explicitly and emphatically denied the former assumption, while Keynes did not explicitly state the second assumption and it is usually glossed over in the literature. If he had made those assumptions clear, most of the controversy could have been avoided. But do the textbooks (elementary or other) which still deal with the multiplier state, or place the necessary stress on, these assumptions?

Samuelson has claimed that the multiplier explains "why an easy money policy is ineffective at the same time that deficit spending may be effective."[57] It does nothing of the kind. What it has done (intentionally or otherwise) has been to misdirect attention from monetary policy as such (concerned with the value of the money unit) to a politically favored form of monetary policy—deficit spending.

Finally, as I have already stated (pp. 230–32, 384), if it can be assumed that there is a high elasticity of supply of services in general (which assumes a society in which there is much easily releasable withheld capacity, and in which, therefore, the money income multiplier is likely to equal the real income multiplier), it must be equally legitimate to assume that very modest price (and wage-rate) adjustments[58] will be sufficient to restore full employment. For if, through a slight fall in "aggregate money demand" (the money valuation of income), a great deal of withheld capacity is induced, then there are reasons for assuming that, conversely, a small cut in certain prices is all that will be necessary to ensure the release of idle capacity. This is not, however, a relationship between elasticities which can be represented in demand and supply schedules, because it depends in

---

[56] Wilson, op. cit., p. 564.

[57] Samuelson, op. cit., pp. 602–3.

[58] I do not suggest that modest price adjustments would be sufficient to ensure *optimal* employment as distinct from *full* employment of resources. The worst evils of restrictionism are by no means expressed in withheld capacity alone.

part upon the release of capacity in one field being the source of demand which induces the release of capacity in noncompeting fields. We are again brought back to the circumstances in which the relevant demand and supply schedules are not independent.

Every increase in utilized capacity induces the release of, or growth in, capacity elsewhere. The value of a *multiplier* in this sense will depend solely (a) upon the degree of withheld capacity or suboptimal employment of resources due to price discoordinations, or (b) in respect of growth calling forth growth, upon the extent to which the flow of services is versatile (as between consumption uses and net accumulation uses) and the rate at which savings respond to changes in entrepreneurial bidding (that is, to interest), which means changes in prospective yields.

The *practical* harm wrought by thinking along "investment multiplier" lines has been that it has caused "investment" (expenditure in the process of net accumulation) to be regarded as a causal factor and not, as it ought to be regarded, as the result of the thrift which recovery normally induces.

But the *intellectual* harm has been indirectly even more serious. The conventional multiplier apparatus is rubbish. It should be expunged from the textbooks, its place being taken by an exposition of the dynamic implications of Say's law.[59]

---

[59] See my *A Rehabilitation of Say's Law* (Athens: Ohio University Press, 1974), esp. chap. 3, "Say's Law Restated," and chap. 7, "The True Multiplier"; and R. Clower and A. Leijonhufvud, "Say's Principle, What It Means and What It Does Not Mean," *Intermountain Economic Review,* vol. 4, no. 2, Fall 1973.

17

The Accelerator Fallacy

A notion which, I believe, is just as fallacious as the multiplier is what has become known as "the accelerator," or "the acceleration principle." Although this notion has an important role in the apparatus which Keynes' disciples have constructed, it was referred to only briefly and casually in *The General Theory*. It is essential to deal with it, however, because it has become an ingredient of neo-Keynesian teachings.

In essence, the theory asserts that increased expenditure on (or demand for) the sort of economic activity which accompanies growth in the sense of the net accumulation of assets (for example, the rate of flow of productive services into the "constructional industries"), is *an acceleration* of expenditure on (or demand for) consumption. Expressed in terms of the life expectancy of assets, the notion asserts that the demand for assets of long life expectancies (for example, constructional goods) is *an acceleration* of demand for assets of short life expectancies (consumer goods, and services consumed as they are rendered). It seems to me that merely restating the proposition in these terms shows its absurdity. Yet the alleged phenomenon is held to constitute an inherent defect of the market economy, engendering "strains" and "disturbances" in the price system. The theory leaves the impression that the rational approach to the problem of restoring full activity in a depression (in which the resources devoted to the replacement or net accumulation of equipment tend typically to be underemployed) must be by way of restoring or stimulating the rate of consumption.

Now as we have seen, the act of consumption by any person is the *extermination* of part of his existing power to demand the product of others, not a creation of that power. But the act of production to replace consumption *is* of course the replacement of power to demand, just as production to accumulate assets is the creation of additional power to demand.

Yet Paul Samuelson says:

> According to this law, society's needed stock of capital, whether inventory or equipment, depends primarily upon the level of income or production. Additions to the stock of capital, or what we customarily call *net* investment, will take place only when income is growing. As a result, a prosperity period may come to an end, not simply because consumption sales have gone down, but merely because sales have *leveled off* at a high level (or have continued to grow, but at a lower rate than previously).[1]

In referring to this "leveling off" in consumer goods sales, or a declining rate of growth in consumer goods sales, Samuelson seems to me to draw a veil over the crucial process which determines the time-spread of the process of embodying productive services into assets of relatively long life expectancies.

If the rate of increase in "consumption sales" falls off, that must be either because savings have increased and the "constructional industries" are producing "constructional assets" at an increasing rate *with prospective ultimate consumption sales rising;* or because the prices of outputs of consumer goods which entrepreneurs judge to be most profitable are compatible with less intensive utilization of the resources which make them, including the equipment that makes consumer goods. Now the pricing of outputs is likely to reflect the pricing of inputs. But the outputs (and/or inputs) of *"constructional"* goods can equally be priced for less intensive utilization of the resources which make *them*. In such circumstances it may not be profitable to replace, let alone add to, the fixed equipment.

However, if one industry is not demanding the services of the constructional industries, that creates the opportunity for other industries to get *their* capital goods cheaply! Of course, under defective coordination in the economic system, that is, under imperfect price flexibility, this will not occur to the same extent.

What, then, is the problem? Naturally a community which does not *demand* growth will not get growth. If people stop offering suffi-

---

[1] Paul A. Samuelson, *Economics* (10th ed.; New York: McGraw-Hill, 1976), p. 260.

cient for assets of long life expectancy to get an increase in the stock of such assets, the industries specialized for growth will stand idle. It might be thought that that is more likely to be due to saving preference rather than consumption preference having been deficient. But these two preferences are the opposite sides of one shield. As I have explained, we ought always to think of consumption-saving preference. (See pp. 292–95, 303–6.)

The point at issue is, then, this: Is there any sense at all in which an increased flow of services into replacement, or an increased demand for these services, can be said to generate (a) an accelerated or magnified flow of services into the net accumulation of long-life assets, or (b) an accelerated increase in demand for certain kinds of services which are typically demanded when net accumulation of relatively long-life assets by the community is in progress? In my opinion, the answer is clearly no.

Or is there any sense in which an increased demand for the services which provide for a certain kind of replacement or net accumulation, namely, that of consumer goods (or relatively short life expectancies), can be said to generate an accelerated increase in demand for the services flowing into the replacement of or into the net accumulation of "constructional goods" (or assets of long life expectancies)? Again, in my opinion, the answer is clearly no.

Samuelson continues:

A simplified arithmetical example will make this clear. Imagine a typical textile-manufacturing firm whose stock of capital equipment is always kept equal to about two times the value of its yearly sales of cloth. Thus, when its sales have remained at $30 million per year for some time, its balance sheet will show $60 million of capital equipment, consisting of perhaps 20 machines of different ages, with one wearing out each year and being replaced. Because replacement just balances depreciation, there is no *net* investment or saving being done by the corporation. *Gross* investment takes place at the rate of $3 million per year, representing the yearly replacement of one machine. (The other $27 million of sales may be assumed to be wages and dividends.) . . .

Now let us suppose that, in the fourth year, sales rise 50 percent —from $30 to $45 million. Then the number of machines must also rise 50 percent, or from 20 to 30 machines. In the fourth year, instead of 1 machine, 11 machines must be bought—10 new ones in addition to the replacement of the worn-out one. Sales rose 50 percent. How much has machine production gone up? From 1 machine to 11; or by 1,000 percent! This *accelerated* effect of a change in consumption or other final items on investment levels gives the acceleration principle its name. . . .

According to the acceleration principle, consumption has to continue to keep increasing in order for investment to stand still![2]

Now Samuelson gets his ratio of 1,000 percent (and here he is simply following all the others who accept the acceleration principle) by *tacitly assuming* that the additional machinery needed for the production of the additional output is provided during the arbitrary period of one year, and that the flow of services into making the additional machinery is spread evenly over that one year. Most economists who attempt to explain the principle (although not Samuelson in the passage referred to) actually use the phrase *"per annum"* of the rate of increase in "consumption," or of sales of consumer goods, *and* of the accelerated rate of increase in demand for machinery. In the enormous literature of this topic, I have been unable to find a single case in which a word like "temporary" qualifies the assertion that an accelerated percentage increase in demand for constructional output is induced. But of course, *if rates of increase* are to be simply compared, it *is* unnecessary to specify any time interval. Thus, with rates of consumption (or sales) of consumer goods, a 50 *percent* increase *per annum* is the same thing as a 50 *percent* increase per week, month, or decade.

In Samuelson's example, for instance, if the process of manufacture of the machinery is assumed to be concentrated within three months, or six months, an increase in the *annual* production of 4,000 *percent* or 2,000 *percent* respectively could have been claimed! The assumption that the provision of the machinery occurs within the space of one year is, indeed, completely arbitrary.

The basic truth is that demand for the provision of any kind of equipment (for replacement or net accumulation) is exactly proportional to the demand for the services—that is, for the final product— that the equipment is *expected* to supply. For demand, considered as a *rate of demand,* is independent of the time interval by which we measure it. When we are concerned with things of which the economic life is less than a year and must therefore be replaced within a year (assuming that the demand for their services continues), we can usefully express the rate of supply, or of demand, as an annual

---

[2] Ibid., pp. 260–61.

rate; but *with things of which the economic life is longer than a year, say ten years, the minimum time unit for comparison with their prospective output is a decade.*

Obviously, then, the acceleration principle does not throw any light whatsoever upon the factors which determine *the period within which the provision of any additional equipment needed during the process of growth happens to be concentrated;* and yet it is precisely that which the student is led to believe that it does. Countless factors determine this period. The current rate of replacement of a product, and the extent to which demand leading to its replacement is believed to be permanent or changing, determine the decision to replace or add to any equipment which makes it. *But the time span* within which productive services will be in course of incorporation into that equipment is determined by supply factors.

If a stable increase in demand for any product is forecast, a *proportional* increase in demand will be induced for the services which flow into replacing the larger volume of equipment which will be needed to manufacture that product in the future; but either the expression of, or the response to, that demand may be discontinuous and sometimes spasmodic. The acceleration principle does nothing to explain the discontinuities of "constructional activity" which those discontinuities of demand and supply bring about.

Demands for equipment (for replacement or growth) from any *individual firm* are likely to be discontinuous, but this is much less likely in the case of any *individual industry*, and least likely of all in the case of *all* activities requiring equipment. Thus, a large steel works will be fulfilling orders for one firm or industry at one time and another firm or industry at another; and when demand for equipment generally is rising (which will tend to be in direct proportion to the magnitude of savings achieved), entrepreneurial bidding based upon individual prospective yields will determine priorities. That is, the sequence in which the orders for plant and machinery from individual firms or industries will be satisfied, will be decided via the price mechanism.

Should there happen to be a great deal of wastefully idle productive capacity in the consumer goods industries,[3] a large recovery in their outputs, due either to coordinative price adjustments in each industry (whether brought about by policy which releases noninflationary market pressures or by unanticipated inflation) or, more

---

[3] Wastefully idle because its services are priced above market-clearing values.

important, to similar causes in noncompeting industries, may be accompanied by relatively little increase in "constructional activity," until the recovery of final outputs is complete. But if the recovery of demand for final products is believed to be stable and permanent, that will mean a more or less equal recovery of demand for the services of and hence for the replacement of the equipment which makes them, that is, a proportional increase in demand in spite of discontinuity in the expression of this demand in individual cases. The principle remains unchanged even when, owing to high durability of the equipment concerned, replacement is necessary only after very long intervals.

On the other hand, should there be idle equipment in "constructional industries" which have been equipped to satisfy demand for expansion, while the full recovery of demand for consumer goods is followed by the resumption of a previous trend toward growing outputs, an abnormally rapid but roughly proportional rate of increase in constructional output may occur.

The extraordinary hold which the accelerator has acquired is inexplicable to me. It has been woven into elaborate treatments of the trade cycle which have been laboriously studied by large numbers of honors and graduate students. But it is a notion which, together with the multiplier, has vitiated attempts of economists to discern the true origins of fluctuations in employment and aggregate income. It has been subjected to a large number of restatements, revisions, and modifications. But it is incapable of useful refinement because it is basically wrong. In the meantime it remains in the textbooks, confusing further generations of students, the less critical of whom are probably destined to be the teachers of the next generation.

18

The Retreat and Prospects

According to Martin Bronfenbrenner, writing in 1947, the term "Keynesian" had already largely lost its meaning as a result of the splitting of the school into two camps, on the Right and on the Left. "The Keynesian Right," he wrote, "have taken policy positions on inflation control not greatly dissimilar from those of monetary theorists who have never seen the Keynesian light. . . . They rely mainly on tight money," he continued, "tax increases, and reduced public spending to curb inflation, look with equanimity on whatever unemployment may result from a 'stabilization crisis,' and distrust direct controls over individual prices."[1] This can hardly be said to be "not greatly dissimilar" to the broad pre-Keynesian position in respect of the situation which has existed since 1945. It is identical with it, as Bronfenbrenner would, I think, now agree. The truth is, I shall maintain, that the Keynesians of this "Right" group have, in fact, been forced to retreat toward the pre-Keynesian position. But their thinking and exposition are still encumbered by all the confusing apparatus which Keynes introduced.

Bronfenbrenner suggested that, had Keynes been living, he would have identified himself with the "Right." If so, he would have had to renounce his teachings of the mid-1930s. For his teachings *did* imply the policies to which the Keynesians of the Left are now obstinately clinging.

It is true that the "Leftist" Keynesians have tended to some extent to replace their master's own theories which new and perhaps even more subtle ones; but this does not mean that their doctrines are

---

[1] Bronfenbrenner, "Some Neglected Implications of Secular Inflation," in Kurihara, ed., *Post-Keynesian Economics,* p. 34 n.

essentially different. And they have this merit as against the Keynesians of the "Right," that the policy implications of *their* teachings are unmistakably clear. "If the choice must be made," says Bronfenbrenner, "they prefer inflation to underemployment," and instead of relying upon interest and the price mechanism to curb the rate of inflation, they believe in the use of controls such as price fixing, official allocation of resources, rationing, exchange control, etc.[2]

We know where we stand with these Keynesians. But where do we stand in relation to the Keynesian "Right"? How much inflation would *they* permit in order to prevent a little unemployment? What criteria have they on this obviously vital point? They have no criteria at all. And what criteria have they for the degree to which the interest and price mechanism should be superseded by "conscious controls"? (See pp. 75–76, 145–46.) The answer, again, is none whatsoever. Is not the absence of any such criteria proof of some inherent defect?

Mabel Timlin, who is one of the leading members of the "Right" group (I hope I do not do her an injustice by including her in Keynesian company), tries to develop Keynesianism by suggesting that the "*monetary* parallel to the classical and neoclassical problem of the allocation of resources is the problem of the structure of prices."[3] This may suggest—quite wrongly—that teaching in the pre-Keynesian tradition did not always see the problem in just that way. But Timlin goes further. She recognizes that, once the relevance of the structure of prices has been perceived, "policy considerations no longer involve simple aggregates such as consumption, investment, saving, and 'the' interest rate but rather rates of consumption of particular types of goods and services, investment in particular markets, and the *asset* structure as well as the *time* structure of market rates of interest."[4] In this passage, she is developing, or rather refining, Keynesian teaching back to what Keynes would originally have regarded as the purest orthodoxy. Moreover, largely because she has again brought into consideration the issues which the Keynesian approach had excluded or obscured, we find that, in respect of actual recommended policy *for the world of 1946,* she takes unequivocally the pre-Keynesian line. Not only does she contemplate

2 Ibid.

3 Mabel F. Timlin, "Monetary Stabilization Policies and Keynesian Theories," in Kurihara, op. cit., p. 59.

4 Ibid., pp. 59–60.

the deliberate use of interest as the means to monetary stability, but she says that "perhaps the logical time for the use of the interest rate as a regulator is *before* an inflationary rise in costs takes place."[5] She says that "attempts to hold to policies of artificially low rates of yield on securities traded in by central banks could be expected to increase existing disequilibria in these markets."[6] There is a "theoretical flaw," she contends, in the policy of encouraging, "through low interest rates, the investment of funds in productive capital contributing to employment."[7] "The *minimum* sound objective" in a postwar period "would seem to be to prevent any extension of accumulations of currency and bank deposits; this would involve yields on securities entering into the portfolio of the central bank high enough to deter any flow of these securities toward the bank. Those who wished to liquidate their holdings would be compelled to offer them at prices that would be acceptable to other potential holders. . . ."[8] "There is no real substitute for adequate control over the quantity of currency and bank deposits, exercised through flexibility of yields."[9] "It is precisely because investment opportunities may be limited that this policy is urged."[10] In other words, avoiding the misleading Keynesian terminology to which Timlin clings, it is precisely because the services which can be embodied into assets of long life expectancy, that is, for growth, are limited, that attempts to "stimulate" this process by fixing interest below the natural level may be purely inflationary.

As I have said, Timlin is assuming the conditions which existed after World War II—conditions which she contrasts with those existing when Keynes wrote *The General Theory*. And as we have seen, there is a general tendency today to say that Keynes really meant his teachings to apply only to a state of unemployment or underemployment; and that it ought to have been realized that, under full employment, his *General Theory* becomes irrelevant. We are told that it is true, as Keynes contended, that savings do not determine "investment" (assets accumulation) but that "investment"

---

[5] Ibid., p. 80.

[6] Ibid., p. 60.

[7] Ibid., p. 62.

[8] Ibid., p. 64.

[9] Ibid., p. 86. She explains the inflationary consequences of maintaining security prices. I became aware of the second edition of her *Keynesian Economics* (1977) too late to make use of it.

[10] Timlin, "Monetary Stabilization," in Kurihara, op. cit., p. 65.

determines savings *up to the point at which unutilized capacity no longer exists.* Beyond that point, savings *do* determine "investment." As soon as the last little bit of idle capacity has been brought into operation, orthodox teachings become unassailable. As Timlin puts it, in the middle thirties, demand for liquidity "constituted the neglected margin."[11] "The postwar situation differed vitally from the prewar situation."[12] Before the war there had been idle labor and equipment in existence. After the war it no longer existed.

What this suggestion of Timlin amounts to is an explanation I (and others) have already suggested, namely, that the "general theory" was a "special theory"—an analysis based upon assumptions which were realistic at a particular period only. It was, I think, Hicks who first used the phrase "special theory" to describe *The General Theory.* But Patinkin (who seems to have studied economics wholly during the Keynesian era, but who has also read the classical economists) argues that "the propositions of Keynesian monetary theory are much less general than *The General Theory* would lead us to believe"; but, he adds, "this in no way diminishes the relevance of Keynesian unemployment theory for the formulation of a practicable full employment policy."[13]

Now we have seen that pre-Keynesian economics always recognized that credit expansion can, in certain circumstances, bring idle resources into utilization (a) to an extent which is *not* inflationary and (b) to a further extent which *is* inflationary; and that insofar as the expansion is *non*inflationary, decisions which result in savings out of increasing *money* income imply decisions to acquire savings out of increasing *real* income (and hence real accumulation of assets).[14]

My argument in Chapters 10 and 11 has shown that this does not justify the conclusion that, even in the presence of withheld capacity, the expression of saving preference (influenced by interest offered and *the form* of current income) ceases to be the *sole* determinant of the rate of assets accumulation. Indeed, the conclusion stands that the achievement of savings *by individuals* is always contributing to net accumulation by the community unless it is being offset by dissavings

11 Ibid., p. 60.

12 Ibid., p. 62.

13 Don Patinkin, *Money, Interest, and Prices: An Integration of Monetary and Value Theory* (2d ed.; New York: Harper and Row, 1965), p. 3.

14 As full employment is approached, however, the repercussions upon real income (out of which real savings are made) gradually cease. Net savings require a bigger sacrifice.

made by others. In other words, unless accumulation of assets (supposed or realized) is occurring, the community cannot be achieving savings (supposed or realized) and vice versa. Hence, far from Keynes' "special theory" assisting in "the formulation of a practicable full employment policy," it obscures the crucial distinction between inflationary and noninflationary coordination, and between inflationary and noninflationary credit expansion.

If Keynes had *really* intended his *General Theory* to be a special theory, he would certainly have brought in the notion of a gradual rise in the ability of savings to determine "investment" as fuller employment is attained. Of course, the attempt to do so would have produced absurd results. Imagine having to contend, for instance, that if "employment" is four-fifths of full, savings will determine four-fifths of "investment" and "investment" one-fifth of savings! Hence the thesis is just as *untenable,* even as a special theory. What can be claimed is that it is more *plausible* when withheld capacity is serious, simply because unanticipated inflation *is* one way of inducing the release of that capacity.

The switch from condemnation of insufficient "effective demand" to condemnation of "excessive demand," or, more recently, "overfull employment," which characterizes the new doctrine of the "Rightist" Keynesians, has merely confounded the confusion.[15] For the latter concepts are no more satisfactory than the former. The term "excessive demand" *could* be used to mean overconsumption (in the sense that, in the light of the collective objectives of a community engaged in the effort of war, for instance, resources *ought* to be released to a greater extent from "excessive" normal uses for the pursuit of war objectives). But if it does not mean this, it can only mean "inflation." Yet when Keynes talked of an *insufficiency* of effective demand, he certainly did not mean deflationary *demand.* If he had, he would have said so, and where we were all puzzled by *The General Theory* we should have understood.

Since his death, we have seen the Keynesians—even those of the "Left"—occasionally demanding that inflation shall be kept in check by the curtailment of "nonessential investment." But they seldom seem to ask that the persistent increase in the number of money units in relation to the flow of real income shall be curbed. They think rather in terms of "controls" to prevent entrepreneurs from reacting

---

[15] It has vitiated also many non-Keynesian contributions when the writers have attempted to use Keynesian concepts.

rationally to the situation which monetary policy creates. Their complaint against "nonessential investment" has not, as far as I am aware, been explained by any rigorous consideration of the criteria of "nonessentiality." Few "Keynesians of the Left" would doubt that government expenditure is always essential; hence the tendency is usually to suggest that private investment is nonessential or less essential.

But neither in title nor by explicit claim did Keynes present his contribution as a special theory. Nor did he himself *explicitly* retract, or rebuke his many influential followers who, throughout the war years, continued to argue (as many still do) for the continuance of low interest throughout the postwar period in order to stimulate investment, maintain employment, etc. Statesmen, governors of central banks, ministers of finance, demagogues, and others were all arguing, up to the time of Keynes' death, for the very policies the disastrous flaw in which Timlin exposes. But Keynes was silent. True, following *The General Theory,* he increasingly seemed to hedge by broad references to the virtues of orthodoxy, a point with which I shall shortly deal. Unfortunately, he was seldom sufficiently explicit. He did not force the bulk of his loyal followers into an opposing camp. To have confessed that *The General Theory* ought to have been named "a special theory"—a theory which provided a justification for what may have been *politically expedient* in the thirties— would certainly have seriously deflated the unprecedented power and influence (for an economist) which he had attained. But in my judgment he had failed to think himself out of the confusions into which a clumsy method had led him.

Timlin appears to think Keynes would have approved of her refutation of what the majority of Keynesians have believed him to have taught. She quotes in this connection the passage in *The General Theory* in which he said: "If our central controls succeed in establishing an aggregate volume of output corresponding to full employment as nearly as practicable, the classical theory comes into its own again from this point onward."[16] She maintains that, when unemployed resources exist, interest below the natural level—what she calls "an artificially low" interest rate—is the appropriate remedy, but it is no longer to be recommended when resources are fully employed.

Yet the vital point of controversy is on this very issue. The trouble

---

[16] Keynes, *The General Theory*, p. 378, quoted by Timlin, "Monetary Stabilization," in Kurihara, op. cit., p. 87.

with using "artificially low" interest to achieve reemployment is that there is never any moment at which it can be legitimately contended that the abandonment of inflation will not mean *some* unemployment, in the absence of the price and cost adjustments which Keynesianism excludes from consideration. This means that, in practice, the classical theory can never be justified!

There is nothing to be gained by blinking the fact that Keynes gave the green light to governments that preferred inflating to taking steps to permit or directly to bring about the coordination of prices. Governments preferred to inflate for exactly the same reasons that have always actuated them, when they have not been restrained by constitutional or legal enactments. As Timlin herself so strikingly puts it:

> Debasement of the currency in the face of difficulties is a very old resort of princes. Modern methods through depreciation are more subtle. . . . Temptations to use these methods to meet contemporary fiscal or political problems may be relatively continuous. Governments may resort to them as drunkards may take to drink, little by little, under the plea of imperative necessity.[17]

The postwar inflations have been in no way different except that the Keynesian philosophy has been available to clothe them with respectability. And this philosophy was announced in "white papers" and other official documents during Keynes' lifetime, with direct quotations from his writings and in his own terminology. He lived long enough to have been able to inaugurate the plowing under of what he had sown. He failed to do so and the modern Western world has reaped the harvest. All he did was to sow doubts, and the full meaning of Keynes' apparent anti-Keynesianism was never perceived.

Nevertheless, it looks as though Timlin was trying, in 1947, with consummate tact, to lead the Keynesians back to orthodoxy. But she will never do that by suggesting that *The General Theory* was orthodox. It can be done only by showing, as she has in fact shown, that Keynes was causing confusion both in thought and action, through diverting attention from coordination through price adjustment.

In the middle 1940s, the Keynesians felt superior and triumphant. During the 1950s they were mostly losing their confidence. Their loss of confidence was manifest, I suggest, in John Hicks' attempt (in

---

[17] Timlin, "Monetary Stabilization," in ibid.

1957) to meet Patinkin's criticisms, and especially in the former's assertion that a "properly equipped 'classic' . . ." would agree with Keynes. Hicks' hypothetical "classic" would argue, we are told, that an

> increase in saving would *directly* reduce the rate of interest, so that employment would increase in the investment-goods trades as it diminished in the consumption-goods trades; but he could (or should) go on to admit that the increase in saving would carry with it a diminution in the velocity of circulation (some of the savings would be hoarded), so that, with an inelastic monetary system, and the fixed money wages that are being assumed, there would still be a net decline in employment.[18]

Well, if Keynes had said anything like this, there would have been little controversy. The answer to him would have been simply that the proposition was stated in an unnecessarily clumsy way. Using the terminology which I have here introduced, the reply would have been:

What you are saying is that an increase in saving preference will, *ceteris paribus,* reduce the natural level of interest. On the (absurd) assumption that monetary policy is inflexible (so that the market rate of interest does not fall in harmony) there will be a deflationary reaction. Similarly, if we make the further (doubtfully justifiable) assumption that an increase in saving preference implies (for some *other* reason) an increase in demand for the services of money, monetary policy being assumed to be inflexible, there will be a further reason for deflation. If therefore deflation is not a deliberate objective (to correct a previous inflation, so as to keep faith with those who had trusted convertibility obligations), it must be regarded as a purposeless deflation due to a defect in monetary organization.[19] And if at the same time the labor unions are allowed to reduce the flow of wages by refusing to permit the product of labor to be priced so as to permit the sale of the full valuable output, serious sociological consequences will follow; and this will be attributable, not so much to the failure to adjust to changes in consumption-saving preference, as to a wholly unintended monetary situation.

---

[18] John R. Hicks, "A Rehabilitation of 'Classical' Economics?" *Economic Journal,* June 1957, p. 279.

[19] Several non-Keynesians would have regarded with sympathy such a criticism applied to the Federal Reserve System in the early 1930s.

The only reason why this sort of rejoinder was not made to Keynes in 1936 was that he did *not* say what Hicks claimed that he *should* have said.

There are plenty of signs that Keynes occasionally felt misgivings. Already, in the last chapter of *The General Theory,* and startlingly so on pp. 379–80, he was paying tributes to the working of a competitive society, and indirectly praising institutions which were completely incompatible with the remedies implied by his analysis. And during the war years, we can discern his reaction against his own teaching. It may well be that, had he lived, he would have become the leading anti-Keynesian. In his *How to Pay for the War* (1940), he appeared to be concerned with the dangers of inflation. But I do not think that, when he wrote that contribution, he was already beginning to see the disastrous consequences which could flow from his own teachings. Had he merely argued that the aim should have been to prevent the necessity of a rationing system which would place an undue strain on administration, or had he urged the necessity of preventing the prices of consumers' goods rising to an extent which would have caused a demand for increased money income, his argument would have been perfectly *understandable.* But his case had not been thought through. It remained woolly. He *may* have been recognizing at last that the speed of inflation must never be allowed to be so rapid that the people are led to expect it and fully to allow for it in concluding current contracts. He *may* also have felt that, if an inflation is allowed to progress too rapidly, the people are likely to demand its cessation. Then suddenly, shortly before his death, he showed much more definite signs of being in retreat. There is a story that, in a conversation with a number of economists toward the end of the war, he showed impatience with what was being said and told one of his best known supporters not to be silly. But reliable evidence of his wavering is to be found in his last *Economic Journal* article, which appeared just before he died.[20] The word "wavering" is not unjust. How else can we regard his assertion that "the classical teaching embodied some permanent truths of great significance," and his reference to "deep undercurrents at work, natural forces, one can call them, or even the invisible hand, which are operating toward equilibrium"?[21] How else can we treat his contrast of "much modern-

---

[20] John Maynard Keynes, "The Balance of Payments of the United States," *Economic Journal,* June 1946, p. 172.

[21] Ibid., p. 185.

ist stuff turned sour and silly" and "the wholesome long-run doctrine"?[22] He used the term "classical medicine" four times in this article. Yet he had been the one who had prescribed champagne for the patient and popularized this pleasant remedy when the castor oil of "classical medicine" had been called for.

But in that article he was hinting at the truth, not proclaiming it. John H. Williams told us that "Keynes changed his mind, and almost the last time I saw him was complaining that the easy money policy had been greatly overdone and interest rates were too low both in England and here";[23] and we know that he expected the great postwar problem to be inflation rather than unemployment. Had Keynes lived, he *might* have led the retreat from his own doctrine.

It is sometimes claimed that even if Keynes' main theories must now be admitted to be fallacious, his contribution at least introduced new and useful tools like liquidity preference, the propensity to consume, the marginal efficiency of capital, etc. But these are all ancient *concepts*.[24] Only the names and uses to which they have been put are new. Fellner thinks that "fundamental-theoretical Keynesianism" and "stagnationist Keynesianism . . . might not survive, or at least not in much strength," but that "cyclical Keynesianism" will continue to be influential doctrine in the predictable future.[25] But in my judgment it is precisely in attempts to understand the nature of cyclical fluctuations that Keynesian teaching and concepts are most seriously defective.

There are some signs, then, that Keynesianism is now being refined back to the pure pre-Keynesian orthodoxy by the "Keynesians of the Right." Indeed, they seem tacitly to have abandoned the notion of unemployment equilibrium, which was the crucial originality of the "new economics" and the "Keynesian revolution." Franco Modigliani, Mabel Timlin, David McCord Wright, Don Patinkin, John Hicks, Robert W. Clower, Axel Leijonhufvud, and Harry Johnson have, I think, led the reaction.

---

[22] Ibid., p. 186.

[23] John H. Williams, "An Economist's Confession," *American Economic Review,* March 1952, p. 14. F. A. Hayek has told me that he had a similar experience.

[24] The most original and useful concept which Keynes introduced, in my opinion, was the notion of user cost. But his discussion of it constitutes one of the most confusing parts of *The General Theory*. It *could* have been used to mean that part of depreciation which is due solely to the use of assets and not the passage of time.

[25] William Fellner, "What Is Surviving," *American Economic Review, Papers and Proceedings,* 1957, p. 67.

So far has the retreat gone that Dudley Dillard (whom I thought of as the most consistently uncritical disciple of Keynes) could remark (in 1956), quite without justification, that "one should bear in mind that Keynes was careful not to say that classical economics is wrong."[26] But as I remarked in my *Keynesianism* (1963), *the Keynesian fallacies remain deeply rooted, and the lag is likely to be long before they are eradicated. In spite of the retreat, there seem so far to have been practically no changes in the textbooks or in undergraduate teaching. Students of this generation are still, on the whole, being trained in defective methods. A minority of them manage ultimately to think their way through. The majority are unable to. The confused thinking on which Keynes' case was framed remains the conventional foundation of the modern teaching of economics.* It is too early to expect that progress in economics will resume perceptibly from its pre-Keynesian achievements, that is, from the stage to which Wicksell, Cannan, H. G. Browne, Mints, Hayek, Viner, E. W. Kemmerer, Lavington, Mises, and Benjamin Anderson had led it in the field of money.

In 1963, I thought that the clear academic retreat from Keynesianism had already been accompanied by a retreat in policy. I was a victim of wishful thinking. The connection between academic thought and political action is always difficult to discern with any certainty. Statesmen and laymen generally who had supported Keynesian policy at one time through an "instinctive" or "common sense" feeling about the appropriateness of the remedies implied, have been shaken by the actual course of events. The quotation from former British Prime Minister Callaghan on p. 13 above is evidence of my contention. It is no longer doubted that, in the long run, repressed inflation breaks down. Expenditure intended to maintain investment and hence employment, in a regime in which prices are no longer powerfully influenced by market forces, is recognized as being incompatible with the hoped-for stability of prices. Moreover, it has become obvious that Keynesianism, especially when it is combined with the policy of the welfare state, is destructive of labor incentives to productivity; and other disastrous sociological results of the Keynesian experiment are being perceived, I think, by an ever-widening circle. In some parts of the world at any rate the lay public is resisting, particularly the middle classes. Thus, as early as 1955, Bowen and Meier deplored

---

[26] Dudley Dillard, "The Influence of Keynesian Economics on Contemporary Thought," *American Economics Review, Papers and Proceedings,* May 1957, p. 77.

the fact that despite all the persuasion of economists and the experience of recent decades, the public and its representatives in the United States cling to belief in the soundness of budget balancing and in the evil of debt. The arguments "that 'we owe it to ourselves' or 'that for every liability there is a corresponding asset' have," they regret, "fallen on skeptical and unwilling ears." Such resistance, they continue, "places grave obstacles in the way of compensatory fiscal policies such as deficit spending."[27] It has been fortunate for the United States that the instincts or common sense of many of the public on the issue happens to have been shrewdly or intuitively intelligent.

Recently the most disturbing experience of all—*anticipated inflation*—has been creating insoluble problems. This phenomenon has arisen, as I have explained, through the reluctance of governments to move too rapidly toward complete totalitarianism. The fact that some parts of the economy have been left free for rational entrepreneurial action by the people has been weakening the political motive for recourse to cheap money; for it has robbed inflation of its crude coordinative power; and when this happens the absurdity of the whole business begins to become obvious to a widening circle. In my *Keynesianism* (1963), I referred to Per Jacobsson of the IMF having expressed the opinion that "world forces" seem to be bringing world inflation to an end. The world forces are simply *anticipation*.[28] Unfortunately, since 1963, the techniques of deceiving the business community about the planned speed and duration of inflation have greatly improved.

Originally, the Keynesians seemed to avoid facing the issue of expectations which lead to product prices rising ahead of costs, when it is generally perceived (or even when it is blatantly admitted) that inflation is intended. Hyman Minsky, who blames modern Keynesianism for the purposelessness of today's inflations (while for some reason defending Keynes himself), *does* recognize that anticipated inflations *are* purposeless. Quite unexpectedly, he almost

---

[27] Harold R. Bowen and Gerald M. Meier, "Institutional Aspects of Economic Fluctuations," in Kurihara, op. cit., p. 164. It *is* true of all borrowing that society owes the debts to itself, and that for every liability there is a corresponding asset—the debt. But this does not imply, as Keynesians appear to infer, that the multiplication of liabilities and debt through credit expansion must not be checked if inflation is to be avoided!

[28] But the problems created thereby were at one time leading to the complaint of a world shortage of liquidity, undeterred by flagrant inflation.

implies that Keynes himself would have recommended the suppression of "wage-push," because inflation can no longer effectively make up the wages it (wage-push) exterminates. He remarks that if there is "an accelerating pace of increases in money wages" (meaning wage rates), *while government policy in these circumstances is deliberately (but quietly) to raise prices* (Minsky expresses the words italicized quite differently, but that *is* his implication), "prices will rise at the same accelerating pace as wages, if not faster because of the influence of anticipated increases." Moreover, he observes that "whenever past wage increases have been validated by subsequent price increases, employers become less resistant to further increases."[29]

Nevertheless, current neo-Keynesians still retain the conviction that circumstances can arise in which, without inflation, there must necessarily be at least *some* wasteful and unavoidable unemployment of labor which cheap money can eradicate. The survival of such ideas can be attributed to a general failure to perceive that the problem is *not* one of achieving "a balance between demand and supply" (as it is often put), both being somehow conceived of as aggregates. What *could* be meant by such phrases is that the release of, or initiation of, pressures to move prices which diverge from market-clearing levels toward those levels will always assist recovery. That *would* mean a continuous balancing of changing individual demands and changing individual supplies. Certainly such changes are vital for the avoidance of wasteful *idleness* or the wasteful (suboptimal) *use of* resources. Ultimately, *it is wholly a question of responding to market signals, and the chief signals are prices.*

It was shortly before Keynes' death that economists whom we now call "neo-Keynesians" or "*pseudo*-Keynesians" (Hutchison's term), alarmed at the consequences of inflation, began to argue that to aim at too low a level of unemployment (which they termed "overfull employment") necessarily threatens an intolerable rise of prices. For the implication is still that there is no conceivable means of dissolving any unemployment which has emerged other than that of reducing the purchasing power of the money unit. Such is blind dogma.

The "classical medicine" (as Keynes surprisingly called it shortly before he died) of achieving an expansion in the real wages flow and the real income flow (with incidentally a greater equality in income distribution as a whole) is via moderate, market-selected

---

[29] Minsky, *John Maynard Keynes,* p. 163.

wage-rate and price adjustments.[30] But to Keynes of *The General Theory,* that had been tacitly ruled out. Actually, it was a remedy which could have been successful if "just a little reasonableness" on the part of the unions could have been called for in permitting coordination in the labor market—downward pressures on those wage rates which were most seriously incompatible with market-clearing values.

I am inclined to think that it was entirely because of Keynes' belated recognition that the "classical medicine" would be effective that, shortly before his demise, the most prominent among his British entourage began to argue *against* aiming at the elimination of too much wasteful unemployment. Some of his disciples who had been closest to him, the most distinguished being Nicholas Kaldor, were warning about the need for strict caution in seeking "full employment" by inflation. Such warnings about the dangers of "overfull employment" were made, however, *without* specific reference to the alternative of "classical medicine." Nevertheless, for a while, *neo-Keynesians did seem to be stressing the ideal of price stability.*

After Keynes' death, however, it took them little time to abandon all ideas of the merits of price stability, that is, of a money unit of roughly constant purchasing power. A decade later, recognizing the anarchy of "wage-push," they have tended rather to emphasize the need for a "wages policy," that is, a scheme under which determination of labor's remuneration could be removed even further from the social forces of the market and dictated by politicians beholden to private interests or by officials responsible to politicians. Thus, after fourteen years of quite rapid inflation, Nicholas Kaldor, instead of continuing to advocate a cautious measure of price stability, was warning the Radcliffe Committee of the *dangers* of price stability.

But there has been little consistency in Kaldor's convictions. Later on, we find not only him but Richard F. Kahn and Joan Robinson also, obviously worried about the "wage-push" phenomenon. They *seem* to have perceived, but failed explicitly to bring out, that wage-push had been causing a contraction of the real wages flow and income flow, thereby precipitating stagflation—unemployment even in the presence of inflation.

Ultimately, however, the "*pseudo*-Keynesians" came to believe that only the direct fixing of the price of labor under "incomes

---

[30] The word "moderate" is justified if only "moderate" inflation is envisaged as the alternative.

policies" could guarantee an acceptably low measure of unemployment. At the same time, and rather contradictorily I feel, some of the self-styled Keynesians have desperately argued that it was wrong even to think or talk of inflation as "a disease." Only unemployment should be thought of as a disease, they have held. It can be cured, they suggest, solely through the wisdom of Keynesian officials, administering small doses of inflation, and not through the release of market incentives for the pricing of inputs and outputs nearer to market-clearing values. Yet that is *presumably* just what Keynes had meant by "classical medicine."

But exactly what *is* the condition of "overfull employment"—"too much employment"—against which the neo-Keynesians were then and still are warning? Such a concept certainly creates difficulties for me. On the face of it, the term is silly. Every progressive society is trying continuously to eradicate existing involuntary unemployment.

All improvements in the material well-being of society (and incidentally in the means for achieving moral and aesthetic ends) have had "economizing-displacement" consequences; and the achievement of economies has permitted presently employed persons to be laid off and diverted to other occupations; or economies have caused equipment to become less valuable or obsolete in its existing fields of utilization; or economies have reduced the value of labor needed for the production of equipment. All technological progress has, indeed, been of this nature: the economizing of men and assets in one part of the economy which raises the real value of employment outlets and yields to investment in all noncompeting activities. Hence the only rational use of the term "overfull employment" seems to be when it means "suboptimal" employment and describes a situation in which men and assets are currently employed at wage rates or yields which are lower than available elsewhere—in other words, that there are too many men or assets employed in that condition.

This clarification of how the market mechanism works is an explanation which pre-Keynesian economists would at once have accepted. But the neo-Keynesians appear not to recognize the explanation. When they talk of "overfull employment," they seem to be concerned about a general condition of society, in which "too much" in some sense is being produced from society's existing stock of resources. They seem indeed unable to throw off the "overproduction" notion. They may be thinking of a particular area, or industry, or occupation, and feel that too little is being produced of some other

things, or else that too little leisure is being demanded (the latter
surely being a value judgment). Or they might be referring to a
deflationary condition which requires credit expansion if the value
of the money unit is not to rise. On other occasions the phrase can
be interpreted to refer to a situation in which "too large" a proportion of the community's flow of services is being embodied into assets
of long life expectancy and "too small" a proportion being invested
in assets of short life expectancy. In that event, they are condemning
time preference (which surely is a value judgment).

Then there are contexts also in which the notion of "overfull
employment" appears to mean that too few people and too small a
part of the assets stock are in *pseudo*-idleness (that is, providing the
service of availability, or ready as reserves) for the maximum
flexibility of adjustment in the system. It is a criticism of entrepreneurial acumen. It alleges a defective assets mix. But if a person *is*
in *pseudo*-idleness, he is, economically speaking, employed.[31] Aggregate output is greater by reason of his being in this condition.

Under these circumstances entrepreneurs promoting wholly new
productive ventures will forecast, and rely upon, consumption-saving
preferences releasing resources from their existing kinds of utilization, and so releasing a sufficient flow of productive services from
versatile assets and versatile complementary labor, for diversion to
different forms of utilization, that is, for embodiment in a bigger
proportion of assets of long life expectancy. If entrepreneurs forecast that such services are insufficiently cheap to offer prospective
yields, that will simply be a market signal that society is insufficiently
thrifty, that is, not demanding enough provision for the future to
justify growth. A judgment of this type may be merely a moral
valuation of society's market-expressed objectives, similar to an
opinion that resources employed in gambling are too great. In other
words, the origin of the judgment may be nothing more than a conviction that thrift is a virtue—a social good, the acquisitiveness of
investors tending *ceteris paribus* to contribute to an expansion of
real income and the mitigation or eradication of poverty. But more
likely the suggestion may be that while there can be nothing wrong
with consumption-saving preference, there are somewhere man-made
restraints which prevent a full response to that preference, even if it
is freely expressed.

Occasionally the new term "overfull employment" seems to refer

---

[31] See my *The Theory of Idle Resources,* 2d ed., chap. 4.

to a state in which latent inflation—an abnormally large investment in money (an exceptionally large M_r)—is in process of being *liquidated,* with the threat that money may be suddenly turned into nonmoney so rapidly that an inflation flare-up is on the horizon. But we have seen that this condition poses no problem; for the liquidation of an abnormal nominal value of money stocks can always be offset by an equal value of concurrent credit contraction, *with no deflationary consequences.* Thus, businessmen can replenish their money inventories out of increased sales instead of by borrowing as much as previously.

In my judgment, then, none of the meanings I have suggested for "overfull employment" is appropriately described by such a term. The concept is defective in itself. And if what we now call "job search" is recognized as a most important form of employment, entrepreneurial in some of its aspects (as I maintained in my *The Theory of Idle Resources*), there is no essential reason for the persistence of any *wasteful* idleness.[32] But if the Keynesians of post–World War II had allowed themselves to perceive this, the validity of the whole core of *The General Theory* with which they had so eagerly and profitably identified themselves would have been threatened. Was this not a potent factor in opinion creation?

Through the lessons of sour reality, then, we have seen the gradual spread of doubts about the soundness of Keynesian doctrines: we have seen the intelligentsia beginning to wonder whether, after all, the price mechanism did not do things better in the days when it was permitted at least some freedom.

In 1968, R. C. O. Matthews, whom we all thought of as a "Rightist" Keynesian, expressed skepticism in the *Economic Journal*. He pointed out that "as compared with the interwar period there has certainly been an increase in effective demand, in the Keynesian sense, relative to supply; but . . . it is nonproven that this has been due to government policy, at least in any simple sense." And he maintained that

the decline in unemployment as compared with before 1914 is to a large extent not a Keynesian phenomenon at all. . . . Throughout the postwar period the government, so far from injecting demand into the system, has persistently had a large current account

---

[32] Most so-called unemployment is either voluntary or productive. Job search and *pseudo*-idleness in particular are productive. See ibid., 2d ed., chaps. 3 and 4.

surplus. . . . This is not to deny that in various postwar years fiscal policy has been adjusted with the object of increasing demand above its existing level. But in the years when this was done it was a matter of reducing the size of the surplus rather than turning it into a deficit. The overall effect has therefore been one of restraint. . . . Part of the reason for low unemployment in the postwar period has been the trend increase in the scarcity of labor relative to capital. This is non-Keynesian, it can confidently be expected to persist, and it has little or nothing to do with government policy.[33]

I have quoted Matthews solely to illustrate how dumbfounded some of the most loyal Keynesians were at the trend of events. But although doubts springing from all these issues have modified public discussion and although there has been some effect upon influential opinion, it is still not certain how far *governments* have learned the lesson from bitter experience. Already, in 1963, I reported that of recent years it had often occurred to me that the politicians *had* seen the light but too late—too late because it then appeared to them impossible to turn back. They would, I said, have liked to return to the security of sound finance, but they were then afraid of taking the unpopular steps needed to maintain or enhance the flow of wages and income. Those of their official advisers who had authority to speak publicly were increasingly hinting at, or exposing with tactful frankness, the folly of creeping inflation. But they seemed not to do so in sufficiently unequivocal language.

Thus, although the clarity of the message contained in the First Report of the Cohen Council was clouded by its being expressed in the fashionable Keynesian language, the gist of that message was wholly anti-Keynesian, and contained advice which is as old-fashioned as the maxim: "Exhortations to businessmen to reduce prices, if indulged in, should, we think, be coupled with exhortations to workpeople and other consumers to increase savings."[34] And the Radcliffe Committee (although its Report was couched—even more misleadingly—in terms of Keynesian dialectics) was forced to confess that the consistency of the objectives of full employment, the avoidance of inflation, and the maintenance of stable exchange rates

---

[33] R. C. O. Matthews, "Why Has Britain Had Full Employment Since the War?" *Economic Journal,* September 1968, pp. 555–69.

[34] First Report of Cohen Council (British Council on Prices, Productivity, and Incomes), para. 158.

were "no longer regarded as self-evident."[35] For many years the gilt-edged market had been realizing that inflation had been "gradually eroding all fixed money values." The authorities have believed, it wrote, that the "chronically weak market" has been "resistant to substantial sales not merely at current prices but at any prices."[36] Anticipated inflation was forcing the Committee reluctantly to a vague recognition of pre-Keynesian teaching. The recourse to a seven percent bank rate in 1957 may have marked the turning point.

But the British government has certainly not yet abandoned the view that the maintenance of full employment and the avoidance of depression may still be wisely sought through monetary policy. Occasional references to the desirability of "reasonable stability" in the value of the pound (with a studious unwillingness to define "reasonable") are by no means convincing evidences of the growth of genuine governmental enlightenment.

In the United States the position is not greatly dissimilar. But Arthur F. Burns suggested that the Keynesian belief that traditional credit methods can "check a boom with dangerous ease" but "do little to speed recovery once a depression developed," had been abandoned officially in the United States; for he referred to this belief as having actuated "earlier policy."[37] What is more, he stated that "the heavy emphasis that the government has recently placed on a restrictive credit policy has served to bring us back to the best thought that ruled on the subject during the 1920s."[38] But Burns did not allow for the political factor, namely, the steady degeneration of representative government from democracy toward totalitarian control, against which Bronfenbrenner had so potently warned the United States in 1955. And his (Burns') term at the Federal Reserve Board meant his presiding over the most serious debasement of the dollar since World War II.

I concluded in 1963 as follows: A formidable barrier to the return to sound policy (not only in Britain and the United States but in all other countries) remains, I believe, in the general failure to perceive or admit that, when depression threatens, the flow of wages and

---

[35] Radcliffe Report (British Committee on the Working of the Monetary System), para. 55.

[36] Ibid., para. 68.

[37] Arthur F. Burns, *Prosperity Without Inflation* (New York: Fordham University Press, 1957), pp. 55–56.

[38] Ibid., pp. 43–44.

income can be maintained or increased through downward wage-rate and price adjustment in fields in which they have been raised under coercion. What governments, or those who influence electorates, have not learned is that competitive cost and price reductions cause the release of idle or wastefully used resources for forms of production (and hence of income) which have been starved of resources.

It has, I hold, been tragic for the world that Keynes' ideas should have had so large an influence in the twenties and thirties; for not only did the political attractiveness of his sort of convictions contribute first to unparalleled depression (see pp. 61–64) and then to an era of debilitating inflation, but even worse, I repeat, *it discouraged thought about fundamental reform.* Yet perhaps, in deploring Keynes' influence in economics, one should really be deploring the degeneration of politics to which I have just referred. For his teachings gave apparent respectability to policies which earlier generations would have regarded as reprehensible.

Not long ago, Professor Max Beloff, sadly viewing the British economy, wrote: "In my view, there is little doubt that the individual who (perhaps unwittingly) most seriously damaged the interests of his native country was Lord Keynes."[39] Of course he acted "unwittingly." But he was, I have long been convinced, and I think I have shown, reckless. Indeed, I had originally thought of entitling my *Keynesianism* "The Curse of Keynes."

It can well be argued, against the stand which I am taking, that in the circumstances which have existed, uniformity among economists could have had no influence. Mere academic teachings would have remained inert unless they were based on hidden assumptions of a politically acceptable kind. Nothing, apart from inflation, could have prevented the trade unions and price rings of Western Europe and the United States from repressing the flow of wages and income, creating unemployment, and precipitating the dilemma of depression or inflation. But those who believe this ought always to express their views in these unequivocal terms. Had Keynes himself so expressed his case, his influence on the world would undoubtedly have been much less. But it might not have been inconsiderable and it would have been exerted in exactly the opposite direction.

In 1963 I wrote: "If perseverance with Keynesianism has, indeed, been due to a failure to understand and not to lack of courage, my contribution may have some influence." Thus far, it has had no

---

[39] Quoted by Robert Skidelsky in *Spectator,* August 7, 1976.

discernible influence whatsoever. As I see things, the apparent revolution wrought by Keynes after 1936 is being reversed by a counter-revolution, initially waged unwittingly by higher critics who tried very hard to be faithful. Whether some permanent indirect benefit to economic science will eventually make up for the destruction and intellectual disorder which the revolution has left in its train, is a question which the future historian of ideas will have to answer.

Appendix

The Retreat as Recorded in David McCord Wright's
The Keynesian System

Although the late David McCord Wright has been largely responsible for forcing the Keynesian retreat, his exposition in *The Keynesian System* takes the form, superficially viewed, of a defense of Keynes against his extreme followers and some of his critics.

Discussing *The General Theory,* he tells us that "the continual switching of assumptions, which goes on through the book, forms a continual trap for the *careless or biased* reader"[40] (my italics). But has it not been equally a continual trap for the most careful and detached reader? Is it bias or carelessness to proceed in the belief that an assumption which is stated on one page must hold on the next page unless it has been explicitly changed? Wright refers to the "caricature of Keynes which is generally preached by his more dogmatic disciples and attacked by his enemies";[41] and he seems to rebuke Keynes' most enthusiastic followers for misunderstanding their master. Yet Keynes lived long enough to renounce the earlier "dogmatic" interpretations, and he did not do so in published writings. Naturally the critics—like policymakers—accepted as the new gospel the uncontradicted interpretations of the "dogmatic dis-

---

[40] David McCord Wright, *The Keynesian System* (New York: Fordham University Press, 1962), p. 47. This important contribution was published while my *Keynesianism* was in the hands of the printers.

[41] Ibid., p. 71. It would have helped if Wright had mentioned a few *undogmatic* disciples, that is, Keynesians who interpret Keynes more or less as he does. I do not know of any other Keynesian who has done so *in writing*. But Abba Lerner (whose 1938 and 1939 articles in the *Quarterly Journal of Economics* would undoubtedly have to be classed as "dogmatic" interpretations) seemed later to stand fairly close to Wright. (Address at the University of Chicago, May 14, 1962.)

ciples"; for the latter had, at any rate, translated the untidy jumble of theorems which makes up *The General Theory* into a more or less intelligible system. Had the skeptics (Keynes' "enemies") any alternative to attacking what they thought were fallacious doctrines which had evolved?

In my judgment (as I explained in Chapters 4 and 5), *the enormous appeal of Keynes' thesis originated precisely in doctrines which were rendered plausible through the obscuring of unrealistic assumptions,* the tacit changing of which Wright has tracked down (obviously with the patience of years of sympathetic rereading). In particular, *the unemployment equilibrium thesis—which he admits must be abandoned—was the main source of the political attractiveness of Keynes' contribution.* If Keynes had presented *The General Theory,* as Wright implies that he did, "not as a 'new economics' but as a convenient new method of analysis, and a shift in policy *emphasis,"*[42] he would not have weakened the authority of pre-Keynesian economists at the very epoch when reliance upon their authority could have saved the Western world from disastrous blunders.

Yet Wright really attempts to restore respect for teachings which Keynes effectively ridiculed. He tries to do this by rationalizing *The General Theory,* that is, by showing what Keynes *ought to have meant.* His rationalization is supported by those few odd passages (most of which I also quoted in 1963) which puzzled and exasperated the persevering and careful reader because of their *unresolved inconsistency* with the main body of the argument.[43] He uses these passages as a justification for a construction which he calls Keynes' "model of a dynamic world."[44] The truth is rather, I suggest, that *The General Theory* models are almost wholly static and flagrantly mechanical. Only occasionally do dynamic insights and realistic assumptions seem to intrude, and then nebulously and inconsistently.

I fear also that Wright tends to accept at their face value Keynes' recklessly unjustified assertions about the teachings of the pre-Keynesians. For instance, which economists believed, as he suggests they did, that "the rate of interest would *always,* or necessarily move

---

[42] Wright, op. cit., p. 67. Wright's italics.
[43] Wright talks of "the two Keyneses" (ibid., p. 75). If there *were* two, it was the one whom Wright refutes so relentlessly who achieved fame, title, and unparalleled academic influence.
[44] Ibid., pp. 66–67.

with profit expectations, and . . . that the desire to save would *always* and necessarily move with changes in the rate of interest"?[45] I cannot recall any example. And far from disturbing any "pleasant illusions" of pre-Keynesian economists on the subject, which Wright believes was Keynes' accomplishment,[46] the true influence of *The General Theory* was (as I have shown) the initiation of a tradition which obstructed the refinement of a perfectly valid general insight into the nature and causes of interest. Nor can I accept the suggestion[47] that pre-Keynesian economists were unaware of that element in the demand for money (a determinant—unless offset—of the relation of *market* interest to the *natural* level) which is due to fear of capital loss from a subsequent rise in interest. I have suggested that it was Keynes' treatment of this possibility which was fallacious. (See pp. 284–86, 348–49.) Again, as far as my reading goes, neither pre-Keynesian nor subsequent non-Keynesian economists have attempted to deny that "savings plans and investment decisions are very different things," as Wright suggests they have done;[48] and it is not a "logical quibble" when economists like myself insist, for reasons quite different from those advanced by Keynes, that, sensibly defined, *the magnitudes* realized "savings" and realized "investments" are identical notions. (See Chapters 13 and 14.)

A large part of the argument which I have here submitted amounts to *a plea for the rejection of much of the rationalized version of Keynes' doctrines which* Wright offered. For instance, whereas he still tried to persevere with the Keynesian tools, fifteen years after the first publication of *The General Theory,* I urged that the whole of that apparatus be abandoned; and whereas Wright claimed that Keynes' models "were merely convenient headings under which to group the important forces shaping the economy,"[49] I have maintained throughout that they are *models which tacitly assume away the important forces shaping the economy.* Curiously enough, Wright himself presented ample evidence to justify my view. The Keynesian tools remain crude, clumsy, and inappropriate. Indeed, the clarity of Wright's own exposition was vitiated whenever he attempted to perse-

---

45 Ibid., p. 9.
46 Ibid., p. 10.
47 Ibid., p. 34.
48 Ibid., p. 42.
49 Ibid., p. 66.

vere with Keynesian concepts.[50] But his penetrating contribution did assist my own aim—that of breaking through a formidable barrier to fruitful thought and action.

---

[50] Thus, his phrase (intended to summarize pre-Keynesian theory), "people will stop saving *and start spending*" (ibid., p. 8; Wright's italics), instead of "start consuming" or "start dishoarding and consuming," leaves the very impression which he is trying to dispel. As I have shown, the convention of considering "saving" and "spending" as alternatives has had seriously adverse consequences upon the thinking both of economists and policymakers.

Index

This book was set in the Times Roman series of type. The face was designed to be used in the news columns of the London *Times*. The *Times* was seeking a typeface that would be condensed enough to accommodate a substantial number of words per column without sacrificing readability and still have an attractive, contemporary appearance. This design was an immediate success. It is used in many periodicals throughout the world and is one of the most popular textfaces in use for book work.

Printed on paper that is acid-free and meets the requirements of the American National Standard for Permanence of Paper for Printed Library Materials, Z39.48-1992. ∞

Book design by JMH Corporation, Indianapolis, Indiana
Typography by Weimer Typesetting Co., Inc., Indianapolis, Indiana
Printed by Worzalla Publishing Co., Stevens Point, Wisconsin